CATALOGUE

OF

HEBREW MANUSCRIPTS.

VOLUME I.

בניות ברמה:

רשימת

כתבי יד שפני טמוני קדש

בבית עקד הספרים אשר למדרש החכמה

בקאנטאבריגיא

(יכוננה עליון אמן)

מלאכת צעיר הצעירים

שלמה בן מאיר

החלק הראשון הזה

כולל הפרק הראשון ובו

ספרי תורה נביאים וכתובים

והפרק השני ובו

פרושים על הספרים האלה

קאנטאבריגיא

בבית הדפוס אשר למדרש החכמה

שנת

ויהי ערב ויהי בקר

לפרט האלף הששי

CATALOGUE

OF THE

HEBREW MANUSCRIPTS

PRESERVED IN THE

UNIVERSITY LIBRARY,

CAMBRIDGE.

BY

DR S. M. SCHILLER-SZINESSY.

VOLUME I.

CONTAINING

SECTION I. *THE HOLY SCRIPTURES.*
SECTION II. *COMMENTARIES ON THE BIBLE.*

Cambridge:
PRINTED FOR THE UNIVERSITY LIBRARY.

CAMBRIDGE WAREHOUSE, 17, PATERNOSTER ROW, LONDON.
DEIGHTON, BELL AND CO., CAMBRIDGE,
F. A. BROCKHAUS, LEIPZIG.
1876.

Cambridge:
PRINTED AT THE UNIVERSITY PRESS,
BY C. J. CLAY, M.A.

TO

יום טוב ליפמן בר מנחם

LEOPOLD ZUNZ

(גדול מרבן שמו)

THE PATRIARCH OF HEBREW LITERATURE

NOW ENTERED UPON HIS EIGHTY-SECOND YEAR

(ימים על ימיו יוסיף אל עליון)

IN GRATITUDE

FOR WHAT HAS BEEN LEARNED FROM HIS WRITINGS

THESE FIRSTFRUITS ARE DEDICATED

BY

THE AUTHOR

אמרו חכמינו זכרם לברכה

הלומד מחברו פרק אחד או הלכה אחת או דבור אחד או פסוק אחד או אפילו אות אחת

צריך לנהג בו כבוד

ואני שלמדתי ממך כמה דברים

על אחת כמה וכמה שצריך אני לנהג בך כבוד

PREFACE.

THE preparation of a printed *Catalogue of the Hebrew Manuscripts in the University Library*, the first volume of which is now published, was entrusted to the present writer by order of the Library Syndicate, June 15, 1868. In accordance with the system of classification adopted in a brief List (of the collection as it then stood) which was approved by the Syndicate earlier in the same year, the descriptions of the Manuscripts are ranged under the following eight heads:

I. Bible; text, with or without commentary.
II. Commentaries on the Bible.
III. Talmudic Literature.
IV. Liturgy.
V. Religious Philosophy.
VI. Qabbalah.
VII. Greek-Arabic Philosophy.
VIII. Miscellaneous matters.

The present volume contains the descriptions of the Manuscripts which fall under the first two of these heads. At the end, it is proposed to subjoin a series of *Excursus*, one on each Section of the Catalogue, in which it will be found convenient to gather together at one view the results which it would be impracticable to bring out with the required clearness on each occasion as it arises. An historical account of the whole collection and its gradual formation, together with the necessary Tables and Indexes, will complete the work.

ואדני יהוה יעזר לי על כן לא נכלמתי

S.-S.

UNIVERSITY LIBRARY, CAMBRIDGE,

ערב שבת קדש ויגש תרל״ו

December 31, 1875.

CORRECTIONS.

ספר שאינו מוגה... אסור לשהותו משום שנאמר ואל תשכן באהליך עולה. בבלי כתובות י״ט :

Page 29, *line* 20, *for* תהיה *read* תהא *or* תהי.

,, 37, ,, 8, *for* Cod. 91 *read* Cod. 92.

,, 39, ,, 28, *and* p. 45, *line* 14, *read* Gerosolomitano.

,, 42, ,, 6 *from below*, *read* Enriquez.

,, 46, ,, 14, *for* Bedarshi *read* בדרשי, *as the Latin name of Bêziers is Biterræ, otherwise written Biteris or Bederis* (בֶּדֶרְשׁ), *the adjective being Biterrensis or Bederensis* (בֶּדֶרְשִׁי).

Page 50, *line* 10, *read* (Rashi, R. Salomo Isacides). *The note on p.* 238 *ought to have stood here.*

Page 50, *line* 17, *for* must have been *read* probably was.

,, 54, ,, 11 *from below, and* p. 61, *line* 13 *from below, for* Haqqalir *read* הקליר. *We have our doubts about the correctness of the common transliteration.*

Page 56, *line* 5 *from below, for* פי׳ (פרק) קושיא *read* פי׳ (פרק) ראשון קושיא.

,, 62, ,, 20, *for* ותתעברי *read* ותתעבר.

,, ,, ,, 6 *from below, for* לוי *read* שי׳, *i.e.* שיחיה.

,, 63, ,, 7. *What is given here under* (20) *should not have been included among marginal additions, as the Table occupies three vacant pages of the volume.*

Page 67, *line* 5 *from below, omit points after* חטאו.

,, 69, ,, 6 *from below, omit comma after* Jahrbuch.

,, 71, ,, 6, *omit points after* שאחרי.

,, 78, ,, 1, *read* Agadic.

,, 79, ,, 9 *from below, for* 21^a—22^b *read* 37^a—38^b. *In the early Constantinople editions the* sheets *are numbered, not the* leaves; *so that leaf* 36 *of the volume bears at the foot the number* כ. *Hence our mistake. The volume was only for a few minutes in our hands.*

Page 80, *line* 14 *from below, for* Festival *read* Festival in Commemoration

,, 81, ,, 14, *for* Destruction *read* Fast in Commemoration of the Destruction.

Page 90, *line* 11, *for* Cabbalah *read* Qabbalah.

,, ,, ,, 5 *from below, for* Add. 518, leaf 76^a *read* Add. 518, leaf 46^a, Add. 1015. 2, leaf 48^a.

Page 92, *line* 4. *This is not clearly expressed. Transpose and read* ... the famous poem said to have been addressed by R. Yehudah b. Shemuel Hallevi in a dream to Ibn 'Ezra.

Page 103, *line* 6, *read* Abigedor.

,, 111, ,, 7 *from below, for* clxix *read* cxlix.

,, 131, ,, 13, *for* lxxxii *read* lxxii.

,, 162, ,, 9 *from below, for* ביניגו *read* בינינו, *and for* גצא *read* נצא.

,, 166, *Note* 1, *read* Yerundi (*i.e.* Gerundi, *and not* Girondi, &c. *Later also in the same Note twice read* Gerundi.

Page 177, *Note* 3, *for* 1507 *read* 1497.

,, 191, ,, 1, *line* 5, *for* תחזת *read* תחזה.

,, 197, *line* 8 *from below. The solution of the abbreviation* ד״ת *ought to have been printed thus:* (דיוקא תנינא or דעתא תניתא). *Compare p.* 225 *of this Catalogue*, Note 1.

CATALOGUE

OF

HEBREW MANUSCRIPTS.

I.

THE HOLY SCRIPTURES.

No. 1.

A roll of goat-skins, some of which are dyed brown, others red, 48 ft. 3 in. × 1 ft. 9 in.; 117 columns, 51 (the latest portion 50) lines; square character, oriental Sephardic hands, ranging from the xth century to the xvth.

[תורת משה]

The PENTATEUCH; defective.

THE roll as it now stands contains Gen. i. 1 to Exod. xxi. 25; Num. ix. 22 to xxvii. 18; and xxx. 9 to Deut. v. 11. It therefore consists of two principal portions (coll. 1—80 and 81—117), with large gaps after each. Five hands are to be distinguished:

A. The original hand: coll. 51—66 and 71—80 in the first portion, and coll. 106—117 in the second.

B. Supplementary to A: the last eleven lines of col. 53 (see below) in the first portion, and coll. 84—87, 92—99, and 103—105 in the second.

C. Coll. 100—102 (one skin only) supplementary to B.

D. Coll. 81—83 (one skin only) supplementary to B.

E. Coll. 1—50 and 67—70 in the first portion supplementary to A; and coll. 88—91 in the second portion supplementary to B.

1. The remaining portions of the original roll (A) are written on brown skins, and contain Gen. xliv. 30 to Exod. ix. 10 (coll. 51—66); Exod. xii. 27 to xxi. 25 (coll. 71—80); Num. xxxii. 20 to Deut. v. 11 (coll. 106—117).

Exodus begins on col. 58, and *Deuteronomy* on col. 111. There is an interval of four lines between book and book, each commencing with a fresh column.

The very small portion of the original handwriting which has not been re-touched (see lines 1—7 on col. 115) gives the impression of belonging to the xth century, and of being the work of an Arabian Sephardi, who was a learned and skilful writer, though not a professional scribe (see Excursus I.). As in all copies intended for public use in the Synagogue, we find here neither verse-marks nor vowel-points nor accents. The י״ה of ביה שמו are here found at the head of a column, and this part conforms in other respects also to the ordinary usages of modern Synagogue rolls, the following few points excepted:

(1) There is no trace of the arched ח.

(2) The scribe occasionally adopts a peculiar form of פ, resembling one פ within another, apparently in order to emphasize the words in which it occurs.

(3) He writes the passage which precedes the Song of Moses and the children of Israel (הבאים &c.) in shorter lines, so as to bring that song into greater prominence (see MS. Add. 652, leaf 47[a]).

(4) There are no traces of תגין.

Another characteristic of this part must be mentioned, although it is not the work of the original scribe. The whole text presents a singularly spotted appearance, which is due to the fact that small portions of the dark surface of the skin have been removed with some sharp instrument, for the purpose of marking the text for reading. A single (or occasionally a double) point after a word indicates the close of a verse; one under a word signifies the half-verse (אתנחתא). Other points are found over, others in the centre of certain letters, pointing in some cases to minor subdivisions of the verse, and in others to the stress to be laid on a word, so as distinctly to pronounce it. In this last case it most frequently occurs in את when coming after a weak letter or a ע. The mark ∴ also occurs at the beginning of a line at intervals, indicating the subdivision of the weekly פרשה into smaller portions for the ז׳ קרואים (see Excurs. I.). As there is no trace of this apparently Arabian practice, except in the earliest portion of the MS., it may be inferred that the marks were made while the original roll was still perfect and in use.

2. The portions of the text written by the earliest hand (B) which has supplied the defects of the original MS., are Gen. xlvii. 11 (אחזה) —15 (col. 53, lines 41—51); Num. xii. 8—xv. 28 (coll. 84—87); xviii. 21—xxv. 15 (coll. 92—99); xxx. 9—xxxii. 19 (coll. 103—105). The skins are very hard and of a reddish brown colour, and may be ascribed to the xiith century.

The passage in Genesis is written on a piece of skin, which has been substituted for the original skin at the foot of col. 53. Even this piece has its interest as affording a proof that the skins written by this scribe in the latter part of the roll were written to supply the defects of the original, and were not portions of an independent roll. The usual מ of ביה שמו (Num. xxiv. 5, מה טבו) occurs in the middle of a column instead of at the head; but there is reason to believe that the writers of this roll belonged to a school which observed a somewhat different rule (see Excurs. I.). The ordinary and the arched ח are used indifferently. There are no תגין.

The peculiar פ is used which is found in A, D, and E. In other respects the writer conforms to ordinary rules; the majuscule י occurs in יגדל (Num. xiv. 17), and the pointed ר in אשר (Num. xxi. 30).

3. The next hand in point of age (C) is only found on one very soft brown skin, containing Num. xxv. 16—xxvii. 18 (coll. 100—102). The ח is arched wherever it is in conjunction with י and there only; e.g. יחלאל, הזרחי, whilst זרח, &c. have the ordinary ח only. The majuscule ן is found in משפטן (Num. xxvii. 5). There are no תגין.

4. The next supply (D) also consists of only one very soft skin, dyed a deep red, and contains Num. ix. 22—xii. 7 (coll. 81—83). The peculiar פ, which is found in handwritings A, B, and E, occurs here in ואף (xi. 33). The usual inverted נ before and after x. 35—36 are here. The arched ח is not found, and there are no תגין.

5. The latest portion of the MS. (handwriting E), which is also the largest of all, contains Gen. i. 1—xliv. 29 (coll. 1—50); Exod. ix. 11—xii. 26 (coll. 67—70); Num. xv. 29—xviii. 20 (coll. 88—91). It is beautifully written, on skins dyed a deep red, in a handwriting of the xiv—xvth century. The skins, which contain the passages in Exodus and Numbers, suffice to show that the parts in this handwriting are not fragments of a roll brought from another quarter, as has been sometimes supposed, but were written to supply the defects of the original (A) after they had once been supplied by a second hand (B). The supplement conforms to ordinary copies in the observance of the rules concerning the majuscules, minuscules, and the pointed words, but there are a few things which deserve special notice:

(1) The arched ח occurs throughout.

(2) The same emphatic פ is found here, which is noticed above. For the same reason we find ספר (Gen. v. 1) with a majuscule ס, and צא (Exod. xi. 8) written with a majuscule צ.

(3) The ך in דרך (Gen. iii. 24) is written backwards (see Excurs. I.).

(4) The ל sometimes has a peculiar hook attached to the upper limb; the heads of all other letters throughout have a stroke on the extreme left.

(5) A somewhat wider space than is usually left between word and word, indicates the close of a verse.

(6) The פרשיות סתומות never begin on a fresh line, but invariably, after a gap, on the same line as the end of the preceding פרשה.

(7) The תגין are only found on three skins (coll. 19—22, 23—25, 47—50); but here they are placed not only over the letters שעטנזגץ but also over כמף, which, it may be observed, are the remaining letters of מנצפך not included in שעטנזגץ (see Excurs. I.).

All parts of the roll, so far as we now have it, whether original or supplied, agree in this, that every column begins with a fresh verse, except of course where the ה of ביה שמו occurs, Exod. xiv. 28 (col. 74).

The following printed description is pasted on the back of the first skin: "This Manuscript on a Roll of Goat Skins dyed red, was found in the Record Chest[1] of one of the Synagogues of the Black Jews, in the interior of Malayala in India, by the Rev. Claudius Buchanan, in the year 1806." See Two Discourses... to which are added Christian Researches in Asia, by the Rev. Claudius Buchanan, D.D. (Cambridge, 1811, 8vo.), pp. 312—315. A supposition existed in the country that the roll was brought to India from Senna in Arabia. This is in a great measure confirmed by the fact that some rolls lately brought, it is said, from the same part of Arabia, are found to possess many of the most striking characteristics of the present one.

This roll has been described, the text fully collated, and some of its peculiarities noticed, by the Rev. Thomas Yeates, who was employed to draw up a list of the collection of MSS. brought from India by Dr Buchanan. We may refer to his printed work[2] for much minute information respecting it, and we need only notice that, among the various readings which he has collected, many, in the more ancient portions of the MS. especially, are due rather to the scribe who re-touched the roll than to the original writers (e.g. נבחלו Exod. xv. 15; וקריב Num. xvi. 5; שרה Num. xxvi. 46, &c.).

[Library-mark Oo. 1. 3; presented in 1809 by Dr Buchanan.]

No. 2.

A roll of 80 goat-skins, some of which are dyed yellow, others brown, 116 ft. 10 in. × 1 ft. 10½ in.; 241 columns, 47—54 lines[3]; square character, fine Sephardic hand of the XIIIth century.

[תורת משה]

THE PENTATEUCH; defective, but made perfect.

Genesis, col. 1; *Exodus*, col. 56; *Leviticus*, col. 109; *Numbers*, col. 145; *Deuteronomy*, col. 196.

This roll, although conforming, on the whole, to the copies ordinarily used by the public reader in the Synagogue, has a few additional points worth noticing:

(1) The whole word בראשית is in majuscules and is so placed in connexion with the following word, as to suggest to the eye the reading בראש יתברא אלהים (see Excurs. I.).

(2) The ש of ביה שמו is here in the שני in Lev. xvi. 7 and not that in 8, which is the one ordinarily placed at the head of a column.

(3) The ט in טוב (Exod. ii. 2), the צ in צא (Exod. xi. 8), the ם in ויהם (Num. xiii. 30), and the נ in ונך (Deut. ii. 33) are majuscules, as are also all

[1] The receptacle for worn out or imperfect copies of the Bible, Prayer-books, &c.

[2] Collation of an Indian copy of the Hebrew Pentateuch...by Thomas Yeates, 4to. Cambridge, 1812.

[3] Most of the columns by the original hand have 49 lines. See Excurs. I.

the letters of ותקח (introductory to the Song of Miriam, Exod. xv. 20), whilst והלטאה (Lev. xi. 30) has no majuscule ל, and תשי (Deut. xxxii. 18) has no minuscule י (see Excurs. I.).

(4) ועשרון (Num. xxix. 15) has both the ר and the ו pointed (see MS Add. 465, leaf 46[a]).

(5) The arched ח is not to be met with here; that letter has, however, a perpendicular stroke on the extreme left of the upper part, as its exclusive characteristic.

(6) The rule of the תגין is carefully observed by the scribe of this MS.; they cease, as a system, at Deut. v. 17; after which they appear, however, occasionally, e.g. xxii. 11 (skin 74, col. 224)[1], &c.

(7) The letters הדבק have a perpendicular line in the centre of the upper stroke (see Excurs. I.).

(8) Corrections are made, if of one or two words only, by inserting them above the line; and if of some extent, by writing them on a separate piece pasted over.

All that remains of the original portion of the MS. is a model of system, correctness and beauty. The defects, which have been supplied by five different hands (B, C, D, E, and F), are as follows:

Gen. vii. 11 (מאות)—xi. 9 (הפיצם), skin 3, coll. 7—10. Supplied, coll. 7 and 10 by B, and 8 and 9 by C, so that the two hands are necessarily contemporary. They contain 47 lines to the column. Coll. 7—9 conform entirely to A; col. 10, however, does so on the first four lines and a half only, after which the ח has a stroke, while הדבק and שעטנזגץ are without strokes and תגין respectively.

Exod. xxi. 28—xxiv. 11, skin 28, coll. 83—85, supplied by D, 62 lines to the column. It conforms here entirely to A.

Lev. xiii. 21 (והיא)—xiv. 23 (פתח), skin 41, coll. 123—125, supplied by E, 54 lines to the column. It conforms here entirely to A.

Num. xxi. 16 (בארה)—xxiii. 18 (וישא), skin 58, coll. 174—176, supplied by F, 47 lines to the column. It has no strokes (on ח excepted) and no תגין.

Num. xxxii. 2 (העדה)—xxxvi. 12 (מטה), skins 63, 64, coll. 189—195, supplied by D, 62 and 63 lines to the column. It conforms entirely to A.

Deut. vii. 22 (מפניך)—x. 8 (בעת), skin 69, coll. 208—210, supplied by D, 58 lines to the column. Here (except on ח) no strokes are found, nor are there any תגין. It conforms to A as that is in this part.

Deut. xxviii. 20 (מעלליך)—xxix. 10 (נשיכם), skin 77, coll. 232—234, supplied by E, 52 lines to the column. It conforms to A, not as that is here, but in the greater part of the roll.

All these supplementary portions, though conforming, as must have been seen, for the most part to the rules observed by the original scribe, are very inferior specimens of handwriting. The parts supplied by D in

[1] This part seems to have been written as a specimen of caligraphy; it is of surpassing beauty and deserves to be called אשורית as defined by המאושר שבכתבים. See Excurs. I.

Numbers and Deuteronomy in particular teem with mistakes[1]. None of these supplements are later than the xvth century; and B and C are but little posterior to A.

This roll, is, on the whole, in a good state of preservation. There is no trace of its earlier history; it seems to have been procured for the University through Mr Yeates for the sum of a hundred pounds.

[Library-mark Add. 289; bought in 1812.]

No. 3.

A fragment of a roll of goat-skins dyed a brownish yellow, 1 ft. 8⅝ in. × 1 ft. 9 in.; 3 columns, 42 lines; square character, fine Sephardic handwriting of the xivth century.

[תורת משה]

THE PENTATEUCH; a fragment.

This is one יריעה of a roll as used by the public reader in the Synagogue. The text reaches from *Genesis* xxxi. 16 (עשה) to xxxiii. 3 (עבר).

The whole copy probably conformed, a few points excepted, to an ordinary Synagogue roll. The ח is not arched but has, as have also the letters הדבקי (see MS. Add. 333), a perpendicular stroke on the upper part, towards the left side. The letters שעטנזגץ have the תגין.

This skin is, no doubt, a remnant saved from a fire, as will be seen from col. 2, and is also otherwise injured. But small fragment though it is, it gives ample testimony to the very great value the ספר התורה must have had, owing to its correctness and beauty.

[Library-mark Add. 860; presented in 1871 by the Librarian.]

No. 4.

A fragment of a roll of goat-skins, dyed a pale yellow, 3 ft. ⅝ in. × 2 ft. ½ in.; 5 columns, 45 lines; square character, Sephardic handwriting of the xivth century.

[תורת משה]

THE PENTATEUCH; a fragment.

This is one יריעה of a roll as used by the public reader in the Synagogue. The text reaches from *Exodus* xx. 7 (אלהיך) to xxv. 22 (שם).

[1] E.g. Num. xxxiv. 25, ולמטן for ולמטה; Deut. vii. 25, where לא is given twice; viii. 5, היום for עם; ib. 9, תצב for תחצב; ib. 17, חחיל for החיל; ix. 15, where באש is given twice and בער not once; x. 1, אל for אלי; ib. ושממם for ושמתם; ib. 4, where הלחות is altogether omitted. Such can hardly be honoured with the name of various readings.

The whole copy probably conformed to an ordinary Synagogue roll, except that the ה is not arched and has not even the stroke so often found on it in lieu of the arch (see Excurs. I.). The תגין now to be found on the letters שעטנזגץ are the addition of a modern hand, to which is also due the re-touching of sundry letters and words.

The ink has run owing to the bad dressing of the skin, and the fragment is much stained and soiled.

[Library-mark, Add. 861; presented in 1871 by the Librarian.]

No. 5.

A roll of 72 goat-skins, dyed a brownish yellow, 152 ft. 4½ in. × 2 ft. ½ in.; 267 columns, 46 lines[1]; square character, fine Sephardic hands of the XVth or XVIth century.

[תורת משה]

THE PENTATEUCH.

Genesis, col. 1; *Exodus*, col. 67; *Leviticus*, col. 119; *Numbers*, col. 161; *Deuteronomy*, col. 217.

Three different hands, of which the first two are those of master and pupil, are distinguishable in this truly splendid MS.; viz.

1. The Master's hand: coll. 1—47 (part), 65—268.
2. The Pupil's hand: coll. 47 (part)—64.
3. The Corrector's hand: passim.

This roll conforms in almost all respects to the ordinary copies as used by the public reader in the Synagogue. There are, however, a few points worth being mentioned.

(1) The ה, as in MS. Add. 289 (see above), is merely provided with a stroke on the extreme left; in Gen. xlvii. 28 (ויחי), and Exod. xxxii. 11 (ויחל), however, it is arched (see Excurs. I.).

(2) The letters הדבקי have a perpendicular line, near the extreme left; but this rule is observed only where the תגין are found on שעטנזגץ. These break off for the first time with col. 100, and although they resume again, they cease to be attended to systematically.

(3) Gen. xxx. 42 (ובהעטיף), xxxiv. 31 (הכזונה); Lev. xi. 30 (והלטאה); Num. xiii. 30 (ויהס); Deut. xviii. 13 (תמים), and xxxii. 4 (הצור), have no majuscules. Exod. xi. 8, however, has a majuscule צ in צא. See Nos. 1 and 2 described above.

(4) The skins are connected with one another by the prescribed תפירת גידין (see Excurs. I.).

This copy was written for a private individual, as may be seen from the ungraceful אל, in the last word (see Excurs. I.). The first owner's

[1] Col. 61 has 47 lines.

name was probably דוד בן יוסף אלפסי, as this name with the addition of ישע (יבוא שלום עליו) is found on the silver pointer (יד), which, with the usual mantle, bells, &c., accompanies this ספר התורה. It was presented by the Jews of Morocco, as a tribute of gratitude, to James Finn, Esq., for services rendered to them by him, while English Consul at Jerusalem.

[Library-mark Add. 333; presented in 1867 by Mr Finn.]

No. 6.

A roll of 82 white roe-skins, 125 ft. × 1 ft. 11 in.; 239 columns, 48—50 lines; square character, Chinese hand of the XVIIth century.

[תורת משה]

THE PENTATEUCH.

Genesis, col. 1; *Exodus*, col. 63; *Leviticus*, col. 114; *Numbers*, col. 148; *Deuteronomy*, col. 196.

The skins are numbered on the back, by the original hand.

The character, although very inelegant, is of considerable interest, as it is an imitation of an ancient character rarely to be met with.

The whole MS. is the work of one man, who, however, must have written it from mere dictation; otherwise we could not account for the frequent and grievous blunders he commits in interchanging א with ה, א with ע, ה with ח, ח with כ, ח with ע, כ with ק, מ with נ &c.[1]

This roll is a great curiosity, not only in the points in which it deviates from, but also in those it conforms to, a ספר התורה, as will be seen from the following statement:

(1) The ordinary rules concerning the interval between פרשה and פרשה are entirely disregarded, the disregard extending even to that between book and book.

(2) On the other hand great care is taken that every column (the 81st and 236th, on which are the ה and ו of ביה שמו, naturally excepted) should commence with a fresh verse and that every column (the 1st, 62nd, 81st, 218th and 225th excepted) should also commence with a ו. (See Excurs. I.)

(3) ביה שמו are placed at the beginning of a column, but of these the י is יששכר (Gen. xlix. 14), the ש is שפטים (Deut. xvi. 18), and the מ is מוצא (Deut. xxiii. 24).

[1] For instance: Gen. xviii. 26, אמצה; xxx. 26 תנא; Ex. xii. 18, בערבעה; Num. vii. 14, אשרה; Gen. xix. 12, החן; xlvii. 17, וינחלם; Gen. vi. 14, והפרת, in which the ה is written for a ח, which itself was a mistake for a כ. A complete list of these interchanges will be found in the MS. notice of the present roll, preserved in the Library.

(4) No notice is taken of the rules concerning the majuscule and minuscule letters.

(5) Of the נקודות בתורה (תיבות) some are pointed and others not.

(6) Of the תגין not the slightest trace is found.

(7) Several of the שמות הקדש שאינם נמחקין (see Excurs. I.) are unceremoniously erased.

It is in an excellent state of preservation.

[Library-mark Add. 283; presented in 1853 by the London Society for promoting Christianity amongst the Jews[1].]

No. 7.

A strip of parchment, $3\frac{3}{8}$ in. × $3\frac{1}{4}$ in.; 22 lines; square character, fine Sephardic handwriting of the XV—XVIth century.

[מזוזה]

A Door-phylactery.

This copy, which conforms, on most points, to a modern מזוזה (see Excurs. I.), has an arched ח in אחד only. In the other words, in which this letter occurs, it has the ordinary form with the addition of a perpendicular line on the upper stroke, towards the left.

On the back, while the שדי can no longer be traced, the כוזו במוכסז כוזו (see Excurs. VI.) is perfectly legible.

This copy is much stained, soiled and torn.

[Library-mark Add. 849, No. 1; found in 1871, lying in an old printed book.]

No. 8.

A roll of 4 strips of parchment, 7 ft. $\frac{3}{4}$ in. × $9\frac{1}{4}$ (to $\frac{1}{2}$) in.; 14 columns, 28 lines; square character, Sephardic hand of the XV—XVIth century.

[מגלת אסתר]

The Book of Esther.

This copy, designed for the use of the public reader in the Synagogue on the festival of פורים, contains:

(1) The three benedictions, which usually precede the reading of this book (column 1), and

(2) the text of the book itself (coll. 2—14).

[1] See the Bp. of Victoria's letter, Jewish Intelligence, XVII. (1851), p. 432, and J. Zedner in Frankel's Monatsschrift für Gesch. u. Wissensch. d. Judenth., II. pp. 56—61.

Whilst agreeing on most points with an ordinary מגלה, this roll presents the following differences:

(1) It has a verse-mark in the shape of a stroke or full stop.

(2) The system of the תגין, although not entirely ignored, is not strictly adhered to, so that whilst the י has them sometimes, the letters שעטנזגץ are often without them.

(3) Several words, originally forgotten, were afterwards inserted above the line.

(4) The letters בדהמת are occasionally provided with a perpendicular line on the upper stroke (see Excurs. I.).

Although this MS. comes from Cochin, in India, it was, probably, written in Spain or Portugal prior to the expulsion (1492—97), and thence carried to India, where Dr Buchanan obtained it from the "Record Chest" attached to one of the Synagogues of the Black Jews. See Collation of an Indian copy of the Hebrew Pentateuch...also a Collation and Description of a MS. Roll of the Book of Esther[1],...by Thomas Yeates, (4to. Cambridge, 1812), pp. 43—48, and this Catalogue, No. 1.

The condition of the MS. is, the first two columns excepted, where the ink has peeled off, tolerably good; the תפירה, however, is loose in some places and the cover is rather faded and torn. The roller, of polished walnut wood, is in good condition.

[Library-mark Oo. 1. 4; presented in 1809 by Dr Buchanan.]

No. 9.

The last strip of a roll of parchment, 10⅝ in. × 1 ft. ⅛ in.; 1 column, 22 lines; square character, German Ashkenazic handwriting of the xv—xvith century.

[מגלת אסתר]

THE BOOK OF ESTHER; a fragment.

This is a fragment of a copy of this Book as used by the public reader in the Synagogue. The text reaches from ix. 22 (טוב לעשות) to x. 3 (the end).

The תגין are worn off, but their existence can be easily traced.

This and three other fragments (MSS. Add. 849, Nos. 3, 4, and 5) were probably in Prof. Larsow's collection, since they appear as No. 21 in Stargardt's Catalogue xciii. (Berlin, 1871), out of which they were bought for this Library.

[Library-mark Add. 849, No. 2; bought in 1871.]

[1] Most of the points given in this Catalogue have escaped Yeates' notice.

No. 10.

A roll of 8 strips of parchment, 9 ft. 1 in. × 4⅝ in.; 27 columns, the last of which is blank, 14—16 lines; square character, Sephardic hand of the XVII—XVIIIth century.

[מגלת אסתר]

THE BOOK OF ESTHER.

This roll, probably intended for Synagogal use by a private individual only, exhibits the following peculiarities:

(1) The ח (except in חור, i. 6, where it is arched) is the ordinary one (see Excurs. I.).

(2) Words affected by a קרי or a יתיר, have over the so affected letters two points or strokes.

(3) The same is the case with respect to certain words, the first or last letters of which give the Most Holy Name, otherwise not to be found in this book (see Excurs. I.).

(4) Of the תגין not the smallest trace can be found here.

The description attached to this copy runs thus:—"This Manuscript was found in one of the Synagogues of the Black Jews of Cochin, in India, by the Rev. CLAUDIUS BUCHANAN, in the year 1806."

The condition of the MS. is good. The roller, made of common wood and painted yellow and red, is somewhat damaged.

[Library-mark Oo. 1. 5; presented in 1809 by Dr Buchanan.]

No. 11.

A roll of 3 strips of parchment 4 ft. 3¼ in. × 10¼ in.; 12 columns, 35 lines; square character, fine Polish Ashkenazic handwriting of the XVII—XVIIIth century.

[מגלת אסתר]

THE BOOK OF ESTHER.

This copy conforms in all respects to an ordinary roll as used by the public reader in the Synagogue on פורים and is, a few corrections excepted, the work of one scribe.

It is one of the finest specimens of writing of the school to which it belongs.

The majuscule ח (in חור, i. 6) has an additional ornament; otherwise that letter is everywhere simply arched and the תגין are executed in a style worthy of their name (crowns).

The MS. is torn in some places and more or less stained and soiled. The writing has, however, suffered but little.

[Library-mark, Add. 862; presented in 1871 by the Rev. William Bailey, of Jerusalem.]

No. 12.

Parchment, 10¼ in. × 7¾ in.; 464 leaves, 4-sheet quires, 2 columns[1], 32—34 lines; square character, the bare unpointed text in a fine Sephardic handwriting, dated 7 Adar 616[2].

[התורה הנביאים והכתובים]

The Bible.

Leaf 1ª, blank; 1ᵇ, *Genesis;* 31ᵇ, *Exodus;* 56ᵇ, *Leviticus;* 73ᵇ, *Numbers;* 97ᵇ, *Deuteronomy;* 118ª, *Joshua;* 133ª, *Judges;* 146ᵇ, *Samuel* (165ª, 2 *Samuel*); 181ª, *Kings* (199ª, 2 *Kings*); 216ᵇ, *Isaiah;* 241ᵇ, *Jeremiah;* 273ª, *Ezekiel;* 300ᵇ, *Hosea;* 304ª, *Joel;* 305ᵇ, *Amos;* 309ª, *Obadiah;* 309ª, *Jonah;* 310ª, *Micah;* 312ᵇ, *Nahum;* 313ᵇ, *Habakkuk;* 314ª, *Zephaniah;* 315ᵇ, *Haggai;* 316ª, *Zechariah;* 320ᵇ, *Malachi;* 322ª, *Psalms;* 360ᵇ, *Proverbs;* 373ᵇ, *Job;* 390ᵇ, *Ruth;* 392ᵇ, *Canticles;* 394ᵇ, *Ecclesiastes;* 398ᵇ, *Esther;* 403ª, *Lamentations;* 405ᵇ, *Daniel;* 415ª, *Ezra* (420ᵇ, *Nehemiah*); 428ᵇ, *Chronicles* (444ª, 2 *Chronicles*); 463ª, subscription and acrostic by the original scribe; 463ᵇ, blank; 464, blank, wanting.

In this volume, which, as a whole, is the growth of many centuries, 6 hands, of which the last only is Ashkenazic, are distinguishable; viz.

(1) The scribe of the text,

(2) The pointer and accentuator,

(3) The writer of the מסרת,

[1] The only exceptions are leaves 40ª (part of the Song of Moses and the children of Israel, which is in אריח על גבי לבנה &c.); 135ᵇ—136ª (Song of Deborah, which is in the same form); 324ª—360ª (the greater part of the Psalms); 361ᵇ—373ᵇ (the greater part of Proverbs); and 375ª—390ª (the greater part of Job); which are all arranged in hemistichs.

[2] According to Jahn's Tables, 7 Adar 4616 corresponds to 18 February 856 of the common era.

(4) The scribe who executed the ornaments,

(5) An occasional corrector, and

(6) An owner who marked the chapters.

1. There is an interval of 3 lines between the various books, the only exceptions being *Habakkuk*, which is preceded by 2 lines only, but which commences on a new page; *Malachi*, which is preceded by almost 3 lines; the *Psalms*, which are preceded by 7 lines, but which commence on a fresh column; *Canticles*, which is preceded by 2 lines only, but which commences on a fresh page; and *Lamentations*, which is preceded by almost 3 lines. The vacant spaces are invariably filled up with part of the word on the next line and, should that not suffice, with the addition of a י (see Excurs. I.). The text differs but little from that of the ordinary printed editions; but there are occasional variations in the arrangement of the פרשיות פתוחות וסתומות, e.g. Gen. i. 6, 14, &c. Although knowing that the last verses but one in Isaiah, Malachi, Ecclesiastes and Lamentations have to be repeated, the scribe is apparently unacquainted with יתקק סימן, but gives the commencement of these verses. To this scribe belong, besides the bare text, the verse-mark throughout, the mark פרש׳ in the Pentateuch, the numbers to the Psalms (149, as cxiv. and cxv. here form one Psalm), the centre-mark (חצי הספר), wherever it is not part of the מסרת, and the following subscription:

אני יעקב הלוי סופר
חתמתי זה הספר
ז׳ לחדש י׳ב׳ הוא אדר
באותיות וכתב הדר
שנת ה׳ת׳ו׳ר׳ה׳ ליצירה
ח׳ק׳ק׳ לבנין בית הבחירה

יזכני ה׳ להגות בו תדירה
ערב ובוקר רמשא וצפרה
קול מבשר ישמע מהרה
בקבוץ עמנו שבעבר נהרה
השב הנזר והעטרה
לבית דוד התפארה
ובית לוי לשיר וזמרה
ישימו כהנים באפך קטורה

The text must have been executed in Palestine, although not at Jerusalem, as will be seen from בקבוץ עמנו שבעבר נהרה (comp. Josh. xxiv. 2, &c. and Is. vii. 20) on the one hand, and the utter silence regarding the Holy City on the other hand. (For further proofs that this Bible was for some time in Palestine see Excurs. I.)

Respecting the time at which it was written, one certainly hesitates at the first moment to accept as true the high age which is ascribed to it in the postscript; and yet a minute and careful examination of the MS. shows that the reasons which have hitherto been alleged are wholly insufficient to condemn it as a forgery. See Kennicott, Dissertatio Generalis...ed. Bruns. (8vo. Brunovici, 1783), pp. 374—376; Zunz, Gesch. und Lit. (8vo. Berlin, 1845), pp. 214—215; and Excursus I. to the present Catalogue, where the history of this MS. is fully investigated.

2. When the bare text of one scribe is provided with vowel-points, accents and emendations by another, there will necessarily be produced a source of various readings; a source of which, though important, but little notice has hitherto been taken in collating MSS. Viewed in this light, this copy, though it is far from being an absolute model of correctness, will prove to be of considerable importance (see for instance Zeph. ii. 3, where instead of תסתרו is תטהרו; which emendation was early effected by a finely executed erasure; it is not noticed by Kennicott). To the pointer, accentuator, &c., probably belong all the older קרי &c., the older few pieces of מסרת and a few marks of הפטרות, all easily recognized by character and ink.

3. The real מסרת, which in its larger form occupies 2 lines on the upper and 3 lines on the lower margins, and in its lesser form the outer margin and the space between the columns, belongs to a third scribe. This מסרת, although it contains a few things (סמנים simple or mnemonics) not to be found in the printed editions, is not of any great value, as in the first place they are very few indeed, and in the second place they are mostly incomplete (see Excurs. I.). To this writer belong the "candlesticks" which adorn the outer margin on pages 1—3 and 16 of every quire (the first quire has them on pages 2—7 and 16). These are said (by Kennicott) to contain מסרת; but such is only the case at the commencement (leaves 1ᵇ—3ᵃ, and even of these 2ᵃ already contains Ps. ciii. in addition) and from leaf 360ᵇ (Proverbs) onwards. Those of the greater part of the MS. have Psalms, the book of Psalms itself having pieces from Chronicles and Ezra-Nehemiah. To this hand belong also some marks for הפטרות, which are easily to be distinguished from those of the other scribes. This scribe has moreover marked the quires in the corner of the upper margin; they are 58 in number.

4. The scribe, who executed the ornamentation in gold and colours, has supplied also, at the commencement of the various books, the word ספר (a fresh book), as is found on leaves 56ᵇ, 97ᵇ, 118ᵃ, 133ᵃ, 216ᵇ, 241ᵇ, 273ᵃ, 300ᵇ, 304ᵃ, 305ᵇ, 309ᵃ (twice), 310ᵃ, 312ᵇ, 314ᵃ, 315ᵇ, 316ᵃ, 320ᵇ, 373ᵇ, 390ᵇ, 394ᵇ, 398ᵇ,

405^b, 415^a and 428^b, or the names of the books, as שמואל and מלכים. The only books which have no ornament at the beginning, are Habakkuk, Psalms, Proverbs and Canticles, which, however, commence on a fresh column, and Lamentations, because its contents are not in harmony with ornamentation (see Excurs. I). To this scribe probably belong also various marks for הפטרות in the respective passages of the prophets; and certain of the older emendations as well as a few pieces of מסרת may also be assigned to him.

5. A fifth hand wrote some corrections which may occasionally be traced (see leaves 323^a, 328^b, &c.). This is no professional scribe but a learned owner. To him also some marks for הפטרות belong. We must not omit to remark on this occasion, that the notices concerning the הפטרות in this MS. are of the highest value, not merely because they form a link in the evidence concerning the time and place at which this MS. existed (as will be seen in Excurs. I.), but because certain passages of the Pentateuch, ordinarily not looked upon as distinct weekly פרשיות, are here specified as such, e. g. ויפן (Exod. xxxii. 15). Compare leaf 50^b with leaf 196^a, &c.

6. An Ashkenazic hand (probably in France or Holland) has marked the Christian division of the Bible into books and chapters throughout. It is, no doubt, this hand, which re-touched the MS. where the ink had peeled off, and it is also the same person who marked the correct positions of certain quires (formerly transposed and now set right) by such phrases as ח׳ דפים נגדך, and י׳ דפים לפניך.

At the end of the volume is a parchment leaf which has apparently at one time preceded a copy of the "tables of the covenant" written within an ornamental coloured border, such as is frequently found in manuscripts of the xiiith century and onwards. It was probably the work of the fourth of the scribes mentioned above. Following this are two paper fly-leaves with Library-marks, and a note on the age of the MS., signed 'Israel Lyons, Junr., 1753.'

The state of the MS. is, on the whole, extremely good, except the first leaf (which is slightly injured, though not in the text), and the margins, particularly the upper one, which are badly cut, so that few traces of the running titles are left.

This MS. is Cod. 89 in Kennicott's list. It was collated by him, but he has certainly amplified the number of the various readings to be found here. Full details of the contents of the margins will be found in the MS. notice preserved in the Library. The מסרת was collated in 1870 by Dr Ginsburg for his projected edition.

This volume, a truly royal gift, was presented to the University by King George I., with the rest of Bp. Moore's collection. In the list of the Moore MSS. it is numbered 1006 (e. 15); from which it is apparent that it must have formed part of a choice collection of early MSS. procured from France shortly after 1697.

[Library-mark, Mm. 5. 27; presented in 1715.]

No. 13.

Parchment, $13\frac{1}{8}$ in. × 11 in.; 246 leaves, 4-sheet quires, 3 columns[1], 37 lines; square character, fine Sephardic handwriting of the XII—XIIIth century.

[התורה הנביאים והכתובים]

The Bible.

Leaf 1ᵃ, blank; 1ᵇ, *Genesis;* 16ᵃ, *Exodus;* 28ᵃ *Leviticus;* 36ᵇ, *Numbers;* 48ᵃ, *Deuteronomy;* 59ᵃ, *Joshua;* 66ᵇ, *Judges;* 74ᵃ, *Samuel* (83ᵇ, 2 *Samuel*); 92ᵃ, *Kings* (102ᵃ, 2 *Kings*); 112ᵃ, *Isaiah;* 125ᵃ, *Jeremiah;* 141ᵇ, *Ezekiel;* 156ᵇ, *Hosea;* 158ᵇ, *Joel;* 159ᵃ, *Amos;* 161ᵃ, *Obadiah;* 161ᵃ, *Jonah;* 161ᵇ, *Micah;* 162ᵇ, *Nahum;* 163ᵃ, *Habakkuk;* 163ᵇ, *Zephaniah;* 164ᵇ, *Haggai;* 165ᵃ, *Zechariah;* 167ᵇ, *Malachi;* 168ᵃ, *Chronicles* (177ᵃ, 2 *Chronicles*); 188ᵇ, *Psalms;* 209ᵃ, *Job;* 217ᵃ, *Proverbs;* 223ᵇ, *Ruth;* 224ᵇ, *Canticles;* 225ᵇ, *Ecclesiastes;* 228ᵃ, *Lamentations;* 229ᵃ, *Esther;* 231ᵇ, *Daniel;* 236ᵇ, *Ezra* (240ᵃ, *Nehemiah*); 245ᵃ, Table of the Christian division into books and chapters; 246ᵇ, blank.

Two principal hands are distinguishable in the text:

The first scribe, who wrote leaves 1ᵇ—168ᵇ (Genesis—1 Chron. ii. 48),

The second scribe, who wrote leaves 169ᵃ—244ᵇ (1 Chron. ii. 48—Ezra-Nehemiah).

There is an interval of 3 lines between the books of the Pentateuch, except that between Exodus and Leviticus there are 4 (see Excurs. I.). Between the Pentateuch and the Prophets 12 lines are left, and within the Former Prophets 3 lines between book and book. The Latter Prophets commence on a fresh leaf (after 14 lines), and the several books thereof have 4 lines. Within the 12 Minor Prophets, which in point of space are as one book (see Excurs. I.), 3 lines are left. The Hagiographa commence on a fresh column after 22 lines. Of these the Psalms and Job are preceded by 4 lines each, Proverbs commence on a fresh leaf after 2 lines, and the Five Rolls on a fresh column after 11 lines. Within the Rolls 4 lines are left between book and book, as is the case also between Esther and Daniel. Between this last and Ezra, which commences on a fresh column, 2 lines are left blank.

[1] The exceptions are leaves 58 (the Song of Moses), 188ᵇ—223ᵃ (the poetical books), which are in two columns and arranged in hemistichs, and 245ᵃ—246ᵃ, which are in six columns.

The vacant spaces are filled up by the two scribes naturally in two different ways, viz.: by the former in putting a מ, or part thereof, and occasionally '', and by the latter in either taking part of the word on the next line, or in putting a Rabbinic א (see Excurs I.). The text has vowel-points and accents; but the system of the former differs somewhat in the two different parts of the MS. Thus while in the earlier part the חטף פתח, even in the דומות (two ב, two ל, &c.), is but sparingly used, the latter part abounds with it. The sign of רפה, which is not found here in the absence of the דגש lene, is found over letters where superficial grammatical knowledge might expect a דגש forte, and think the omission thereof a mere accident. The text is remarkably correct and the various readings are of considerable value.

The מסרת, which occupies, in its larger form 2 lines on the upper and 3 lines on the lower margin, and in its lesser form the outer margin and the spaces between the columns, is the most complete yet discovered, unless in a special book thereon. There is very little of value in the printed editions which is not noticed here, while there is much here not to be found in them. Various readings are given here in the margins from the following sources: (1) מגה (in the second part מוגה or בספר מוגה), 167; (2) יפה, four; (3) גד, one; besides ס״א and מסורת (these last mostly in the latter part). The margins are also rich in sopheric rules and literature (see Excurs. I.). It must be added that, as in the text, so also in the מסרת, the scribes of the earlier and later parts of the volume must have drawn from a similar (if not the same) source; as, except a slightly different spelling and a preponderance of the one codex over the other, they both quote the same standard copies, and give the same kind of mnemonics in Aramaic (סימנים בלשון תרגום). These latter are of particularly great value here (see Excurs. I.). To the first scribe belong the plain mark פרש in the Pentateuch and the numbering of the first 21 quires, and to the second scribe the numbers to the Psalms (149[1], as cxiv. and cxv. here form one Psalm).

Leaves 245ª—246ª are occupied by a Table of the Christian division of the several books of the Hebrew Bible, drawn up by R. Solomon b. Ismael, and written in mixed Rabbinic and current character (משיטה). If not copied by the same scribe as the latter part of the text (which seems not altogether impossible), it cannot well be later than the early part of the xivth century, or at least a hundred years before the date of R. Isaac Nathan, whose concordance, begun in 1437, is usually considered the first instance of the Jewish adoption of the Christian chapters for any purpose. The introduction shows that it was here used for the purpose of ready reference in the continually recurring controversies with the Christians.

Begins (leaf 245ª):

אלו הן פרקי הגוים הנקראים קפיטולש של ארבעה ועשרים ספרים ושמות כל ספר וספר בלשונם והעתקתים מהספר שלהם שיוכל אדם להשיב להם

[1] It should also be mentioned that Ps. קי״ז (cxvii. of the editions) here includes the first four verses of the following Psalm.

תשובה מהרה על שאלותם שהם שואלים לנו בכל יום על ענין אמונתנו ותורתנו הקדושה ומביאים ראיות מפסוקי התורה הן מנביאים או מספרים אחרים ואומרים לנו ראה וקרא בפסוק פלוני שהוא בספר פלוני בכך וכך קפיטולש מהספר ואין אנו יודעים מה הוא הקפיטולש ולהשיב להם מהרה תשובה לכן העתקתים פה.

ספר בראשית נקרא בלשונם גֶ̃נִישִׁי

פרק ראשון בראשית ברא אלים

שני ויכלו השמים

Ends (leaf 246[a]):

ל׳ו ויקחו עם הארץ את יהואחז.,

עוד יש להם ספר אחד נקרא מַקָבֶיבְש והוא מגלת אנטיוכוס.,

נשלמו פרקי הגוים מכל כ״ד ספרים והעתיק אותם ר׳ שלמה בן איסמעאל מן הספרים שלהם כדי שיוכל אדם להשיב תשובה מהרה על כל שאלותם.

Some way down the page is the following note, partly obliterated, possibly in the same handwriting as the above table:

סכום פסוקי עשרים וארבעה שתי רבוא ו···· אלפים ושבע מאות וארבעים ושבעה לא יתר לא פחות וסימן רכב אלהים רבותים אלפי שנאן

But we have to notice, besides these principal writers, a few others who have left their mark on this MS.; viz.

The scribe who supplied the running titles to the various books on the upper margin. He still keeps to the original division, as may be seen from his treating Samuel &c. as one book. The writing may be attributed to the latter half of the xivth century.

His successor, however, of scarcely a hundred years later, adopts the Christian division and carries it systematically through. The work of this writer is easily discerned; it is mostly executed in red, or attention is drawn to it by a design in that colour. To him belong also the few pieces of ornamentation in red and gold which disfigure the original designs done in ink (leaves 2[b], 4[a], 11[b], 58[a], 58[b] and 59[a]).

To another scribe again (of the xvith century) is due the division of the Psalms into seven parts, for the purpose, no doubt, of reciting them in the course of the week (see Excurs. I.). This division and its purpose can only be guessed from the א ב ג ה ו placed at the end of Psalms xxi., xxxviii., lviii., lxxxix., and cxiv., the ד being probably omitted after lxxii., because that is the end of a book. To this writer belongs also סימן יתקק on leaf 168[a].

In what estimation this MS. was held for its correctness and its excellent מסרת, may be seen from a description on a leaf of paper which formerly covered leaf 1[a], but which now forms a fly-leaf at the beginning of the volume. It runs thus:

ספר ארבעה ועשרים כתוב מכתיבת יד בקלף דוכסוסטום עם נקודות וטעמים ואותיות קטנות עם גדולות מעשה ידי אומן על יד סופר מהיר

ומובהק ובקי בסדר הפרשיות ובמסרות מסרה גדולה וקטנה כתובים סביבות הגליונות כאשר יראה הרואה עם ציון הפרשיות פתוחות וסתומות ולא נודע הכותב אל מי מקדושים ישמח הקורא ויגל הכותב אמן׃

This description, belonging to the xviii—xixth century, expresses great admiration indeed; but the praise it bestows on the MS. is far from overstating its merits. On the contrary, they are understated; for the Table, which, though last in order, is by no means least in importance, is not mentioned.

The greater part of the MS. is much stained and soiled, and numerous leaves are more or less injured, particularly 1, 9—19, 33, 176, 192 and 246. The writing is also in some places scarcely legible, and the margins, which must have been of large dimensions (see leaves 229 and 244), are now considerably cut. Nevertheless one may safely assert that few Biblical MSS. extant are of such value.

This volume has not been used for any printed edition, but a full collation of the text &c. will be found in the MS. notice preserved in the Library. The מסרת was collated in 1870 by Dr Ginsburg.

[Library-mark, Add. 465; bought in 1869 from H. Lipschütz of Cracow.]

No. 14.

Parchment, 7 in. × 4⅞ in.; 288 leaves, 6-sheet quires, 2 columns[1], 32 lines; square character, fine Sephardic handwriting of the xiii—xivth century.

[התורה הנביאים והכתובים עם מורה הנבוכים]

The Bible with the מורה of Rabbi Moses ben Maimon; defective.

Leaf 1a, probably blank, wanting; 1b, *Genesis;* 37a, *Exodus;* 68a, *Leviticus;* 90a, *Numbers;* 121b, *Deuteronomy;* 149b, *Joshua;* 169a, *Judges;* 187b, *Samuel* (212a, 2 *Samuel*); 232a, *Kings* (256b, 2 *Kings*); 280—288 and all that followed wanting.

The interval of lines between the various books is unequal and seems chiefly to have been determined by the necessities of ornamentation. Thus while Exodus, Leviticus, Samuel and Kings are preceded by 5 lines, Numbers is by 4, Deuteronomy by 6 and Joshua by 1 line only. (As a defect oc-

[1] The only exceptions are leaves 47b—48a (part), which contain the Song of Moses and the children of Israel and the Song of Miriam; 147a—148a, which contain the Song of Moses; 172b, which contains the greater part of the Song of Deborah; and 229b—230a, which contains the Song of David. The Song of Miriam is written over the whole page without metrical form, while that of Moses is in hemistichs; all the others, however, are in אריח על גבי לבנה &c. (see Excurs. I.).

curs immediately before Judges, we cannot say whether any, and if so, how many, lines were left before that book.) The scribe has left, however, independently of the above, at the commencement of each book, in accordance with the ordinary and non-Jewish custom of his time, a space of 3 or 4 lines for the insertion of ornamental initial letters. The subdivisions of the Pentateuch have 3-line, and the other books 4-line initials. Besides these the MS. has other ornaments of various kinds, as animals &c., illustrative of the events narrated in Holy Writ (leaf 4[b] an ark, 5[b] a dove, 6[a] a rainbow, &c.). These are more numerous in the Pentateuch, where they are chiefly placed at the commencement of the weekly פרשיות. They are all executed either in gold or colours or in both together. The names of the weekly פרשיות in the Pentateuch and of the several books in the Prophets are to be found in the outer corners of the upper margins. The הפטרות are marked at the respective passages in the Prophets.

The vacant spaces at the end of a line are mostly filled up by one or more letters of the first word on the next line and occasionally by a ז (see Excurs. I.). The text, which is provided with vowel-points and accents, has now and then the sign of רפה over the א, when quiescent, to prevent the insufficiently informed from pronouncing it (as לאדני &c.). This copy can vie in correctness with the finest productions of the school to which it belongs.

The מסרת, which in its double form, although mixed up, is represented on the outer margin and on the space between the columns, is rather scanty, but nevertheless not without value. It has some of the Aramaic mnemonics (סימנים בלשון תרגום, see Excurs. I.); it has some rarer pieces of the ordinary מסרת, which are only to be found in the מסרת הגדולה as a special book (compare the אכלה ואכלה, ed. Frensdorff, Hannover, 1864, 4°.); it has some sopheric rules of great importance, throwing light on some difficult passages in the commentators on the שלחן ערוך יורה דעה (see Excurs. I.), and it quotes the standard codices ירושלמי, מוגה and the הללי (the first several times, the second on leaf 97[b], and the last on 132[a]).

The following leaves are either partially or totally wanting: 1—2 (all), 3 (part), 10 (almost all), 11 (all), 12 (part), 157, 159, 160 (all), 162, 163 (part), 165, 166, 168, 280—288 and all after these (totally). The defects caused thereby in the text are

Genesis: i. 1—iii. 7 (בראשית to עירמים) and single words or letters in iii. 14—16, and iv. 24—v. 1; xvi. 5—xvii. 20 (חמסי to יוליד) are almost gone, and xvii. 23—xix. 13 (וימל to גדלה) and 22, then a portion of 32—33; and finally xx. 4—6 (הגוי to כפי) are entirely gone, and

Joshua: x. 12—41 (ואת to יהוה); xii. 5—xv. 9 (חשבון to ותאר); xviii. 16 (על פני גי); xxi. 6—xxii. 27 (אשר to לבנינו); xxiv. 3—33 (את יצחק to אפרים the end of the book).

Where ordinarily the מסרת in its larger form is to be found, this copy has the מורה הנבוכים of Maimonides, according to Ibn Tibbon's translation. This occupies 3 lines on the upper and 4 lines on the lower margins and conforms, on the whole, to the printed editions. It reaches from i. to ii. 16, and is defective in various places, owing to the loss, either total or partial, of several leaves.

Begins (leaf 3[a]; ed. Sabionetta, 1553, leaf 8[b]):

בה מתכונת הגשמים ...

Breaks off (leaf 279[b]; ed. Sab., leaf 93[b]):

... כן תתחייב הרחקה יותר גדולה ממנה.

An owner, of the xv—xvith century, has arbitrarily divided the whole Prophets for purposes of recitation in connexion with the weekly פרשיות of the Pentateuch. With the פרשה of משפטים ends 2 Kings, with which the MS. breaks off; and from the fact that the owner just mentioned has written, at the end of the volume as it now stands, the words תרומה דברי ירמיהו, we gather (1) a confirmation of what we suspected before (seeing that 2 Kings ended on the third leaf of a 6-sheet quire), that this volume is only the earlier portion of a whole Bible; and (2) that that Bible conformed to the rules of the Babylonian Talmud, that Jeremiah should succeed Kings (see Excurs. I.).

[Library-mark, Add. 468; bought in 1869 from H. Lipschütz.]

No. 15.

Vellum, 10 in. × 7½ in.; 499 leaves, mostly 5-sheet quires, 3 columns[1], 28 lines; square character, German Ashkenazic hand of the xiv—xvth century.

[התורה הנביאים והכתובים]

THE BIBLE, in three parts; defective.

I. PENTATEUCH AND PROPHETS: Leaf 1, blank, wanting; 2[a], *Genesis;* 33[b], *Exodus;* 59[b], *Leviticus;* 78[a], *Numbers;* 103[b], *Deuteronomy;* 127[a], *Joshua;* 144[a], *Judges;* 160[b], *Samuel* (182[b], 2 *Samuel*); 199[b], *Kings* (219[b], 2 *Kings*); 239[a], *Isaiah;* 266[a], *Jeremiah;* 299[b], *Ezekiel* (320 wanting); 328[b], *Hosea;* 332[b], *Joel;* 334[a], *Amos;* 337[a], *Obadiah;* 337[b], *Jonah;* 338[b], *Micah;* 340[b], *Nahum;* 341[b], *Habakkuk;* 342[b], *Zephaniah;* 343[b], *Haggai;* 344[b], *Zechariah;* 349[b], *Malachi;* 351[b], Table of הפטרות (according to the Ashkenazic rite); 353, probably blank, wanting. The defect at leaf 320 is Ezek. xxxvi. 11 (כי אני)—xxxvii. 17.

II. FIVE ROLLS: Leaf 354[a], *Ruth;* 356[a], *Canticles;* 358[a], *Ecclesiastes;* 362[b], *Lamentations;* 365[a], *Esther.*

III. REST OF THE HAGIOGRAPHA: Leaf 370[a], *Psalms;* 404[a], *Proverbs;* 415[b], *Job;* 429[a], *Daniel;* 439[b], *Ezra* (446[a], *Nehemiah*); 455[b], *Chronicles* (473[a], 2 *Chronicles*); 491—499, wanting, that is, xxxii. 21 (פנים) to the end.

[1] The only exceptions are leaves 42[b]—43[a] (the song of Moses and the children of Israel, the first half of which is in אריח &c., whilst the latter half is in the form of a chessboard); 124[a]—125[b] (the Song of Moses, which, although written in two columns, reads from column to column as hemistichs); 147 (Song of Deborah, in אריח &c.); 197[b]—198[a] (Song of David, in אריח &c.); and 369[b] (containing the end of the book of Esther, and which is written in a single column).

Three hands are distinguishable in this MS.:

(1) The writer of the text;

(2) The pointer, accentuator, &c., possibly a son or grandson of the original copyist;

(3) The writer of the מסרת.

I. There is an entire want of system respecting the interval between the various books, the scribe's principal aim seemingly being to commence every book (and in the Pentateuch every weekly פרשה) with a large initial word. In the larger divisions these initial words are of larger dimensions; some of them, however, have never been executed. The scribe has a few peculiarities which are well worth recording. (1) To fill up vacant spaces he uses the following expedients: he either dilates a letter in the usual way, or he dilates it in an ornamental style (ـ··· — ···ל=ל, 96ª; ـ··· — ···ם=ם, 149ᵇ &c.); or he takes a letter or more from the word on the next line; or finally, he puts one ׳ or more or a ה in Rabbinic character (see Excurs. I.). (2) The final letters כנפץ rarely reach below the line. To this scribe belong also: (1) The word הפטרה, attached to the respective passages in the Prophets, the fuller heading of which he does not trouble himself to specify, as he furnishes a special Table for that purpose. (2) The names, on the recto page, of the various books (the Pentateuch excepted), which are by him separately paged. (3) The numbers to the Psalms (147, as xlii.—xliii., lxx.—lxxi., and cxvii.—cxviii. here form single Psalms; see Excurs. I.)[1]. The text, particularly in the Pentateuch, is more correct than one would have expected from an Ashkenazic copy. The last page of the Pentateuch is arranged in an ornamental manner, and it closes with the following subscription by the original copyist, the first three words of which are almost erased (leaf 126ª, col. 3): אני הסופר משה בר אליעזר אשר כתבתי לעצמי ולרצוני הש׳ (השם) יזכני שיהיה לזרע זרעי עד עולם ברוך הש׳ לעילום אשר הביאני עד הלום ויביאני הלאה לכתוב עשרים וארבע.

II. This copy is provided with vowel-points and accents by another, though not much later, hand. Here also some peculiarities are worth noticing: (1) The קמץ חטוף, except in כל, is formed as if it were a חטף קמץ. (2) The קמץ occurring under a ך is strictly placed under, and not within, it. (3) The שוא, in a similar case, is mostly left out altogether. (4) The בגדכפת, when liquid, have a רפה sign. To this scribe belong also: (1) the indication, at the respective פרשיות in the Pentateuch, of the page on which the prophetic portion is to be found, and (2) some of the amounts of verses contained in the פרשיות and books of the Pentateuch. At the end of the Pentateuch, on the upper margin, he has made the following entry in Rabbinic character: אני ליזר סימנתי ההפטרת אצל פרשיותיהן. This ליזר (that is אליעזר) is probably the son or grandson of the original copyist.

III. The מסרת, mostly written in a mixed character (Rabbinic and cursive), is of some extent in the Pentateuch and the book of Esther, although

[1] The actual numbering does not extend beyond 144.

but rarely to be met with in the other books. The handwriting may be of the early part of the xvith century. The following authorities and standard codices are quoted:

(1) ר׳ אושעי׳;

(2) the author of the פרחון;

(3) קמחי[1];

(4) מ״ש׳ (probably מאיר שפירץ, see R. Elia's מסורת המסורת, p. 77);

(5) רמ״ח (probably ר׳משה חזן, see ib. 76);

(6) ע״ה (no doubt the עין הקורא);

(7) ר׳ מאיר (possibly the same as No. 4);

(8) the ספר ירחו (probably the same as the חומש ירחו, see מסורת, p. 78);

(9) the ספרי אספמיא (unquestionably Sephardic Bibles, and perhaps the הללי, the מוגה, the יפה, the גד, &c., see No. 13 of this Catalogue);

(10) רי״ן (either ר׳ יעקב נקדן, see מסורת, 77; or ר׳ יוסף הנקדן, see Maimonides, משנה תורה, book אהבה, in the הלכות ספר תורה, viii., where in the הגהה to Leviticus, a disciple of R. Meir of Rothenburg mentions one of this name as the author of a תקון סופרים); and

(11) the גויל (perhaps identical with the ספר תורה corrected by בן אשר, which is supposed to be identical with the ירושלמי, see מסורת, p. 17, and משנה תורה, as above; compare also Geiger's interesting article in the כרם חמד, ix. pp. 61, 62).

To this scribe belong also: (1) The titles of the פרשיות of the Pentateuch (in the corner of the recto page); (2) the consecutive paging of the MS. (in the corner of the verso page); and (3) the greater portion of the specifications of numbers of verses at the end of the פרשיות and the books of the Pentateuch, &c.

Two owners' names are to be found:

On leaf 2ª: זה הספר של הח׳ (החכם) המ׳ (המובהק) כ׳מ׳ה׳ר (כבוד מורנו הרב רבי) יצחק שמעון הי״ו; the last abbreviation standing for ה׳ישמרהו ויחיהו (Ps. xli. 3).

On leaf 97ª is the entry:

יצחק אלמידה ב׳כ׳ר (בן כבוד רבי) שלמה אלמידה נרו לא תכבה א׳כ׳י׳ר (אמן כן יהי רצון) ב׳נ׳ל׳ך ו׳א׳ע׳י ל׳ק׳י; where ב׳נ׳ל׳ך ו׳א׳ע׳י stands for נותן ליעף כח ולאין אונים עצמה ירבה (Is. xl. 29 with ברוך prefixed); and ל׳ק׳י for לישועתך קויתי י׳י (Gen. xlix. 18).

The following leaves are damaged, the greater part of them having been cut on the lower margin for the sake of the vellum: 2, 4, 6, 7, 11, 17, 18, 28, 31, 36, 53, 56, 102, 106, 114, 115, 121—141, 158, 159, 191—193, 206—214, 257, 260—263, 294, 307—309, 314—326, 329, 331—339, 344, 355—370, 404, 405, 407, 409—446, 454—463, 470—476, 485—486.

[Library-mark, Add. 466; bought in 1869 from H. Lipschütz.]

[1] On the word ירחע (1 Chron. ii. 34) the following remark is to be found on leaf 456ᵇ: לא נמצא בבל הקריא׳ חו׳ע מותא׳ כי אם בשום ירחע ולולי כי עבד מצרי היה לא נקרא שמו כן קמחי.

No. 16.

Parchment, $10\frac{5}{8}$ in. × $8\frac{1}{2}$ in.; 336 leaves, 4-sheet quires, 2 columns[1], 26 lines; square character, fine Sephardic handwriting of the XIII—XIVth century.

[התורה והכתובים]

The PENTATEUCH and the HAGIOGRAPHA.

Leaf 1ª, blank; 1ᵇ, *Genesis;* 36ᵇ, *Exodus;* 67ᵇ, *Leviticus;* 89ᵇ, *Numbers;* 119ᵇ, *Deuteronomy;* 146ᵇ, blank; 147ª, *Chronicles* (168ª, 2 *Chronicles*); 195ᵇ, *Psalms;* 244ᵇ, *Job;* 265ª, blank; 265ᵇ, *Proverbs;* 282ᵇ, *Ruth;* 285ª, *Canticles;* 287ᵇ, *Ecclesiastes;* 293ᵇ, *Lamentations;* 297ª, *Esther;* 303ª, *Daniel;* 315ᵇ, *Ezra* (323ᵇ, *Nehemiah*); 335ᵇ, blank: 336, probably blank, wanting.

There is an interval of 3 lines between Genesis and Exodus and of 4 lines between the other books of the Pentateuch. The Hagiographa commence on a fresh leaf after more than 3 columns blank. The Psalms begin on a fresh column after 10 lines blank. (The separate books thereof have intervals of 2 lines, the second having 1 blank at the foot of the preceding page; and there are single blank lines between the several alphabetic divisions of Ps. cxix. The number and divisions are as in the modern editions; but the marks have been forgotten in viii., mistaken in xxxii., forgotten in liii., mistaken in liv., forgotten in lvi. and lxv., mistaken in lxxxiv., and forgotten in cix. and cxix.) Between the Psalms and Job 5 lines are left, and between that and Proverbs a whole page. Seven lines, across the page, are left between Proverbs and Ruth, 5 lines between that and Canticles and Ecclesiastes; and 6 between that book and Lamentations (which has a blank line between most of the alphabetic divisions in chapter iii.). Three lines are left between Lamentations and Esther; 4 between that book and Daniel, and 12 between that and Ezra, which commences on a fresh column (see Excurs. I.).

The text is a model of beauty and correctness, and in strict accordance with the מסרת, neglecting now and then the traditions of the Babylonian Talmud (see Excurs. I.). In the Pentateuch the MS. has on the margins, within an elaborate design in gold, a פ to mark the weekly פרשה, and, in gold or colour, a ס to mark the סדר according to the מסרת (see Excurs.

[1] The only exceptions are leaves 47ª and 47ᵇ (part), which contain the song of Moses and the children of Israel, and which is written in אריח על גבי לבנה &c. (see Excurs. I.); 143ᵇ or 145ª (part), which contain the Song of Moses and which is metrically arranged; 158ᵇ—159ª, which contain the Thanksgiving of David; and 195ᵇ—282ª, which contain the three poetical books metrically arranged.

I.), whilst in the Psalms the numbers are given in ordinary ink. To fill up the vacant spaces, the scribe frequently inserts ״, such being the upper part of a ע; sometimes, however, the latter part of a ח, and occasionally a portion of the first word of the next line (see Excurs. I.). The text has vowel-points and accents, the sign of רפה over בגדכפת, when liquid, the same over ה when quiescent, and now and then also over quiescent א, for two of this nature standing together only one sign being used.

The מסרת in its larger form occupies, as a rule, 2 lines on the upper and 3 lines on the lower margin; and in its lesser form, though not exclusively, the inner and outer margins and the space between the columns. The larger מסרת is sometimes exhibited in ornamental work, animals, &c., designed to illustrate events related in the text (for instance, leaf 2[b] a serpent, 13[b] a ram, 315[b] a lion, &c.). At the end of the weekly פרשיות in the Pentateuch and at the end of all the separate books in the volume, the number of the verses contained therein is given, mnemonic signs, many of which are not extant in print, being added in the Pentateuch. Most of the books have also, at the proper places, the centre-mark (חצי הספר), the Pentateuch even having the mark רביעית התורה, and the Hagiographa (as one book) that of חצי הכתובים. Although here, as everywhere else, where it is subservient to purposes of ornamentation, the מסרת is far from being complete (see Excurs. I.), it is yet of especial value for the following reasons: (1) It records Aramaic mnemonics (וס׳ בל׳ תרג׳), some of which are not to be found in print or even in our MSS. (see Excurs. I.); (2) it records readings from three standard codices, the הללי, the מוגה and the יפה (see No. 13 of this Catalogue); and (3) it is particularly instructive in sopheric rules (see Excurs. I.).

Leaves 241—248 are by another and perhaps later hand; yet written according to the system of the whole MS.

Later hands have added a number of various readings of considerable importance, under the heading of ס״א, and have provided the Pentateuch with the mark of the open and closed chapters (פרשיות פתוחות וסתומות) according to Maimonides (להר״ם).

Several of the leaves (1—16, 64, 146, 156, 203, 229, 248, 273—281 and 284) are more or less damaged in the outer and lower margins; but the MS. is, on the whole, in very good condition.

The following owners have inscribed their names in this volume. Leaf 1[a]: (1) J. V. (Vita); (2) דוד אברהם חי; (3) Leone Vita; (4) Felice Vita; (5) יהודה חיים פברי (da Fabriano?); leaf 335[b]: יצחק שומאל (שמואל?) חי; and, on a fly-leaf at the beginning, צבי ליפשיץ.

[Library-mark, Add. 652; bought in 1870 from Samuel Schönblum of Lemberg.]

No. 17.

Parchment, $13\frac{7}{8}$ in. × $10\frac{1}{4}$ in.; 456 leaves, 4-sheet quires, 2 columns, 26—27 lines; square character, fine French Ashkenazic handwriting of the XIII—XIVth century.

[התורה עם תרגום אונקלוס : חמש המגלות : ההפטרות
כמנהג האשכנזים : איוב ודברים הרעים שבירמיה]

The PENTATEUCH with the Aramaic paraphrase of אונקלוס; the FIVE ROLLS; the PROPHETIC PORTIONS according to the Ashkenazic rite; JOB and certain passages in JEREMIAH; defective.

Leaf 1, *Genesis;* 86ᵇ, *Exodus;* 160ᵃ, *Leviticus;* 212ᵇ, *Numbers;* 283ᵇ, *Deuteronomy;* 346ᵃ, *Canticles;* 349ᵃ, *Ruth;* 352ᵃ, *Lamentations;* 355ᵃ, *Ecclesiastes;* 361ᵃ, *Esther;* 367ᵇ, *Prophetic portions;* 420ᵃ, *Job;* 438ᵇ, *Jeremiah.*

The intervals between the various books are unequal; but each of these has a large initial word. In the Pentateuch there is between the weekly פרשיות a line left with a פ and sometimes with פפפ, which here stand simply for פרשה and not for פתוחה, as the ס never occurs, and the פרשיות פתוחות וסתומות are not marked with letters. The vacant spaces are filled up with part of the word on the next line and occasionally with a Rabbinic א (see Excurs. I.). The MS. has numerous designs of animals &c., which are chiefly found either at the end of quires or at the commencement of a book. Sometimes they are executed in matter of מסרת.

The text (with very few exceptions, which occur principally at the הפטרות and are pointed out there by the scribe, as on leaf 385ᵃ, between the columns) has vowel-points and accents. The קמץ חטוף is invariably given by חטף קמץ, except in the word כל; and the letters בגדכפת when liquid have the sign of רפה.

The whole of this arrangement extends also to the תרגום, which follows every verse of the text in the Pentateuch. While the text offers, except positive mistakes, no various readings, the תרגום has some variants of value, in the hand of the original copyist, and not a few of even greater value by a later Sephardic hand, probably that of a learned owner. These latter are to be found on the outer margin and are in Rabbinic character. Unfortunately, they cease at leaf 84ᵇ (not quite the end of Genesis). It is worth noticing that there is no תרגום to the sacerdotal benediction (Num. vi. 24—26, see No. 19 of this Catalogue), while there is to Gen. xxxv. 22 (see Excurs. I.).

The מסרת which accompanies the whole MS. (except on a few pages where the defect is pointed out by the scribe, see leaves 382ᵃ and 402ᵇ), occupies, as usual, in its larger form the upper and lower margins and in its lesser form the outer margin and the space between the columns. It accompanies not only the various books which are in the volume but also the prophetic portions. As far as the matter goes, it would not be without value; but serving as it does for ornamental purposes, it suffers from incompleteness.

The principal interest of this copy lies in the peculiarity of its composition. Not that this is the only, or even a rare, instance, seeing that

Kennicott's codices 191, 196, 212, 223, 371, 383, 489, 589, 593, 624 and 631, consist more or less of the same component parts. But it gives us the opportunity to notice here what had apparently not been noticed before: that this and similar volumes ought to be looked upon more in the light of service-books than actual parts of a Bible. They would thus seem to have an intermediate value, for critical purposes, between the text found in a Bible and that in an ordinary מחזור. Thus the *Pentateuch* and the תרגום are here for the lessons to be read out on the various Sabbaths (and their eves), festivals, &c. The same is the case with the *Five Rolls*, which are here given in the order in which they are read in annual course, on the five occasions, Passover, Pentecost, the 9th of Ab (the anniversary of the destruction of the Holy Temple), Tabernacles, and the feast of Purim. The *Prophetic portions* are, as will be easily seen, the twin lessons of those from the Pentateuch. But *Job* and certain parts of *Jeremiah* are for the 9th of Ab and for mourners on other days also. See טור אורח חיים (by Jacob b. Asher), chap. 554, where we read: כל המצות הנוהגות באבל נוהגות בט' באב אבל קורא הוא באיוב ובדברים הרעים שבירמיה.... ובאשכנז נהגו לקרות פרשת קרבו גוים לשמוע אחרי שקראו דברים הרעים שבירמיה. See also טור and שלחן ערוך יורה דעה (by Jacob b. Asher and Joseph b. Ephraim Caro), chap. 384.

The following leaves are wholly wanting: 1—16, 137—152, 157[1], 450, 452, 453, 455 and all after 456; and the following leaves are more or less mutilated: 72, 302—303 (almost gone) and 368 (principally in the lower margin).

The MS. commences (leaf 17ᵃ, Gen. xi. 17):

מאות שנה ...

and breaks finally off (leaf 456ᵇ, Jerem. xxiii. 28):

...הנביא אשר אתו

On leaf 283ᵇ, is the following entry in Spagnol: אישטי ליברו איש די משה קאנפילייש אי' קון' יעקב קאנפילייש מיהן די מירקאר אישטאאש מישנות מירא דידאר מיאלנו ראש ראש אוהון... The writer of this is not the same who wrote the marginal emendations of the תרגום, mentioned above.

[Library-mark, Add. 464; bought in 1869 from H. Lipschütz.]

No. 18.

Parchment, 7⅛ in. × 5¼ in.; 206 leaves, 4-sheet quires, 2 columns[2], 28 lines; square character, fine Sephardic handwriting of the XIVth century.

1 Leaf 157 has been supplied by a later hand. The תרגום is neither pointed nor accentuated, lacks the מסרת, and is otherwise inferior. It is numbered 157*.

2 The exceptions are leaves 46, 139ᵇ—140ᵇ, 152 and 159 containing the Song of Moses and the children of Israel, the Song of Moses, the Song of Deborah, and the Song of David respectively; and all of which are given in אריח &c.

[התורה : ההפטרות כמנהג הספרדים : חמש המגלות]

The PENTATEUCH, the PROPHETIC PORTIONS according to the Sephardic rite, and the FIVE ROLLS, in three parts; defective.

I. GENESIS—EXODUS. Leaf 1[a], *Genesis;* 36[a]—65[b], *Exodus;* 66, probably blank, wanting.

II. LEVITICUS—DEUTERONOMY. Leaf 67[a], *Leviticus;* 87[b], *Numbers;* 116[a]—142[a], *Deuteronomy;* 142[b], probably blank, but 142 is wanting.

III. PROPHETIC PORTIONS—LAMENTATIONS. Leaf 143[a], *Prophetic portions;* 187[b], *Ruth;* 189[b], *Canticles;* 192[a], *Esther;* 198[a], *Ecclesiastes;* 203[a], *Lamentations.*

No system is observed in the intervals left between the books; but the scribe has left a space varying from 5 to 8 lines (16 in the case of Genesis) at the beginning of each book. In Genesis and Leviticus, which begin separable portions of the MS., the initial word is given in gold within a coloured design; in the other books of the Pentateuch the word ספר (a fresh book) is found, as in No. 12 described above. The third separable portion commences with the word הפטרות (the general superscription) and בראשית, in gold and colours, the headings of the several הפטרות being alternately in red and blue. In the Rolls, except Lamentations, which is without ornament (see Excurs. I.), the headings are designs in red, into which, in the case of Canticles and Ecclesiastes, the initial word is worked in ink. In the Pentateuch the weekly פרשיות are distinguished in the margin by a small design with פרש׳ in colours. To fill up the vacant spaces the scribe either puts a ׳ (or two or even three), such being the upper part of a ש, or he puts the first letter or so of the word on the next line (see Excurs. I.). On the other hand when he has not ample room to finish a word on the line, he puts its last letter or two in the margin, but at a certain distance from the word to which it belongs (e.g. הבאי ם).

The MS. has vowel-points and accents, and the sign of רפה on בגדכפת when liquid. It also has a scanty supply of the מסרת in its lesser form, which in most cases does not go beyond the noting down of the קרי &c.

The following peculiarities of this MS. are worth noticing:

(1) The הפטרות of the feasts and fasts do not stand by themselves but are incorporated among those of the weekly פרשיות. Thus between those for צו and שמיני the five for Passover are inserted; between those for במדבר and נשא the two for Pentecost, and again between those for דברים and ואתחנן the two for תשעה באב and the other fasts are given. From the piece left on leaf 183[a], which is for שמחת תורה, we see that the same system must have been observed respecting those for New Year, the Day of Atonement and Tabernacles.

(2) This rule is, however, not observed with respect to the הפטרות for

the Sabbaths of חנוכה, which are indeed neither given in the course of those for Genesis, nor even alluded to anywhere else throughout the MS.

(3) The הפטרות for the four פרשיות, that for the Sabbath and New Moon, and that for the Sabbath which is the eve of a New Moon, are given at the end.

(4) The הפטרה for אחרי מות commences (leaf 162[a]) at Amos ix. 6.

(5) The arrangement of the מגלות is remarkable. They follow in the order of the yearly reading, only reversed, Pentecost, Passover, Purim, Tabernacles and 9 Ab; commencing with *Ruth* it would seem for the very purpose of closing with *Lamentations* (see Excurs. I.).

The leaves wanting are: 3 (Gen. iii. 17 to v. 16); 6 (Gen. ix. 9 to xi. 7); 142 (Deut. xxxiv. 11 to the end); 175—182 (Is. l. 4, in the הפטרה for עקב, to Josh. i. 1, in the הפטרה for שמחת תורה).

At the foot of Leaf 1[a], is written: פקדון ניחמי הנק׳ ר׳ שמואל פ... . Another hand has noted the defect in the הפטרות and has supplied the missing matter in Genesis on two leaves of paper (numbered 3* and 6*) in an oriental Rabbinic character. At the end of the book another hand has written the following note: זה החומש הקדיש שלמה אוליאייא בכ״ר משה נ״ע (נוחו עדן) לקהל קדוש קהל קריריד והקדישו לכפרת נפש בנו ידידו היקר והמשכיל משה תנצ״בה (תהיה נפשו צרורה בצרור החיים) והלוקחו ומשיבו על מקומו יבמה. The third abbreviation is an allusion to 1 Sam. xxv. 29, and the last stands either for יבורך מן השמים or ישא ברכה מאת ה׳ (Ps. xxiv. 5). The word קריריד was first written קריריט, but the writer has inserted a pointed ד over the ט.

[Library-mark, Add. 469; bought in 1869 from H. Lipschütz.]

No. 19.

Parchment, 7⅝ in. × 6¼ in.; 152 leaves[1], 4-sheet quires, 19 lines; square character, Sephardic handwriting of the XII—XIIIth century.

[התורה עם תרגום אונקלוס]

The PENTATEUCH with the Aramaic paraphrase of אונקלוס; defective.

Leaf 1 of the first remaining quire and all that preceded, wanting; 2[a], *Numbers* vi. 14; 94[b], *Deuteronomy*.

[1] Only 19 quires remain out of the whole volume, and the numbering of the leaves only relates to these quires.

To judge from the only instance in our hands, the interval between the various books was determined by the designs the scribe wished to place there. Before Deuteronomy is a 6-line space exhibiting various animals, &c., all in ink. A small embellishment is also found on leaf 132[a], for the פרש (the weekly פרשה of ראה). To fill up the vacant spaces of the line the scribe uses chiefly a letter, or letters, from the first word on the next line, and now and then also a ט (see Excurs. I.), as on leaf 48[b], &c.

The text has vowel-points and accents. The various readings, which are not a few, do not elevate themselves beyond what is commonly to be found in other MSS. of this class.

The תרגום, however, which follows the text verse by verse, and to which also the vowel-points and accents extend, is of great importance, as, in the considerable variants it exhibits, there are many which are superior to the ordinary readings in the printed editions. The sacerdotal benediction (Num. vi. 25—27) is without תרגום (see No. 17 of this Catalogue).

There are emendations both of the text and of the תרגום, either in square character or in Rabbinic, partly by the original copyist and partly by an owner. They are easily to be distinguished from one another.

Numerous leaves are stained, soiled, and torn; and the following are almost or entirely lost: leaf 1 of the first remaining quire and all that preceded it, that is all before קורבניה (Num. vi. 14 in the תרגום); 17 (x. 36 text to xi. תרגום); 24 (xiii. 30 תרגום to xiv. 7 תרגום); 33 (xvi. 11 text to xvi. 23 text); 40 (xviii. 22 text to xviii. 32 תרגום); 146—151 (Deut. xvi. 12 text to xix. 10 תרגום), and all after 152[b], which breaks off: כי יהוה אלהיך עמך (xx. 1 text).

On leaf 50[a], occurs the name of יוסף אלכעלי; on 104[b] that of דוד אלכעלי; and on 94[b], the names of אברהם and שלמה can be traced.

This MS. is not noticed by Kennicott; but a full account of the various readings, both in text and תרגום, will be found in the MS. notice of it preserved in the Library.

[Library-mark, Dd. 11. 26; added to the collection between 1657 and 1752.]

No. 20.

Parchment, 15 in. × 12 in.; 121 and 72 leaves, mostly 4-sheet quires, 2 columns[1], 28—31 lines; square character, French Ashkenazic handwriting of the XII—XIIIth century.

[הנביאים והכתובים]

The PROPHETS and HAGIOGRAPHA; defective in the middle.

[1] The exceptions are, Frag. I., leaves 21[b]—22[a] (Song of Deborah), and 74[a]—75[a] (Song of David), both of which are in אריח &c.

Fragment I. The first 16 quires of the original volume. Leaf 1[a], blank; 1[b], *Joshua;* 18[b], *Judges;* 35[a], *Samuel* (57[b], 2 *Samuel*); 76[b], *Kings* (100[a], 2 *Kings*); 121[b], *Jeremiah*, breaking off with ויגע על פי, i. 9, as the end of the last remaining quire of this portion is wanting.

Fragment II. The last 9 quires of the original volume. Leaves 1—4 of the first remaining quire of this portion are wanting; 5[a], *Ezra* ii. 1 (12[a] *Nehemiah*); 23[b], *Chronicles* (44[a], 2 *Chronicles*); 71—72, probably blank, wanting.

From the fact that the Latter Prophets commence with Jeremiah, and that the Hagiographa end with Chronicles, it is clear that this MS. was written in conformity with the order recorded in the Talmud Babli, בבא בתרא, 14[b].

There is an interval of 3 (almost 4) lines after Joshua, and of 4 lines after Judges, Samuel and Kings. After Ezra (Nehemiah) there are 13 lines left to the foot of the page, so as to allow Chronicles to commence on the reverse of the leaf. The mode of commencing the books is worth notice. Joshua begins, as in a Sephardic MS. of the period, without any distinctive initial; while in all the other books the first word is made to occupy the centre of a line, but is in the ordinary character. The MS. thus affords an example of the gradual development from the simplicity of the Sephardic school to the large ornamental initials of the later Ashkenazic MSS. The vacant spaces at the end of lines are filled up with part of the word on the next line, and occasionally by a ׳ (see Excurs. I.). The MS. has vowel-points and accents. The letters בגדכפת when liquid have the sign of רפה, and the קמץ חטוף (except in כל) is always represented by a חטף קמץ.

So far goes the work of the original copyist, whose name appears to have been יעקב, and who is probably the ancestor of the Nathan who writes at the end of the volume: זה הכתובים ושמונה נביאים שלי נתן ב״ר יעקב סופר ז״צל מאיברא. This abbreviation stands for זכר צדיק לברכה (Prov. x. 7). It may be mentioned that Kennicott's Cod. 50 was written in the year פז (1327) by one Jacob b. Nathan of Evreux (מאייברא), who was probably a descendant of the above.

The מסרת (which is here confined to the קרי and similar notes) as well, as also a good many corrections, are due to another owner, Sarah the daughter of שמריה. This woman was probably then unmarried, as she has made the following note immediately underneath the above-mentioned entry:

זה הכתובים ושמונה נביאים שלי שרה בת החבר שמריה ז״צל

The running titles on the upper margin, the superscription at the commencement of some books, the pagination and the numbering of the Christian chapters, are due to another owner: ברוך בן מ ... (leaves 112[b], 113[a], &c.), between whom and the two previous owners several centuries must have elapsed.

In the xviii—xixth century this MS. was owned by R. Moses Hirsch, חזן at Jassy (in Moldavia), whose son שלמה is mentioned (Frag. I., leaf 50[a]). This R. Moses, in the course of his travelling to the Holy Land, presented it to a young man, Isaac, son of the physician Samuel Hallevi Ashkenazi (Frag. II., leaf 40ᵇ)[1]. The latter, although of Ashkenazic extraction, as his name indicates, was probably an Arabic-speaking Sephardic Jew, as will be seen from Frag. I., leaf 50ᵃ.

What we have of the MS. is in good condition.

[Library-mark, Add. 467; bought in 1869 from H. Lipschütz.]

No. 21.

Parchment, 12 in. × 10 in.; 196 leaves, 3-sheet quires, 2 columns[2], 19 lines; square character, fine Sephardic handwriting of the XIII—XIVth century.

[נביאים הראשונים]

The Former Prophets.

Leaf 1ᵃ, blank; 1ᵇ, *Joshua;* 29ᵇ, *Judges;* 57ᵇ, *Samuel* (93ᵇ, 2 *Samuel*); 124ᵃ, *Kings* (161ᵇ, 2 *Kings*); the last column blank.

There is an interval of 4 lines after Joshua, and of 3 after Judges and Samuel. No majuscule letters occur in this copy.

To fill up the vacant spaces the scribe inserts one ׳ or more; most commonly, however, two, such being the upper part of a צ (see Excurs. I.). They are found not merely at the end but also in the middle of a line.

The MS. has vowel-points and accents. The sign of רפה is written over the letters בגדכפת when liquid, and over ה at the end of a syllable, to mark the legitimate absence of the מפיק (the Tetragrammaton naturally excepted). The same sign is also found over א when quiescent.

The קרי and כתיב, the חסר and יתיר are noted; but of the מסרת in the usual acceptation of the term there are only slight traces[3]. The codex הללי is referred to five times[4]. The first three chapters of the book of

[1] The note on the outer margin of leaf 40ᵇ is as follows: והיתה התורה הזאת לעד ולזכרון ליניק וחכים הבחור החשוב הר"ר (הרב רבי) יצחק השם ישמרהו בן לכבוד הגביר הנדיב החכם רופא מומחה כ"ש (כבוד שמו) מוהר"ר (מורנו הרב רבי) שמואל הלוי הש"י (השם ישמרהו) ה"ה (הלא הוא) אשכנזי : מפני שמי נחת הוא מאתי מתנה נתונה בעברי דרך פה לעלו' לארץ הקדושה : יום שלישי שהוכפל בו ב' פעמים כי טוב : אלה הדברים אשר דבר משה צבי הירש חזן דק"ק (דקהלה קדושה) יאס. The year is not given.

[2] The only exceptions are leaves 34ᵇ—36ᵃ (Jud. iv. 18—v. 31, the song being אריח על גבי לבנה &c.) and leaves 120ᵃ—121ᵇ (2 Sam. xxi. 15—xxii. 51, the song being merely arranged in poetical stichoi).

[3] See leaves 23ᵇ and 103ᵇ, where the only instances of the larger and the lesser מסרת are found, and leaf 100ᵃ, where the מדנחאי are quoted.

[4] Leaves 10ᵃ (Joshua viii. 22, where לו stands for להם and between the

Samuel have a superscription, on the upper margin, in an old Sephardic hand; 1 and 2 Sam. and 1 and 2 Kings have English titles, and the chapters are regularly marked throughout in pencil, probably by Kennicott, who collated the MS. It is Cod. 90 in his list. He attributes it to the end of the XIVth century.

Notes, in Sephardic handwriting, probably of ownership, occur on the first and last pages, but they have been carefully erased, with the exception of the signature יצחק אברבנאל, which occurs several times on leaf 1ᵃ. This is either the celebrated Don Yitzchaq Abarbanel, or his grandson mentioned by the author of the מאור עינים[1]; more probably, however, the former. The volume was subsequently in possession of the Leyden orientalist, Erpenius, whose collection of oriental MSS. was purchased after his death by George Villiers, Duke of Buckingham, who was then Chancellor of the University. After his assassination they were presented to the University by his widow.

[Library-mark, Ee. 5. 8; presented in 1632 by Catherine, Duchess of Buckingham.]

No. 22.

Parchment, 12 in. × 10 in.; 196 leaves, 3-sheet quires, 2 columns, 21 lines; same handwriting as the preceding MS.

[נביאים האחרונים]

THE LATTER PROPHETS.

Leaf 1ᵃ, blank; 1ᵇ, *Isaiah;* 46ᵇ, *Jeremiah;* 106ᵃ, *Ezekiel;* 156ᵃ, *Hosea;* 162ᵃ, *Joel;* 164ᵇ, *Amos;* 170ᵃ, *Obadiah;* 170ᵇ, *Jonah;* 172ᵇ, *Micah;* 176ᵇ, *Nahum;* 178ᵃ, *Habakkuk;* 179ᵇ, *Zephaniah;* 182ᵃ, *Haggai;* 183ᵇ, *Zechariah;* 192ᵃ, *Malachi;* 194ᵇ col. 2, 195, 196 blank.

There is an interval of 3 lines between each of the larger, and of 2 (or almost 2) between each of the Minor Prophets, these last being looked upon as one book.

It must be understood that, in all points not specially mentioned here, this MS. agrees with No. 21, as they are unquestionably the work of the same copyist. There are, however, a few things in which the uniformity is not complete. (1) The vacant spaces are filled up by ׳ or ״, never more.

columns is כן בהללי); 50ᵇ (Jud. xvi. 23, where אויבינו stands for אויבנו, and on the outer margin is כן בהללי ובמוגה אויבנו; on מוגה see No. 13 of this Catalogue); 93ᵇ (1 Sam. xxxi. 12, where in reference to ויקחו we read on the outer margin בהללי וישאו); 103ᵃ (2 Sam. x. 3, where on ולרגלה the outer margin has בהללי ולרגלה); and 143ᵇ (1 Kings xii. 2, where on שלמה המלך between the columns is כן בהללי).

[1] See leaf 9ᵃ in the Mantua edition of 1574, where he says: פרנסי ק״ק... פירדה כמו חשר אב לאביונים דון יצחק אברבניאל בן בנו של המחבר הגדול נוחו עדן.

(2) The sign of רפה is frequently omitted over the quiescent א. (3) The מסורת is considerably more developed here, and even the Aramaic mnemonic (וסימנ׳ בלש׳ תרג׳) is found, although but rarely (see leaf 6b &c. and No. 13 of this Catalogue).

In Isaiah i—xxxix. there are running titles, giving the book and (Christian) chapter in the same Sephardic Rabbinic hand which occurs in Samuel in the preceding volume. Jeremiah, Ezekiel, Hosea, Joel and Amos have the Latin names prefixed in a xvith century hand; and Kennicott has frequently added the English names of the books at beginning and end.

This MS. is Cod. 91 in Kennicott's list. It was collated by him for his edition, and is assigned by him to the xivth century.

The only traces of ownership are entries on the last leaf (in Hebrew) and on the first (apparently in Spanish or Italian); but they are now entirely illegible. There is a high probability that as the preceding volume this also belonged to Abarbanel, as it did subsequently to Erpenius.

[Library-mark, Ee. 5. 10; presented in 1632 by Catherine, Duchess of Buckingham.]

No. 23.

Parchment, 5½ in. × 7¾ in.; 1 leaf, wanting top and bottom, 2 columns, originally 21 lines; square character, French Ashkenazic handwriting of the xiii—xivth century.

[שמואל]

SAMUEL; a fragment.

This fragment contains only 2 Samuel xxii. 5—31 (תמים דרכו), and even in this a line is wanting at the head and another at the foot.

Being part of the Song of David, it is written in אריח, &c. (see Excurs. I.)

There are vowel-points and accents; and the mark of רפה over בגדכפת when liquid. The קרי, &c. is the only trace of מסרת, this MS. possesses.

[Library-mark, Add. 849. 3; bought in 1871.]

No. 24.

Parchment, 8⅝ in. × 3½ in.; the outer half of 1 leaf, originally 28 lines; square character, French Ashkenazic handwriting of xii—xiiith century.

[ירמיהו]

JEREMIAH; a fragment.

This fragment contains only xxiv. 4—xxv. 10 (יהוה אלי לאמר to וקול שמחה קול...), and even in this two lines are wanting at the foot.

It has vowel-points and accents, and the mark of רפה over בגדכפת when liquid.

The MS. as a whole seems to have had no מסרת beyond the קרי, &c.

The contents are marked on the fragment in the handwriting, apparently, of Dr. Steinschneider, of Berlin.

[Library-mark, Add. 849. 4; bought in 1871.]

No. 25.

Vellum, 12 in. × 8⅜ in.; 555 leaves, 6-sheet quires, 2 columns[1], 22 lines; square character, fine German Ashkenazic handwriting, dated Friday 21 Tebeth 5107[2].

[הכתובים (בלי חמש המגלות) עם התרגום ופרושי רש"י הרמ"בן וחכם אשכנזי פלוני אלמוני:]

THE HAGIOGRAPHA (without the Five Rolls) with the תרגום and the commentaries of RASHI, RAMBAN, and an anonymous German author; in three parts.

I. PSALMS and PROVERBS with תרגום and RASHI. Leaf 1ª, *Psalms;* 174ª, *Proverbs.*

II. JOB with תרגום and RAMBAN. Leaf 232ª, *Job;* 306ᵇ, blank; 307, probably blank, wanting.

III. DANIEL and EZRA (-NEHEMIAH) with RASHI; CHRONICLES with תרגום and Pseudo-RASHI. Leaf 308ª, *Daniel;* 329ª, *Ezra* (343ᵇ, *Nehemiah*); 364ª, *Chronicles* (446ᵇ, 2 *Chronicles*); 555ᵇ, subscriptions by the scribe.

The books (Nehemiah and 2 Chronicles of course excepted) commence on fresh pages with large initial words on illuminated ground with various designs, that prefixed to Job representing Job and his wife and Satan (see chap. ii. 7—10). The Psalms are distinguished by 2-line initial words; lxx. and lxxi. here forming one Psalm. There are also large initial words to Ps. lxxviii. 28 (the centre of the book), and to cxv. 12, and cxvi. 12, where those Psalms are divided for liturgical purposes. Further there are large initial letters to each of the twenty-two portions of Ps. cxix. The first four verses of Ps. cxviii. form the conclusion of the preceding one (as in No. 13). To fill up the vacant spaces, one or two letters are inserted at the end of

[1] The exceptions are leaves 160ª, 160ᵇ, 173ᵇ, 231ᵇ, 306ᵇ, 363ᵇ, and 554—555ᵇ.

[2] This is, however, according to Jahn's Tables, Thursday, January 4, 1347.

the line, mostly part of the next word, but occasionally also a Rabbinic ח or part of one, indicating the name of the scribe (see Excurs. I.). The MS. has vowel-points and accents and the mark of רפה over בגדכפת when liquid. The running titles of the respective books are written on the lower outer margin of the recto pages, but are now mostly cut away by the binder.

Although 3 lines are left on the upper and 4 lines on the lower margin, evidently for the addition of the מסרת, there is none to be found there. In the Psalms certainly we find at lxxviii. 38, חצי; in וכנה (lxxx. 16) a minuscule (instead of a majuscule) כ; and at the end of books 2, 3 and 4 the remarks נשלם ספר...פתוחה ב׳ שטין; but in other respects even the first points of מסרת, as the קרי &c., are very rarely noticed.

In the books which are provided with תרגום the verse of the text is succeeded by that of the Aramaic paraphrase, which is pointed, accentuated &c., in the same manner as the text (Chronicles excepted, where of the accents the סוף פסוק alone is noticed). The תרגום conforms on the whole to that found in the printed editions.

The Commentaries, occupying the outer margins and serving mainly purposes of ornamentation, are far from being complete. They are, in most cases, considerably shorter than those to be met with in the printed editions, although occasionally also somewhat fuller. There is, enough, however, of the matter here, to identify them. The authorship of those on Job, Daniel, Ezra (-Nehemiah) and Chronicles will be fully discussed in Excurs. II.

At the end of Chronicles (leaf 555[b]) is the following subscription by the original scribe, in square character: חזק ונתחזק חיים הסופר לא יוזק; and between the lines he has added in Rabbinic character: סיימתי הכתובים עם התרגום בשנת חמשת אלפים ומאה ושבע לבריאת עולם בששי בשבת באחד ועשרים יום לחדש טבת[1]. He was clearly a German; for on the margin of leaf 551[a], in reference to 2 Chron. xxxv. 16, he has: ווערליך דשט הוביש (Wahrlich das ist hübsch), while on the margin of the last page of Ezra (-Nehemiah), where he found the arranging of the text, so as to produce a particular design, rather tedious, the words ווי לנגא נוך (Wie lange noch) occur opposite the centre, and מיך שלאפערט (mich schlaefert's) at the end of the foot. See also leaves 367[b], 437[a], and 462[b].

That the MS. has been in the hands of a Sephardi may be gathered from the fact, that marginal numbers have been put to the Psalms in a Sephardic hand of the XIV—XVth century. They differ somewhat from the ordinary numbering, though at the end they amount to the usual 150. The same hand has marked הק״ז in the margin against the date in the subscription of the scribe on leaf 555[b]. The following names of ownership occur on the fly-leaf (556[b]) at the end of the volume: (1) יהודה ן׳ נחמיאש; (2) שמואל טרטרו, and (3) אבא שאול בן סרויה (all of which are Sephardim). Subsequently the MS. came into possession of Erpenius, apparently in

[1] Besides the subscription and the allusions at the end of the lines, as mentioned above, the scribe has clearly indicated his name on leaf 208[a] by a little ornament placed against the word לחיים (Prov. xix. 23), which occurs at the beginning of a line; see also leaves 177[a], 179[b], 188[a], and 462[b].

company with the Abarbanel copy of the Prophets (Nos 21 and 22 above), and it appears in the printed list of his MSS. (Amst. 1625, 4to.). A few calculations in Erpenius' hand occur on leaves 156[a] and 556[b].

In 1715 the תרגום to Chronicles (otherwise only known from an imperfect copy at Erfurt) was edited from this copy by Wilkins[1]. The whole MS. was collated by Kennicott for his edition and he has written the English names of the books at the beginning and end of each. It is marked Cod. 91 in his list.

[Library-mark, Ee. 5. 9; presented in 1632 by Catherine, Duchess of Buckingham.]

No. 26.

Parchment, $7\frac{1}{4}$ in. × $5\frac{1}{2}$ in.; 30 leaves, 5-sheet quires, 27 lines; the text in square character and the commentary in Rabbinic, fine Sephardic handwriting of the XIV—XVth century.

[משלי עם פרוש ר׳ עמנואל בן שלמה]

PROVERBS, with the commentary of R. 'Immanuel b. Shelomoh; defective.

Begins (leaf 1[a], introduction):

אמר עמנואל בכ״ר שלמה זצ״ל אחר שבח האל על רוב נעימותו וכל תגמולוהי עלי אומר כי הספר הזה והוא הנקרא משלי שלמה חברו שלמה :ע״ה (עליו השלום) להוסיף ביאור בסודות שמצא בתורה ובסתריה....

Breaks off (leaf 30[b], commentary on v. 1):

...ואמ׳ הט אזנך ולא אמ׳ תן לבך וכיוצא בו מפני,

After the introduction, the text and commentary are written alternately, a passage of the one followed by the corresponding passage of the other. The text is provided with vowel-points and accents, and has in most cases the sign of רפה over the letters of בגדכפת when liquid. It reaches from i. 1 to v. 6.

The commentary is found in the edition of the כתובים printed at Naples about 1486; but the author's name in the introduction is there given עמנואל בן יעקב, and the whole is printed from a very inferior MS.

The scriptural text in this copy, being only secondary to the commentary, cannot be expected to have much critical value. It is, however, on the whole, fairly correct, and, as it proceeds, it is even rhythmically arranged. The commentary is free from most of the worst mistakes which

1 ...תרגום Paraphrasis Chaldaica in librum priorem et posteriorem Chronicorum...e MSto. Cantabrigiensi descripta ac cum Versione Latina in lucem missa a Davide Wilkins. Amstelaedami, 1715. 4°.

appear in the printed edition. The corrections on the margin by the original copyist, whose name appears to have been ,שמעיה (see leaf 7[b]), are partly words or sentences occasionally omitted by him, but partly also various readings either suggested by himself or found in MSS. of considerable value.

Two notes are given (leaves 16[b] and 23[b]) by an Ashkenazic owner, whose name does not appear. Another by an Italian (also anonymous) owner of the xvith century (leaf 24[b]), runs as follows: עד כאן חסר מן הספר ואשמיאילך היינו עד פסוק ארח חיים פן תפלס נעו מעגלותיה. This note shows that the present fragment was employed by him to complete the copy described below, No. 27.

[Library-mark, Add. 383. 2; bought in 1867 from H. Lipschütz.]

No. 27.

Paper, in quarto, 7¼ in. × 5½ in.; 166 leaves, 3-sheet quires, 35 lines; Rabbinic character, French Ashkenazic handwriting of the xiv—xvth century.

[משלי עם פרוש ר' עמנואל בן שלמה]

Proverbs, with the commentary of R. 'Immanuel b. Shelomoh; defective.

Begins (leaf 25[a], in the commentary iii. 28):

החולים עם היותם טובים שבמזונות לבריאים....

Ends (leaf 163[b]):

....כלומר אינה צריכה שתתהלל או שיהללוה אחרים כי מעשיה הם שיהללוה:
עוצו עיצה ותופר דברו דבר ולא יקום כי עמנואל:
אלהי אקרא יומם וליל במשכבי לא אירא בחצות ליל:
חזק אברהם ולא יוזק לעולם:
רב ריבי וגאליני אל הזכיני לראות בבניין אריאל
מה טובו משכנותיך ישראל:

The text, which is written alternately with the commentary, as in No. 26, is in somewhat large Rabbinic character, without vowel-points and accents. It is fairly correct. The commentary is greatly superior to that found in the Naples edition. The subscription consists of a verse of Isaiah (viii. 10), applied to the author of the commentary, and an acrostic containing the scribe's name אברהם, and, between the ב and the ר, the words חזק &c. inserted.

Besides the defect caused by the loss of leaves 1—24 and 37—48, the scribe has left 157[a]—160[a] blank in consequence of a defect in his copy. The last has been supplied by a later hand (see below).

Leaf 164 contains two theologico-philosophical notes, anonymous, but probably by the author of the commentary. The first begins:

ביאור יין המשומר בענביו מששת ימי בראשית (T. B. Berakhoth, 34^b) ידוע ומפורסם כי ר"זל (רבותינו זכרונם לברכה) דברו במדרשיהם דרך משל וחידה על הדרך שדרכו הנביאים ע"ה (עליהם השלום).... See MS. Add. 539, p. 150^b.

The second begins:

מזבח הקטרת אשר היה בהיכל: היה להטיב רוח המקום ההוא.... See MS. Add. 539, p. 151^b.

The earliest trace of ownership is found in the supply of the defect at leaves 157^a—160^a. An Italian scribe of the xvth century has copied on a 5-sheet quire of paper (leaves 157*—166* as now numbered, 35 lines, Rabbinic character) the corresponding passages; but he has supplied more than was necessary. He begins with the text of xxx. 24 and continues to the commentary xxxi. 16 (ותדריכם אל עבודת האלהים וקרא עשיית) below which he adds the following:

זה אינו לא מן השמים ולא מן הארץ זה החלק הראשון והחלק השני הוא שלא השלמתי אותו:

This clearly shows that the scribe of the supply was not the owner, but somebody employed by him to copy the missing portion from a MS. in some distant library. The same copyist has added overleaf an explanation of 2 Kings ii. 9. It begins:

ויהי נא פי שנים ברוחך אלי ענינו שמן הרוח האלהי הנאצל עליך יהיה ממנו אלי כפלים ממה שנאצל עליך....

It is not quite finished. This also is probably by the author of the commentary, as it is written in his style.

Leaf 164^b contains two censors' entries: (1) Fra luigi... and (2) Dominico Gerosolimitano, found in so many Italian books.

On leaf 165^b we have the following marks of ownership: Il presente שיר השירים ומשלי sopra עמנואל è di Sanson Sacerdote D. Modone[1]; and below it: זה הספר הו' מהצעי' שמשון כהן מודון וסי' (וסמנו) לעבדו שכׄםׄ אחד (Zeph. iii. 9). The pointed word gives the initials of the owner's name. This MS. came subsequently into the possession of his biographer, Samuele Vita della Volta[2] (see כרם חמד, ii. p. 114), who inherited it from his father. Later again it came into the hands of R. Marco Mortara[3], Chief Rabbi of Mantua.

[Library-mark, Add. 383. 3; bought in 1867 from H. Lipschütz.]

[1] R. Sanson D. Modone was one of the Rabbis of Mantua, and secretary of the congregation in the xvii—xviiith century. He is author of several valuable works. He was born 1679, and died 1727, aged 48.

[2] Samuele Vita della Volta was a physician and an author of some note at Mantua. He was born 1772, and died 1853. See Steinschneider, Cat. Lib. Heb. in Bib. Bod., No. 7353.

[3] The name is Mortara and not Mortera, as Steinschneider (Bod. Cat. p. 1759, No. 6409) writes it.

No. 28.

Parchment, $14\frac{7}{8}$ in. × $10\frac{1}{4}$ in.; 22 leaves, the text 25—30, square character, and the commentary 58—73 lines, mixed (square and Rabbinic) character; fine French Ashkenazic handwriting of the XIII—XIVth century.

[איוב עם פרוש חכם צרפתי פלוני אלמוני]

JOB, with the commentary of an anonymous French Rabbi.

The text is written in alternately indented lines, without, however, being metrically arranged. The vacant spaces of a line are filled up with one letter or more of the next line, and occasionally also with the upper part of a פ (see Excurs. I.). It is provided with vowel-points and accents, and has the sign of רפה over בגדכפת when liquid. As a production of the school to which it belongs it is remarkably correct.

The commentary occupies the three outer margins.

It begins (leaf 1ª):

איש חכם גדול וגאון הדור האשים כל המפרשים הוא רבי׳ שמואל ז״ל (זכרו או זכרונו לברכה) איש שר וגדול לפי שמצא ויהי איש גר בירכתי הר אפרים ושמו מיכה והעניין מוכיח שם שהיה לו פסל ולא ידעתי מי הביאו בצרה הזאת. כי גם שם קוראו איש לפי שהיה ידוע בימים ההם לעשיר ונכבד ויהיה על דרך אלקים אחרים לפי דעת החושבים כן. כי אין אל רק אחד. ופי׳ איש שר וגדול....

Ends (leaf 22ª):

...למשנה ולא דקדק המקרא :

As a literary production it is, certainly, the best explanation of Job that ever fell into our hands. The author seems to have been contemporary with both Ibn 'Ezra and Qimchi, both of whom he quotes (the former almost on every page and the latter on leaves 14ᵇ and 18ᵇ). Besides these he quotes the following authorities:

(1) רב׳ סעדיה (leaf 7ᵇ).

(2) מנחם (leaf 10ª).

(3) דונש (leaves 10ª, 16ª and 19ᵇ).

(4) אבן גיאות (leaves 8ᵇ and 17ª).

(5) ר׳ משה הדרשן (leaf 19ª).

(6) ר״ש (Rabbenu Shelomoh? the quotation is certainly to be found in Rashi; leaf 12ᵇ).

(7) בעל החיוג (also חיוג and Ibn חיוג, and who is also meant by המדקדק הראשון; leaves 2ª, 3ª, 4ª, and 17ª).

(8) אבן גנח (leaf 17ª).

(9) בעל הפרחון, also אבן פרחון (leaves 7ᵇ and 13ª).

(10) רבי' שמואל (leaves 1^a, 3^a, 3^b, and 11^a).

(11) רבי' יעקב (leaves 1^b, 4^a, 8^b, 10^a, 11^a, 12^b and 16^a).

(12) ר' יוסף קרא (leaves 8^a and 15^b).

(13) בעל המסורת, also simply המסורת (leaves 3^a and 15^b).

(14) המדקדקים, also חכמי הדקדוק (leaves 2^b and 17^a).

(15) מדקדק גדול (leaf 10^a).

(16) הפרשנים (leaves 2^a, 2^b and 15^a).

(17) ר' אליעזר מבאייצי (of Beaugency, repeatedly and mostly with approval; leaves 1^b and 2^a).

(18) ר' אליעזר (probably the same as the foregoing; leaves 3^b, 4^a, 4^b, 7^a, 7^b, 8^a, 10^a, 12^b, 13^b, 18^b and 19^b).

(19) ר' אליעזר מבאלגייצי (probably the same; leaf 14^b).

(20) ר' אליעזר מבאגצי (probably the same; leaf 15^a).

(21) רבינו הגדול (leaves 18^a and 18^b).

(22) רבי' שמעון מפי אבי אביהם עליהם השלום (leaf 7^b).

(23) אבי זצ"ל (leaves 6^b, 7^b, 11^b, and 15^b).

(24) דודי ר' בנימין (leaf 8^b).

It is singular that the author of a commentary of such excellence should have remained unknown. The frequent recurrence of the phrases שיטת and ע"ד will enable any one to identify it, if existing elsewhere. The בלע"ז, which amount to twenty-one, are French. A glossary on the Bible, with French interpretations, now in the University Library at Leipzig, MS. 102, is apparently drawn from a commentary on the whole Bible by the author of the present one on Job. See Delitzsch, Jesurun (Grimmae, 1838, 8vo.), p. 241, Zunz, Gesch. und Lit., p. 82, and Excurs. II., where later communications from Professor Delitzsch will be found, as well as further details concerning this commentary.

This MS. was bound up formerly with the כתובים of the first edition of the Rabbinical Bible (Venice, Bombergi, 1518), and in that state formed part of the collection of יצחק (בן מנחם ?) פראגי, which was imported from Italy in 1647 by George Thomason, the London bookseller. The volume occurs on p. 47, among the *Libri Hebraici in folio*, in his catalogue (Lond. 1647, 4to.). The collection was bought by the House of Commons, and presented to the University. The present MS. and the printed כתובים were not bound together until they came into the possession of יצחק פראגי, when the leaves were numbered throughout in ink, 1—183 (כתובים), 184—205 (Job). This fact is further confirmed by the circumstance that the three censors' marks (dated 1595, 1597, and 1618) are found, not at the end of Job, but at the end of the כתובים which precede it.

The condition of the MS. is, on the whole, good, except that it has suffered somewhat from damp, and it has been reduced to single leaves by the binder's knife. The damp, however, has brought out a fact which we should not otherwise have known; for the first and last pages contain impressions of ink from the pages which formerly stood next them. There is not sufficient to show what preceded; but it is clear that the Job was followed by a copy of the תרגום on Ruth, written in three columns, in somewhat smaller square character by the same scribe as this Job, and with a larger initial ויהי for the beginning of the text.

[Library-mark, Dd. 8. 53; presented in 1647 by the House of Commons.]

No. 29.

Paper, in quarto, $8\frac{1}{16}$ in. × $5\frac{1}{2}$ in.; 118 leaves, 5-sheet quires, 19 lines; the text in square character, and the paraphrase in Rabbinic, Italian handwriting of the xvth century.

[חמש המגלות עם התרגום]

The Five Rolls with the Aramaic Paraphrase; defective.

Leaf 1, probably blank, wanting; 2[a], *Ruth* (4 and 7 wanting); 13[b], *Canticles;* 36[b], *Ecclesiastes;* 70[b], *Lamentations;* 85[b], *Esther* (108 wanting); 116 blank; 117—118, probably blank, wanting.

The first word of each verse in the text is in large Ashkenazic character, and the rest in Sephardic; while the תרגום is in smaller Italian Rabbinic.

Every book begins with a fresh page, except Esther; probably from the wish to avoid closing even a page with the end of Lamentations (see Excurs. I.). The vacant spaces on the lines are mostly filled up with one or more letters of the first word on the next line; occasionally, however, with a ד (see Excurs. I.). The text is fairly correct and is accompanied by the primitive מסרת, marking (mostly on the outer margin) the קרי, כתיב, חסר, יתיר, the centre-mark, the number of verses, &c.

The תרגום, which follows every verse of the text, is of considerable value, and far superior to the printed editions, both in what it gives and in what it omits, e.g. Esther ix. 25 (see Excurs. I.). It has occasionally also readings on the margins, which are worth examination. Both text and paraphrase are now and then found pointed, accentuated, and provided with the mark of רפה over בגדכפת when liquid. At the close of the תרגום the scribe has added כבודך יי', a formula constantly to be found in Italian, and occasionally also in French MSS., and probably adopted by the scribes from their Catholic contemporaries.

Below the end of the paraphrase (leaf 115[b]) occur the entries of the Censors, with the usual Revisto per me: (1) Pietro Martire, and (2) Antonio Fran' Enriqnez...1687.

On leaf 116[b] are the following marks of ownership: (1) Io uitell uiterbo, and (2) Io Giuachino Scialom abitante di Vrbino.

The MS. has suffered both from fire and water; yet not so as to injure the writing.

[Library-mark, Add. 436; bought in 1867 from H. Lipschütz.]

No. 30.

Parchment and paper, in quarto, $7\frac{1}{4}$ in. × $5\frac{1}{2}$ in.; 60 leaves, 5-sheet quires, 28—29 lines; Rabbinic character, Italian handwriting of the xvth century.

[שיר השירים עם פרוש ר׳ עמנואל בן שלמה]

Canticles, with the Commentary of R. 'Immanuel b. Shelomoh; defective.

Begins (leaf 2ª):

שיר השירים אשר לשלמה אמר עמנואל בכ״ר שלמה זצ״ל אחרי הודות לי׳ יתע׳ (יתעלה) על טוב גמולותיו אומ כי הספר הזה על דעת רז״ל הוא מבחר הספרי שנאמ׳ ברוח הקדש...

Ends (leaf 60ᵇ, with the commentary):

....ודמה במרוצתך ובבריחותך לבריחת הצבי או לעופר האילים ולך לך על הרי בשמים ושם אבוא אחרייך

The text, which is written alternately with the commentary, is distinguished by being in somewhat larger Rabbinic character. It is provided with vowel-points, accents, and the sign of רפה over the letters of בגדכפת when liquid. It is not of much value, particularly with respect to the vowel-points, which are rather carelessly applied. The commentary, however, which has never been published, is of great value. It is, like all the Biblical commentaries of this gifted author, of philosophical tenour, but rather diffuse, as was the fashion of his time. To him this book is Holy of Holies, not in the sense used both by Jews and Christians, who treat it as a symbol of God and the congregation of Israel, but because it is a symbol of the separate intellect and the human soul. In this view he had been preceded by R. Mosheh Ibn Tibbon, who had explained this book so before, only without entering into such minute detail. He composed this commentary at the request of the sages of Rome, as may be gathered from the following passage in the introduction:

ובראות חכמי רומה מה שכתב החכם הנז׳ (הנזכר) נכספו לבוא לחדריו והפצירו בי בגזירת האהבה לחבר ביאור הספר הזה על הדרך אשר דרך החכם הנז׳ ולהעמיק על פרטיו ולחדש בהם חדושי׳ לא נזכרו בספרו....

Those who will differ from him in the process of symbolisation will scarcely help agreeing with him in the division of the book, in which he succeeded better than any one before or after him, owing, probably, to his poetical spirit (see Excurs. II.).

On leaf 2ª the letters א׳ ס׳, which seem to be library-marks, identify this MS. together with the other two MSS. bound with it, as having been in the possession of the father of Samuele Vita della Volta, the physician, after having previously belonged to R. Sanson Modone (see description of No. 27 of this Catalogue). On the same page is the signature ארי' צבי ליפשיץ, H. Lipschütz. The label on the back, פירוש עמנואל על שה"ש ומשלי כ"י (כתב או כתיבת יד), is in the writing of R. Marco Mortara.

Leaves 1 (blank) and 10 are wanting, and leaf 2 is only to be read with difficulty; otherwise the MS. is in good condition.

[Library-mark, Add. 383. 1; bought in 1867 from H. Lipschütz.]

No. 31.

Paper, in quarto, 8 in × 6 in.; 60 leaves, 4-sheet quires, the introduction, preface, and analytical index 30 and the body of the work 32 lines; the text in Sephardic square character, and the rest in mixed (Rabbinic and cursive), Italian handwriting of the XVIth century.

[שיר השירים עם פרוש ר' דוד בן אברהם פרווינצאלי]

CANTICLES with the commentary of R. David b. Abraham Provenzale.

The introduction, after leaf 1 (blank), begins (leaf 2[a]):

בהנוא (בשם ה' נעשה ונצליח אמן) כי שמעתי דבת רבים מרחיבים פה ומאריכים לשון לדבר על המלך שלמה חכם מכל ונביא ה' תועה לאמור כי יצא מלפני ה'....

The preface begins (leaf 14[a]):

ראה ראיתי אני הצעיר באלפי מבני בלי שם את דברי הספר החתום הזה. ונתון אל לבי לרדת לסוף עומק כונתו מפי המפרשים חדשים גם ישנים....

The commentary itself begins (leaf 17[a]):

אם אמרתי אספרה כמו הנה כל הקושיות או הספקות הנופלות בזה הדבור הנכבד שיר המעולה והעולה על כל השירים וקדש קדשים....

Ends (leaf 60[a]):

....ולז"א (ולזה אמר) ברח לך אל המקום הנאות ואתה בטוח שמה כי לא יחטאו לך ותמיד שבחך בפיהם ואז יהיה משכנך בתוכם לעולם כמ"ש (כמה שנאמר) וידעו הגוים כי אני ה' מקדש את יש' בהיות מקדשי בתוכם לעולם אכי"ר:

The text is now and then provided with vowel-points and accents. It is followed by a commentary well worthy of consideration. The author mentions his own name, David, on leaf 8[b] (see Excurs. II.). He divides this sealed book into 5 נתחים and 19 חלקים of 6, 4, 3, 3, and 3 respectively, and explains it both literally and mystically (נגלה ונסתר) in a way which reminds us strongly of Don Abraham b. Yitzchaq Hallevi's commentary, only that this is the more valuable because the more natural of the two. Under נגלה this book is treated as an idyll, and under נסתר as representing God and the congregation of Israel (see description of MS. Add. 378. 2, below, and Excurs. II.). It is a compromise between the philosophical and poetical schools on the one hand, and the mystical and believing schools on the other hand—a task for which our author was well fitted, as he united in himself, in a singular degree, these apparently contradictory qualities. He was a contemporary of the celebrated author of the מאור עינים, by whom both he and his brother Mosheh were much respected for their learning and piety (see Excurs. II.). While the body of the work was copied by somebody else, the introduction, preface, &c., are apparently an autograph, as are also the numerous notes with which the margins of the work itself are filled.

On leaf 60[b] is the Revista of the censor, Dominico Gerosolimitano.

On leaf 2[a] is written א· צ"ט, probably the number of the volume in the library of the father of Samuele Vita della Volta. The label on the back, פי' שיר השירים כ"י, is in the writing of R. Marco Mortara.

The MS. is, on the whole, in good condition.

[Library-mark, Add. 636; bought in 1870 from S. Schönblum.]

No. 32.

Paper, in folio, $11\frac{3}{8}$ in. × $7\frac{3}{4}$ in.; 14 leaves, one 7-sheet quire; the text Sephardic square character, and the rest in 34—38 lines mixed (Rabbinic and cursive), Italian handwriting of the xvith century.

[שיר השירים עם פרוש לועזי פלוני אלמוני]

CANTICLES with the commentary of an anonymous Italian Rabbi.

The introduction begins (leaf 1[a]):

הקדמת הספר· חכמי האמת אשר זרח עליהם אור הקבלה האמתית גזרו אומר שהנשמה היא עצם רוחני דק מאד. עד כי שלמי' וכן רבים גזרו אומר שהיא חצובה מתחת כסא הכבוד....

The commentary itself begins (leaf 2[a]):

שיר השירים במדרש שיר שהוא על כל השירים הכונה ששירת הנשמה גדולה משירת המלאכי' כמו שדרשו על קדמו שרים אחר נוגני'....

Ends (leaf 13[b]):

....על הרי בשמי׳ היינו בין ההדסי׳ שהם הצדיקי׳ שב״נע (שבגן עדן) שנק׳ הרי בשמי׳ שריחם נודף וכל זה אמרו לחוזק התשוקה לחזות בנועם ה׳ כי באור פני מלך חיים. בריך רחמנא דסייען

The text is without vowel-points and accents. It is surrounded on the outer and lower margin by the commentary, which is not without merit. The author explains this book as treating of the human soul, somewhat in the style of R. Mosheh Ibn Tibbon and R. 'Immanuel b. Shelomoh, to whose high conceptions, however, he cannot elevate himself. Otherwise, he seems to have been a man of great Talmudic learning, well read in the poets of our nation, acquainted with those who wrote in Italian, and quite fit for the style of דרש in which he explains this book.

The authorities and books he names are: (1) רש״י; (2) רא״בע; (3) רמ״בן; (4) המליץ (Yeda'yah Penini Bedarshi); (5) עבודת הקדש (R. Meir Ibn גבאי); (6) מקראי קדש (R. Yoseph סמיגה); (7) מאמץ כח (R. Mosheh Almosnino); (8) גליקו (R. Elisha'); (9) ר׳ יהודה הרופא (Leo Hebraeus, i. e. Don Yehudah b. Yitzchaq Abarbanel) whose Dialoghi di Amore he mentions several times.

For specimens of explanation, see Excursus II.

The MS., although somewhat injured, particularly on the lower margin, is in fair condition.

[Library-mark, Add. 860; bought in 1872 from Fischl Hirsch of Halberstadt.]

No. 33.

Parchment and paper in quarto, $8\frac{1}{2}$ in. × $5\frac{3}{4}$ in.; 130 leaves, mostly 10-sheet quires (the outer and inner sheets parchment, the rest paper), 21—22 lines; mixed (square and Rabbinic) character, inelegant and careless Greek Sephardic handwriting dated 22 Adar 5170[1].

[מגלת אסתר עם פרוש ר׳ שמריה האיקריטי : פרוש על תלמוד בבלי מסכת מגלה פרק ראשון לר׳ שמריהו הזקן האיקריטי : מדרש מגלת אסתר :]

ESTHER, with a CRITICAL COMMENTARY by R. Shemaryah of Crete; defective. COMMENTARY on Talmud Babli MEGILLAH, section 1, by R. Shemaryahu the elder, of Crete (b. Eliyyah Happarnas of Rome). A MIDRASH on ESTHER.

[1] According to Jahn's Tables, 22 Adar 5170 corresponds to 26 Febr. 1410.

A quire or more is wanting before leaf 1; 1[a], *Esther*, with subscription by the scribe; 8[b], *commentary* on T. B. *Megillah* with subscription by the scribe; 111[b], medical recipe; 112[a], *midrashic* commentary on *Esther;* 127[b]—128[b], blank; 129—130, probably blank, wanting.

1. ESTHER, with a CRITICAL COMMENTARY.

Begins (in the text, vi. 4):

לאמור למלך לתלות את מרדכי על חעץ אשר הכין לו : שאל אם יש בחצר אחד מן השרים יועציו לשואלו מה כבוד יעשה למרדכי : ...

Ends (in the commentary, last verse):

.... מיוחס לפעול. הטעם לכל הזרע שממנו נזרע.
הודיעני אורח חיים שבע ‖ שמחות את פניך נעימות ‖ בעצתך תנחני ואחר כבוד ‖ תקחני בימינך נצח מי לי ‖ בשמים ועמך לא חפצתי ‖ בארץ : כי עמך מקור ‖ חיים באורך נראה אור :. נכתב זה הפירוש של מגילה על ידי לי שמריה בכ"ר ישמעאל זצ"ל וכתבתיו לנכבד כ"ר יהודה ורילא בן המשכיל כ"ר שמואל ורילה נתצ"בה (נפשו תהי צרורה בצרור החיים) והיתה מנוחתו כבוד והשם יזכנו להורישו לזרעו אחריו ואל יאכלו זרים חילו אמ' בן יאמר האל.

The apparent confusion in the colophon arises from Ps. lxxiii. 24, 25, having been put in as an after-thought. The abbreviation נתצ"בה is an allusion to 1 Sam. xxv. 29.

The text is without vowel-points and accents, and is not distinguished from the commentary even by having exclusively the ordinary verse-mark. The commentary, which follows the text paragraph by paragraph, reminds one of the style of the great Ibn 'Ezra, of whom it is quite worthy. One would indeed unhesitatingly have ascribed it to him, as a third commentary on this book, were it not for the fact that quotations from this very commentary occur in the מנות הלוי of R. Shelomoh אלקבץ, where it is distinctly attributed to R. Shemaryah of Crete (see Excurs. II.). The phrases in definition mostly employed by the author are: ...הטעם and מקיצה (refers to, governs, &c.).

2. COMMENTARY on (the agadic part of) the first section of MEGILLAH, by R. SHEMARYAHU the elder.

Begins (leaf 8[b]; Talmud, leaf 2[b]):

אמר ר' ירמיה בר אבא ואיתימ' ר חייא בר אבא מנצ"פך או סוןץ"ףך צופים אמרום פי' אלה חמשת אותיות הבאות בסופי התיבות נביאים אמרום ולא משה רבינו ....

Ends (leaf 111[b]; Talmud, leaf 17[a]):

.... קל וחומר שינתן ענין יעקב לסימן ששהה בבית עבר י"ד שנה שאע"פ (שאף על פי) שאינו אמת למתבוננים בעניין מכל מקום אין שקרותו מבואר כשיקרות אזינך שבר קפרא קורא אזניך כדי לתתו לסימן.

זהו פירו׳ מגלת אסתר שפירשו וחברו הרב הגאון זקיני רבינו שמריהו הזקן ואני שמריא בכ״ר ישמעאל נכדו זכותו תגן עלינו אמן העתקתיו מספרו אלף המגן לנכבד הייקר והמשכיל עטרת בחורים והדר זקינים כ״ר יהודה ורילא בכ״ר שמואל מ״כ (מנוחתו כבוד) והשם יזכינו להוליד בנים ולהורישו להם יחד עם כל מה שימצא לו ולא יאכלו זרים חילו אמ׳ ואמ׳.

This commentary (on a part of the Talmud which is replete with interest for critics, as it treats on the origin of the Septuagint version of the Pentateuch and other points of importance) is a testimony to the author's great learning and critical tact and acumen. (On his identity with R. Shemaryah of Negroponte, see Geiger, החלוץ, ii. pp. 25 and 158, and אוצר נחמד, ii. p. 94.) In the course of this essay he mentions the following authorities: (1) רש״י (whom he generally calls ר״ש); (2) בעלי התוספות; (3) ר׳ אברהם (Ibn 'Ezra); (4) הר״ם (Maimonides); (5) הרמ״בן, and none later, although he wrote it as late as 1309 (see Excurs. III.). The following works of his own are also mentioned therein: (1) Commentary on the Pentateuch and on other parts of the Bible, and (2) on (the agadic part of) the treatises of the Talmud, Shabbath, Synhedrin, &c. (see Excurs. III.). One would be inclined to think that what is given by the scribe as a subscription was in reality an erroneous superscription to the next work, but for a superstitious medical recipe (beginning: קח חלב כלבתאי שחורה ומשח פי הרחם ותתעבר וזונתך) standing between this and the next work. It is, however, quite possible that the foregoing commentary on *Talmud* Megillah, treating naturally on various passages of the *book* Megillah, was viewed by this not very learned copyist as a commentary on Esther itself.

3. A MIDRASH on ESTHER.

Begins (leaf 112ª):

אריות של זהב חלולים עומדי׳ משני צידי הכסא והיו מלאים כל מיני בשמים...

Ends (leaf 127ª):

....יש אומרים החריב אכסדרא שלו והוציאו משם והכינו והשיב הקב״ה (הקדוש ברוך הוא) מחשבתו בראשו ונתלה הוא ובניו ככה הק״בה יקלקל מחשבות של כל אוייבינו מעלינו ומכל עמו ישראל ונאמר אמן ואמן תם ונשלם על ידי שמריא בכ״ר ישמעאל זצו״ל (זכר צדיק[1] וחסיד לברכה) והשם יזכינו לימות המשיח מהרה ביימינו וכתבתיו לנכבד הייקר והמשכיל עטרת בחורים והדר זקינים כ״ר יהודה ורילא בכ״ר שמואל מ״כ ציטדין דפטרש בכ״ב לאדר שנת הק״ע ליצירה השלמתיו זה.

This Midrash, copied apparently from an inexact MS., corresponds in the beginning with the דמות כסא שלמה המלך (see Jellinek, בית המדרש, II. pp. 84, 85) and from leaf 113ᵇ to the end with the מדרש אבא גוריון (Ibid. I.

[1] זצו״ל is not equivalent to זצוק״ל as Luzzatto (אבני זכרון, Prag, 1841, 8vo. p. 17, Note 4) and Zunz (Gesch. u. Lit. p. 456) think. See Index of Abbreviations at the end of this Catalogue.

pp. 2—18), and is more or less taken from the תרגומים, but particularly from the second תרגום or Jerusalem paraphrase of the book.

On leaf 77[a] occurs the following note by the copyist:

כ״ב שו״ל כתיבה ונייר וקלף.

There are no traces at all left by former owners, except, on leaf 127[b], the following entry, גומא פַּפְּרִיטִיקוֹ כי חיות שְׁטַנוּמֵיגִיש (Exod. ii. 3 and i. 19), in Greek Sephardic Rabbinic handwriting of the xvth century. The book afterwards belonged to Erpenius.

The condition of the MS., but for the defects, is excellent.

[Library-mark, Mm. 6. 26. 2; presented in 1632 by Catherine, Duchess of Buckingham.]

II.

COMMENTARIES ON THE BIBLE, WITHOUT THE TEXT.

No. 34.

Parchment, $10\frac{1}{4}$ in. × 8 in.; 178 leaves, 4-sheet quires, 2 columns, 33—35 lines; mixed (square and Rabbinic) character, Italian and Greek Sephardic handwriting of the XIII—XIVth century.

פירוש התורה לרבי' שלמה זצ"ול

COMMENTARY on the Pentateuch by R. Shelomoh b. Yitzchaq of Troyes (Rashi).

Leaf 1[a], blank; 1[b], *Genesis;* 48[a], *Exodus;* 94[a], *Leviticus;* 121[a], *Numbers;* 150[a], *Deuteronomy;* 176[b], blank; 177 and 178, probably blank, wanting.

The weekly פרשיות have at the beginning a large initial word, and at the end .... חסלת פרשת (those of נצבים and וילך are treated as one). The various books have at the end a rhyme probably belonging to the scribe, whose name must have been Abraham, as whenever the word אברהם occurs, he has placed a little ornament against it.

This MS. is, if not one of the oldest, certainly one of the most correct copies of this work, and surpasses, both in what it has and in what it omits, the printed editions. It is to be regretted that Dr. A. Berliner, the latest editor of Rashi on the Pentateuch (Berlin, 1866, 8vo.), whose labours are very meritorious, knew nothing of this MS., which would, while confirming him in most of his views, have checked him in a few things which he has advanced without sufficient grounds (see Excurs. II.).

Later hands, Sephardic as well as Italian and Ashkenazic owners, have left their mark on this MS., partly by corrections and partly by questionable ornaments. The former are mostly to be found on the outer margins, and the latter chiefly at the commencements of the various books. Now and then these are also to be met with in other places, where they serve the purpose of illustrating various passages. No names, however, are given. On leaf 1[a] is the name of Isaac Angiolo, and on the outer margin of leaf 130[b] (which has been cut) we read: ...ן אברהם יאודה זלה״ה (זכרונו לחיי העולם הבא) whilst on one of the fly-leaves at the commencement שמואל דוד לוצאטו[1] י״ב תמוז תר״א occurs. See Catalogue de la Bibliothèque ... redigé par son fils Joseph (Padoue, 1868, 8vo.), p. 10, No. 94. To this distinguished scholar is due the re-touching of the MS. towards the end.

Leaves 1—2, 7—8, 12, 14, 16, 21, 24, 33—34, 36—37, 44, 54, 60—61, 71, 98, 103, 119, 155, 163—176 are slightly injured, yet so as to affect the writing in two places only, so that the MS. is on the whole in a good state of preservation.

[Library-mark, Add. 626; bought in 1870 from S. Schönblum.]

No. 35.

Paper, in quarto, $8\frac{5}{8}$ in. × $5\frac{7}{8}$ in.; 122 leaves, 6-sheet quires, 26 lines; Rabbinic character, Greek Sephardic handwriting of the XIVth century.

[פרושים על פרושי רש״י והראב״ע על התורה ודברים מדברים שונים]

Supercommentaries on Rashi and Ibn 'Ezra on the PENTATEUCH, together with various other matters; defective.

1. ספר השגות שהשיג הרב אברהם ב״ר דוד ז״ל על רבינו שלמה הצרפתי י״ל (יהי או יִזָּכֵר לברכה) בפירוש התורה.

STRICTURES on RASHI'S COMMENTARY on the PENTATEUCH by R. ABRAHAM B. DAVID.

The copyist's admonition runs thus:

אני מפים לכל מי שיהיה הספר הזה בידו שלא יפרסמינו ברבים:

Introduction begins (after leaf 1^a blank, 1^b):

מפני שראיתי בפי׳ התורה המכונה לרש״י הצרפתי ז״ל הגדות ופירושי׳ (נוטים מן דרך כוונת התורה במקומות הרבה ומקצתם הם הפך מהכונה הנכונה) ....

Work begins:

סדר בראשית. אותם הדרשות שהוא מזכיר שראשית הוא מפני שנקראו ישראל ראשית כמבואר והתורה ראשית. אע״פ שלא היה כן הכוונה באותה המילה אינו מזיק אבל ההגדה שאחז״ל שהשמים נבראו מאש וממים (לא הבין הרב) ....

[1] S. D. Luzzatto was born at Trieste, Aug. 22 (not 25, as Steinschneider, Cat. Lib. Heb. in Bib. Bod. p. 1633, No. 6193, writes), 1800, and died as Professor in the Collegio Rabbinico, at Padua, Sept. 29 (not 30, as Stern, Liber Responsionum . . . Vindobonæ, 1870, 8vo., in a note to Luzzatto's letter, has), 1865.

Ends (leaf 11[a]):

....או משה רע״ה (רבנו עליו השלום) זה השיעור יותר מעוג שהיה רשע גמור
אלא האמת כי כל אותם הדרשות בדו אותם בליבם תועי רוח והיו חוטאים
והחטיאו את תורת יו״י תמימה משיבת נפש : נשלמו השגות שהשיג ה״ר אברהם
ב״ר דוד על רש״י יצו״ל (יהי או יִזָּכֵר צדיק וחסיד לברכה) על ידי לי (שבתי) הצעיר
בן החבר ר׳ (ישעיא) כהן והמחוקק בלב״ו (Bilbao) בן הרב מ׳ (מורנו) יהודה כהן
בלבו : ברוך יו״י שלי כתבתי.

This book of strictures is of the greatest importance both on account of the literature it contains, which is apparently unique and is certainly of the highest order of merit, as also on account of the freedom, bordering on disrespect, with which the author speaks of the otherwise universally venerated Rashi, whom he once (leaf 9[a]) calls שרי״ל. (See Excurs. II.)

Our author, as will be seen, partly from his calling Rashi הצרפתי, but more so from his style, must have been himself an Arabic-speaking Sephardi. He must have lived between 1204 and 1411 (probably in the XIIIth century), as he mentions Maimonides with the term ז״ל and is in his turn so spoken of by the copyist, although it is certainly possible that this last ז״ל refers to his father only. Respecting the author's identity we can only negatively say, that he is neither the R. Abraham Hallevi b. David (דאוד) who wrote the ספר הקבלה, and who suffered martyrdom in 1180, nor the Abraham b. David who wrote the השגות on the משנה תורה of Maimonides. The former, apart from the improbability of his quoting the מורה, would not have spoken so disrespectfully of Rashi (of whom, perhaps, he had never heard, as he does not mention him in the ספר הקבלה, although he mentions Rabbenu Tam his grandson with respect). The latter, on the other hand, would not have so idolized Maimonides as our author emphatically does. Should Jellinek's theory (Beitraege, I. p. 75 and בית המדרש III., Anhang, p. XLIII. Note 16, based on R. Mosheh Cordovero's פרדס רמונים XII. and Dukes' נחל קדומים p. 3), that R. Yoseph הארוך is the author of the commentary on the ספר יצירה commonly ascribed to רא״בד, turn out to be incorrect; and should, after all, that commentary belong to a R. Abraham b. David; then we should feel inclined to identify this our author with the commentator of the ספר יצירה, as he is unquestionably a solid cabbalist as well as a deep thinker (see Excurs. VI.).

Most of the more disrespectful phrases have been crossed through and replaced by such as are somewhat more respectful towards Rashi. They are the work of later hands (Ibn Tarshish a Greek Sephardi and Shelomoh a Greek Ashkenazi; see later).

2. [לקוטים שונים] COLLECTANEA VARIA.

Begin (leaf 11[b]):

אלהי אבי להיות לי בעזרי. אומר במסכת׳ סופרי׳ שאין מברכין על הלבנה
עד שתתבצץ פי׳ עד שתאיר מאורה בטוב מלשון בוצינה דנהורא....

End (leaf 16[a]):

....ל׳ לגיהוץ ולתספורת מכאן ואילך אמ׳ הב״ה (הקדוש ברוך הוא) וכי אתם מרחמי׳ עליו יותר ממני עכ״ל (עד כאן לשון) רב יהודה.

לשבתי

והשלמתיו לשבח האל חי, אשר בו נפשי אזי ורוחי:
אותי יעזור ויחכם לבבי, וגם אזכה ללמדם בנוחי:

כהן

These collectanea are of varying value even as they are by various authors and on various matters. They may, however, be reduced to the following chief points:

a. Sayings of the Rabbis;
b. Calculations in the style of Notaricon (נוטריקון);
c. Difficulties, questions and answers;
d. Symbolical interpretations of certain customs;
e. Ordinary explanations of certain customs;
f. Explanations of biblical passages, (in one of which R. Shemuel מאשפירא is mentioned);
g. Halakhic quotations from Rabbenu Yonah (b. Abraham of Gerona), and R. Asher (b. Yechiel) the well-known רא״ש;
h. Extracts from the Babylonian Talmud.

3. [חדושי רבנו ישעיה הכהן (בן עמנואל ?) על רש״י על התורה].

Supercommentary on Rashi on the Pentateuch by R. Yesha'yah Hakkohen (b. 'Immanuel ?); defective.

16[b], *Genesis;* 26[b], *Exodus;* 43[a], *Leviticus;* 48[a], *Numbers;* 52[b], *Deuteronomy.*

Begins (leaf 16[b]):

עמי עש׳ו (עזרי מעם יי׳ עשה שמים וארץ Ps. cxxi. 2) בס״ד (בסיעתא דשמיא) ברצון האל בראשית ברא.....פרש״י אמר ר׳ יצחק....והקשה מורי אדרבה לא היה לו להתחיל אלא מהמילה שהרי המילה היתה קודם לכן וזו היא מצוה ראשונה......

Ends (leaf 55[a]):

....וכולן (זבולן) בגימטריא חילזון (חלזון). חסלת זאת הברכה.

אל הסופר תן מנוח, רבו ציריו מני ארבה:
אל נותן ליעף כח, ולאין אונים עוצמה ירבה:

The following points, resulting from a careful investigation of this MS., are worth noticing:

(1) The author mostly calls Rashi, even as he is called by both R. R. Yesha'yah of Trani (grandfather and grandson) by the name of המורה (occasionally המורא and once המורה הגדול), which is against the theory of Azulai (who restricted it to R. Yesha'yah I.) and his annotator Isaac Benjacob (who in extending it to R. Yesha'yah II., restricted it to these

two). This theory was adopted by the great Munk, who, on the strength of this appellation, vindicated to R. Yesha'yah I. a work in the Paris collection (No. 366 in the new Catalogue). This work, however, belongs to him, although for other reasons. Zunz, *Zeitschrift für die Wissenschaft des Judenthums* (Berlin, 1823, 8vo.), pp. 367-368, has shown that even the תוספות called him sometimes so; and indeed this "Prince of commentators" has been called by many others also המורה, i. e. the teacher *κατ' ἐξοχήν*.

(2) Yesha'yah of Trani, the elder, is here quoted as ריב"מ and also somewhat fuller רבי' ישעיא ב"מ זצו"ל (leaf 31[a]); and, perhaps, the י"ש זצו"ל may be the same.

(3) Our author, although called in the superscription by a later hand (see below) ר' ישעיא השני, cannot have been a grandson of the foregoing, and much less the well-known R. Yesha'yah b. Eliyyah. (See MS. Add. 169.)

(4) The commentary is full of גמטריאות, halakhic discussions, and agadic sayings, which prove the author to have been a Talmudist of no mean capacity. Each of the numerous difficulties raised either by the author himself, or by his teacher, concludes, if remaining without a solution, with ורפיא. (See No. 36 below, p. 64, Note 2 (1)). Now and then the author supplies us with corrected readings of the Rashi-text.

(5) The author quotes his teacher continually by the phrases והקשה מורי, or והקשה רבי, וקשיא לרבי, ותירץ מורי or ותירץ רבי, and מפי ה"ר (הרב רבנו) יצו"ל, without giving his name (in one place, leaf 26[b], he certainly says ותירץ מורי ה"ר אברהם; see, however, 12, below). This teacher, as well as he himself, possessed the Midrash השכם. See Zunz, Gottesdienstl. Vortraege (Berlin, 1832, 8vo.), p. 281, and Excurs. III. of this Catalogue.

(6) The author must have lived in the XIII—XIVth century as he quotes ר' יצחק (perhaps R. Yitzchaq of Russia); R. Yehudah (b. Shemuel) החסיד, who died 1216, (see description of MS. Add. 669. 2 below), and R. Mosheh מקונצי (of Coucy ?). Besides these he quotes ר"ת (רבנו תם, i. e. R. Ya'aqob b. Meir), R. Ya'aqob of Orleans, Rabbenu Tobiyyah, Ibn 'Ezra, Rabbenu Chayyim, a Rabbenu מ"מ זצ"ל (leaf 35[a]), a סגן לויה (39[a]), his contemporary מפי ר' יהודה הלוי (perhaps the same as the foregoing), הרב אשכנזי (leaf 49[a], margin), Rabbenu Shemuel and Rabbenu Mosheh of Coucy (מקוצי).

4. פי' מוסף של פסח. Explanation of the טל of R. El'azar Haqqalir. Begins (leaf 55[b]):

קחה חידות ופירוש פסח ישנות . במוסף התבונן הנפשות :
ובו תבונה רב ודעת הקדושים . וכל דברי גבורות וחלושות :
ותמצא חן וחסד טוב וכל ת־ אותיך לך ביאות וחשות :
נאום תְּשבִי קטון קומה ושפל בנו חבר (ישעיא) הוא קדושות :
בדעתו אביעה חידות בדעתו של הב"ה . אביע כמו יום ליום יביע אומ'....

Ends (on אבי ישנה ... in the last poem but one; leaf 63[b]):

....ישראל שנקראת ישנה שנ' אני ישנה וליבי ער קול דופק פתחי לי אחותי רעייתי וכתי' (וכתיב) שראשי נמלא טל קווצותי רסיסי לילה. תם ונשלם. שבח לבורא עולם . פירוש בדעתו אביע למוסף. לשבח לשם שהוא מוסיף.

There can be very little doubt that this explanation belongs to the school of Rashi, if not to that celebrated teacher himself, as it is quite in the style of his time and school. (See MSS. Add. 394. 1 and 2; and Add. 561, marginal literature.) The poem given above belongs only partly to R. Shabbethai (anagrammatically תשבי), the chief copyist. See תקון מדות הנפש by R. Shelomoh b. Yehudah Ibn גברול (in the collection גורן נכון, Riva di Trento, 1562, 4to.) at the end. In a highly valuable MS. which among other matters contains also this work of גברול, and which belongs to Fischl Hirsch of Halberstadt, the poem here imitated, is to be found at the commencement of the just-named work.

5. [שני שירים]. Two Poems, occupying leaves 63ᵇ—64ᵃ.

The first is the famous piece, in 23 lines, all ending in ין or ים, by R. Abraham Ibn 'Ezra, beginning:

באתי ביום צום בית אנוש צר עין...

and ending:

...וזכור לאברהם ספרדי אשר, יוקם ברוב ימים ושבעתים:

See Biscioni, Bibl. Hebr. Flor. Cat. (8vo. ed.), pp. 325, 459.

The second is a poem, apparently addressed to Maimonides, in 16 lines, all ending in סים. It begins:

לך הרב למישור כל רכבים...

and ends:

וקם שבט ומחץ פאתי, צר אל עמים ירומם פה ונסים „ תם ונחתם:

6. [פרוש סודות אבן עזרא על התורה לר' יוסף אבן כספי]

Supercommentary on R. Abraham b. Meir Ibn 'Ezra on the Pentateuch, by R. Yoseph b. Abbamari b. Yoseph b. Ya'aqob Ibn Kaspi of Argentière[1].

Begins (leaf 64ᵇ):

פירו' סודות של (אבן כספי) על רבי אברהם בן עזרא: ומאל עזרי. פרשת בראשית אמר רבי' (רבינו) אב"ע (אבן עזרא) זצ"ל בהקדמת פי' התורה דרשו קדמונים שהתורה קדמה לעולם אלפיים שנה ואמ' כי אנינו כמשמעו....

Ends (leaf 87ᵃ):

....שהוא נכון לבוא אל בית השם שהוא ציור ליבי לא ציור דמיוני הנאמ' עליו קרוב אתה בפיהם ורחוק מכליותיהם „ נשלם ספר ויקרא „ תמו סודות של אבן עזרא שפירשם אבן כספי על ידי אני תולעת ולא איש (שבתי) בן החבר ר (ישעיא) בן כבוד הרב רבי יהודה כהן בלבו השם יקיים בי מקרא שכתו' לא ימושו מפיך ומפי זרעך אמר השם מעתה ועד עולם וסימן לימו"ז ווזאימו"ע אמן חזק.

As is supposed, R. Yoseph Ibn Kaspi wrote three supercommentaries on Ibn 'Ezra on the Pentateuch, one on the simply difficult passages, of which there are not a few, and another on the theosophical or rather theologico-philosophical (in rare cases also on the astronomical and mathematical)

[1] מכספי המקום, München, Cod. 61; see Kirchheim, ...עמודי כסף (Frankfurt a. M., 1848, 8vo.), p. I. Note 1.

passages, which are doubly difficult, and are mostly spoken of by Ibn 'Ezra himself as סודות. The present commentary is to be identified with the latter; see MS. Add. 510. 2. leaves 69ª—96ª. (On the third see Steinschneider, in Ersch and Gruber's *Encyklopaedie*, Sect. 2, Theil 31, pp. 68 and 69; Geiger, Jüd. Zeitschr. vi. p. 124; MS. Add. 857. 2, and Excurs. II. of this Catalogue; and for the introduction and the supercommentary on Num. and Deut. see later.)

7. שאלות לאבא אוריון. QUESTIONS and ANSWERS on VARIOUS MATTERS.

Begin (leaf 87ª):

אומר דילטורין פי׳ רכיל מנלן״ י״ל (יש לומר) כי דלטור בגימטרי׳ רכיל....

End (leaf 88ª):

.....ואמרו רז״ל הנולד אדום ממתינים לו עד שיבלע דמו וזה נבלע לעולם ונשאר כך„ סליקו שאלות ותשובות לאבא אוריון בעזר השם.

The author's name is, no doubt, fictitious, and the literature, consisting of questions and answers, is only true as far as the facts underlying the questions are concerned. The answers are mostly explanations in Hebrew גימטריא even of Greek words. (For similar practices, however, see both Talmudim passim.)

8. קושיות ותירוצים. HALAKHIC DIFFICULTIES and ANSWERS.

a. On the laws concerning the Day of Atonement, according to Maimonides.

Begin (leaf 88ᵇ):

על הלכות י״ה (יום הכפורים) פרק ראשון · אומר ומהו חייב על עשיית מלאכה ביום זה אם עושה ברצונו בזדון וכו׳ וא״ת (ואם תאמר) מה הוצרך לומ׳ ברצונו כי פשיטא כיון שעושהו בזדון שברצונו הוא....

End (leaf 91ª):

....ובהכי סמכה דעתו דחולה ולא מאכילינן ליה „ תמו קושיות ותירוצים של י״ה על מהר״ם (מורנו הרב רבי משה).

These halakhic difficulties and answers extend over certain points of the first two sections of the law to be observed on the Day of Atonement (משנה תורה, book זמנים, Hilekhoth שביתת עשור). Although it says, on leaf 90ª, תשלום פ״ב (פרק ב׳) מהלכות י״ה, such is not the case, as it treats to the very end of the article on the laws concerning a person being sick and the permission to take food in such a case. In the course of this short article we read: ...כך פי׳ החבר ר׳ אליעזר ז״ל ור׳ משה י״ל (יחי לעד) פירש...

b. On the laws concerning the sounding of the Shophar on a New Year's Day.

Begins (leaf 91ᵇ):

הלכות שופר פי׳ (פרק) קושיא הר״ם במז״ל. אומ׳ אע״פ שלא נתפרש בתורה תרועה בשופר....ארציכם וא״ת היאך הוא לומד מכאן אם מג״ש (מגזרה שוה) תרועה....

Ends (leaf 91ᵇ):

....וכתי׳ זיכרון תרועה יהיה לכם · לא מצאתי יותר.

This occupies one point only in the first section of these laws (משנה תורה, Book זמנים, Hilekhoth שופר, &c.).

9. קושיות אחרות (ודברים אחרים). OTHER DIFFICULT QUESTIONS and VARIOUS OTHER MATTERS, occupying leaves 91b—94a.

a. On the formula על נטילת לולב, beginning:

למה אנו מברכין על נטילת לולב ולא על נטילת אתרוג....

b. On Ibn 'Ezra's explanation of Gen. iii. 18, beginning:

צחות כתב ר' אברהם א"ע (אבן עזרא) ז"ל בפי' התורה פרש' בראשית וקוץ ...פי' תיבת קוץ הוא פעל שלם....

c. On Ps. xci. 11 &c., beginning:

קבלה וחידוש. כתי' כי מלאכיו יצוה לך לשמרך בכל דרכיך שנים וכתי' חונה מלאך השם סביב ליראיו אפילו אחד....

This is not identical with No. 134. F. in Ghirondi's Library, catalogued by Steinschneider (Berlin, 1872, 8vo.).

d. On Job xxviii. 12, explained in the style of גמטריא and beginning:

והחוכמה מאין תמצא אמ' מאין בגימטריא ק"א....

e. On six points, four of which explain sayings of the Rabbis, while two refer to medical matters. They are introduced by the catechetical phrase התדע; for example:

התדע למה אחז"ל (אמרו חכמינו זכרונם לברכה) רוב הממיזרים פקחים" אמ' דעו כי הממזר לא יהיה לבד מנואף ומנואפת....

f. On the difference made by Maimonides, between the number of the leaves required in the myrtle and the willow of the brook (used on the Feast of Tabernacles). It begins:

זאת התשובה השיב ה"ר רבי' משה ע"ה על השאלה ששאלו לו חכמי זמנו....

At the end we read:

זו הועתק מהעתקת חכם אחד שהעתיקו בלשון ערבי ממענה החכם ה"ר רבי' ע"ה.

See טעם זקנים (Frankf. a. M. 1854, 8vo.), pp. ע"ה and 75, and חמדה גנוזה (Königsberg, 1856, 8vo.), pp. 5 and xxxiv. This MS. has כל instead of ר"ל; but there is little doubt that אֲבָל is the right reading.

10. [שירים שונים]. VARIOUS POEMS, occupying leaves 94a—95a.

a. החרז לתשבי (the principal copyist, whose anagram this is), beginning:

צביי היבין צרי צירי שפתו....

b. ריב הלחם עם היין, beginning:

בין רעים שמעתי תוכחות....

See Assemani, Bib. Apost. Vat. Codd. MSS. Cat. (Romae, 1756, Folio), Tom. I. No. 303. 3, p. 290.

c. ריב חיות ועופות, beginning:

אל בוראי ראשית הכל בו רבו מהללי....

See Assemani, ibid.

d. Copyist's thanksgiving, beginning:

נשלם בעזר כל עונה.

11. [תפלת הקדיש]. ON THE PRAYER יתגדל, &c., occupying leaves 95b—97b.

a. Explanation of this prayer by R. Shelomoh of Paris, beginning:
פי׳ קדיש לרבי׳ שלמה גאון מפריש זצ״ל. יתגדל ויתקדש על שם והתגדלתי והתקדשתי והיאך יוכל להתגדל שמו של הב״ה שמא חס ושלו׳ כביכול חסר הוא אין ודאי חסר הוא דכתי׳ כי יד על כס יה נשבע הק״בה....

See Assemani, ibid. 16 (p. 292).

b. Reason for the recitation of this prayer, beginning:
מצאתי טעם בקדיש . מפני מה תיקנו שעונין הקהל אמן יהא שמיה רבה... והן שבע תיבות כנגד....

12. [פרוש על ההגדה לר׳ ישעיה הכהן (בן עמנואל ?)]

EXPLANATION of the DOMESTIC SERVICE on the FIRST TWO PASSOVER EVENINGS, by R. YESHA'YAH HAKKOHEN (b. 'Immanuel ?).

Begins (leaf 98[a]):
הגדה להרב החסיד הגאון רבינו ישעיא מורינו ורבינו הא לחמא ענייא דאכלו וכו׳ בירושלמי (בירושלם) שמספרים ארמית לכן מספרים לשון זה משום שמחה....

Ends (leaf 104[b]):
....ואחר שיגמור הלל מה שרגילין להוסיף שבחות הרשות בידם ואחר כך מברך על כוס רביעי בורא פרי הגפן ועל הגפן. אילו דברי הרב הגדול הגאון רבינו ישעיא זצ״ל.

The author of this is unquestionably identical with the author of the supercommentary on Rashi on the Pentateuch (see 3 above), and must, therefore, not be confounded with either of the RR. Yesha'yah of Trani. In the course of this explanation the author mentions his teacher (נשאלתי מרבי...ואמר לי...), although not by name. He further mentions a certain R. Yitzchaq (of Russia ? or is this his teacher, as he says, leaf 100[a], משם מורי הרב רבי׳ יצחק זצ״ל ?), besides R. Qalonymos (תנא ה״ר קלונימוס) and R. Yesha'yah, whose נימוקים he speaks of (R. Yesha'yah of Trani I.).

13. [חדושים וכו׳ על אבלות]. EXTRACTS from the TALMUD, and NOVELLÆ, on MOURNING AFFAIRS, &c., occupying leaves 104[b]—105[b].

a. חידוש beginning:
בשמת בנו של רבן יוחנן בן זכאי נכנסו תלמידיו לנחמו....

b. גימגום beginning:
ראיתי בתוספות שמקשינן על ההוא שאומ׳ בכתובות מבטלין תלמוד תורה....

c. חידוש beginning:
ונשאל מרב פלטוי גאון נוהגין אצלינו בשעה שחוזרין בבית (מבית) הקברות.

14. [סדר התשובה [לר׳ אלעזר מגרמיזא. RULES for PENITENCE, by R. EL'AZAR B. YEHUDAH B. QALONYMOS, commonly called R. EL'AZAR OF WORMS.

Begins (leaf 105[b]):
הא לך סדר התשובה והלכותיה לכל עבירא ועבירה והם מיסוד ה״ר רבי׳ אליעזר בן רבי׳ יהודה כאשר קבל מרבי׳ יהודה מרישבורק (Regensburg) אב

החוכמה בין רבינו שמואל אשר היה בן רבי׳ קלונימוס הזקן מאספסייא בן רבינו יצחק בן הרב רבי׳ אלעזר והם קיבלו רב מרב וגאון מגאון וחכם מחכם עד משה מסיני „ והיה האיש ההוא אשר תקף יצרו....

Ends (leaf 116ª):

....והנינותיך המה יהמו עלי יהיו לרצון אמרי פי והגיון ליבי לפניך י״וי צורי וגואלי״ תם סליקו עניני תשובה כאשר סידרם רבינו החסיד הגדול והפרוש הרב רבינו יצחק זצו״ל וחיברם כבר הגאון ה׳ר אליעזר מגרמישין (Worms) בן רבי׳ יהודה כאשר קיבל מרבי׳ יהודה אב החוכמה מרנשבורק (Regensburg) ז״ל וכתבתים אני (שבתי) בן (החבר ר׳ ישעיא) כהן בן (הרב) ר׳ יהודה כהן (בן הרב חמובהק רבנא) משה (עבד) האל בן (הרב) ר׳ שבתי בן (מורינו הרב הגדול רבנא) ישעיא (גאון בן רבינו) עמנואל זצו״ל השם יזכיני להגות בו אני וזרעי וזרע זרעי ככתו׳ לא ימושו מפיך ומפי זרעך ומפי זרע זרעך אמ׳ השם מעתה ועד עולם „ חזקו ידים רפות וברכים כושלות אמצו אמן.

These rules, which are to be found in the author's רוקח (Cremona, 1557, Folio), leaves 6ᵇ—9ᵇ, at the end of the Responsa of R. Meir b. Barukh of Rothenburg (Prag, 1608, Folio), and elsewhere, differ considerably from the printed editions (see later).

15. [סודות בקבלה]. Cabbalistic Matters, occupying leaves 116ᵇ—119ª.

a. On the Most Holy Name, beginning:

בס״ד בי׳ יה סודו . דע כי השם הנכבד נכתב ואינו נקרא ככה...

See Ibn 'Ezra on Exod. xxxiii. 23, and the supercommentators in מרגליות טובה (Amsterdam, 1721, Folio), leaves 50ᵇ and 84ᵇ—85ª. Towards the end this article is somewhat cabbalistically treated.

b. On the name ירושלם, beginning:

והנה אגלה לך סוד ירושלם ולמה חסרים. דע כי מספר ירושלם הוא פּוֹרֹשׁ....

See Assemani, No. 103. 6, p. 72.

c. Calculation in connexion both with the Most Holy Name and the spelling of ירושלם, beginning:

וזה סוד החשבון אבגדהוזחטי בראשית המניין שהוא א׳ עד תכליתו שהוא י...

d. On the Most Holy Name, beginning:

דע לך בני כי זה השם שאני מפרש לך עתה הוא סוד גדול ומופלא....

e. On humility, &c., beginning:

כשהוא מוכיח את עצמו ונותן דין הבורא מעצמו.

and ending:

...ויכנעו עמי אשר נקרא שמי עליהם״ תם בתם על איש צעיר ולא תם (שבתי בן החבר ר׳ יהודה הכהן) בלבו.

Leaf 119ᵇ is blank.

16. [לקט השכחה]. A Note, occupying leaf 120ª. It begins:

ויקרא אכתבנו. זה שייך בפ׳ (בפרשת) וארא וי״ל (ויש לומר)זה שאומ׳ שסירטו בהי שר״ל (שרצונו לומר) שפרעה סירט את משה....

This reference is wrong; it ought to be בא instead of וארא; see leaf 28^{a} at the bottom. Leaves 120^{b}—122^{b} are blank.

So far goes the work of the principal one of the two original copyists and first owner, whose name, as we have repeatedly seen, is Shabbethai Bilbao[1]; Ḥe is, apparently, a descendant of R. Yesha'yah Hakkohen. His fellow-copyist, who was a peninsular Sephardi, wrote but little in this volume; all that belongs to him is found on leaf 56^{a}. But two later hands, whose work is of no small value, have left their mark on this MS.:

I. The first of these is Ibn Tarshish, a Greek Sephardi. To him are due:

(i) The crossing through of all the disrespectful terms in which Rashi is spoken of by R. Abraham b. David, and the substitution, in some places, of other and more respectful terms.

(ii) The erasures of the names of the principal original copyist and his immediate ancestors, against whom Ibn Tarshish seems to have had a spite. (Is it because he considered R. Shabbethai Bilbao dishonest in claiming for himself and his parentage titles and literature which were not theirs?) Thus he carefully erased the superscription of 3 and, leaving only the two words of the rhymes ישרים ... עברים, he puts the following instead: בסימנא טבא ובנחשא מעליא חפץ הש׳ בידי יצליח בהתחילי לכתוב חידושים בפי׳ התורה על רש״י לרב הגדול רבינו ישעיא השני ת״נ״צ״ב״ה....., whilst, inconsistently enough, he puts at the end of this commentary נשלמו חידושי תורה לרבור׳ ישעיא כהן תנצ״בה. See also this description (15. e.) on his bringing out, by an ingenious erasure, the damaging phrase "ולא תם בלבו", &c.

(iii) The marginal additions as follows:

(1) 16^{b}—18^{b}. Explanations of sundry passages in the Parshiyyoth בראשית to לך לך. They are superscribed טעמי בראשית, and are by ה״ר אברהם or א״ע, i. e. R. Abraham b. Meir Ibn 'Ezra and by מה״ר אלעזר קרובי, R. El'azar, a relative of the scribe, but chiefly by ב״ש, or הרב״ש, i. e. R. Yoseph בכור שור.

(2) 21^{a}. Explanation of Gen. xxv. 6, which is ascribed to מה״ר אהרן זצ״ל.

(3) 25^{b} and 26^{b}. Explanation of Gen. xlvii. 28, Ex. ii. 23, and iii. 19, which are ascribed to R. Yoseph קרא.

(4) 27^{a}. Explanation of Ex. ii. 4, ascribed to הרא״ש, i. e. R. Asher b. Yechiel, and of Ex. iv. 10, ascribed to the foregoing R. Yoseph.

(5) 28^{a}. Explanation of Ex. x. 14 by an anonymous writer.

1 "Sabbathai fils d'Isaïe Kohen de Saint Jean d'Acre," who copied No. 698 in the Paris Collection is, no doubt, the same. Assemani (No. 105. 11, p. 76), mentions a R. Mikhael (מכיאל) b. Shabbethai Kohen 'בלבו' (which he erroneously writes Belibo), who is probably a son of our scribe.

(6) 33[b], 34[a], and 43[a]. Additions to R. Yesha'yah's commentary.

(7) 50[a]. Remarks (superscribed גליון) on Num. xiii. 1 and 16, in which last place we read .... ונראה לי אבן תרשיש.

(8) 50[b]. Remarks (superscribed גליון) on Num. xiii. 3, and 23, in which last place .... אמ׳ תרשיש occurs, and on the same passage with reference to Ex. xiii. 16, in which R. Yehudah Hakkohen ב״מז״ל is mentioned.

(9) 51[a]. Remarks (superscribed גליון) on Num. xvii. 18, in which וה״ר יהודה חסיד occurs.

(10) 120[b]. Extract from the T. B. Synhedrin 56[b] on the commandments given by God to the first man.

(11) 122[a]. Entry of the birth of Mikhael Bilbao (?), running thus:

נולד בני מיכאל ביום ב׳ לחדש ניסן שנת הקע״א וסימנו הופיע מהר פארן ואתא מרבבות קדש מימינו אש דת למו הש׳ יחייהו ויגדלהו בתורה ובמצות אמן.

(According to Jahn's Tables, 2 Nisan 5171 corresponds to 27 March 1411.) This is possibly R. Shabbethai's own son, only that the entry was made for him by Ibn Tarshish. See the foregoing Foot-note.

II. The second of these is a Greek Ashkenazi, named Shelomoh (see below), of the latter part of the xvth century. To him are due even more important additions:

(i) Various Rabbinical sayings on leaf 1[a] which are a continuation from what at one time preceded this volume in a former binding (see MS. Add. 377. 2).

(ii) Part of the phrases in replacement of those crossed through by Ibn Tarshish in R. Abraham b. David's Strictures on Rashi.

(iii) Marginal additions as follows:

(1) 12[a]. An extract from Qimchi.

(2) 48[a] and 55[b]. Emendations on the commentary of R. Yesha'yah Hakkohen and on that of the טל of R. El'azar Haqqalir.

(3) 63[b]. An extract from the ספר האמונות of R. Se'adyah Gaon referring to matter on leaf 64[b] in Ibn Kaspi's supercommentary.

(4) 64[b]—70[b]. Additions to Ibn Kaspi's supercommentary on Ibn 'Ezra on the Pentateuch, consisting of the preface to the whole, and the supercommentaries on Numbers and Deuteronomy. The preface begins לא מפני היותי איש חכם, and not איש סכל (שכל), as the first four MSS. cited by Steinschneider read.

Deuteronomy ends:

וזה שאמ׳ החכם ראב״ע סוד גדול . תמו ונשלמו ביאור הסודות של החכם ר׳ אברהם אבן עזרא . והמפר׳ הזה הוא אבן כספי וכן נתאמת לי שכך הוא (שלמה)״ ברוך נותן ליעף כח . סליק . ולפי הנראה שהמחבר אבן כספי ביאר אחר חיבור זה גם סודות וטעם ערכים (see MS. Add. 510. 2, leaf 96[b]) וסוד

הייבום וסוד הציץ והתפלין וסוד האהבה והיראה וכתבתיהו בסוף ספר מאמר השכל וע״ש (ועיין שם).

(5) 87ª. A reference to Ibn Kaspi's supercommentary on Ibn 'Ezra on the Pentateuch.

(6) 92ª. A note on the orthography of the name עקיב' with traditions from R. Shemuel מבבנבערק and R. Yitzchaq אור זרוע מאושטריך. See R. Yitzchaq b. Mosheh of Vienna's אור זרוע (Zitomir, 1862, Folio), p. 5.

(7) 92ᵇ. Explanations of Mishnah Sotah, III. 4, beginning:

הא דאמרינן במס' (במסכת) כתובות בפ' (בפרק ה') רוצה אשה בקב וטפלות....

(8) 105ᵇ—106ª. The סוד התשובה of R. El'azar of Worms, beginning:

עמ״י אחל סוד התשובה מיסוד הרב רבי אליעזר מגרמייזא זצ״ל איה״ן איה״ן עש״ו סוד התשובה שלח לנו.... הקבה.

See כל בו, Siman 67, to which this is, although shorter towards the end, greatly superior. The abbreviation איה״ן איה״ן is אנא יהוה הושיעה נא אנא יהוה הצליחה נא, Ps. cxviii. 25.

(9) 106ᵇ. An extract from R. Yonah's חיי עולם (towards the end), commencing: ...תמיד בכל חדש יתענה.

(10) 106ᵇ—108ª. A מוסר by Rabbenu Ephraim in תשר״ק with the acrostic אפרים. It commences:

תזעק נפשי ותתעברי מפני חבוט הקבר...

and ends:

כי יי' גמל עלייכי "תם ונשלם מוסר זה שיסד רבי' אפרים ז״ל"

(11) 107ª. An index of the 29 paragraphs of the סדר התשובה, the numbers being placed in accordance with this index at the side of each paragraph (107ª—115ᵇ).

(12) 109ª. Another reading of the text.

(13) 109ᵇ. A consultation or response by R. Meir b. Barukh on the penitence required by a woman, who killed her own child accidentally by lying on it while asleep. See עיר מקלט, in יד כל בו (Amsterdam, 1727, folio), leaf 50ª, § XXXIV.

(14) 110ª and 111ᵇ. Extracts from the חיי עולם, on taking an oath and other matters.

(15) 114ª. On warming oneself on a Sabbath in the nursery. It commences: ....על עבירה חייב אדם לעשות תשובה, and in the course of the note we read:

אבל כת' ה״ר אלכסנדרי בן הר״ר יצחק ב״ר מאיר מדורא (Düren) וז״ל (וזה לשונו) שמעתי מאבא מרי הר״ר יצחק לוי כשלמד תורה לפני מורי' הר״ר טוביה בצרפת ובא לשם ה״ר יחיאל מפריש וראה שהיו יושבים אצלו.......

(16) 114ᵇ. The וידוי extracted from the כתר מלכות of R. Shelomoh הקטן אבן גבירול. It commences: ...אשמתי בתורתיך, and ends with the words: אלך בלא חמדה.

(17) 115ª. A מוסר extracted from חובות הלבבות of R. בחיי b. Yoseph

Ibn בקודה. It commences: נפשי הכיני צדה, and ends with the words: כן איש נודד ממקומו.

(18) 116[b]. Explanations of the calculation of the numerical value of the Most Holy Name.

(19) 117[b]. A טעם בנגלה on ירושלם being spelled without the י, which the copyist had heard from the mouth of R. Abraham b. Shemuel.

(20) 120[b]—121[b]. A table of the contents of the whole volume as formerly bound (MS. Add. 377), now consisting again of eight separate volumes; from which we see that at that time it consisted of at least 700 pages, of which now a good many are unfortunately lost; see MS. Add. 377. 1. Begins:

עמ״י עש״ו לסמן זה הקובץ אגרת התשובה וחסידות ומיני מוסרים ממה״ר אביגדור כ״ץ (כהן צדק)....

Ends:

ספר בן סירא ק״ף עד ר״ג.

(iv) The titles of the various works and essays, which are to be found in the corner of the upper margins, and the pagination (where the pages and not the leaves are counted) which is to be found in the corner of the lower margin of the recto pages.

A still later owner, a German Ashkenazi, Abraham b. Eli'ezer Hallevi of quite modern date (see leaf 116[a], where תקעו לפ״ק (לפרט קטן), *i.e.* 1816, occurs), has written the following on leaf 119[b]:

אל אלהי אבי בעזרי אברהם בר אליעזר שמו סג״ל (סגן לויה).....אמי מורתי מרת מינדל בת יהוד׳ סג״ל ז״ל....

This owner seems to have dealt in lottery shares, as the numbers there given apparently indicate.

As for the state of the MS., leaves 1—18, 22, 28 have suffered from damp, 29 and 67 are wanting, 30—33 are partly destroyed, 34—36 are only a little damaged.

[Library-mark, Add. 377. 3; bought in 1867 from H. Lipschütz.]

No. 36.

Paper, in quarto, $6\frac{7}{8}$ in. × $5\frac{1}{4}$ in.; 120 leaves, 4-sheet quires, 27 lines; Rabbinic character, fine German Ashkenazic handwriting of the XIVth century.

ביאורים [על פרוש רש״י על התורה לחכם אשכנזי פלוני אלמוני]

Supercommentary on Rashi on the PENTATEUCH by an anonymous German Rabbi; defective.

Leaf 1, *Genesis* (1—16, 32, wanting); 52ª, *Exodus;* 82ᵇ, *Leviticus;* 93ª *Numbers;* 106ª, *Deuteronomy*.

Begins (leaf 17ª, on Gen. xx. 5[1]):

....כיון שתהרוג אותי שאני גוי גם צדיק תהרוג וזהו אברהם על שלא גילה לי שהיא אשתו....

Ends (leaf 120ᵇ, on Deut. xxxiv. 10):

..אשר ידעו יי׳ פנים אל פנים כדכתי׳ פה אל פה אדבר בו במראה ולא בחידות ותמונת יי׳ יביט: סליק ביאורים.

Our author makes Rashi, by commenting on him, his chief means of commenting on the Pentateuch. While mostly approving of what Rashi says, the difficulties he raises against him are raised in order the more clearly to bring out his author's meaning. But although Rashi is our author's chief authority, and although גמטריאות, and such like, are his favourites, he is by no means uncritical as a commentator, nor contemptible as a grammarian. In pursuance of his critical aim, he brings not merely his own difficulties to bear upon Rashi, but also those of others, and chiefly those of R. Chizqiyyah b. Manoach, which, as in the original, he cites by the phrase חז״ק[2]. The chief importance of this commentary, however, consists (1) in the valuable readings of the Rashi-text (see for instance leaf 88ᵇ, which has a piece not to be found anywhere else, leaf 104ᵇ, &c.); (2) in the curious anti-christian passages it contains (see leaves 20ᵇ, 48ᵇ, 49ª, 66ᵇ, 74ª, 89ª, and 114); and (3) in the illustrations, due originally to the author himself, of the text (see leaves 32ᵇ, 77ª, 78ᵇ).

Our author (who composed also a commentary on Aboth, see leaf 98ª, and of whom more will be found in the description of MS. Add. 669. 2, which is full of most interesting matter) was a German of the xɪɪɪth century, as may be inferred from the German words[3] found in this commen-

[1] It is only by the forgetfulness either of the author himself or of one or the other of the scribes that Gen. xx. 5 is placed here; a few lines later the earlier verses of xix. 26, &c. are explained. See for somewhat similar instances on leaves 62ᵇ, 64ª, 66ª, and 94ᵇ, where, however, the emendations are preceded by the phrase . . . שכחתי.

[2] R. Chizqiyyah b. Manoach prefixes the phrase חז״ק, whenever he has a difficulty against Rashi such as either he cannot solve at all, or only unsatisfactorily, or after a great deal of trouble. In such a case he uses it for the following threefold reason: (1) it being in a certain sense the same as ורפיא (a term current for such difficulties in the xɪɪɪth century; see No. 35. 3. (4) of this Catalogue); (2) it being part of his own name חזקיה; and (3) it being the abbreviation of חזי קושיא (which solution alone explains the ...על ריש״ occasionally following it). The statement of Zunz (Gesch. u. Lit. p. 92), Seine eigenen Bemerkungen bezeichnet die Chiffer חזק, is therefore incomplete.

[3] These amount to 57, and are to be found on leaves 27ª, 36ᵇ, 50ᵇ, 85ᵇ, 86ª, 90ª, 96ᵇ, and 109ᵇ. There are also five French words to be met with. The two on leaf 61ª are Rashi's, the one on leaf 112ᵇ is taken from the שוהם, while the one

tary on the one hand, and the authorities quoted therein on the other hand.

The following are the authorities whom he quotes :

(1) אבא מורי זצ״ל (leaves 18^a, 19^b, 22^a, 34^a, 52^a, and 65^b).

(2) His contemporary שמעתי מפי ר׳ יעקב אננער (leaf 18^a).

(3) ובספר נמצא מר׳ יהודה החסיד, also simply החסיד (23^b, 53^b, and 98^b).

(4) חומשים מדויקים (leaf 23^b).

(5) מסורה (leaves 23^b, 87^b, 94^b, and 95^a).

(6) הקדוש ר׳ יצחק משפירא (leaf 35^b).

(7) חז״ק (leaves 39^b, 40^b, 45^a, 59^a, 61^a, 70^a, and חזקוני distinctly, leaf 40^a).

(8) His contemporary שמעתי מפי ר׳ ויבש[1] אורי (leaf 40^a).

(9) יצחק ב׳ר שמואל (leaf 43^a). (10) רבנו חננאל (leaf 43^a).

(11) הערוך (leaves 43^a and 72^a).

(12) His contemporary ושמעתי מה״ר יהודה הכהן (leaf 43^b).

(13) Anonymous but contemporary authors מפי אחרים שמעתי (leaf 44^b).

(14) הרר״א (leaf 46^a, also הר״א and ההר״א, leaves 59^b, 60^a, and 92^b).

(15) פענח רזון (רזא) (leaf 51^a).

(16) בכור שור, also מה״ר יוסף בכור שור and ר׳ בכור שור (leaves 51^a, 59^b, 60^a, 78^b, and 106^b).

(17) הרי״ח (R. Yehudah Chasid ? leaves 55^b and 78^b).

(18) His contemporary ושמעתי מן הר״ר בנימין (leaf 56^b).

(19) ר׳ מנחם אשר (חבר ספר) שכל טוב (leaf 57^a).

(20) His teacher כמו שקבלתי ממורי הח״ר משולם מקולונייא (leaf 57^b).

(21) ר׳ משה הדרשן (leaf 65^b). (22) הקדוש מדאייט (leaf 71^b).

(23) הר״ר יעקב מאורלנייש, also הר״י מאוריינש (leaves 72^b and 90^b).

(24) ר״י בשם ר׳ יוסף and ר״י (leaves 74^b, 79^b, and 80^a).

(25) ר״ת (leaves 76^b and 97^a). (26) רשב״ג in answer to ר״ת (leaf 76^b).

(27) הר׳ משה (leaves 83^a and 85^a).

(28) הג״ן[2] (גן עדן ?). See Neubauer, in Geiger's *Jüd. Zeitschrift*, IX.

on leaf 63 and the other on leaf 115^b, although not traced as yet, were probably taken by our author from some other French commentator.

[1] ויבש, when belonging to an Ashkenazi, and particularly when either preceded or followed by אורי, is equivalent to Phoebus and not to Vivas, as Zunz (*Gesch. u. Lit.* p. 104) thinks.

[2] The current opinion is that it is called הג״ן, from being a commentary on the Pentateuch, which consists of fifty-three (נ״ג) weekly Parshiyyoth. See Zunz, *Gesch. u. Lit.* p. 78, and Neubauer, in Frankel's *Monatsschrift*, XXI. p. 182.

p. 230; but the MS. there described seems to contain a work later than the genuine (leaf 84ª).

(29) מהר"ם (leaf 89ᵇ). (30) ר' שלמה (not Rashi; leaf 91ᵇ).

(31) הר' יוסף (twice leaf 92ª).

(32) הר' יוסף קרא (leaves 95ᵇ, 112ª, and 119ᵇ).

(33) הר' חיים (leaf 95ᵇ).

(34) רבנו טוביה, the grandson of R. Yehudah החסיד (leaf 98ᵇ).

(35) ר"ח (not חזקוני; leaf 101ᵇ). (36) הר' ברכיה (leaf 103ᵇ).

(37) ר' שמואל (leaf 112ª). (38) השוהם (leaf 112ª).

(39) אבי עז' (not Ibn 'Ezra, unless the interpretation be forced; leaf 119ᵇ).

(40) דנש (leaf 120ᵇ).

(41) הפייט (leaves 61ᵇ, 67ª, 71ª, 101, and 116ª).

But, besides the literature to be found in the ordinary place, that to be met with on the margins must not be neglected, as it contains matters of importance which have escaped the otherwise very exact scholars, the late S. D. Luzzatto[1], who, as its last owner[2], described this MS. in the כרם חמד (VII. pp. 68—69), and the venerable Zunz, who adopted the results of this description in his *Gesch. und Lit.* (pp. 103—104). The margins, then, contain, besides the emendations and additions on leaves 21ª, 23ᵇ, 62ᵇ, 68ª, 69ᵇ (this last is superscribed תוספת), 70ᵇ, 75ᵇ, 78ᵇ, 80ᵇ, 81ª, 93ª, 94ª, 95ª, 95ᵇ, 96ª, 101ᵇ, 107ª, and 113ª, by the original scribe himself, also literature by others, viz.:

(1) By a German Ashkenazic hand of the early part of the XIVth century. This hand wrote on leaves 22ᵇ, 36ᵇ, 54ª, 55ª, 59ª, 62ª, 62ᵇ (in which ר' אביגדור is quoted), 63ª, 67ª, 69ᵇ, 70ª (in which this R. Abigedor is surnamed הצרפתי), 71ª, 71ᵇ, 79ᵇ, 82ᵇ, 84ª, 86ª, 86ᵇ, 88ᵇ (in which מהרא"ש י"ץ is quoted; this is, no doubt, R. Asher b. Yechiel, who died October 25[3], 1327, and who, as י"ץ is equivalent to ישמרהו צורו, must have been then alive), 89ª, 89ᵇ, 90ª, 90ᵇ, 91ª (in which the לקח טוב is quoted), 92ª, 94ª 96ᵇ, 97ª (in which הר' יוסף, and again מהרא"ש י"ץ, are quoted), 97ᵇ, 98ª, 101ª, 101ᵇ, 102ª and 105ª.

(2) By another German Ashkenazic hand, also of the XIVth century, though later, which wrote on leaf 76ᵇ.

[1] Thus so important a name as that of R. Asher b. Yechiel, which is twice to be found, is not mentioned by him, whilst R. Eli'ezer of Forchheim, not to be found here at all (see MS. Add. 669. 2, leaf 54ᵇ), is said to be mentioned here.

[2] This MS. is described by his son Joseph, in his *Catalogue de la Bibliothèque de litterature hebraïque et orientale de feu Mr. Samuel David Luzzatto de Trieste .... Padoue*, &c. p. 9, No. 87, as containing שני פירושים על התורה אחד בקרב הדף ואחד בגליון...., which statement is entirely incorrect.

[3] Zunz, Monatstage . . . (Berlin, 1872, 8vo.) p. 58.

(3) By a third German Ashkenazic hand of the xvth century, which wrote on leaves 80ª, 84ª, 84ᵇ and 86ᵇ.

(4) By an Italian hand of the xv—xvith century, which wrote on leaves 67ª—71ª and 72ª—72ᵇ. It is this owner, probably, who wrote also the Arabic numbers on the lower margin of the verso-page, and who had the MS. mounted and bound.

The label on the back שני פירושים על התורה כ"י is apparently in the writing of the last owner, S. D. Luzzatto, who acquired the volume at Trieste in the summer of 1841; see כרם חמד, vii. pp. 55 and 68.

The condition of the MS. is not very satisfactory, every leaf having been so badly cut as to require being mounted; nevertheless very little, comparatively speaking, of the literature has been lost, and the paper is very stout.

No. 37.

Paper, in quarto, 8½ in. × 6 in.; 29 leaves, 30 lines; Rabbinic character, Greek Sephardic handwriting of the xvth century.

[פרוש על פרוש רש"י על התורה לחכם יוני פלוני אלמוני]

Supercommentary on Rashi on the PENTATEUCH by an anonymous Greek Rabbi; defective.

Leaf 1ª, *Genesis* (16 wanting); 17, *Exodus;* 26ᵇ, *Leviticus;* 28ᵇ, *Numbers;* 29 and all leaves afterwards wanting.

Begins (leaf 1ª):

בראשית פיר"ש לא היה...להת...הזה למה התחיל...וקשה לעולם יתחיל מהחדש הזה...

Breaks off (leaf 28ᵇ; on Num. xvi. 1—4):

וא"ת למה אמ' גם לוי: והלא גם הוא היה צדיק. י"ל אותו לא בקש רחמים. א"נ (אי נמי) בן לוי ר"ל (רצונו לומר) שעשה לוייה לקורח שהיה רשע: ויפול על פניו פרש"י מפני המחלוקת שכבר זה בידם סרחון רביעי וא"ת והלא שבט לוי לא חטאו....

This Supercommentary is written in the style of the North French Rabbis, as exhibited in the תוספות on the Talmud Babli as also in their Additamenta to Rashi on the Pentateuch. Every paragraph commences here more or less with וא"ת, to which a וי"ל is given. The literature is often also the very same in substance if not in wording; see דעת זקנים (Livorno, 1783, Folio), passim. It is, however, very short, and it strikes one as if it were a mere extract from a larger work; observe for instance that between the Parashah of תזריע (in Lev.) and that of קרח (in Num.) nothing is to be found.

Our author must have been a Greek, as we see from leaf 12[b], where he says גינסיא של מלכים לשון יון ינוסיאה, and leaf 27[a], where he says לקיץ המזבח לשון יון פְּרוֹסְפָּאִי. The only authorities he quotes besides Rashi, whom he mostly calls ר״ש only (see No. 33 above), a phrase to which later, particularly French, writers have a great objection, are: Rabbenu חננאל (leaf 14[b]), רבינו טוביהו (ib.), (Coucy ?) רבי משה מקונצי (leaf 24[b]), and ר׳ אברהם מגרמישא (leaf 25[b]). See Excurs. II.

A later, very inelegant, trembling, and apparently old hand, has occasionally put a remark on the margin (see 15[b], 22[a], &c.), mostly emendations or summaries. There are no other traces of ownership. The MS. afterwards belonged to Erpenius.

The condition of the MS. is very bad, half of leaves 1—4 having been cut off, whilst what we have is much soiled and stained, making the writing illegible in various places. It is also somewhat worm-eaten, and has suffered both from fire and water.

[Library-mark, Mm. 6. 26. 1; presented in 1632 by Catherine Duchess of Buckingham.]

No. 38.

Paper, in quarto, 8⅜ in. × 5¾ in.; 104 leaves, 4-sheet quires, 34 lines; Rabbinic character, Italian handwriting; dated Friday, 13 Sivan, 20 June, 5296 (1536).

חדושים על רש״י [על התורה לר׳ עובדיה מברטנורא הראשון.]

Supercommentary on Rashi on the PENTATEUCH, by R. 'Obadyah of Bertinoro, the elder.

Leaf 1[a], *Genesis*; 28[a], *Exodus*; 56[a], *Leviticus*; 76[a], *Numbers*; 91[a], *Deuteronomy*; 103[a], subscription by the scribe; 103[b]—104[b], blank.

Begins:

בראשית ברא וכו׳ אמ׳ ר׳ יצחק....קשה איך אמ׳ שמצות החדש היא ראשונה והרי קודם זה יש המילה וגיד הנשה שנצטוו קודם לכן. י״ל שכל המצות כולן נאמרו למשה רבינו ע״ה....

Ends:

.....ומראש הררי קדם וכו׳ שהרריה מקדימין לבכר בישול פירותיהן ד״א (דבר אחר) מגיד שקדמהברייתן לשאר הרים דהשתא אתי שפיר לשון הררי קדם שנבראו מקדם.

לשוני ופי נערכה   בפי׳ וזאת הברכה
אודה לאל בורא שמשי   שעזרני בספר חמשי
ויתן לעבדו עזרה   בפי׳ ה׳ חומשי תורה
כן לעד יאיר עיני אורה   לעסוק ולהגות בכל התורה.

ותשלם מלאכת הקדש זה ספר חדושים על רש״י ז״ל על ידי יהודה עמ״י יזיי״א (יראה זרע יאריך ימים אמן) בכאמ״ר (בן כבוד אבי מורי רבי) שמואל ז״ל איש פירמו (Fermo) היום יום ו׳ י״ג לחדש סיון כ׳ יוניו שנת ה׳ אלפים ורצ״ו לבריאת עולם ה׳ יזכני להגות בו ובכל ספרי הקדש אותי וזרעי וזרע זרעי עד סוף כל הדורות אמן ואמן.

בנ״לך ואע״י כבודך ה׳

חזק ונתחזק הסופר והקורא לא יזק לא היום ולא לעולם עד שיעלה פול בסולם אשר יעקב אבינו חלם אמן כן יהי רצון אמן.

The abbreviation עמ״י is Ps. cxxi. 2, and that of יזיי״א is Isaiah liii. 10, with אמן added; for the פול (פיל) בסולם as well as for חמור בסולם and שור בסולם see Excurs. VIII.

This commentary was first printed (Pisa, 1810, 4to.), under the title of עמר נקא, from a copy made by the scribe who wrote the present MS. It has been since reprinted (Czernowitz, 1857, 8vo.), but this reprint is full of inaccuracies. The title of the edition (עמר נקא) is neither one given by the author himself, who seems not to have named the book at all, nor that given by the copyist, who calls it in both MSS. ספר חדושים על רש״י ז״ל; but is a fancy-title bestowed by the first editor R. Ya'aqob Nuñez Vais[1], who wished in עמר to give anagrammatically and this again in initials only, רבי עובדיה מברטנורא, and who united with it the phrase, Dan. vii. 9, as he considered this work to be clear and pure.

Concerning the author himself we need only observe that this is the celebrated commentator of the משנה. See *Zunz*, on geographical literature of the Jews, No. 66 (in Asher's edition of the Itinerary of R. Benjamin of Tudela, London and Berlin, 1841, 8vo. II. pp. 267—268); *Neubauer*, who has published two most interesting letters which our author sent from Palestine to his father and brother in Italy (in the third volume of the *Jahrbuch, f. d. Gesch. d. Jud. und d. Judenth.* pp. 192—270); and Excurs. II. to this Catalogue where the relations of the book both to the written work and oral communications of his teacher will be discussed.

The copyist, whose name we know to have been יהודה, has placed a small

[1] R. Ya'aqob b. Yitzchaq Nuñez Vais was Rabbi of Leghorn; see Ghirondi, תולדות גדולי ישראל (Trieste, 1853, 8vo.) p. 132, Nos. 9 and 10.

ornament against that name wherever it occurs throughout the MS. besides the mention thereof in the subscription as given above.

The fly-leaves at the commencement contain interesting notes in which R. 'Obadyah Sforno's, R. Yitzchaq Kohen's and an anonymous owner's own calculations of coins, weights and measures mentioned in the Talmud (and some also of those in the Bible) are given. Leaf 104[b], also by an anonymous owner, has a few sayings of the Rabbis; and occasionally with explanations.

On leaf 1[a] on the upper margin is to be found the following entry:

אשר חנן אלקים את עבדו יואב בכמוהר״ר עבדיה ז״ל מטיוולי (Tivoli) קניתיהו באנקונה (Ancona) בעד ה׳ פאולי ה׳ יזכני להגות בו אני וזרעי וזרע זרעי עד סוף כל הדורות אכי״ר.

On leaf 104[b] occurs, probably, another owner's name:

כמה״רר חנני׳ פרופס מימודלייאנו (Modigliana) יצ״ו (ישמרהו צורו וגואלו).

The former note is in Italian current and the latter in Sephardic Rabbinic character. The label on the back, חדושים על פיר״שי עה״ת (פרוש רש״י על התורה) MS. 1533 (mistaken for 1536) is apparently in R. Marco Mortara's handwriting.

The MS. is, the fly-leaves excepted, which are somewhat worm-eaten, in excellent condition.

[Library-mark, Add. 395; bought in 1867 from H. Lipschütz.]

No. 39.

Paper, in quarto, 8¼ in. × 6¼ in.; 108 leaves, mostly 6-sheet quires, part, 25 lines, mixed (Rabbinic and current) character, Italian handwriting, and part, 27 lines, Rabbinic character, Sephardic handwriting; both contemporary and of the XVIth century.

[פרוש על פרוש רש״י על התורה וישוב קושיות הרמב״ן עליו לר׳ יעקב קניזל]

Supercommentary on Rashi on the PENTATEUCH, with reference to Nachmanides' strictures, by R. Ya'aqob Cañizal; incomplete.

Leaf 3[a], *Genesis*; 50[b], *Exodus*;...

Begins:

בהנו״א כתב רש״י ז״ל בראשית ברא א׳ א״ר יצחק לא היה צריך להתחיל התורה וכו׳ ומה טוב היה שרש״י יפרשהו אלינו. וכבר הקשה הרמב״ן ז״ל על מאמ׳

ר׳ יצחק ואמ׳ כי צורך גדול הוא......וכמו שתראהו בארוכה בספרו..ואני אומ׳ שהקושיא שעשה הרמב״ן ז״ל על מאמ׳ ר׳ יצחק אם הוא היה עושה הקושיא יותר חזקה.....

Breaks off (leaf 100[b], Exod. xxi. 36):

....ר״ל שמ״ש (שמה שאמר) והמת יהיה לו חוזר לניזק ולא למזיק שאם לא כן מה היה צריך הכתו׳ (הכתוב) לומר שיהיה המת למזיק שאחרי....

Printed with three other commentaries, perhaps at Constantinople, 1525[1]. See De-Rossi's *Annales Hebræo-Typographici, ab An. MDI ad MDXL* (Parmae, 1799, 4to.), Part II. No. 13, p. 45. Steinschneider, Bod. Cat. No. 5515, and Zedner, Cat. of the Heb. Books in the British Museum, p. 677.

On comparing this copy with the printed edition, we find that not only is the latter a mere short extract from the author's work as exhibited in this copy, but that a good many of the explanations given here and found there, are there wrongly attributed to one or the other of the three other commentators, and particularly to R. Shemuel Almosnino.

The author was a Spanish Sephardi (probably of Cañizal), living in the latter part of the xvth century. See leaf 16[b], where on Gen. xviii. 21 he says:

הכצעקתה של מדינה. הוקשה לו שהי׳ שיאמ׳ הכצעקתם שהם חמשה עיירות לז״פ (לזה פרש) שיחזור לשם מדינה שהוא כולל מקומות הרבה כמו שאומרי׳ בלשון לע״ז קונדאדו או מרקשדו, &c.

See also leaf 99[b], where on Ex. xxi. 20 he says:

....וכי יכה·····שסותר את כולו כמו שפי׳ (שפרש) בעל הליכות עולם.

The הליכות עולם was composed in 1467; see the description of MS. Oo. 1. 35. 6 below. The De-Rossi MS. 355, which seems to contain the present work also, was copied in 1508. These facts are enough to settle the author's country and date within narrow limits.

Although copied by two different anonymous copyists, the whole MS. was executed contemporaneously, as may be seen passim on strict examination. At first sight one would certainly take leaves 3[a] and 26[b], which are in mixed Italian character, to have been written as a supplement.

The Italian copyist, who was, no doubt, the first owner of this MS, has on some of the margins and on portions of leaves 46[a], 103[a]—104[b], and 108[a], some additional notes, consisting partly of corrections and partly of supplements. Another anonymous Italian, who was probably the next owner, has enriched many of the margins with very learned and most interesting notes which he always introduces by ולי התלמיד. And a still later, also anonymous Italian owner, has also several notes, in one of which (leaf 34[b]),

[1] According to Carmoly, *La Famille Almosnino* (extrait du Journal l'Univers Israélite, Numéros de Janvier, Février et Mars, 1850), p. 6, these Commentaries were probably printed at Salonika towards the middle of the xvith century.

he mentions his teacher מהר"ם יצ"ו (R. Meir Katzenellenbogen, of Padua ?). The two latter owners have also left us their explanations of, and extracts from, the Talmud Babli, the Midrashim, the 'Arukh, and the works of R. David Qimchi and R. בחיי b. Asher on various passages of the Bible, &c., and which are to be found on the leaves left blank by the original scribes.

The following leaves were left blank by the original scribes: 1—2, 7 (the weekly Parashah of בראשית is here incomplete), 45ᵇ (part)—46ᵇ (which reads on nevertheless), 85ᵃ and ᵇ (which reads on), 100ᵇ (part)—108ᵇ.

Leaf 1ᵃ has the following little poem in a Rabbinic Sephardic hand (not that of one of the original scribes):

מה לך עצל עד אן תישן„ הן הנמלה אגרה לה בר„
לא ראיתי חתול ישן„ אשר תוך פיהו בא עכבר„

Corresponding with these lines we read in an Italian current hand:

היום ד׳ אלול השצ"ג קניתי הספר הזה מר׳ יהושע פירושה[1] מוכר ספרי׳ ממנטווה (Mantua) יאמי"ץ.

This is, no doubt, the signature of Leon[2] Modena, the abbreviation being יהודה אריה ממודינא ישמרהו צורו (ישמרני צורי); see MS. Dd. 10. 14. 7. The volume afterwards belonged to Yitzchaq (b. Menachem ?) פראגי.

The condition of the MS., as far as it goes, is excellent.

[Library-mark, Dd. 10. 14. 2; presented in 1647 by the House of Commons.]

No. 40.

Paper, in quarto, $8\frac{1}{8}$ in. × 6 in.; 196 leaves, 8-sheet quires, 34—40 lines; mixed (Rabbinic and current) character, Italian handwriting of the XVIth century.

[פרוש על פרוש רש"י על התורה ודברים שונים ממחברים שונים]

Supercommentary on Rashi on the PENTATEUCH, together with various other matters by various authors; defective.

1. פרוש על פרוש רש"י על התורה לר׳ מנחם בן דניאל בן דוד בן משה ממודינא.

[1] For Yehoshua' b. Yehudah Shemuel Perugia, see Steinschneider, Cat. p. 3019, No. 3029.

[2] This famous man is commonly, but by mistake, called either *Leo di*, or *da*, or *de*, Modena. His signature in Italian is to be found in the Bodleian (MS. Arch. Seld. A. 47).

SUPERCOMMENTARY on RASHI on the PENTATEUCH by R. MENACHEM B. DANIYYEL B. DAVID B. MOSHEH OF MODENA.

Leaves 1, 2, blank; leaf 3, probably blank, wanting; 4, blank; 5[a], *Genesis;* 28[a], *Exodus;* 51[b], *Leviticus;* 65[a], *Numbers;* 76, blank; 77[a], *Deuteronomy.*

Preface begins (leaf 5[a]):

הצעיר

מכל מלמדי השכלתי כי עדותיך שיחה לי (Ps. cxix. 99)
נחלתי ערותיך לעולם כי ששון לבי המה (Ibid. 111)
חלקי ה׳ אמרתי לשמור דבריך (Ibid. 57)
מה נמלצו לחכי אמרתיך מדבש לפי (Ibid. 103)

בכ״מר דניאל ממודינה יצ״ו בכמה״ר דויד איש מודינה זצ״ל בכמה״ר משה ממודינה זלה״ה זה הוא החבור קטן הכמות שתקנתי לפי מעוט השגתי אני קטן המחוקקים צעיר התלמידים נבזה וחדל אישים זעירא דמן חבריא כפי מה אשר הורוני מורי ואלופי ורבותי ומלמדי להועיל....

Introduction begins (leaf 6[a]):

עמ״י בהנו״א עש״ו בראשית כשברא הקב״ה את עולמו לא עלה במחשבה באיזה אות תהיה לו ראויה להתחיל....

Work begins (ibid.):

בראשית ברא פרש״י א״ר יצחק לא היה צרי׳ להתחיל וגו׳ פי׳ שהיה די שיקצר בדברי׳ ולא יאריך כ״כ (כל כך) בספורי׳ ושיאמ׳ כי בששת ימי׳ עשה ה׳ את השמי׳ ואת הארץ ואל יאריך לספר את ענין המבול וכל הנמשך. ופי׳ לא היה צרי׳ להתחיל תורת של ישראל אלא מהחדש הזה לכם כי כל זה היא תורה של בני נח....

Ends ('eaf 85[b], on xxxiii. 25):

...וכן א״ל (אמר לו) ברזל ונחשת מנעליך התיר לו נעילת הסנדל„ עד הנה חזק ה׳ את ידי׳„

תם ונשלם תהלה לאל עולם: סכום פסוקים של כל התורה חמשת אלפים ותשע מאות וארבעים וחמשה: חזק הסופר ואמיץ הקורא: בנל״ך ואע״י:

In explaining Rashi, our author is particularly desirous to point out the necessity which brought that great teacher to use such and such a word, or to come to such and such a conclusion. In this endeavour he is mostly successful; not so, however, when he explains the Scriptural word independently, which he generally does by means of גמטריאות, or ראשי תבות, and סופי תבות, and the like. In such a case he rarely gives anything new worth having, although, judging from what he reproduces, he must have been an enormous reader. The work before us is the result of weekly lectures given to his disciples, as may be seen from leaf 28[a], &c., and the MS. as such is an autograph, as the numerous alterations, emendations and additions, to be found on every page, sufficiently shew. The author is an Italian, and lived in the XVIth century (see later).

The following notes by the author are to be found on leaves originally left blank by him.

A. At the commencement:

(1) On the fly-leaf. Various short sentences, both halakhic and agadic, taken from the Bible, Talmud Babli, the Midrashim, the sayings of Ben-Sira and the Philosophers of the middle ages. These are introduced by לזכר טוב יהיה אמן.

(2) Leaf 1^a. An extract from T. B. 'Abodah Zarah, 20^b, commencing:
בה"א (בשם ה' אמן) בריש ע"ז סוף פ"ק (פרק קמא) לפני אידהן דף כף ת"ר (תנו רבנן) ונשמרת מכל דבר רע....

(3) Leaf 1^b. Various matters of cabbalistical and philosophical import, commencing:
בהנו"א השם בן ד' אותיות עולה למספר כ"ח....

(4) Leaf 2^a. Logico-grammatical observations, some פרפראות, and a חדוש on the connexion between the names of the Patriarchs and the Tetragrammaton, which the writer had heard from the mouth of a Rabbi from the Holy Land. The first commence שבעה דברים בדקדוק, and are signed תלמיד המדקדקים מטֹי יפרֹח; the second commence:
הדרשנים אמרו על דרך פרפרת אֹשר קֹדש ידיד מֹבטן ר"ת אקים....
and the third commences:
חידוש שמעתי מפי רב אחד מארץ הקדושה אֹברהם יֹצחק יֹעקב ר"ת....
Compare R. Ya'aqob b. Asher on Ex. iii. 14.

(5) Leaf 2^b. Various agadic and halakhic extracts from T. B. Baba Metzi'a and Baba Qama, commencing:
בבבא מציעא פ' הזהב אמר רב יהודה לעולם יהא אדם זהיר בתבואה בתוך ביתו....

(6) Leaf 4^a (leaf 3 wanting; see above). Scriptural explanations extracted from the commentary of R. David Qimchi, commencing:
פי' כתובים מורכבים מספר יחזקאל לפי פי' רד"ק. ויבא אותי....פי הקמחי משתחויתם מלה מורכבת....

(7) Leaf 4^b. An extract from the Yalqut in explanation of 1 Chronicles i. 54, commencing....בדברי הימים פי' שמעוני גבי אלוף עירם, two talmudical sayings, an explanation of Ps. vii., a mnemotechnical sign for the time of the exile of the Jews from the Spanish peninsula, a grammatical piece, and a few Rabbinical sayings.

B. At the end:

(1) Leaf 85^b. A remark made by the Emperor Octavianus, when about to be crowned, and a remark made by Ibn 'Ezra (?) on the human brain and its three chambers; commencing: כתוב בספר הרומיים שאוקטבייאנו.... and אמר ר' אברהם ב"ע יש באיש... respectively. (See 12. e. below.)

(2) Leaf 86^a. On the order of the Haphtaroth, and an extract from the

Midrash on the value of peace; the former commencing: בשנת עבור כשחולקין ...ראשי המטות, and the latter ....אמרו במדרש שלו׳ זה תורה

(3) Leaves 86[b]—87[b]. Explanation of various passages in the Five Megilloth, with special reference to Rashi, and done mostly in the style of גמטריא; commencing:

בשיר השירים ישקני....פרש״י פה אל פה דייק כן שנ׳ פיהו הל״ל (הוה ליה למימר) פיו....

(4) Leaves 87[b]—88[b]. On the Mishnah Aboth, particularly on Peraqim 3, 4, and 5. In the last-named Pereq additions are to be found to the printed matter in Rashi's commentary; commencing:

בפ״ג דמסכת אבות ר׳ שמעון או׳ ג׳ שאכלו...כשאתה מחשב מנינו של כ׳ תמצא מנינו ל׳....

(5) Leaf 88[b]. An extract from Don Yitzchaq Abarbanel's נחלת אבות, commencing:

אל תהיו כעבדים....הזהיר האדם שלא תהיה עבודתו....

This differs somewhat from the printed edition.

2. [זאת חקת הפסח].

Matters in connexion with Passover, partly halakhic and partly agadic, occupying leaves 89[a]—110[b].

A. Halakhic matter, occupying leaves 89[a]—108[b].

(1) [חדושים על הרמב״ם בהלכות חמץ ומצה]. Novellæ on the laws concerning leavened and unleavened food, as expounded in Maimonides' משנה תורה, Book זמנים. They explain sundry passages in all the eight Peraqim of these Halakhoth, and are, probably, by the before-mentioned R. Menachem.

Begin (leaf 89[a]):

חדושי׳ בהלכות חמץ ומצה בהרמב״ם כפי אשר הורוני מורי: התחיל יש ג״ מצות עשה וה׳ לא תעשה ואחר מפ׳ הלאוין תחלה י״ל דרכו כן להתחיל בלאוין תחלה על דרך סור מרע ועשה טוב....

End (leaf 91[b]):

....נאם הכוסף לדעת כונת האוסר את הכלים כמ׳ פלו׳ ב״ז לדבר יהב״ל לו לספיר׳ רצ״א לפ״ק אירע מעשה כך באריין (Reggio).

The author conscientiously gives his authority whenever he owes an idea to anybody. Thus 90[b], in giving an explanation of a certain passage, he has זה העתקתי מתוך הרמב״ם אחד; a little later again he has, כך מצא׳; leaf 91[b], נעתק זה מסביב מרבינ׳ אשרי בכתב. As will have been seen, at the end is attached a letter (by R. David of Imola?) which treats on kindred matter.

(2) [חדושים על הסמ״ג בהלכות חמץ ומצה]. Novellæ on the same laws

as expounded in R. Mosheh b. Ya'aqob[1] of Coucy's ספר המצות[2]. They explain sundry expressions in the 76th chapter of the negative commandments, and are, probably, also by the before-mentioned R. Menachem.

Begin (leaf 92ᵃ):

חידושים בחמץ ומצה בסמ״ג על הלאוין בסימן ע״ו : אסור לאכול חמץ ביום י״ד למ׳ לא אמ׳ שיהיה בו לאו לפי שסובר שאין לאו לאוכל....

End (leaf 93ᵃ):

....אינו אסו׳ גמור שנוכל לומ׳ בעוד שהכלי פולט אינו חוזר ובולע לכך אמר נכון „ תוספת „ ע״כ „

(3) [חדושים על הסמ״ג בהלכות חמץ ומצה]. Novellæ, by R. Eliyyahu, on the same laws as expounded by the Semag, and illustrated by R. Yoseph Qolon b. Shelomoh. These Novellæ, although here distinctly ascribed to R. Yoseph Qolon, belong to him only in part, and are only so far entirely his, as on his views, R. Eliyyahu, an Italian Rabbi of the xv—xvith century, who is the collector of the whole, founded most of his own observations to which he strung those of other authors. They consist of eight groups, occupying leaves 93ᵇ—108ᵇ, as follows:

a. Explanation of chapter 76 of the Semag (negative commandments) by R. Eliyyahu, beginning:

חידושים שחבר מהררי״ק זצ״ל על הסמ״ג בהלכות חמץ ומצה : אסור לאכול חמץ ביום י״ד מחצות היום וכו׳ כלומ׳ אפי׳ לר״ש דפליג אדר׳ יהודה... (Leaves 93ᵇ—99ᵇ).

In the course of this explanation we read (leaf 94ᵃ):

....צריכני לבארו ע״פ מהררי״ק ז״ל אם יזכני ה׳ ואני מצאתי בקונטרס אחד בשם מהררי״ק....

and again (leaf 95ᵃ):

....ולי הצעיר אליהו הוקשה לי....

To these Novellæ is attached a Responsum by R. Yisrael Isserlein (תרומת הדשן, No. 121).

b. R. Yoseph Qolon's own wording in explanation of the passages in the Semag, ch. 77 and 78 (negative commandments), commencing:

מצא׳ זה הלשון מועתק מכתיבת יד מהררי״ק זצ״ל ואין צ״ל שלשם כך הפי׳ וכו׳ משמע שהיינו יכולין לפ׳ בענין אחר שמתוך אותו פי׳ היינו למדים שצריך שטיפת צונן כנ״ג.... (Leaves 100ᵃ—100ᵇ.)

[1] Ya'aqob, and not Yitzchaq, as Krafft and Deutsch (*Catalogus Codicum Manuscriptorum, Bib. Palat. Vindobonensis*, II. p. 58) write.

[2] This ספר המצות is commonly called סמ״ג (ספר מצות גדול), in contradistinction to the עמודי גולה or סמ״ק (ספר מצות קטן או קצר) by R. Yoseph b. Yitzchaq of Corbeil.

c. Views of R. Chayyim חדר, on the phrase of the Semag (ch. 77 and 78, negative commandments): ....ולפ"ז יתישב בקדרה של נחשת.... conveyed in a letter to R. Eliyyahu (?) commencing:

והא לך מה שכתב החסיד איש אלקי' כמהר"ר חיים חדר זצ"ל: עַל אשר בקשת ממני לבאר לך דברי סמ"ג בענין ולפ"ז יתישב בקדר' של נחשת עם יתר גמגומין הקשין שם בדבריו אף כי ידעתי כי אין בבאורי טעם וריח מ"מ אכתוב לך אשר בידי לקיים ודברת בם ולא בדברי' בטלי' ואפר' תחלה דעת הסמ"ג....

In the course of this letter R. Chayyim mentions his father: והפי' הזה שמעתי מ"ה א"א יצ"ו...., without, however, giving his name. (Leaves 100ᵇ—102ᵃ.)

d. R. Eliyyahu's own views on the same phrase of the Semag, and the one just preceding the above-mentioned one, commencing:

אמנם או' אבי אמי רבי חיים כהן דאסור תרומה קל וכו' יש לתמוה מה עלה על דעתו להקשות מההיא דירושל' דמפ' בהדיא.... (Leaves 102ᵃ—103ᵃ.)

e. The same phrase explained by an anonymous author, commencing:

מצא' דעת אחרת. ולפ"ז יתישב אף בקדרה של נחשת. ר"ל לפי שפי' רבי' חיים כהן מגעיל ג"פ בחמין שר"ל בכלי שני.... (Leaf 103ᵃ.)

f. On successive paragraphs of the same chapters of the Semag, commencing respectively:

(1) מאני דקוניא; (2) חטה שנמצאת; (3) וכן בשר מליח; (4) אבל בשומן, and to the end of chap. 79, which is the end of the Halakhoth. In the course of this treatise we meet (leaf 105ᵇ) with the phrase ותי' מו' הגאון, without giving the name of this teacher, and (leaf 107ᵃ) מצאתי בגליון בהיותי בפימונטו (Piedmont)..., without saying of what book (the Semag or R. Yoseph Qolon's work?). (Leaves 103ᵇ—107ᵃ.)

g. Explanation by R. Shimshon of Chinon of a Talmudic passage (Yerushalmi Terumoth xi. 4); the whole ending:

...מרבינו שמשון מקינון (Chinon) עכ"ל. לפי הנ"ל הלשון מוטעה קצת העתקה שלפני: תמו החידושי' ממהררי"ק זצ"ל בסמ"ג על הלאוין תל"ח (תהלה לאל חי)
(Leaf 107ᵃ—107ᵇ.)

h. Explanation of chap. 39 of the Semag (affirmative commandments), commencing:

ואתחיל בע"ה (בעזרת השם) בעשיין בסימן נ"ח להשבית חמץ: ואו' ר"ת דבטול מועיל משעת הפקר: וכו' וק' אם בטול מועיל מטעם הפקר לר' עקיב' אמאי אינו מועיל אמפרר וזורה לרוח....

The נ"ח ought to be ל"ט, and the ר"ת ought to be ר"י, i. e. רבנו יצחק, and not רבנו יעקב. To this short commentary are added a few customs with respect to Passover mentioned in various books, and, among others, some found on the margin of a Semag, &c. These notes probably belong to R. Menachem, as they are worded in his style. (Leaves 107ᵇ—108ᵇ.)

B. Aagadic matter, occupying leaves 108^{b}—110^{b}.

(1) [שאלות ללילי פסחים]. Questions to be put by the children to their parents on Passover night during the domestic service.

Begin (leaf 108^{b}):

אלו הן קושיות לישאל בלילי פסחים : למה ועצם לא תשברו בו וכן הוא או׳ ואכלתם את הבשר הבשר ולא גידין ועצמו׳ אכילת הטלה הוא להראות בו בעשותנו רצון הבורא השרי׳ של מעלה תחת רשותינו ....

End (leaf 109^{a}):

....לכן תקנו לנו ד׳ כוסות בליל פסח.

That children should put questions respecting matters in connexion with the redemption of Israel has a foundation in Ex. xii. 26 and xiii. 14, although it is, certainly, there spoken of conditionally only. See T. L. Kingsbury, *Spiritual Sacrifice* (London and Cambridge, 1868, 8vo.), Note F. The present questions are very short, which is, however, not their only merit, as there are some interesting points touched upon. They are pieces from various authors, the collector of which is, no doubt, our R. Menachem. The following piece deserves to be specially pointed out; it is to be found on leaf 109^{a}:

במוצאי פסח הולכין אל נהר ואומרין תשליך במצולות ים כל חטאתם ויש בזה סוד....

(2) [קושיות ללילי פסחים]. More difficult questions in connexion with the ceremonies of Passover.

Begin (leaf 109^{b}):

ולא יפחתו מד׳ כוסות פי׳ כנגד ד׳ לישני גאולה והוצאתי והצלתי וגאלתי ולקחתי וכו׳ וק׳ דא״כ שמ׳ ליבעי ד׳ לחמין ....

End (leaf 110^{b}):

....וידענא מוקדם ללא ידענא וכן נראה במרדכי גדול פ״ק דפסחים דף רנ״ד.

Being designed for riper scholars, it is unavoidable that occasionally some halakhic matters should be mixed up with the agadic, the latter alone being the tendency of the questions. These questions, although they also are short, are somewhat longer than the foregoing, and belong to various authors, among whom are R. Yoseph Qolon and others. At the end is attached an explanation of T. B. Synhedrin, 12^{a}, given by R. Yehudah of Montereale, apparently, to R. Mordekhai of Modena. It begins:

הגאון כמהר״ר יהוד׳ ממונטריאלו זצ״ל פי׳ לי הא דאיתא בפ״ק דסנהדרין גבי אמ׳ ר׳ יהוד׳ מעשה בחזקיהו ....

and ends:

....אי אפשר להתחיל שום הזא׳ והיינו דנקט מספר ב׳ ימי׳ : נעתק זה מספר הגאון כמהר״ר מרדכי ממודינה א״ש זצ״ל.

This R. Mordekhai is, no doubt, the grandfather of the celebrated Leon Modena. His לקוטים in manuscript are often quoted by Azulai (ברכי יוסף, Livorno, 1774), whose copy of them is probably that now in possession of S.

Schönblum, of Lemberg. See *Catalogue d'une Collection Anconienne* .... Leopol. (1872 ?), pp. 5 and 6, No. 32.

3. [במגלת ספר כתוב].

MATTERS IN CONNEXION WITH PURIM, partly agadic and partly halakhic, occupying leaves 110ᵇ—113ᵇ.

A. Agadic matter, occupying leaves 110ᵇ—111ᵇ.

(1) [דברי אגדת מגלה]. On various agadic passages in the Talmud Babli Megillah. These explain only a few sundry pieces of that treatise, and belong probably to R. Menachem.

Begin (leaf 110ᵇ):

על הדרשות ממגלת אסתר במסכת מגילה פרק מגלה נקראת: מסיק בגמ׳ דיש הפרש בין ויהי לויהי בימי....

End (111ᵃ):

....אחר רוחצו לקח רבי׳ יחיאל זצ״ל האגן שבו המים מיד השר ושתה הרחיצה ההיא לפני המלך והשרי׳ ואמ׳ בזה אני חפץ שהוא מותר לי וביין איני חפץ כי הוא אסור לי והמלך שמח על הדבר ויאהבהו כפלים.

In illustration of T. B. Megillah, 13ᵇ, and Esther iii. 8, a most interesting story is told respecting the relation of R. Yechiel (b. Yoseph) of Paris to the King of France, of his time (Louis IX.), which, although mixed up with much fabulous matter, contains, no doubt, more than one historical fact. The same story is somewhat differently worded in שלשלת הקבלה (Amsterdam, 1697, 8vo.), leaf 44ᵇ.

(2) [קצור דרשת אבן שועיב לפרשת תצוה וזכור]. Abridgment of the Sermon of R. Yehoshua' Ibn Sho'eib for the Sabbath preceding the Festival of Purim.

Begins (leaf 111ᵃ):

דרשה לפורים הוצא בקצור מן ספר אבן שועיב: אמ׳ ז״ל זכור את אשר עשה לך כו׳ יכול בלב כשהוא או׳ לא תשכח....

Ends (leaf 111ᵇ):

....אורה זו תורה שמחה זה י״ט ששון זה ברית מילה דכתי׳ שש אנכי על אמרתך ויקר זה תפלין׳׳

There is nothing original in this abridgment, which merely consists of short extracts from the Talmudim, Midrashim, and other Rabbinical writers. Compare the Constantinople edition[1] of Ibn Sho'eib's Derashoth, leaves 21ᵃ—22ᵇ. The merit of re-extracting them belongs, no doubt, to R. Menachem.

B. Halakhic matter, occupying leaves 111ᵇ—113ᵇ.

(1) [חדושים על הרמב״ם בהלכות מגלה]. Novellæ on the laws concerning the reading of the book of Esther on, and other laws pertaining to, Purim, as expounded in Maimonides' משנה תורה, Book זמנים. They ex-

[1] Printed Friday, 12 Adar 1523. There is a blur in the last figure of the printed date; but 1523 is, according to Jahn's Tables, the only year in the decade in which 12 Adar fell on a Friday.

plain sundry passages in both Peraqim, and are, probably, by R. Menachem.

Begin (leaf 111[b]):

בהלכות מגילה על הרמב"ם : הענין הזה של מגילה אמתי היה לפי שנבוכדנצר שלח ישראל בגלות בבל. . ∴.

End (leaf 112[b]):

....אין מדקדקין פי' לראות אם הוא רמאי כמו שעושין שאר פעמי' כשנותנין צדק' אבל כאן כל הפושט ידו ליטול נותנין לו :

As is in the nature of this subject, some agadic matter is mixed up therewith.

(2) [חדושים על הסמ"ג בהלכות מגלה]. Novellæ on the same laws, as expounded by R. Mosheh b. Ya'aqob of Coucy. They explain sundry expressions in the ספר המצות, Appendix iv., and are, though founded on R. Yoseph Qolon's views, probably by R. Eliyyahu; see 2. A. (3) above.

Begin (leaf 112[b]):

על הסמ"ג והיא מצוה רביעית מדברי סופרים : הכל כשרין לקרות המגילה ור' יהודה מכשיר בקטן מה דעת חכמים דפסלי בקטן לפי שהקטן יש בו ב' דברי' מדרבנן....

End (leaf 113[b]):

....ולא מטו שלוחי תשרי דגזרי' בההוא דוכת' דניסן אטו תשרי דעבדינן תרי יומי כדאית' בספ"ק דר"ה :

Although it says, leaf 113[a], תם, such is only the case with respect to a single phrase; but the article is treated on to the very end of leaf 113[b]. As in the preceding number the subject is unavoidably connected with agadic matter even in its halakhic part.

4. [זאת חנכת המזבח].

MATTERS IN CONNEXION WITH THE FESTIVAL OF THE RE-DEDICATION OF THE TEMPLE IN THE TIME OF THE HASMONEANS, occupying leaf 114[a]—114[b]

(1) [חדושים על הרמב"ם בהלכות חנכה]. Novellæ on the laws concerning the lights of the festival of Chanukkah, as expounded in Maimonides' משנה תורה, book זמנים. They explain sundry phrases in both Peraqim, and are, probably, by R. Menachem.

Begin (leaf 114[a]):

בהלכות חנוכה על הרמב"ם : הדליקו נרות המערכ' ח' ימי' למה הוצרך כ"ב זמן עד שיהיה להם שמן טהור....

End (ibid.):

....נר ביתו קודם משום שלום ביתו ודוק :

The text of the Rambam is here irregularly commented on, earlier things being taken later, and later things earlier. The author had also, apparently, other readings in the Rambam-text before him.

(2) [חדושים על הסמ"ג בהלכות חנכה]. Novellæ on the same laws as expounded by R. Mosheh b. Ya'aqob of Coucy. They explain sundry phrases in the ספר המצות, Appendix v., and are, though founded on R. Yoseph Qolon's views, apparently by R. Eliyyahu.

Begin (leaf 114ª):

על הסמ"ג והיא מצוה חמישית: דאי לא אדליק מדליק אינמי לשעור׳ מאי בניהו פי׳ דאי לא אדליק מדליק א"צ שיתן בו כ"כ שמן....

End (leaf 114ᵇ):

....לכ"ש לא צריכ׳ דלא א"ר יוחנן בחנוכה"

The story of Rabbi (Rabbenu Haqqadosh, the editor of the Mishnah) and Antoninus[1], introduced here in explanation of להפר בריתי, &c., is corruptly given.

5. [על חרבן בית המקדש].

MATTERS IN CONNEXION WITH THE DESTRUCTION OF THE HOLY TEMPLE, occupying leaves 114ᵇ—115ª.

(1) [חדושים על הרמב"ם בהלכות תשעה באב]. Novellæ on the laws concerning the 9th of Ab, and other fast-days, as expounded in Maimonides' משנה תורה, book זמנים. They explain sundry expressions in the last Pereq (v) of the Hilekhoth תעניות, and are, probably, by R. Menachem.

Begin (leaf 114ᵇ):

בהלכות ט"ב בהרמב"ם פ"ה מהלכות תעניות: יש שם ימי׳ שכל ישראל פי׳ שם מצוי כמו שפי׳ בתחלת חבורו יש שם מצוי ראשון גבי הקב"ה....

End (leaf 115ª):

....פי׳ אפונין הוא מיני קטנית הנקראין בלע"ז ציריש וכן תמצא כשתעיין במפרש בספר דניאל בתחלתו"

(2) [חדושים על הסמ"ג בהלכות תשעה באב]. Novellæ on the same laws as expounded by R. Mosheh b. Ya'aqob of Coucy. They explain sundry phrases in the ספר המצות, Appendix iii., and are, though founded on R. Yoseph Qolon's views, apparently by R. Eliyyahu.

Begin (leaf 115ª):

על הסמ"ג במצות ט"ב והיא מצוה שלישית: עטרות של מלח ושל גפרית פרש"י בשלהי מס׳ סוטה ענין עטר׳ שעושין מאבן מלח....

End (ibid.):

ולהסיר השיער כך פי׳ רשב"ם בפ׳ חזקת הבתים: תם:

[1] According to Rapoport, ערך מלין (Prag, 1852, 4to.), p. 123, this is Marcus Aurelius; see also Bodek, Marcus Aurelius Antoninus .... (Leipzig, 1868, 8vo.), passim.

Attached to these Novellæ are the following pieces: (1) R. Aharon Hallevi, on סעודה המפסקת; (2) R. Shelomoh b. Abraham Ibn אדרת, on the week in which the 9th of Ab falls; (3) R. Meir b. Barukh, of Rothenburg, on the commencement of the month of Ab; (4) A הגהה, from the book גבור, on שני תבשילין in the סעודה המפסקת; and (5) an anonymous writer (probably R. Menachem himself), on the kindred passage in T. B. Betzah 15b (Mishnah ii. 1).

6. [יום כפרים הוא].

Matters in connexion with the Day of Atonement, occupying leaves 115b—116b.

(1) [חדושים על הרמב"ם בהלכות יום הכפרים]. Novellæ on the laws concerning the Day of Atonement, as expounded in Maimonides' משנה תורה, book זמנים. They explain certain phrases in all the three Peraqim of the Hilekhoth שביתת עשור. These are apparently by R. Menachem.

Begin (leaf 115b):

בהלכות שביתת עשור בהרמב"ם : למה קורא להלכות י"ה שביתת עשור לישנא דקרא נקט....

End (leaf 116a):

....אבל בי"ה אין מוצא חטא לקטרג עליהם „

As is the author's wont, he mixes a little Agadah with the Halakhah, which alone is here his chief aim. (The רבי' שמואל בר' אהרן, to be found here, is only quoted from the תוספות of T. B. Berakhoth 8b כאילו.)

(2) [חדושים על הסמ"ג בהלכות יום הכפרים]. Novellæ on the same laws as expounded by R. Mosheh b. Ya'aqob of Coucy. These explain sundry phrases in the ספר המצות, chapter 69 (not 61) of the negative commandments, and are apparently by R. Menachem.

Begin (leaf 116a):

בסמ"ג בסימן ס"א (ס"ט) : שהאוכל מאכלין הראוין כבותבת וכו' ושערו חכמים שאין בית הבליעה וכו' השותה משקין הראוין לאדם כמלא לוגמיו וכו' ומתקיף לה בגמ' מאי שנא אכילה דלכ"ע ככותבת....

End (leaf 116b):

...אבל האזרח האמו' בסכות בא למעט את הנשים „

The piece of Piyyut[1] quoted by the Semag is thus explained:

אחר גמר מצוי אכול דצוי ורצוי פי' אחר גמר הימי' שנ' בהם דרשו ה' בהמצאו אלו ימי' שבין ר"ה לי"ה אכול לחמך שמח ורצוי מצוי לשון בהמצאו דצוי לשון שמחה „

[1] It belongs to R. Shelomoh b. Yehudah Habbabli. See Zunz, *Literaturgeschichte d. synag. Poesie* (Berlin, 1865, 8vo.), p. 234, Note 2, where to the reference "Tos. Sabbat 114b" is to be added ואמאי.

7. [בחדש השביעי].

MATTERS IN CONNEXION WITH THE 1ST, 2ND, AND 15TH—22ND DAYS OF THE MONTH OF TISHRI.

(1) [חדושים על הרמב"ם בהלכות שופר סכה ולולב]. Novellæ on the laws concerning the sounding of the Shophar, the sitting in the Sukkah, and the handling the "four plants," as expounded in Maimonides' משנה תורה, book זמנים. These extend to all the Peraqim of the Hilekhoth שופר סכה ולולב, and are, apparently, by R. Menachem.

Begin (leaf 116[b]):

בהלכות שופר סוכה ולולב בהרמב"ם ממהררי"ק : ג' תקיעות ג' ג' ג' שיעו' תקיע' כג' תרועות שיעו' תרועה כג' יבבות....

End (leaf 120[a]):

...וכן משמע במסכת בבא מציעה פ' הזהב ממגיד משנה ופ' אלו מציאות :

The following few remarks are indispensably necessary: (1) Although distinctly stated to be R. Yoseph Qolon's, there is little doubt that in their present state these Novellæ are only founded on his views, but are worked up by R. Menachem; (2) the paragraph on לולב, on leaf 117[a] in the middle of the Hilekhoth שופר, is only by mistake there; and (3), that in the Hilekhoth סכה there are a number of בלע"ז (which are, of course, Italian). The following few lines (from leaf 117) especially deserve to be quoted: (Pereq i.) ....לפי דעת העמוד יברך לשמוע ואנו עושין כהרמב"ם ולפי הסמ"ג יברך התוקע בתוך הבור לפי שהיונים ;(.Pereq ii) and ;לתקוע והאשכנזי' עושין כסמ"ג... גזרו שלא יעשו המצות והחסידים שבהן היו תוקעין לתוך הבור או לתוך המערה כדי שלא ישמעו קולם. On אנדרוגינוס we read (leaf 117[b]): ....והוגד לי שכן הוא שהוא בריה בפני עצמ' דומיא דכוי שגם הוא בריה בפני עצמה ולא הכריעו בה חכמים....

(2) [חדושים על הסמ"ג בהלכות שופר סכה ולולב]. Novellæ by R. Menachem on the same laws, as expounded by R. Mosheh b. Ya'aqob of Coucy. These explain sundry phrases in the ספר המצות, chapters 42—44 (affirmative commandments), and are, although founded on the views of several authors, apparently, worked up by R. Menachem. They consist of eight groups, occupying leaves 120[a]—133[a], as follows:

a. Explanation of chap. 42, by an anonymous writer, beginning:

בדיני שופר על הסמ"ג סימן מ"ב : כה אמר אשחר, אני אל אל אשחר, יתן בפי דבר לו שחר, והיא נכון כשחר, וטוב מחרוץ ומכל מסחר, מלבא ומלכי ישפר, ותיטב לה' משור פר, מקרין ומפרים בהלכות שופר : אין לי אלא במדבר בר"ה מנין דא"כ מה בא ללמדנו הג"ש מתרוע' לתרוע'....

In אשחר the name of the author is probably hidden, although there is no indication to mark it as an abbreviation. This "explanation" is, perhaps, the first recension by R. Shemuel Chizqiyyah רומליי. See d. below. (Leaf 120[a]—120[b].)

b. Explanation of the same chapter, according to R. Yoseph Qolon, by R. Eliyyahu, beginning:

ממהררי"ק שנ' ובהקהיל את הקהל תתקעו ולא תריעו מכלל דיש במסען תקיעה ותרועה וק' איך משמ' תאמ' שר"ל ובהקהיל את הקהל עשו תקיע'....

That this cannot be R. Yoseph Qolon's own explanation will be seen, in spite of the superscription, from the following: ....ונר' למורי רבי' מהררי"ק הק' מהררי"ק, (leaf 121[a]) דלפי הגמ'.... (leaf 121[b]) and chiefly from the next paragraph. But, apart from all this, the language is identical with that of the before-mentioned R. Eliyyahu. (Leaves 120[b]—122[a].)

c. Explanation of the same chapter by R. Yoseph Qolon, in his own language, beginning:

מצות עשה של תורה לתקוע בשופר וכו' נ"ל שחולק על ר"מ ודעתו שחולק עליו בנוסח הברכה....

The author continually quotes his father (R. Shelomoh), א"א ז"ל (leaf 122[b]), כך תירץ א"א (leaf 123[a]), אאז"ל הביא בחדושיו (leaf 125[a]; compare also leaves 126[a], 127[a], and 127[b]). That this is R. Yoseph Qolon's own explanation will be best seen from the following phrase which is much in his usual style. After a goodly number of difficulties raised by him against his author, he says (leaf 123[b]): לכן נר' לאחוז בזה דרך אחד יתישבו כל הספיקו' ויתלבנו דברי הסמ"ג כי שפתיו ברור מללו וזה כי אחז צדיק דרכו הקצר' לשנות המשנ' ולפר' אותה בלשון קצרה.... (Leaves 122[a]—127[b].)

d. Explanation of the same chapter by R. Shemuel Chizqiyyah רומליי (conveyed in a letter to R. Menachem ?), beginning:

הא לך מה שפי' לי הותיק והאלוף כמהה"ר שמואל חזקיה רומליי זצ"ל: תנן שיעו' תקיע' כתרוע' ושיעו' תרוע' כג' יבבו' ויש בריית'....וטרם אפרש לך לשון הסמ"ג ותכלית כונתו בזה המאמ' כפי הנר' מתוך לשונו אודיעך כי מסקנת הגמ' בפי' המשנה הזאת....

and ending:

....אם גניח' הוא או יללה ודוק: עכ"ל הותיק האלוף כמהה"ר שמואל חזקיה רומליי זצ"ל. One R. Shemuel רומילי died Oct. 13, 5336 (1576); see תפארת אדם, in נפוצות יהודה (Venezia, 1589, 4to.), leaf 156[b], and Zunz, Monatstage.... (Berlin, 1872, 8vo.), p. 57. (Leaves 127[b]—129[a].)

e. Explanation of the same by an anonymous disciple of R. Yoseph Qolon, beginning:

התקין ר' אבהו בקיסרי קשר"ק פי בלא קש"ק וקר"ק כי מעיקר' סבר דאין הפסק' מעכבת....

and ending:

דכל הקולות כשרין בשופר.

The latest authority he quotes is his teacher מהררי"ק. (Leaf 129[a]—129[b].)

f. Responsum on the necessary and right condition of the Shophar, &c., addressed by R. Shelomoh טרבוט[1], to R. Levi, father-in-law of R. Yoseph Qolon, the writer's son; beginning:

והא לך מה שכתב בתשובה האשל הגדול כמהר״ר שלמה טרבוט זצ״ל אביו של האשל הגדול כמהר״ר יוסף קולון זצ״ל על זה: למרבה המשרה, אבא בקצרה, ואשיבנו על ד״ת, איש בריתי ושלומי, בשרי ועצמי, הח״ר לוי שיחי׳, גור אריה, לגוי גדול יהיה, ראה ראיתי כתבך אל בני חתנך שי׳ לכתוב לך דעתי על הא דכתב רב יהודאי גאון דק״ל כתרי לישני דר׳ יוחנן לחומר׳ ומביאו הסמ״ג ועל זה כבר נלחמו ראשוני׳ ואחרי׳ שכתבת להודיעך דעתי אכתבנו לך אני כאשר אמרתיו באשכנז על מעשה שהיה והודו לדברי.... (Leaves 129ᵇ—130ᵃ.)

g. Explanation of the foregoing by R. Yoseph Qolon, as reported to, and by, R. Benedetto Achseldara[2], and the latter's difficulties against that explanation; beginning:

פי׳ נאה ומקובל מצא׳ אשר שמע מהר״ר בנידיטו אכסילדרא אשכנזי זצ״ל ממהררי״ק על מה שכתו׳ בסמ״ג בהלכות שופר והק׳ על פירושו ז״ל בסימן מ״ב: ופסק רב יהודאי גאון.... והני תרתי לישני איתנהו בגמ׳ על המשנה וז״ל המש׳ ניקב וסתמו....

In the course of this essay we read:

כך שמעתי כאשר כתבתי בשם מהררי״ק ואני צעיר התלמידי׳ בנידיט אכסילדרא ק׳ לי על פירושו ואי אפשר לי להעמיד שהוא מפורש לפי לישנא האמור בו....

The above essay is, as far as is reported in his name, in reality by R. Yoseph Qolon himself, as the style amply testifies. (Leaves 130ᵃ—131ᵃ.)

h. Explanation of the further phrases in the Semag, chap. 42, by R. Yoseph Qolon, beginning:

ותוקעין ומריעין כשהן עומדין תימ׳ הא קא עברי בבל תוסיף וכ״ת כיון שנפטר ה״ל כשלא בזמנו....

[1] טרבוט (טְרֵבוּט) is no doubt the French Trévout, and the representative either of the German Drehfuss, or Dreifuss (a name common among South-German Jews to this day, and pronounced by them, in common with all other South-Germans, *Trehvuss* and *Treivuss* respectively), or of the French town Trévoux (Ain). It is known that not only was R. Yoseph Qolon's father surnamed הצרפתי, but that many others bearing the family name of טרבוט were additionally called הצרפתי, e.g. R. 'Azriel (see 19 below; MS. Add. 405, leaf 1ᵃ, &c.). Settling in Italy, where the Jews read it טְרָבּוֹט, this name became, conformably to the genius of the vernacular, Trabotto and Trabotti. This will remove Steinschneider's difficulty (Bod. Cat. p. 1501 in No. 5944). For טריויש see the geographical index at the end of this Catalogue.

[2] Achseldara is only the Italian form of the common German name Achselrad (אכסלרד), which in its turn, as a Jewish proper noun both for an individual and a family, is chiefly adopted because it is confounded with Alexander (אלכסנדר), a name, since the time of Alexander the Great, very common among the Jews. See MS. Add. 405. 2.

and ending:

אלא במקו׳ שיש שם ב״ד קבוע והלכ׳ כר׳ אלעזר. (Leaf 131ᵃ—131ᵇ.)

(3) [חדושים על הסמ״ג בהלכות סכה]. Novellæ on the laws concerning the Festival-Tabernacle. These explain sundry phrases in the Semag, chap. 43 (affirmative commandments), and belong to R. Yoseph Qolon.

Begin (leaf 131ᵇ):

בדיני סוכה בסמ״ג בסימן מ״ג ממהררי״ק: עושה דופן שיש ברחבו יתר על טפח וכו׳ ומסיק רבא דצריך לעשו׳ לה צורת פתח....

End (leaf 132ᵃ):

....ולא היו משלימין אותו אח״כ: תם ״ תם ״

Attached to these Novellæ are the following pieces: (1) A notaricon, commencing: אמרתי אעלה בתמר; (2) the views of R. Ya'aqob b. Yaqar, on the benediction שהחינו with respect to the לולב, commencing: השיב רבי׳ יעקב בר יקר דזמן לולב לא תקנו....; (3) on דבר האבד, commencing: ר׳ בון בר ממל אמר אלו היה לי מי שימנה עמי התרתי בשר בכור....; and (4) on the lawful size of a סכה, commencing: אמ׳ רב שמואל בר רב יצחק אמ׳ רב הונא הלכ׳ צריכ׳.... These are extracts from the Talmud, Rab Alphes, Rabbenu Nissim, the Tosaphoth, and Rabbenu Yesha'yah the latter (b. Eliyyah of Trani). (Leaf 132ᵃ—132ᵇ.)

(4) [חדושים על הסמ״ג בהלכות לולב]. Novellæ on the laws concerning the "four plants" on the Festival of Tabernacles. These explain sundry phrases in the Semag, chap. 44 (affirmative commandments), and belong, no doubt, though founded on R. Yoseph Qolon's views, to R. Menachem.

Begin (leaf 132ᵇ):

במצות לולב בסמ״ג בסימן מ״ד ממהררי״ק: מנהג פשוט לכל יודעי דת ובן אומ׳ מהררי״ק בשם הראב״ד וגדולים אחרי׳ הנוטל לולב....

End (leaf 133ᵃ):

....בימינו שהוא שמאל כל אדם ״ תם ״ ״

Attached to these few Novellæ are the following pieces: (1) An explanation of הדם שוטה, commencing: הדם שוטה קרי ליה לפי שעליו הולכין שלא כסדר....; (2) explanation of T. B. Sukkah, 33ᵇ, extracted from Rabbenu Nissim; (3) on the Eighth Day of solemn Assembly being an independent Festival (and not a part of that of Tabernacles), with the mnemosyna פזר קשב explained, extracted from the Abudrahim; (4) the חידה, by Rabbenu Tam (R. Ya'aqob b. Meir, Rashi's grandson), on the רביעית, or quarter of a log of the Scriptures, (equivalent to the space of an egg and a half) commencing: חרוז שעשה רבינו תם על רביעית של תורה: רביעית הנמצא, השלך החוצה...., with explanation; (5) explanation of the same with regard to the religious bath (מקוה); and (6) cabbalistic transmutations (צרופים) &c. of חלם, and hints as to their testifying to the eternity of God; see 12. f. below. (Leaf 133ᵃ—133ᵇ.)

8. [מעשיות ותשובות].

PRACTICAL DECISIONS and RESPONSA on religious matters, collected by R. MENACHEM.

Begin (leaf 134[a]):

מעשה בא בהר שהביאו גוים דגים ביום אחרון של פסח הסמוך לשבת....

End (leaf 135[b]):

....ובודאי כמו שאסרו מלאכה בהמ׳ בשבת כך אסרו בתוך המועד כו׳: ושלום מני ישעיה: הגהה:

(1) [מעשיות].

These Ma'asiyyoth contain the records of the following decisions: (1) commencing ... מעשה בא בהר (at Montpellier), in which the great men of Lunel decided against R. Asher b. Meshullam, who took the more lenient side; (2) commencing: ... אם יש מנודה בעיר; (3) commencing: מעשה בא לידינו החכם ר׳ אליה הורה להתיר ... in which it says: מירקות שנתבשלו....; (4) commencing: מעשה היה בהר בדגים שניטגנו במחבת בשמן ....ונמצא בין קרבי הדגי׳ שרץ קטן...., in which R. Abraham declared the fish unfit for food, whilst R. David b. R. Reuben differed from him: (5) commencing: מעשה היה בהר בקער׳ חולבת שאינה בת יומ׳ ....; (6) commencing: מעשה שהיה שנפל בתוך התנור מגבינת....; (7) commencing: מעשה בא לידינו בקדר׳ של בשר שאינה ב״י...., in which occurs: ....והתיר החכם ר׳ אליה הלוי התבשיל; (8) commencing: מעשה בא לידינו באשה שלשה עסה והפריש׳ חלה ואח״כ..., in which occurs: ...והורה החכם ר׳ אליה הלוי; (9) commencing: מעשה אחר היה שאחר שהפריש׳ חלה הניח אותה על השאור....; (10) commencing: מעשה היה שנשחטו ג׳ תרנגולו׳ ונתנבלה אחת..., in which the חכמי צרפת are mentioned, and at the end: ....וכי האי גוונא בא בעיר מונפשליר (Montpellier) והתירו הר׳ שלמה ב״ר אברהם ז״ל. Attached to this last are two philosophico-agadic pieces, commencing .... וכמה זעמו רגע and שור שהקריב אדם הראשון respectively.

(2) [תשובות]. Responsa.

These Responsa are mere extracts from larger works, and particularly from R. Yoseph Qolon's: (1) commencing: ועל ברית מילה.... (Shoresh 179); (2) commencing: ועל הדלקת נר חנוכה.... (Shoresh 184); and (3) commencing: לכבוד הנכבד והיקר והנעים אחי ורעי רבנין עטרת שלום מאתי אשר על החותמ׳ הבא להסיעך על אשר כתבת מהו להשכיר חמורו בח״ה ויש מתירין....

The author is a R. Yesha'yah, who signs the letter as before stated.

9. [פסק ר׳ דוד מאימולה להתיר בשר לצלי בלא מליחה].

DECISION of R. DAVID OF IMOLA, allowing MEAT to be ROASTED WITH FIRE without SALTING.

Begins (leaf 136^a):

להפקת רצון וחפץ אלו היקרים י״ץ ואני בבואי מבית אבי מאימולה ומארץ מולדתי מבולוניא (Bologna) ....

Ends (leaf 137^a):

....אינו בולע מהדם שבשפוד ע״כ: הרי ברור כשמש כי אפי׳ הראב״ד והרשב״א שהחמירו מזולתם מודין הן דאין צריך מליח׳ לצלי כמו לקדירה: זהו הנר׳ לע״ד ואני העבד הקטן מזומן כל ימי צבאי עלי ארץ לשמור ולעשו׳ ככל אשר תצוני ואחלה פני אל ויחנך ואת המרומם אדו׳ גבירי אישך יצ״ו עם רב שלום בניך ושלום. הצעיר הלא מסתתר בסתר מדבר כדברי׳ האלה כי לא נסה דומם ונסתרה דרכו (דוד) פה בסלע משכן לו כ״ה לספירה פר״ח (1528): חלק לה ה׳ שמן ששון וטעם בבינה ויראתו לה למנה. המעטירה המפוארה מרת פומינה (Pomona ?) מב״ת (מנשים באהל תברך Jud. v. 24) אשת למרומם כמ׳ דניאל גבירי יצ״ו ממודינה ואליהם שלו׳ רב מאריי׳ ושלו׳ מססולי׳ (Sassuolo).

This 'Decision' is of moment, not merely on account of the great learning and liberality of the author displayed therein, but also and chiefly for the following reasons: (1) We meet here with a woman, not only of great piety, but Talmudic learning too, as to her this learned epistle is addressed, and (2) we learn from this that this was the mother of our R. Menachem. See next paragraph.

10. [העתקות מספרים שונים נעשו על ידי ר׳ מנחם בן דניאל ומשפחתו].

EXTRACTS from various sources, made by R. MENACHEM and other members of his family.

(1) [מגלת יוחסין]. Register of births and deaths.

Begins (leaf 137^b):

עמ״י גד גדי בהנו״א וסינוק לא עש״ו: ארחמך (1508) ה׳ חזקי: וזה סימן טוב ....

Ends (leaf 138^a):

....והיא בת כמ״ר חיים טרבוטי נ״ע שנפטר יום ה׳ י״ז אייר כ״ג אפרי׳ שי״א ... (April 23, 1551).

a. The births contain the following names: (1) Menachem[1] Manuel (מניאל) b. Daniyyel b. David, born Sabbath, Shebat 8, Dec. 30, 5269 (1508); (2) Abraham[2] b. Daniyyel, born at Reggio, Tammuz 16, 5271 (1511); (3) the Twins, Rosa (named after her paternal grandmother) and Ya'aqob (after his maternal grandfather), born at Reggio, Thursday, Nisan 6, March 11, 5278 (1518), the children of Daniyyel of Modena; (5) Yitzchaq, son of Daniyyel b.

[1] This is the author of the first and other pieces in, and the copyist of the greater part of, this volume.

[2] This is a poet of some talent, and the author of Cod. Bisliches, 72, now in the Bodleian. See Zunz, הפליט (Berlin, 1850) p. 25, and *Literaturgesch d. synag. Poesie*, p. 535. Zunz seems to identify ארייו with Arezzo, whilst we identify it with Reggio. See p. 75 above, 2. A. (1).

David, born at Reggio, Ab 15, July 30, 5280 (1520); (6) the first-born David Bentzion b. Abraham b. Daniyyel, born at Reggio, Elul 7, August 30, 5301 (1541), and redeemed at Forli (פורלי); (7) David, son of Menachem Laterinaro (לאטרנארו) and of Rosa bath Daniyyel, born at Modena, Friday, Sivan 12, May 26, 5302 (1542); (8) Nechamah (נחמה), daughter of Mordekhai Chazaq, born Ab 15, July 13, 5287 (1527); and (9) Leah, the daughter of Chayyim Trabotti, born Sabbath, Elul 11, August 22, 5294 (1534). These last two were successively the wives either of R. Menachem or of Ya'aqob of Modena; and Leah was clearly divorced.

b. The deaths contain the following names: (1) Yitzchaq b. Daniyyel b. David, died July, 5303 (1543); (2) Mordekhai Chazaq, d. Marcheshvan 16, 5307 (1546); (3) Nechamah, his daughter, d. Shebat 18, January 25, 5311 (1551); (4) Chayyim Trabotti, d. Thursday, Iyyar 17, April 23, 5311 (1551).

(2) [מדרשים, קבלה, חדות ופרושם]. Agadic and cabbalistic sentences with their explanation, and enigmas and their solution; occupying leaves 138ᵇ—139ᵃ. These are anonymously given, and contain: (1) commencing: ...ר׳ יוחנן פתח עד שיפוח היום...זו אזהרה לאדם; (2) commencing: אסור על אחת הוסיף תשעה... להסתכל בקשת ועיין בזוהר....; (3) commencing: אם תכפול חצי השם; פירוש על א׳ הוסיף ט׳ הרי עשר....; (4) commencing: מה תצעק; מסוד הגלגול הבל הוא משה...; (5) commencing: עדת קרח בסוד הגלגול... אלי מ׳ יום...; (6) commencing: מעשה באדם אחד שהיה זהיר במצות ציצית....; (7) commencing: חכמות נשים בנתה ביתה...מעשה היה באשה אלמנה....; (8) commencing: אמרו חכמים חצר גדולה יש למתים....; (9) commencing: ; and (10) commencing: .

11. [מסעות ר׳ יעקב בן נתנאל הכהן].

Travels of R. Ya'aqob b. Nethaneel Hakkohen in the Holy Land.

Begin (leaf 139ᵇ):

אני יעקב ב״ר נתנאל שהלכתי וטרחתי ועזרני השם שהכניסני לארץ ישראל וראיתי קברי אבותי׳ הצדיקי׳ שבחברון....

End (leaf 140ᵃ):

....שם המדינה טורסין. כאשר זיכני לכתוב אותו כן נזכה לבא שמה ולמות שם נשלמו דברי יעקב הכהן מכל הראיות שראיתי בארץ ישראל.

Although these, as all similar travels, must be used with great caution, there is a great deal of true and interesting information to be found therein; compare our description of MS. Add. 431, יוחסין השלם (ed. Filipowski, London and Edinburgh, 1857, 8vo.), p. 228, and Zunz, on geog. lit. of the Jews, No. 47 (in Asher's Benjamin of Tudela, ii. p. 258).

12. [לקוטים שונים].

Collectanea Varia, occupying leaves 140ᵇ—157ᵇ.

These Collectanea are by various authors, and on various subjects, but may be reduced to the following nine chief points:

a. Extracts from the Babylonian Talmud. These are mostly without the smallest commentary; but generally the name of the volume, and the leaf where they occur, are given. Towards the end a small index for finding the דיני הרשאה is given. (Leaves 140[b]—142[a].)

b. Extracts from various Rabbinical authorities, such as the Tur, Rabbenu Nissim, and R. Yoseph Qolon. (Leaves 142[b]—143[a].)

c. Extracts from Cabbalistic authorities. These are mostly anonymously given. The subjects treated on belong to the range of practical Cabbalah. (Leaves 143[b]—144[a].)

d. Cabbalistical essays by R. Yoseph b. Abraham Ibn ג׳קטילה on the Rabbinical saying: ראויה היתה בת שבע לדוד מששת ימי בראשית (T. B. Synhedrin 107[a]), and other Rabbinical sayings. (Leaves 144[b]—146[b].)

e. A piece headed:

וזה מצאתי מפרשת כי תשא

It consists of two extracts from Ibn 'Ezra's shorter commentary on Exodus, followed in each case by extracts from Ibn Kaspi's supercommentary on the סודות of Ibn 'Ezra.

The first is on Exod. xxxi. 3 (ed. Reggio, Prag, 1840, 8vo. p. 96), and begins:

בחכמה ובתבונה אמ׳ אברהם ב״ע ז״ל כבר פרשתי בספר משלי לך ובקש מה בין זה לזה

The extract which follows, beginning: אמ׳ אברהם ב״ע יש באיש שלשה חדרים ...... is generally supposed to be a piece of Ibn 'Ezra's lost commentary on the Proverbs[1], but it is in reality only Ibn Kaspi as above, as may be seen from the fact that ורבי׳ משה ז״ל (Maimonides) is here quoted, though no doubt it gives the substance of what Ibn Kaspi found in Ibn 'Ezra's lost commentary.

The second is on Exod. xxxii. 5 (ed. Reggio, p. 99), and begins:

אמ׳ אבן עזרא אני אגלה לך סוד העגל ברמיזות והמבין מלאכת השמים ידע צורת העגל

It is followed by an extract from Ibn Kaspi's supercommentary, beginning with the words: למה הנה סתם דבריו ואני אפרש לך קבלתי: See MSS. Add. 377. 3, leaf 83[a]; Add. 510. 2, leaf 86[a]; Add. 433, leaf 137[b]; Add. 518, leaf 76[a], and p. 74 of this Catalogue. Compare also

[1] It may be as well to remind the reader that the commentary attributed in the printed edition to Ibn 'Ezra belongs not to him, but to R. Mosheh Qimchi. See Reifmann, ציון, I. p. 76. This fact was unknown to Wolf (I. p. 894), Uri (No. 157), and De-Rossi (No. 694. 3).

MS. Add. 510. 1, leaf 70[b], 9 lines from below, אמר יוסף עד היום לא ראיתי פירושו על ספר משלי אך מצאתי כתוב על שמו כי ג׳ חללי׳... In the printed edition, leaf 81[a], it runs somewhat differently. (Leaf 147[a].)

f. Extract from the cabbalistical essays of R. Yoseph Ibn גקטלא; a continuation of d. above. See 7. (4) above, at the very end. (Leaves 147[b]—148[a].)

g. Biblical verses containing the various Names of God, to which are added the names of the Angels, corresponding with each of the Ten Sephiroth, &c. They are one hundred in all. Selected by the foregoing Cabbalist, who is here called ר׳ יוסף גוטילה. (Leaves 148[b]—150[a].)

h. Biblical, Talmudical, and Rabbinical sayings, philosophico-cabbalistically explained. They include explanations of (1) the wording of a passage in the Prayer-Book, commencing: וחננו מאתך דעה; (2) the Biblical passage, 1 Sam. ii. 8; (3) the Mishnah Aboth.... ואל תהי רשע; (4) the Talmudic passage on יין המשומר בענביו (see the description of No. 27, above); (5) the work of the Tabernacle in the wilderness; and (6) the Biblical passages, Ex. xxxiii. 22, and Job xi. 15. They treat further on (7) the altar of incense (see the description of No. 27, above); (8) מטטרון, the שר הפנים; and (9) the duty of every Israelite to have a right conception of God (directed against the evils springing from anthropomorphism). They explain (10) the words בקי, כור, הדרוקן and ירח בול; (11) the difficult words occurring in 2 Kings xvii. 30 and Isaiah iii. 18—23, &c. (a large number of these being also translated into Italian); (12) the Biblical passages, Prov. iii. 6 (extracted from R. 'Immanuel b. Shelomoh's commentary), Deut. xxxiii., Judg. v., the Midrashic and Talmudical passage, Synhedrin 91[b], &c. They contain also (13) a few other short Rabbinical sayings, without commentary; (14) an extract from the introduction to the book Yetzirah, and the commentary, ascribed to R. Abraham b. David (see Excurs. VI.); and (15) the Alphabets belonging thereto. (Leaves 150[b]—155[a].)

i. Poems and Explanations:

A. Poems. (1) A Hymn called עץ חיים, on the thirteen articles of the Jewish religion. It is an imitation of the well-known יגדל, and consists of 14 lines all ending in תו. It commences: נמצא בעולם יש, and ends: ומי יחקור עד סוף תכונתו. (2) A poem in 4 lines, inviting the learned to cling to this 'Tree of life'. It commences: שלחו נבונים יד בעץ חיים.... (3) An enigma on the author's name, commencing: לשם הורי שאלוני.... All three are by Matithyah יד״ד.

B. Explanations. (1) Remarks on T. B. Pesachim, 49[b]; (2) on the genealogy of Eldad and Medad; (3) on the creation of the first man; (4) on the ass on which Abraham rode when about to sacrifice Isaac;

(5) an extract from the Minchath Yehudah (by R. Yehudah b. Eli'ezer) on Gen. xxxi. 33, with reference to the Midrash Rabbah thereon; (6) explanation of Gen. xiv. 18, and Exod. xvi. 4, by R. Aharon (a contemporary of the collector). Attached to these is the famous poem by R. Yehudah b. Shemuel Hallevi, said to have been addressed to Ibn 'Ezra in a dream, in which the former invites him to 'sing' in the better world, and Ibn 'Ezra's answer thereto. It is here superscribed: ... חידה מר' יהודה הלוי ז"ל. (Leaves 155ᵇ—157ᵇ.)

13. [חידת הראב"ע ופרושה מר' יצחק בן משה הלוי].

The Riddle of R. Abraham b. Meir Ibn 'Ezra on the Litteræ Quiescentes, and the explanation thereof, by R. Yitzchaq b. Mosheh Hallevi, commonly called Prophiat Duran.

Begins (leaf 158ᵃ):

את דבר חידתי.... זאת החידה, אשר כל יציץ זיוה הדרה והודה חברה החכם הראב"ע ז"ל על אותיות אהוי ונשאל עליה להוציא לאור תעלומ' החכם הגדול מאשטירו פרופייט דוראן הלוי וכה השיב וכה אמר: הנה תפארת השלמי' רלב"ג ז"ל אמ' בפירושו לספר משלי....

Ends (leaf 159ᵇ):

....עד אשר תתחטאו העיר בכל זה למה שבחידה מן העומק: סליק לק"י.

This famous Chidah, which precedes in the printed editions Ibn 'Ezra's preface to his commentary on the Pentateuch, and the solution of which has been for a considerable time a matter of controversy, is here explained by one who was not merely best qualified to explain it on account of his intimate knowledge of the philosophy and grammar peculiar to its author, but also on account of his thorough acquaintance with, and experience in explaining, Ibn 'Ezra's Biblical commentaries and other works; (see the description of MS. Add. 433 below). This explanation is not identical with that of the "Quiescentia" to be found in the לוית חן, as Friedlaender and Kohn (מעשה אפֹדֿ, Wien, 1865, 8vo. p. 11, v.) think; but is identical with Cod. Flor. xlii. x (p. 310), and Cod. De-Rossi, 835, 3°. (On the name Prophiat Duran and its equivalent אפֹדֿ, see our remarks in *A descriptive Catalogue of the Arabic, Persian and Turkish Manuscripts in the Library of Trinity College, Cambridge*... Cambridge, 1870, 8vo., Appendix, p. 220, Note 1, and the description of MS. Add. 391. 4). Attached to this are the following pieces:

a. (1) Short sayings of the philosophers, commencing: החכם חכם בעודו ... דורש החכמה; (2) a few Rabbinical sayings, commencing: מאן דמשתעי בהדי ריש לקיש בשוקא...; (3) a few lexicographical statements commencing: .... א"ע ערב לשון ערוב. These are in their turn succeeded (4) by other remarks within the province of grammar, philosophy, and theology, which end with an extract from the נחלת אבות by Don Yitzchaq Abarbanel, and another extract from the ספר עולם קטן.

b. A poem on the thirteen Articles of Religion, in imitation of יגדל, and consisting of 16 lines, of which the first two are, however, introductory, and the sixteenth has a concluding character; so that, strictly speaking, it treats, as in the original, on the subject in thirteen lines. It has the acrostic of משה, and is here ascribed to R. Mosheh de' Rossi of Cecina or Cesena (ציסינה). It is introduced by אלו הן י״ג עקרים שסדרם כמה״ר משה מן האדומי יש״ר (יחי שנים רבות) מציסינה., and commences .... משוך אל חסדך, תנה לי הודך. Zunz, *Literaturgesch. d. synag. Poesie* (Berlin, 1866, 8vo.), p. 510, ascribes it to the author of the book התדיר (Mosheh b. Yequthiel of Rome). In any case the author is not the father of the celebrated author of the מאור עינים. (Leaves 159b—160a.)

14. [לקוטים מגדולי הראשונים על מסכת שבועות לר׳ יוסף הלוי].

COLLECTANEA from VARIOUS EARLY RABBINICAL AUTHORITIES on the TALMUDICAL TREATISE SHEBU'OTH, by R. YOSEPH HALLEVI.

Begin (leaf 160b):

איתמר מתפים בשבועה אביי אמ׳...וק״ל כרבא...ואני יוסף הלוי פי׳ דמתפים בשבועה לאו כשבועה דמי היינו לענין קרבן....

End (leaf 165a):

....משמתינן ליה על תנאי שיהא בשומתא אם הוא חייב ואינו משלם הרא״ש פסק כלישנא קמא:

The latest authority quoted is the הגהות הראש. The author's name occurs three times (leaves 160b [twice] and 164b); the last time it says, respecting a remark on נקיטת חפץ by R. Asher b. Yechiel: והחמירו בשבועת הדיינין זה הוספתי מדעתי אני יוסף. Perhaps this is the R. Yoseph Hallevi, who put the questions concerning the Sephiroth to R. Meir Ibn גבאי (see 16 below). It must be remarked that the very learned S. Sachs (הפליט p. 53, Note) doubts the existence of such a personage, &c. altogether. Attached to these are extracts (1) from the סמ״ק (see above, p. 76, Note 2); (2) the Tosaphoth; (3) the Talmud Babli; and (4) from the מנחת יהודה, on Ex. xiv. 15, xv. 21, and xvi. 1. (Leaves 165a—167b.)

15. [רמזים על מצות שונות ודברים מדברים שונים].

SYMBOLICAL INTERPRETATIONS of VARIOUS LAWS of SCRIPTURE, RABBINICAL SAYINGS and CABBALISTIC MATTERS.

Begin (leaf 168a):

בהנו״א ענין פרה אדומה יראה שהוא להכניע גאון לב האדם אשר לא הביא צוארו בעבודת האל ית׳....

End (leaf (171b):

....שבעה על גבי שנים עשר עכ״ל שם הנ״ל.

The matters contained here are: (1) on the Red Heifer[1]; (2) on the same subject, extracted from the חשק שלמה, a philosophical commentary on the Kuzari[2]; (3) on the superiority of the law of circumcision to that of the Sabbath, extracted from the same; (4) on vacuity, extracted from the same; (5) on the Agadah T. B. Berakhoth 3ª[3]; (6) on the Agadah T. B. Pesachim, 54ª; (7) on the five meanings of 'before,' extracted from the before-mentioned commentary; (8) on the representation of God in man, extracted from the same commentary; (9) explanation of two phrases in the Kuzari respecting Christianity and Mahommedanism, and (10) explanation of the Ten Sephiroth, and the introduction to the Sepher Yetzirah. Attached to these are a few cabbalistical remarks by a contemporary of the copyist, R. Pinechas Eliyya of Mele[4] (אליא ממילי; see 18 below); commencing: אם תראה אותיות נסתרות שיוצאין מאדם .... Among other sayings, the witty saying: העבר אין, העתיד עדיין, ההוה כהרף עין, הזמן מנין, is stated by a later optimistic scribe thus to have come down to him:

העבר ... עין, דאגה מנין'

16. [פרושים על הספירות].

COMMENTARIES on the TEN SEPHIROTH, occupying leaves 172ª—176ᵇ.

a. [תשובות שאלות לר׳ עזריאל]. Questions and answers by R. 'Azriel of Gerona, beginning:

שאלות תשובות בקבלה האיי״ל. שאל השואל מי יכריחנו להאמין שיש לעולם מנהיג. תשובה כמו שאי אפשר לספינה בלא קברנט ....

The greater part of this is printed under the title of פירוש עשר ספירות (Berlin, 1850, 8vo.); but from the commentary דרך אמונה (re-printed from the Padua ed. of 1567) as well as also from MSS. Add. 400. 10, and 406. 2, it is easily seen that this MS. contains in the additional matter nothing but literature systematically and legitimately belonging thereto. (Leaves 172ª—175ᵇ.)

[1] This is identical with the matter given by Neubauer (Bod. Catal. of Heb. MSS., No. 221. 10, col. 39) as belonging to הצדיק 'Immanuel.

[2] Puttick and Simpson, Cat. for Dec. 13, 1869, p. 15, No. 258, have on this work the following remarks, the author of which is probably Steinschneider: Salomo Ben Jehuda, called Salmon Vivas de Lunel.... The author was a pupil of Menachem ben Salomo (Frai Maimon), and only 13 years of age when he wrote this work. According to Zunz (הפליט, in the description of Cod. Bisliches 18, p. 13), however, Frat (not Frai) Maimon was called R. Shelomoh b. Menachem; compare also Mortara in אוצר נחמד II. p. 210, Note, and the description of MS. Add. 666, in the present catalogue.

[3] Instead of R. יוסי, the commentator read R. ישמעאל.

[4] Mele, and neither Mile, as Zunz (*Gesch. u. Lit.* p. 260), nor Melli, as Luzzatto (אוצר נחמד II. p. 12), write. One R. Pinechas Eliyya b. Tzemach Eliyya flourished about 1573 at Mantua. See Lampronti ,פחד יצחק, letters חל, leaf 24ª.

b. [פרוש להרמב"ן]. Explanation of the ten Sephiroth, by R. Mosheh b. Nachman (?), beginning:

יתברך שם הבורא ית' שהוא חי וקיים לעדי עד והוא ברחמיו יאיר עיני בתורתו ויחשכני משגיאות. ראשית כל דבר שהוא ראשית לכל והקדמון לכל והוא נעלם מכל והוא נקר' עלת העלות ואין לומר עליו לא יש ולא אין כי הוא נסתר מן המלאכים ק"ו ממנו....

We read here towards the end the following:

מלאך אלקי' ואני הצעיר בבית אבי משה ב"ן ז"ל המפרש עושה מלאך אלקי' מוכרת.... See Cat. de la Bibl... Luzzatto... par son fils Joseph, p. 13, No. 113, XII.

17. [מצות תפלין והנחתן בחול המועד].

Responsum (?) on the Tephillin, and the duty of putting them on on the Middle Holidays, by an anonymous Italian Rabbi.

Begins (leaf 177[a]):

לענין תפלין. התוכפן ומברך זו אחר זו בלי שום הפסק זוכה ונוצח במלחמה....

Ends (leaf 177[b]):

....ועושין המצוה כהלכתה: תם.

In the course of this Responsum (?) we read:

י"א שגם בחול המועד אין להניח תפלין....וגברה ואת המחשבה אצל קצת מהמורים מפני מה שמצאו כתו' בספר הזוהר שהמניח תפלין בחול המועד חייב מיתה וגם שמעתי אומרי' כי בא במדרש הנעלם בשם ר' עקיבא שאסור להניח תפלין בחול המועד ואלו כלם דברי' תמוהים בעצמן מתמיהים ומבהילים לרכי הלב...גם הנמצא כתוב בספר הזוהר שהמניח תפלין בחולו של מועד חייב מיתה כ"כ תמיה שמורה על בטולו ואיך אפשר שבעל הזוהר שהיה רשב"י לפי מה שיחסוהו אליו יאמר כן....אלא שדברי' אלו אינן עיקר לא בזוהר ולא במדרש הנעלם אלא טעות יצא מתחת ידי כותב והכניסום ולא ממנו....

Leaf 178[a] is blank.

18. [לקוטים בקבלה לר' פנחס אליא (בן צמח?) ממילי].

Collectanea Cabbalistica, &c. by R. Pinechas Eliyya (b. Tzemach ?) of Mele.

Begins (leaf 178[b]):

בהנו"א בס"ה (בספר הזוהר) תנינן תלתא דרגין אינון ומתקשרן דא בדא....

Breaks off (leaf 180[b]):

....צפרתא ישראל ואת הצפור לא בתר עד קרסוליה....

These collectanea contain, besides a number of extracts from the Zohar and other cabbalistic works, also some רמזים, &c. See 15 (10) above. Leaves 181—183, of which the latter two may have been blank, are wanting; leaf 184 is blank.

19. [סדר סבוראים גאונים ופוסקים לר' עזריאל (בן יחיאל?) טרבוט צרפתי].

Brief History of the Saburaim, Geonim and other Deciders, by R. 'Azriel (b. Yechiel?) טרבוט, the Frenchman.

Begins (leaf 185[a]):

ראשונה אחר רבינא ורב אשי שהיו סוף הוראה עמד רב אחאי:....

Ends (leaf 185[b]):

....ומקצתם כתבו פסקי הלכות ותשובות שאלות וספר מיוחד. לא נמצא על שמם „ עכ"ל מהר"ר עזריאל טרבוט צרפתי זצ"ל.

One R. Yechiel b. 'Azriel טרבוט flourished in the year 1573 at Pesaro (פיסארו). At that time his father, who is probably the author of this Seder, was dead. See Lampronti, פחד יצחק, letters חל, leaf 25[a], and below in the paragraph on owners.

Attached to this is a kindred piece, commencing:

רש"י היה זקנו של הרשב"ם....

and ending:

רשב"א הוא רבי' שמשון ב"ר אברהם משנץ: „ (Leaf 186[a]);
and another piece containing Talmudical explanations of various verses in Holy Writ, but particularly of Haggai (Pesachim, T. B. Pereq 1, leaves 16[b]—17[a], &c.), as also other extracts, both halakhic and agadic, beginning:

משה ואהרן בכהניו...וארז"ל שקול שמואל כנגד משה ואהרן....

and ending:

וכן לא תאכלו על הדם שפירשו בו רבו' כמה דברים. (Leaves 186[b]—187[b].)

20. [פרקי דרך ארץ].

The Talmudical Treatise on Good Manners:

Begins (leaf 188[a]):

הלכות דרך ארץ. מי שהוא תלמיד חבר לא יאכל מעומד....

Ends (leaf 188[b]):

....זה בית המקדש שיבנה במהרה בימינו אמ'. הדרך עלך דרך ארץ..

These Peraqim correspond on the whole, although there are many different readings in the text, with Peraqim v—ix in the מסכת דרך ארץ זוטא, which is to be found in the מסכתות קטנות attached to the Talmud Babli. Leaves 189ª—193ᵇ are blank, and leaves 194—196, probably blank, are wanting.

Of the owners, who, down to about 1560, and perhaps for almost a century later, were members of the author's and principal scribe's family, we know after that time nothing with absolute certainty. Between 1642 and 1685, however, this MS. must have come into the hands of R. Abraham Yoseph Shelomoh b. Mordekhai Graziano, chief Rabbi of Modena, who acquired it from the heirs of his predecessor in office, R. Nethaneel b. Binyamin Trabot[1], as a Note, to be found on leaf 5ª, shows. It runs thus: ב"ה ה' מנת חלקי וכיסי אשר קניתי ס' הנכבד והנורא הזה אשר הוא פי' על רש"י בתורה וחדושי' אחרי' על כל פ' ופרשה מאת יורשי הגאון מופת הדור האשל הגדול כמוהר"ר נתנאל טרבוט בכמה"ר בנימן טרבוט זצ"ל במעות מנויות, ע"י הסרסור והאמצעי הנעלה כמה"ר יוסף יצ"ו בכמ"ר אדונירם מירם מויניייולא (Vignola) ז"ל ויש גם בזה הס' לקוטים וחדושים רבים מחכמים שוני' כאשר עיניך לנוכח יביטו דברי חכמים וחידותם והיה זה פה מודונא (Modena) בשנת (no year is given) לפ"ק ולוי"א (ולמזל ולברכה יהיה אמן) והכל שריר וברור וקים. It is he who wrote the double, though imperfect, index on leaf 1ª and 1ᵇ, and provided most of the treatises and other separable parts of literature which are to be found in this truly remarkable literary repository, with superscriptions. These, although far from being exhaustive, bear testimony to this owner's great learning; and only one who has catalogued this MS. can understand his difficulties. His signature is found numerous times in this volume, chiefly at the commencement or end of a new treatise. It runs mostly: איש גר (אברהם יוסף שלמה גראציאנו) אנכי בארץ חאוע (חרפת אדם ובזוי עם

[1] R. Nethaneel b. Binyamin Trabot (טראבוט), a relative of the family טרבוט of France (see 19 above, and Azulai, שם הגדולים, under יחיאל), was alive, at all events, in the year 1642, as there is a Responsum of his, bearing that date, to be found (Lampronti, פחד יצחק, letters מש, leaf 228ª). According to Ghirondi (תולדות גדולי ישראל p. 34, No. 81) R. Graziano was a descendant of R. Nethaneel Trabot; a statement which is adopted by the great Zunz (Monatstage, p. 60); but this is impossible, as the above note clearly shows, in which G. speaks of R. Trabot as of an entire stranger. The mistake originated, no doubt, in the following way: Ghirondi confounded R. Nethaneel *Segré*, who is said by Nepi (זכר צדיקים לברכה in Ghirondi's ת"ג"י", p. 5) to have been R. Graziano's uncle, with R. Nethaneel *Trabot*, and thus calls Graziano נכדו של הגאון רבינו נתנאל טרבוט . . . Upon this Zunz translates this נכדו, which is used among the Italian Jews not merely for grandson but also for nephew, by "ein Enkel von Natanel Trabot," whilst, as must have been seen, the only relation subsisting between RR. Trabot and Graziano is that of predecessor and successor. (The word נכד is found in the sense of nephew even among the French Jews of the xi—xiith century; see Pseudo-Rashi, i. e. רשב"ם on T. B. Baba Bathra 109ª, ומשני', &c. Compare in the English A. V. Gen. xxi. 23, with Isa. xiv. 22 and Job xviii. 19.)

(Ps. xxii. 7); sometimes it is less full. After his death[1] this volume came into the hands of one of his family, a son, or a nephew, and subsequently into those of R. Chayyim Graziano (his grandson or grandnephew), who possessed it in the years 1735—44, as a loose leaf, to be found in this MS., bearing those dates, and on which two miracles wrought by God for R. Chayyim are recorded, will testify. From that day to the day when it came into the possession of the University, its history is a blank.

The state of the MS. is, on the whole, good.

[Library-mark, Add. 539; bought in 1869 from H. Lipschütz.]

No. 41.

Paper, 8 in. × 6 in.; 137 leaves, 4-sheet quires, 54—60 lines; mixed (Rabbinic and current) character, German Ashkenazic handwriting of the XVI—XVIIth century.

[גור אריה לר׳ ליווא בן בצלאל]

Supercommentary on Rashi on the PENTATEUCH, by R. Löwe b. Betzaleel, chief Rabbi, successively, of Posen, Cracow, and Prague; defective.

Leaf 1, *Genesis;* 49ᵇ, blank; 50ᵇ, *Exodus;* 95ᵇ, *Leviticus;* 126ᵇ, *Numbers;...*

Begins (leaf 1ᵃ; on Gen. vii. 12):

....ואלו היה מנין החדשים מניסן א״כ (אם כן) נחה התיבה בתשרי על הרי אררט והיה לכתוב עוד....

Breaks off finally (leaf 137ᵇ; on Num. xxix. 6):

...ונסכו ולא כתב ונסכיהם אע״ג (אף על גב) דבחג כתיב ונסכיהם ומפרשינן על שני תמידים....

Twice printed (Prag, 1578, Folio; Warszawa, 1862—1863, Folio).

The author was at what may be called in some respects a Jewish Classical period (we remind the reader only of Yoseph Caro, Shelomoh Alqabetz, Mosheh Cordovero, Mosheh Isserls, Shelomoh Loria, Mordekhai Yapheh, the great 'Azaryah de' Rossi and others who lived at that time), one of the foremost men. He was celebrated as Talmudist, Grammarian, Philosopher and Cabbalist, and justly so. He is known in literature as the מהר״ל מפראג, whilst he is commonly called the "high Rabbi Löb". As such he is on account of his practical Qabbalah, the hero of the nursery to this day; and

[1] R. Graziano died, according to the statement of R. Chananeel Nepi (ז״צ״ל in Ghirondi's תולדות גדולי ישראל, p. 5), on Sabbath חיי שרה 5445 (Nov. 4, 1685); see also Zunz, Monatstage..., as above.

stories are still told of him, which fill the youthful mind with awe and delight at the same time. A valuable contribution to the history of his descendants, many of whom have attained great eminence in Jewish literature, will be found in the dedication of the בן יוחאי (Wien, 1815, Folio) to the spirits of his parents by the highly-gifted author, R. Moses *Kunizer* (as in the Lithograph prefixed to המצרף II. Prag, 1857, 4to., and not Konitz or Kuniz as Steinschneider and Zedner write it), who, according to an extract from the Register of the "Holy Brotherhood" (חברא קדישא[1]), died at Pest, 27 Shebat 5597 (Feb. 2, 1837), as Rabbi of Buda. R. Kunizer was both by his father and his mother a descendant of our author.

This MS. is, apart from its defects, inferior in many ways, copied as it is by an ignorant or thoughtless copyist, on very bad paper, and having some of the margins badly cut. On the other hand, it seems to have been copied from a better copy, probably a second revision, as it has some readings which are superior to those in the printed editions.

The following are the defects besides those mentioned as existing at the beginning and end: (1) leaves 21, 33—34, 102, 109, 117—118, and (2) several quires between the leaves now paged 124, 126. It is interesting to know that this MS. was carried to the Black Jews of Cochin, from whom Dr Buchanan obtained it in 1806, as is stated on the printed label which is attached to this as well as to all the Buchanan MSS.

[Library-mark, Oo. 1. 19; presented in 1809 by Dr Buchanan.]

No. 42.

Paper, 8 in. × $5\frac{7}{8}$ in.; 30 leaves, mostly 4-sheet quires, 30 lines; mixed (Rabbinic and current) character, Sephardic handwriting of the XVII—XVIIIth century.

[גור אריה לר' ליווא בן בצלאל]

Supercommentary on Rashi on the PENTATEUCH, by R. Löwe b. Betzaleel; incomplete.

Begins (leaf 2ª):

בהנ"וא בראשית אמר ר' יצחק לא היה כו' בראשית ברא שאע"פ שאין ספור א' בתורה שלא לצורך אפילו אחות לוטן תמנע כדאיתא בפרק חלק אחר ששם תורה אינו נופל אלא על מצות התורה שהרי לשון תורה הוא לשון הוראה....

[1] This חברא is on the Continent an independent corporation, with privileges and duties of its own, whilst in England, where the Hebrew congregations are comparatively of recent growth, the duties of attending to the sick, dying and dead, belong to the congregation itself.

Ends (leaf 30[b]):

....ומ״מ (ומכל מקום) כאשר הרשעים נמצאים שייך באותו זמן התעצבות כי מצדם היתה התעצבות אשר ברא האדם ואם לא היה בבריאות עולם הצדיקים עיקר למה בראו כי הוא בראו ופעלו ישתבח האדון הכל ויוצר בראשית:

חסלת פרשת בראשית.
המאירה כעששית:

Leaf 1[a] has an ornamental design, representing Aaron and Moses, two Angels holding the two tables of the covenant, &c.; within has been left a vacant space, evidently to place the title of the book, which is, however, left blank. With leaf 2[a] begins the text, the first word of which is in larger character, within a small ornamental border.

This MS., although exhibiting no outward traces of connexion with No. 41, was, probably, copied when that MS. had become defective. The copyist, however, proceeded no further than the first weekly Parashah (בראשית), perhaps, because at that time the defect of the other had not spread farther.

It is, on the whole, well copied, the only mistakes occurring in it being German words, which the copyist, naturally, did not understand. Like the foregoing MS. it differs sometimes, for the better, from the printed editions, which leads one to believe that this also was copied from a revision made after 1578.

This copy was probably executed in Cochin whence Dr Buchanan obtained it in 1806, as the label states. The label on the back has in an inelegant Sephardic hand (not that of the copyist) פרשת בראשית.

[Library-mark, Oo. 1. 35. 1; presented in 1809 by Dr Buchanan.]

No. 43.

Paper in quarto, $7\frac{3}{4}$ in. × $5\frac{5}{8}$ in.; 132 leaves, 6-sheet quires, variable number of lines; mixed (Rabbinic and current) character, Italian handwriting of the XVIth century.

[פרוש על פרוש רש״י על התורה לחכם לועזי פלוני אלמוני]

Supercommentary on Rashi on the PENTATEUCH by an anonymous Italian Rabbi; defective.

Leaf 1, blank; 2, *Genesis* (2—20 wanting); 47[b], *Exodus;* 78[b], *Leviticus;* 100[a], *Numbers;* 115[a], *Deuteronomy;* 121—136, the greater part probably blank, wanting.

Begins (leaf 21[a]; on Gen. xviii. 1):

....וירא. פתח האהל בגימטר׳ להכנים את האורחים. יוקח נא מעט מים... גימ׳ מכאן זכו לבאר....

Breaks off (leaf 120b; on Deut. xxxii. 30):

....הרי במדה טובה אחד אינו רודף כי אם מאה לכל היותר....

Although the greater portion of this work consists of disconnected collectanea, and these again of גמטריאות, נוטריקון, סופי תבות, ראשי תבות and such like, it is nevertheless of considerable value for the following reasons. In the first place, it comments on the really difficult passages of Rashi. Then, very many of the explanations by the earlier Rabbis and many of the גמטריאות it gives are not to be found in the Minchath Yehudah and "Ba'al Hatturim" (the ordinary repositories for similar literature). Then again, we become, by this work, acquainted with names, which if otherwise not entirely unknown, are certainly not named in connexion with literature of this kind. And, finally, we find here readings of Rashi, not ordinarily to be found (e.g. leaf 106a, &c.).

The economy of this work is as follows. After having given the ordinary וא"ת, or ותימא, to which the well-known וי"ל succeeds, the author gives the גמטריאות, &c., and finishes up with a באור המלות, in which the difficult phrases of Rashi are explained by means of Targum, Midrash and Talmud in general, the technical terms being given בלע"ז, i.e. in the Italian vernacular (of which we have here several hundreds). The Decalogue of Exodus has a באור הלוחות (63b), and occasionally the author gives an additional remark under the name of הגהה (59b) and תוספתא (75a), &c. An antichristian passage of some interest is also to be found here (45a); comp. Berliner, Pletath Soferim (Breslau, 1872, 8vo.), p. 35. The Parshiyyoth ואתחנן, עקב, ראה and כי תבא are not commented on (see, however, later).

In addition to the Tanna debe Eliyyahu, Rabbenu Se'adyah, Rab Hai Gaon, Rabbenu Chananeel (37a), the 'Arukh, Ibn 'Ezra, Rashbam, R. Yoseph קרא, Rabbenu Tam, Maimonides (87a), R. Elyaqim, R. Chizqiyyah b. Manoach, R. Yehudah b. Shemuel (החסיד), R. Yehudah (simply, 53b), R. Mosheh of Coucy, R. Abraham of Coucy (74b), Nachmanides and R. Shemaryah of Crete (מניגרופונטיש; see p. 48 of this Catalogue), our author quotes also:

(1) His teacher, whom he does not further specify.

(2) מהרי"ק (R. Yoseph Qolon b. Shelomoh טרבוט, 70b; see p. 85 of this Catalogue).

(3) הרב הגדול כמו"ה אבא מרי זל"ה (44b and 66a; who is probably the father of R. Eliyyah Chalphan, fl. 1550).

(4) ספרדי אחד, whom he does not further describe.

(5) The ג"א (גור אריה, i.e. R. Löwe b. Betzaleel? 39b; see Numbers 41 and 42 of this Catalogue).

(6) ה"ר הושעי' (63a).

(7) R. חיון (which of the many of this name?).

(8) מפי חכם גדול (65b).

(9) The Ba'ale Haqqabbalah (72b).

This MS. seems to be an autograph.

A second hand gives, on the numerous pages left blank by the first scribe, additional literature much in the style of the original author. This matter is given sometimes under the name of הגהה or תוספתא, and sometimes under the name of extracts. The second author's or collector's name is R. Yehudah (40b; see next Number of this Catalogue). He is, like the original author and scribe, an Italian, as may be seen from his hand and the בלע"ז, which latter are, though not as numerous as his predecessor's, still plentiful enough to confirm this fact. This scribe has also provided the MS., the original portion of which he has re-inked in various places, with Arabic numerals, to insure the correctness of the גמטריאות, both those given by his predecessor as well as those by himself. The half-brackets to mark the separate passages of the original MS., and the hand to draw the reader's attention to a valuable passage, are also his work. But the chief interest attaching to this scribe's work is to be found in the anti-christiana it contains, and which, though sometimes identical with those given in the before-named Pletath Soferim, are here more correctly given[1].

The following are the authorities and works quoted by the author, in addition to such as are identical with those that had been named by the original author:

(1) The Zohar (a portion of the extracts from which is given in Hebrew);

(2) R. David Qimchi;

(3) Rabbenu Yesha'yah (see p. 53 of this Catalogue);

(4) The Tzaphenath Pa'neach; (5) The Gan;

(6) R. Yaa'qob b. Asher b. Yechiel (from whose פי' התורה, or טעמי המסורת, he borrows various passages for the last three out of the four[2] Parshiyyoth in Deuteronomy which had been left without a commentary by the original author);

(7) R. בחיי b. Asher; (8) The Chinnukh;

[1] E.g. the unintelligible מושר, which Berliner (p. 34, כ) emends into מאשה, and which must be as unsatisfactory afterwards as it was before, is simply מישר, i.e. מישראל as is here (leaf 118a) distinctly given. The mistake in the MS. before Berliner, originated no doubt in the י being elongated into a ו and the stroke after the ר being left out. (Felix qui potuit rerum cognoscere causas!) According to this MS. this antichristian passage is to be found in the books צפנת פענח and הגן.

[2] There is a heading on leaf 116a, which shows that this scribe intended also to give for ואתחנן extracts from the Ba'al Hatturim; a promise, however, which was never fulfilled.

(9) The 'Aqedath Yitzchaq; (10) The Tzeror Hammor;

(11) The Mizrachi (as he believes, לפי דעתי);

(12) R. Yonah בקלם (46[a]); (13) R. Yoseph Hakkohen;

(14) R. Simchah b. Shelomoh of Ashkenaz (32 ; see next Number of this Catalogue);

(15) R. Abigeder;

(16) R. Asher Ashkenazi (51[b], upper margin; this last word is crossed through and replaced by Tzarephathi). These last three were contemporaries of the author.

The following pages are yet entirely blank (not to speak of most of those that are so partly only): 1[b] (1[a] having now an entry, that July 15, 1525, the locust visited Monte אלבורו and the road of סיניגאלייה [Sinigaglia], besides various medical recipes for headache and intermittent fever, of the efficacy of which the writer is so convinced, that he says: ודבר ברור אין צריך מופת), 22[a], 29[b], 43[a], 54[a], 58[a], 76[b], 77[a], 84[b], 98[b], 99[b], 101[a], 108[b], 114[b], 115[b], 116[a], and 117[a].

Leaf 45[a] has an erased antichristian passage, re-written by a third hand; no doubt, an owner, who must have been an Italian of the middle of the xviith century.

Leaf 21[a] has פירוש על פירוש רש"י עה"ת by an Italian hand, also of the xviith century, though somewhat later than the foregoing. The same page has the Library-mark, ב' ל"א, which identifies this MS. as having belonged to the father of the physician Samuele della Volta of Mantua (see p. 39 of this Catalogue), whilst the חדושים על פירש"י עה"ת כ"י, on the label on the back, belongs to that Samuele himself. The above Library-mark also occurs on leaf 1[b].

The censor's entry on leaf 21[a] (lower margin) shows that this MS. was in 1634 already defective; this entry is partly in Italian and partly in Latin, and runs thus: Rivisto il di 31 Agosto 1634, presente me Za (Fra ?) Mori Avelio de mandato R[mi] Inq[ris].

The before-specified defects excepted, this MS. is in good condition.

[Library-mark, Add. 404; bought in 1867 from Ḣ. Lipschütz.]

No. 44.

Paper, in quarto, $7\frac{5}{8}$ in. × $5\frac{5}{8}$ in.; 298 leaves, mostly 4-sheet quires, 30 lines; Rabbinic character, Italian handwriting of the xvith century.

[פרושים על התורה ודברים שונים לחכמים שונים]

Commentaries on the PENTATEUCH and other matters by various authors.

1. [לקוטים על פרשת בראשית ופסוקים אחרים בתורה ממחברים שונים]

COLLECTANEA ON THE PERICOPE בראשית AND SOME OTHER VERSES OF THE PENTATEUCH, TAKEN FROM VARIOUS AUTHORS.

These occupy leaves 1[a]—12[b], and contain the following pieces:

(1) [פרוש מלת בראשית]

Explanation of the word בראשית, beginning:

בראשית אין לשון אחרית אלא בזמן והזמן נופל עם התנועה היומית....

and ending:

כי העדר האור החשך וטעמו לגזור ולשום גבול וכו׳...

This explanation is similar to, if not identical with, one to be found in a MS. in the possession of Carmoly, and which is described by Kirchheim in Frankel's *Monatsschrift*, IV. p. 108. Comp. also Auerbach in Geiger's *Jüd. Zeitschrift*, IV. p. 299, Note, and Steinschneider, *ibid.* VI. p. 126. (Leaf 1[a].)

(2) [מעשה בראשית]

Essay on the prominent acts of the creation.

Begins (leaf 1[a]):

בראשית ברא אלהי׳ . ר׳ בו פתח ביום ההוא כרת ה׳ את אברם ברית לאמר
בחמשה ענינים נאמר הברית. אחד הוא ברית (הבשר או המילה) שנ׳ בו והיתה
בריתי בבשרכם לברית עולם . השנית ברי׳ הקשת...

Ends (leaf 8[a]):

...הה״ד עושה מלאכיו רוחות עשה לא נאמר אלא עושה שהוא עושה בכל־יום:

This essay contains nothing, which in its isolated ideas and links could not be traced to the Talmudim, Midrashim, the Zohar (which is here given both in the original and in Hebrew), the Tiqqunim, the קנה, &c.; as a whole, however, it is new and of considerable interest. It imitates successfully the language of the ancient Rabbis, and the interpretation reaches from Gen. i. 1—7. It is, probably, the work of an Italian Rabbi, and belongs, perhaps, to the very author of 2, 4, &c. below. Attached to this is a (תוספת), beginning (leaf 8[a]):

הפסוק הראשון של מעשה בראשית....ברא אלקים את ס״ת אמת...

and ending:

...וזהו הפן הראשון של ראש דברך אמת

(3) [לקוטים על רש״י על פרשת בראשית]

Collectanea on Rashi on the pericope בראשית.

These contain sundry remarks on Rashi's explanation of Gen. iv. 5 and 15. (Leaf 8[a].)

(4) [נוסחא אחרת [מפרוש מלת בראשית

Another mode of explaining the word בראשית, beginning:

בראשית יש שואלין למה תחלת התורה בְ ולמה שואלין והנה מלת בראשית תורה כי בְ ראשית או בית ראש...

and ending:

....הם ישראל שמקיימי׳ המצות בעולם הזה וזוכין בעולם הבא . לא מצאתי יותר .

This explanation certainly excels in ingenuity all others regarding the transposition of the letters of this word, although it occasionally re-produces matter which we know from the "Ba'al Hatturim". The author having given, among others, several cabbalistic explanations without feeling any compunction at doing so, one is rather surprised to find that, on explaining that בראשית is equivalent to רב אשית, he should proceed:

סוד מופלא ירמוז בו לשר הפנים ואין זה מקומו...

Comp. 4, below. (Leaves 8ᵇ—9ᵃ.)

(5) [פרוש שמות הקדושים]

Explanation of the Most Holy Names, beginning:

אהיה בחשבון מרובע ר״ל שתרבע כל אות מאותיותיו כולל שני שמות מן הכנויים...

and ending:

...אם ירדוף אחד אלף ואלף אחד מפני גבורת אחד.

This explanation establishes, in a mathematico-cabbalistic way, the meaning of אהיה, the Tetragrammaton, אחד, אלהים &c., and the reason of their being called so. The author does this, partly in the style of Ibn 'Ezra in his Excursus to Exodus, and partly in the style of R. Yoseph Ibn גקטילא in his Ginnath Egoz, Sha'are Orah, Sha'are Tzedeq, &c., none of which, however, he mentions here. (Leaves 9ᵇ—10ᵃ.)

(6) [גמטריאות, ראשי תבות וסופי תבות]

Explanations by means of comparing the numerical value of words and developing, from the initials or finals of a word, a new word. In this way are here explained Ex. xxxii. 19, and 23; Num. xi. 27; Isa. xix. 1; Ex. xix. and xvii. 11; Ps. clxvii. 18, cvii. 20, and xcvi. 11; Ex. iv. 14, and iii. 13; Esther v. 4; Deut. xxx. 12. (Leaf 10ᵃ.)

(7) [באור מקצת סוד המספר להראב״ע]

Explanation of part of Ibn 'Ezra's mathematical Excursus in his commentary on Exodus.

Begins (leaf 10ᵇ):

כתב אב״ע כי בהתחבר אחת לאחת ישוב ראש המספר . פי אם תחבר אחת לאחת יהיו בְ ונקראו שנים ראש המספר...

Ends (*ibid.*):

...ולכן אם תעשה דבר אחד שיהיה ארכו ב̄ ורחבו ב̄ וגבהו ב̄ יעלו כלם כשבור שמנה . תם . אמר.

This explanation follows the text closely and is absolutely mathematical.

(8) [באור על הראב״ע בפרשת כי תשא]

Explanation of Ibn 'Ezra's commentary on the pericope כי תשא, beginning:

אמר אברהם המחבר כי השם הנכתב ואינו נקרא ככה הוא שם העצם והעצם הוא הכבוד . פירוש השם של ד׳ אותיות...

and ending:

...והוא אסמכתא למה שאנו מכנים שמו של הקב״ה במלת שמים כמו ויהי מורא שמים עליכם . תם זה הפירוש.

The explanation found in this anonymous piece is essentially identical with that given by R. Shelomoh Ibn Ya'ish the younger (MSS. Add. 400. 12, leaf 37[a], and Add. 510. 2, leaf 38[a]). The writer, however, does not acknowledge the source of his information, but in this he is not singular; see further under No. 47 of this Catalogue. (Leaves 11[a]—12[a].)

(9) [באור סוד גן עדן לר׳ שלמה ן׳ גברול לחכם אחד פלוני אלמוני]

The view of גברול on Gen. ii. 8—15, explained by an anonymous author.

Begins (leaf 12[a]):

בראשית אב״ע ודע כי כל מה שמצאנו הוא אמת וכן היה ואין בו ספק גם יש לו סוד כי מאור השכל יצא החפץ...והמלה כי מכח המלאכים יצא החפץ נשמת האדם...

Ends (*ibid.*):

...ולזה מיתתם נעלמת לכך תמצא בהם לקיחה:

The mystical passage here explained has been preserved by Ibn 'Ezra in his commentary on the Pentateuch. See the fragment of the שטה ראשונה on Genesis, published by Mortara in Otzar Nechmad, II. p. 218, and comp. also Steinschneider in Pletath Soferim, p. 45. The explanation given here is one more contribution to the many (see, for instance, MS. Dd. 4. 2), which profess to illustrate the famous passage; and a most interesting and sensible one it is.

2. [פרוש על פרוש רש״י על התורה לר׳ יהודה בן שלום הלוי?]

SUPERCOMMENTARY ON RASHI ON THE PENTATEUCH, BY R. YEHUDAH B. SHALOM HALLEVI (?).

13[a], *Genesis;* 42[a], *Exodus;* 52[b], *Leviticus;* 69[b], *Numbers;* 81[a], *Deuteronomy.*

Begins (leaf 13[a]):

עמ"י עש"ו בהנו"א פרשת בראשית . בראשית . קרשו ענין קרח וכפור ובלע"ז גלאצה . ירופפו ענין שבר . . .

Ends (leaf 96[b]):

. . . ומנלן דאקרי שמים כתיב הכא לרוכב בערבות וכתיב התם לרוכב (רוכב) שמים בעזרך ׳

The author seems originally to have intended to give only short explanations of the difficult words (מלות זרות) and phrases of Rashi (המורה 17[b]), in which the בלע"ז, in Italian, played a prominent part. He made afterwards, under the name of (תו'(ספות and הגהות, considerable additions, which fact alone accounts for the many irregularities in this commentary, where later things are earlier and earlier things later commented upon. These additions, which contain sometimes also direct explanations on the Pentateuch, are made, partly by applying the literature of the Targumim (in which our author is particularly well versed), Talmudim, Midrashim and later Rabbinical writers, and partly by applying exegetical matter belonging to himself. In this latter he digresses sometimes into a regular Derashah, in the so-called Melitzah-style (comp. leaves 18[a]—23[b], 34, 37[a], &c.). Taken as a whole this commentary is very good, and the numerous Le'azim are of the highest merit.

The author, apparently a physician (26[b]), was an Italian of the xvith century (91[b]), and his name was probably R. Yehudah b. Shalom Hallevi (61[b]). Like the second author and scribe of the preceding number (MS. Add. 404), his name is Yehudah, like him he mentions R. Simchah b. Shelomoh Ashkenazi as his contemporary (84[a]), like him he is very fond of Qabbalah[1] (24[a], 76[b], 94[b], &c.), and like him he uses constantly גמטריא and נוטריקון for purposes of explanation. Yet not only does the literature in both MSS. considerably differ, but even the style thereof is far from identical; in consequence of which facts one hesitates in declaring both authors to have been one and the same person. However, great as the neglect may be into which the author has fallen, so that his very name cannot now be fixed with certainty, there must have been a time when both he and his work were well known and looked upon as of considerable authority, as may be seen from the fact of our anonymous copyist continually referring to ס"א and נוסחא אחרת.

The authorities quoted in this work contain, with the exception of one, or perhaps two persons, no name not well known. The exceptions are the R. Simchah mentioned before and R. Mosheh of Matha-Mechasya, in whose

[1] He sees the effects of Qabbalah, where ordinary people would perhaps not see them; thus he says of שלש לשונות בחרדל (24[a], quoted by Rashi from the Gemara, T. B. Baba Metzi'a, leaf 86[b]), that it is a סוד עמוק מי ימצאנו!

name he gives an explanation of Deut. xv. 19, and who, perhaps, was his contemporary.

3. [פרפראות על התורה לרבנו יעקב בן אשר בן יחיאל]

PARPERAOTH on the PENTATEUCH, by R. YA'AQOB B. ASHER B. YECHIEL.

97ᵃ, *Genesis;* 119ᵇ, *Exodus;* 142ᵃ, *Leviticus;* 150ᵃ, *Numbers;* 157ᵃ, *Deuteronomy.*

Begins (leaf 97ᵃ):

עמ״י עמ״י עש״ו פירוש התורה לרבינו יעקב ז״ל בעל הטורים בן הרב רבינו אשר ז״ל והם טעמי המסורת ופרפראות וגמטריאות של כל סדר בהנו״א לק״י בראשית יש במדרש שלכך פתח בבית ולא באלף לפי שבית היא לשון ברכה...

Ends (leaf 165ᵇ):

...בגי חסר אלף שלא ידע איש את קבורתו ואפי׳ משה רבינו ע״ה אלא יחידו של עולם ברוך הוא וברוך שמו וברוך זכרו לעולם ועד אמן כן יהי רצון . תם ונשלם שבח לאל בורא עולם.

This work has been printed numerous times, both with and without the sacred text. On comparing this MS. with the matter to be found under the name of בעל הטורים in the Warsaw Bible edition of 1860 (the Lemberg and Hanover editions are not in the Library), we find that the remark חסר מההעתק (leaf 122ᵃ) is not justified, as nothing worth mentioning is there missing. On the other hand, however, this like the Warsaw edition, can scarcely be the whole work (בעה״ט הארוך), despite the assertion to be found on the label on the back of this MS. (see later).

4. [לקוטים על התורה]

COLLECTANEA on the PENTATEUCH.

166ᵃ, *Genesis;* 181ᵇ, *Exodus;* 203ᵇ, *Leviticus;* 213ᵃ, *Numbers;* 226ᵇ, *Deuteronomy.*

Begin (leaf 166ᵃ):

ליקוטים על החומש . בראשית . נוטריקון בתחלה ראה אלהים שיקבלו ישראל תורתו . ד״א בראש(י)ת (?) ולזה רמזו בראשית ולזה רמזו רבותינו ע״ה שיתא אלפא הווי עלמא...

End (leaf 233ᵃ):

...ואמר והסוד אך אלקים יפדה נפשי, רמז בזה אל ההשארות שהוא הדבוק האמתי . תם ונשלם שבח לאל בורא עולם.

These Collectanea consist chiefly of גמטריאות, נוטריקון and other matter kindred to that of the "Ba'al Hatturim", but are by no means confined thereto. There are to be found, in addition, a piece of מסרת (178ᵇ), the explanation of various pieces of Rashi, extracts from, and explanations of, Ibn 'Ezra, Nachmanides and sundry cabbalistic matters, some of which agree, nay, are almost identical, with the matter to be found in 1 above.

The author, or rather collector, is apparently identical with that of 1 and 2 (see leaves 172ª—177ᵇ, 187ª—198ᵇ, &c., where the same kind of Derashah in the same kind of Melitzah-style is to be found), and perhaps also with 5 below (where the same kind of literature is to be met with, and the same cabbalistical predilections manifest themselves). He is, in any case, a man who combined great familiarity with profane as well as sacred lore.

The following authorities and works, some of which are but little known, are quoted by him:

(1) ציצירונו and his work דיוינאציאוני (214ᵇ, Cicero, *de Divinatione*).

(2) ספרי זוטא (215ª, the matter is to be found in the Siphré before us).

(3) 'Arukh (passim).

(4) R. Yesha'yah (167ᵇ; see this Catalogue, p. 53).

(5) The Moreh (Maimonides, passim).

(6) החכם הרמב"ן (172ª, meaning Nachmanides as cabbalist; and הרמב"ן simply, passim).

(7) Franco (206ª, one of Ibn 'Ezra's commentators, and called Ibn רש"ף, by R. Shemtob b. Yehudah Ibn Mayor, see MS. Add. 433, passim, and Steinschneider in Geiger's *Jüd. Zeitschr.* VI. p. 122).

(8) Don Yoseph Ibn וקאר (232ᵇ, see Steinschneider in Ersch and Gruber's *Encyklopaedie*, Sect. 2, Theil 31, p. 100).

(9) R. Yitzchaq עראמה (189ᵇ, the author of the 'Aqedath Yitzchaq).

(10) R. Yehudah מכבי of Recanati (169ª, see MS. Add. 512).

(11) The author's own ספר הפשטים (also פי' פשוטים 204ª, 206ª, 233ª, &c.).

(12) His teachers (רבותי, without however specifying them by name, passim). It must also be remarked, that numerous explanations on Ibn 'Ezra on the Pentateuch, given anonymously, are by Shelomoh b. Ya'ish the younger (see MSS. Add. 400. 12 and 510. 2).

5. [לקוטים אחרים]

OTHER COLLECTANEA.

These occupy leaves 233ᵇ—257ᵇ, and contain the most heterogeneous matter, as follows:

(1) A disquisition on the sin in connexion with the golden calf, as recapitulated in Deut. ix. 7, &c. It begins:

זכור אל תשכח וכו' זה הפסוק כולל לכל הרעות שעשו ישראל במדבר...

In the course of this disquisition, R. 'Obadyah Sforno, who died after 1550, is here mentioned with the addition of ז״ל, i.e. as already dead. (Leaves 233[b]—234[a].)

(2) A calculation of the dimensions of the Tabernacle, beginning:

המשכן היה ק׳ על נ׳ וכשתכה (multiply) ק על נ (50 × 100) יעלו . . .

This is purely mathematical, and for the better understanding of the reader, Arabic numerals are used in many points of the process. (Leaves 234[b]—235[a].)

(3) A piece of the פרקי שירה (wherein the whole of nature is said to sing God's, the Creator's, praises in appropriate biblical verses). Here we have only the verses said to be recited by the heavens, the earth, leviathan, the fishes, streams and wells. (Leaf 235[b].)

(4) Notice of a Roll of the Pentateuch said to be found at Avignon and to be written on skins, and concerning which there is a tradition (?) that it was executed by Ezra himself. It begins (leaf 235[b]):

שמעתי כי נמצא בעיר אביניון ספר תורה ישן . . .

(5) Reconciliation of the apparently contradictory Solomonic verses in Prov. xviii. 22 and Eccl. vii. 26. It begins (leaf 235[b]):

שלמה המלך ע״ה אמר מצא אשה מצא טוב ובמקום אחר הוא אומר ומוצא אני מר ממות את האשה . . .

(6) Explanations of Ex. ii. 2, beginning (leaf 235[b]):

ראיתי באור על ויפן כה וכה שהיה עומד בספק . . .

(7) Testimony of the collector (or scribe) that the Rabbis of Mantua allowed prayers to be recited on a Sabbath for a person dangerously ill. (*ibid.*).

(8) Disquisition on, and explanation of, biblical verses.

a. Deut. xviii. 9, beginning:

בפרשת שופטים לא תלמד . . . גם זו מצוה מבוארת . . .

b. Deut. vii. 9, beginning:

בפרשת ואתחנן . וידעת . . . וידעת מיציאת מצרים . . .

c. Deut. iv. 19, beginning:

אשר חלק . . . כבר פירשתי אשר חלק . . .

These three pieces are anonymously given, but are extracts from Nachmanides' commentary. (Leaves 236[a]—237[a].)

d. Deut. iii. 25, &c., beginning:

בפרשת ואתחנן אעברה נא ... אמר המחבר ר׳ עמנואל ז״ל ראיתי להרחיב המאמר בזה הפסוק בעבור אשר ראיתי הטעות הגדול אשר נכנס בלבות האנשים והוא מה שיזכירוהו תמיד מענין משה רבינו ע״ה שיאמרו עליו שנתירא מן המות ...

This is, no doubt, an extract from the commentary on the Pentateuch by the celebrated poet 'Immanuel b. Shelomoh, a MS. of the whole of which is to be found in the De-Rossi collection at Parma[1]. (Leaves 237ᵇ—238ᵇ.)

(9) Explanation of the difficult talmudical passage (Babli, Chullin 60ᵇ) on Gen. i. 16. It begins:

ביאור על מאמר רז״ל ויברא אלהים את שני המאורות הגדולים ... אע״פ שהאמת הוא כפשוטו ממש שהחמה והלבנה שניהם מאורות גדולים ...

This, as is natural, is an allegorical explanation, and by no means to be rejected. From the conclusion it would seem that it formed the epilogue of a lecture. (Leaves 238ᵇ—239ᵃ.)

(10) Midrashic explanation of Ps. lxxviii. 38, beginning (leaf 239ᵇ):

והוא רחום ... עון יש לו ה׳ שמות עון פשע מעל ...

(11) Reconciliation between Ex. xx. 13 (Deut. v. 17), and Jer. xlviii. 10, beginning (*ibid.*);

כתיב לא תרצח וכתוב אחד אומר (ו) ארור מונע חרבו מדם ... זה שהוא נושא אשה זקנה ...

(12) Two matters in connexion with the services in the synagogue, beginning respectively (*ibid.*):

אין נופלין על פניהם אלא במקום שיש בו ס״ת ...

and האנשים שנושאין ילדיהן בבית הכנסת ...

(13) Questions and answers, mostly on ritual points. Three excepted, they commence all with ...למה, e.g. למה נהגו לומר בשבת פורים סוכת שלום They are different from those mentioned in this Catalogue, p. 57. (Leaves 239ᵇ—240ᵃ.)

(14) Midrashic explanations of the following biblical verses:

a. Ps. clxix. 5, beginning:

ירננו על משכבותם . אמרו חכמים חצר גדול יש למתים ...

[1] See "Commento sopra il Pentateuco (פי׳ התורה) del Rab. Emmanuele figlio di Salomone, secondo il cod. Derossiano 404, inedito ed unico, publicato da Pietro Perreau" in Merx' Archiv für wissensch. Erforsch. d. A. T., Erster Band, 1867—1869, pp. 363—384. Although Abbate Perreau says there "continua" there is nothing further to be found down to this day (Band II. Heft II. 1872).

b. Ruth i. 2, 4, 14, 12, 13 (in this order), ii. 2, beginning (leaf 240[b]):

מחלון וכליון לא כך שמם ולמה נק׳ שמו מחלון שהקב״ה מחה אותו מן העולם...

(15) Disquisition on the parallel passages of 2 Kings xvii. 37—xix. 7, and Isa. xxxvi. 22—xxxvii. 7, beginning:

בספר מלכים וגם בספר ישעיה ויבא אליקים...הנה יש בפסוקים האלה שאלות ראשונה איך סדר מעלות שלשת אלה עבדי המלך חזקיה...

and ending:

...להאמין בה׳ ובישעיהו עבדו וביאור יתר הדברים והמלות אשר בפסוקים האלה תקח מדברי החכם אבארבאנילו.

It will be seen, from Don Yitzchaq Abarbanel being called "Abarbanelo," that the author of this must have been an Italian; and indeed, this little disquisition has other Italian terms also, e.g. מאייור דומי (Majordomo), סיקריטאריאו (Secretario), &c. (Leaves 242[a]—243[b]; 241 being blank.)

(16) [לכבוד האמת ולחרפת השקר]

Essay in praise of Truth and depreciation of Untruth, beginning:

שבח אל האמת וגנות אל הַשקר. מה נמרצו אמרי יושר ושמעו אמרי הקדמונים כי נעמו...

and ending:

...אך גם מלספר שמועה יקשה על שמעה להאמין אותה פן כשמעה שיאמר דבר שיהיה אצלם כמעט מכת הנמנעות יחזיקוהו לבדאי ושקרן ונקלה לעיניהם:

This essay, resting on the argument that אמת consists of the first, middle and last letters of the alphabet (see MS. Dd. 14. 10. 2, leaf 1[a]), develops this and other kindred matters, as בגד, &c. most ingeniously, with the purpose of shewing the praiseworthiness of Truth and the blameworthiness of Untruth. It is written in the before-mentioned Melitzah-style, and seems to have been a lecture, or the latter part of one. It belongs, if we may judge from the style, to the collector himself; in any case it is most interesting. (Leaves 244[a]—247[b].)

(17) Explanations:

a. Of Prov. xxviii. 16, beginning:

משלי כ״ח ד׳ (so) נגיד חסר תבונות...הפסוק הזה קשה והמפרשים כתבו עליו איש הטוב בעיניו גם רד״ק האריך עליו ואומר אני שמלת חסד משמשת גם כן לרב מעשקות...

b. of the words צדק, רשע and their derivatives צדיק and רשע, beginning:

צדק. צדק נבדל מצוקה (מצדקה), כי צדקה נאמרת...

The author quotes the Ethics of Aristotle (probably the Hebrew version). He appears to have been acquainted with Latin. (Leaves 248[a]—249[a].)

(18) Four anecdotes about Diogenes, beginning:

כתב עוד דיאוגיני הפילוסוף שהאיש הצדיק והישר הוא חפשי . . .

These anecdotes are very interesting, but, except a few deviations, are known. (Leaves 249[a]—250[a].)

(19) Essay on the sojourn of Israel in the wilderness, beginning:

הנה האנשים אשר הכו בסנויר הפתיות יחשבו שאת אשר הניע ה׳ אבותינו במדבר . . .

This essay attempts to prove the superiority of the material and moral advantages of Israel's life in the wilderness over those of their life in the promised land. It is written in the Melitzah-style, and is not without merit. (Leaves 250[b]—252[a].)

(20) Explanation of Ps. xlv. 17, beginning:

תחת אבותיך . . . כל המפרשים פרשו הפסוק הזה דרך העברה ולא שתו אל לבם כמה מן היעוד וההצלחות נכללו בו . . .

In this explanation, also written in the Melitzah-style, the commentary of R. 'Immanuel (b. Shelomoh) on the Psalms is mentioned. (Leaves 252[b]—253[a].)

(21) Comparison between the spider and the merchant, beginning:

ואמרתי אני כמקרה העכביש גם אני יקרני . . .

This comparison is made in the Melitzah-style, and is both well conceived and executed. (Leaf 253[a]—253[b].) Leaf 254[a] has a heading identical with 238[b]; but the scribe, having found out that the matter had been given before, omitted to proceed further; and the leaves down to 257[b], inclusive, are blank.

6. [כתוב יושר דברי אמת]

On the Proper Forms of the Hebrew Alphabet.

Begins (leaf 258[a]):

בהנו״א אלו הם כל התיבות מהאלפא ביתא והספר הזה מפרש כל הדברים וא׳ מהם לא ישכח כל הקורא בו . ראשונה . א . נקודה ראשונה העליונה כמין יוד . . .

Ends (leaf (260[a]):

. . . כשתשים כל העשרות לאחדים :

This so-called book is the result of a combination of Midrash, Halakhah and Qabbalah, as will be best seen from the following authorities quoted therein:

(1) אלפא ביתא של ר׳ עקיבא (in letters ח and ט).

(2) רש״י (in letter ח). (3) ר״ת (in letters ה, ח and ט).

(4) רבינו שמחה (in letters ב, ז, ל and ש).

(5) חסיד (R. Yehudah, in letters א, ב, כ, ל, ף, צ and ת).

(6) יראים, also R. Eli'ezer of Metz, (in letters א, ט and פ).

(7) רוקח (in letter פ). (8) סמ"ג (in letters ה and ש).

(9) רמב"ן (in letter ו). (10) אור זרוע (in letter ת).

(11) הגהות מימניות (in letters ה, ח and ט).

(12) רא"ש (in letters ב and ה). (13) תמונה (in letters ל and ת).

(14) מהרי"ת (in letters ה and ח).

(15) ואני...ראיתי or ואני המחבר קבלתי (in letters ל, ם, פ, ק and ת).

(16) בעל תפלין בחבור שלו (in letter ש).

7. [ערכי מלות קשות בתלמוד]

DIFFICULT TALMUDICAL WORDS AND PHRASES EXPLAINED.

Begin (leaf 260[a]):

בהנו"א מלות זרות (בתלמוד). אגסים אמונייגש בלע"ז אומן פי' מקיז דם...

End (leaf 294[b]):

...תתמרח. ער שתתמרח התבואה. פי' עד שמטהר (שתטהר) התבואה מן התבן ופי' מרח מלשון וימרחו על השחין.

This little book is of great value. Difficult words and phrases of Talmud (and Midrash, and occasionally also rare words of the Bible) are therein briefly explained. Sometimes there is also the Italian added to such explanations. The author makes judicious use of the Targumim, Rashi (passim, and to whom any French word, to be found here, belongs), the 'Arukh (in letters ז, ט, ל and ק, and from which the לשון יון on leaf 275[a], is probably taken), and Maimonides (to whose Mishnah-commentary the לשון ישמעאל on leaf 270[b] can be traced). There is, unfortunately, a little disorder in the arrangement observable, particularly in the letters ב and ג; and now and then one and the same thing is given twice, or even thrice. Numerous pages are also either entirely or partly blank.

8. [ערכי מלות ארמיות וקשות במקרא]

DIFFICULT ARAMAIC WORDS AND PHRASES IN THE BIBLE EXPLAINED.

Begin (leaf 295[b]):

מלות זרות מספר דניאל אזדא הלכה וכן בדברי רז"ל...

End (leaf 298[a]):

...לאסורין פי' או לעונשו ממון או לאוסרו בבית הסהר:

These explanations comprise the books Daniel and Ezra, and are identical with the greater part of the Appendix (באור המלים) of R. David Qimchi's *Shorashim*, but with the occasional addition of the בלע״ז, in Italian, thereto.

9. [לקוטים קטנים]

SHORT COLLECTANEA.

These occupy leaf 298[b], beginning:

שמות שבעה (שבע) חכמות ...

and ending:

... ויען איוב ופזים.

These Collectanea consist of two groups: (1) containing a number of technical terms of philosophy, theology, astronomy, &c. in Hebrew and Italian; and (2) the various names in Hebrew for heaven, soul, lot, lion, together with the explanation of the word Pizmon.

The last leaf (298[b]) has the name of the well-known Italian censor Dominico Gerosolomitano.

The following marks of ownership are to be found in this MS.:

(1) זה קנין כספי ידעיה בכמ׳ ר׳ ליאונתי ז״ל (Leaf 1[a]). The words ידעיה בכמ׳ ר׳ ליאונתי have been inked out, and the last word is consequently uncertain.

(2) (Perugia) זה שמי לעולם יהודה שמואל בכמ״ר אלייה ז״ל מפירושה (Leaf 1[a]). This whole entry has been crossed through, but is yet legible. This is not the Yehudah Shemuel of Perugia mentioned before in this Catalogue (p. 72, Note 1), although they were probably related to one another.

(3) The Library-mark ה׳ ה׳ כ״ז, which identifies this MS. as one of the books which at one time belonged to the father of the Physician Samuele della Volta. It occurs on leaf 1[a], and on the fly-leaf at the beginning. It is this owner, probably, who has added the word מהשרש after דניאל in the heading on leaf 295[b].

(4) The פירושים עה״ת כ״י, on the label on the back, is in the handwriting of R. Marco Mortara (see p. 39 of this Catalogue). This title was afterwards incorrectly amplified by the seller into:

פירושים (שונים מלוקטים מראשונים) עה״ת (ועל מדרשים פי׳ בעל הטורים הארוך שבח האמת וגנות השקר בסדר א״ב וגם פי׳ המילות בסדר א״ב) כ״י.

The MS. is in very good condition.

[Library-mark, Add. 396; bought in 1867 from H. Lipschütz.]

No. 45.

Paper, in octavo, $5\frac{3}{4}$ in. × $4\frac{1}{8}$ in.; 32 leaves, 4-sheet quires, 23 lines; mixed (Rabbinic and current) character, Sephardic handwriting of the XVIIIth century.

[פרוש על פרוש רש"י על התורה לחכם ספרדי פלוני אלמוני]

Supercommentary on Rashi on the PENTATEUCH by an anonymous Sephardic Rabbi; incomplete.

Begins (leaf 1[a]):

בראשית... אין המקרא... משום דאי אפשר לפרש מלת בראשית כמשמעה ענין התחלה ותהיה סמוכה למלת ברא מפני שאי אפשר שתהיה סמוכה בפועל שעבר גם אי אפשר שתהיה סמוכה במלה חסרה כמגיד מראשית אחרית...

Breaks off (leaf 27[a]):

....וא"ת ולמה לא פירש מלת הכזונה כמשמעה הנפקרת לזנות ויהיה פירוש את אחותינו כדלעליל (כדלעיל) יש לומר מפני שלא יוכל לפרש את עם אחותינו אלא כשיוסיף מלת עם על מלת הכזונה לומר הכמו עם זונה יעשה עם אחותינו ואינו יכול להו׳ ׀

Although this commentary is neither old nor original (see later), it is much to be regretted that we have scarcely a fifth part of what it probably was in its entirety (see leaf 18[b], where it refers to this commentary on Num.). The author possesses great familiarity with the literature of the Bible, the Talmudim and Midrashim, and the writers thereon, together with a thorough knowledge and appreciation of Hebrew grammar, as well as also considerable critical acumen, so that, in spite of his predilection for midrashic matter, he does not lose himself therein. He is fully aware of the importance of good editions, and the various readings to be found therein; and occasionally he tells us what readings in the Targum and Rashi he had before him and where he found them. See leaves 13[a], 17[b], 18[a], 18[b], 19[a], 19[b] (כן מצאתי בספר רש"י שנדפס בקושטנדינא[1]), 22[b], &c.

[1] We may, by the way, throw light on a curious passage in Rashi and his commentators, which has given Berliner, his latest editor, and many others before him, some trouble. The passage is on Gen. xix. 36; and it is the reading of עדותן with a ד instead of the nonsensical ערותן with a ר. The phrase is then ...וראיה מב'ר, which is emended by Berliner into מת'׳, it being his impression

The following authorities (besides, of course, Rashi) are quoted by him:

(1) דרך המסורת (13ᵃ, 22ᵇ).

(2) The בעל הערוך (13ᵃ, 17ᵇ). (3) רשב״ם (3ᵇ, 6ᵃ).

(4) רבנו תם מארולייניש (R. Ya'aqob of Orleans, 11ᵇ). He is so surnamed to distinguish him from Rashi's grandson, R. Ya'aqob b. Meir of Rameru. R. Ya'aqob of Orleans was killed at London on the coronation-day of Richard Cœur-de-Lion, 1189.

(5) התוספות (11ᵇ).

(6) רד״ק, with or without the addition בשם אביו (2ᵇ, 20ᵃ, 21ᵇ).

(7) רמב״ן (6ᵃ, 11ᵃ, 13ᵃ, 21ᵇ twice, 24ᵇ, 26ᵃ; the הרב רבי משה בן, 24ᵃ, means the same; and the רמב״ם, 20ᵇ, is, no doubt, a mistake for the same).

(8) חזקוני (13ᵃ, 19ᵃ, twice, 19ᵇ, twice). (9) רשב״א (18ᵇ).

(10) בעל הפליאה (2ᵇ). (11) מזרחי (10ᵃ, 16ᵇ, 18ᵃ, 20ᵃ, 21ᵇ).

(12) עין יעקב (23ᵇ). (13) צרור המור (23ᵇ, 26ᵇ).

(14) פריצול (R. Abraham Farissol) on Job (1ᵇ).

(15) שלחן ערוך (16ᵇ).

Thus it will be seen that our author could not have written before the xvith century. But we have reason to believe that he belonged to an even later period, that his name was R. Yoseph b. Mosheh Zakkai, that he was Rabbi of the congregation of Cochin, in India, and author of various other compilations of Halakhic import. (See, for instance, MS. Oo. 1. 33. 3.)

The copyist of this MS. is, apparently, identical with that of MS. Oo. 1. 35. 6, &c., whose name is there distinctly given as Levi b. Mosheh בלילא.

A later Sephardic hand, which wrote a piece of the Rashi-text on Gen. xxxii. 5, is to be found on leaf 25ᵇ.

This MS. having been obtained by Dr Buchanan from the Jews of Cochin, who, because they had no practical use for it, had placed it in their "Record Chest," it will surprise no one that it is in a rather precarious condition. Thus leaf 1 is much injured, whilst the other leaves are much soiled and stained. Leaves 28—29, no doubt blank, are wanting; leaves 27ᵇ, 30—32 are blank.

[Library-mark, Oo. 6. 71. 1; presented in 1809 by Dr Buchanan.]

that מב׳ר ought to be solved into מבראשית רבה, when and where, however, the reference would be wrong. But the matter is very simple. מב׳ר is the abbreviation of מבוררת (the ו between the ב and the ר having been in a mistake changed by a scribe into a stroke, while the stroke at the end fell out entirely). The reading therefore is: ...עדותן בדלת לשון עדות וראיה מב(ו)ר(רת) ואלה בתולי בתי ... עדות בתי. Compare leaf 19ᵇ of this MS.

No. 46.

Paper, in quarto, $8\frac{3}{4}$ in. × $5\frac{3}{4}$ in.; 392 leaves, 6-sheet quires, 19—28 (the later portions mostly 24) lines; Rabbinic character, partly oriental Sephardic, partly Greek Sephardic and partly Italo-Greek, handwriting, ranging from the middle of the XIVth to the middle of the XVth century.

[פרוש על התורה לר׳ אברהם בן מאיר אבן עזרא יליד טוליטולה]

Commentary on the PENTATEUCH, by R. Abraham b. Meir Ibn 'Ezra (הראב״ע[1]) of Toledo; defective.

Leaves 1—13, wanting; leaf 14ª, *Genesis;* 75ᵇ, *Exodus* (97, 108, 189, wanting; 194, blank); 252ᵇ, *Leviticus;* 301ª, *Numbers* (310—313, wanting); 345ª, *Deuteronomy;* 392ª, the author's concluding poem, preceded by the scribe's, or the editor's, rhyme; 392ᵇ, record, by the editor, of the author's day of death, succeeded by a mnemosynon of the latter.

Begins (leaf 14ª, on Gen. iv. 22):

לך כמותם וכמוהו ויקח האיש נזם זהב ...

Ends (leaf 392ª):

... המורא הגדול· מעמד הר סיני·
חסלת פר״ש וזאת הברכה, בעזרת אשר לו המלוכה,
נגמר פשט התוֹרה שחבר החכם
אבן עזרא, בעוז צור רואה ולא יֵרָא·

[1] הראב״ע, i.e. HArab Rabbi Abraham Ben 'Ezra; see this Catalogue, pp. 51, 61, 105, 106, &c. He is also called אב״ע, i.e. either Abraham Ben 'Ezra, or IBn 'Ezra; more probably the latter (ibid. p. 55). He is also spoken of as ב״ע (ibid. p. 90), and finally also as א״ע (ibid. p. 57, &c.). Yet, it must be confessed, that ordinarily he is spoken of as "Aben Ezra," and that all these abbreviations are but rarely used, even by the learned. This is owing, besides to other causes, chiefly to two. In the first place, Ibn 'Ezra has never been a very popular author (such as Rashi, Redaq and others), and in the second place, the pronunciation of the abbreviation has too little certainty (Harabe', Haraba', Harave, Harava, &c.) to be commonly used. This fact will somewhat qualify, although it will not entirely do away with, C. Taylor's censure of Friedländer, for having neglected to mention in the introduction to his translation of Ibn 'Ezra's commentary on Isaiah, the abbreviation ראב״ע (Academy, 1 Dec. 1873, p. 451).

לדור דורים שנותיך אלהי, וחיינו מתי מספר ספור(ים.)
ואתה חי וקיים לעדי עד, בלי תכלה וכל דורות ודורים(.)
ושוכן עד וקדוש רם ונשגב, ועושה טוב ומטיב לישרי(ם.)
(ו)מדריכם בדרך הישרה, ותקראם ישרים גם טהורים.
בחסדך אל אלהים למדני, לתורתך ואבין הסדרים.
ועזרני להתחכם בדתך, ואדעם יהו על פי סדורים.
(כ)שם יה שעזרתני בטובך, וכתבתי לשר כל הספרים.
והשלמתיו בארבע׳ אלפים, תשע מאות וגם שבע ועשרי׳
(ש)נת ששית למחזור רֹסֹ ברומי, שנת רצון שנת תפקוד אסורים.
(ב)יום ששי ביום טובה ושמחה, לאדר בו עשית נס לעברים.

וביום שני בראש חדש הראשון שנת תתקכה לפרט נפטר ר׳ אברהם אבן עזרא ז״ל והוא בן ע״ה שנה ושם לעצמו סימן בכתב ידו ביום שנפטר, ואברם בן חמש שני׳ ושבעים שנה בצאתו מחרון אף ייי.[1]

Ibn 'Ezra is more than merely known to, he is very famous in, the learned world, both Jewish and Christian; and his commentary on the Pentateuch, in particular, has been printed numerous times[2]. Nevertheless, or, perhaps, because of these facts, we feel persuaded that the student of Hebrew literature will read with considerable interest the following description of a MS., lately acquired by the University, containing as it does that Pentateuch-commentary, with, however, many noteworthy additions and peculiarities. Not that we think that this MS. is necessarily a unique one; on the contrary, we have reason to suspect, that MSS. of the Vatican (xxxix. and ccxlix. 3; see Footnote 1 below), of the Paris Library (New Catalogue, No. 177, p. 19) and of the Court-Library of Vienna (No. 39;

1 This subscription, although not entirely free from mistakes, makes good sense; and is, on the whole, more correct than either the subscriptions to be found in the Vatican MSS. (Assemani, pp. 29 and 209), or that of the MS. preserved in the Court-Library of Vienna (Krafft and Deutsch, xxxi. p. 34). For further information see Excursus II.

2 Without the biblical text it has been printed, at least, three times (Napoli, 1488, Folio; Qostandinah, i.e. Constantinople, 1514, Folio; Amsterdam, 1721, Folio); with the Bible-text, however, times too numerous to be specified here. The so-called *Brief commentary* on Exodus, the greatest part of which is embodied in this MS. (see our description a little later on), has been printed only once; comp. this Catalogue, p. 90.

see Footnote 1, as before), contain something kindred. But, as those MSS. have either never been properly examined, or, at all events, have not been fully described, we will give the results of a careful investigation of the volume before us; and these they are:

A.

Internal Matters in connexion with this MS.

a. The deviations from the text as extant in the printed editions amount to several hundreds, and consist partly of mere substitutions (sometimes of a phrase, a word, or even a letter only), partly of omissions and partly of additions.

1. Even the mere substitutions are of great importance, inasmuch as they often throw light on certain passages otherwise unintelligible[1].

2. The omissions are owing partly to accident, i.e. either to the forgetfulness of the immediate scribe, or to the fact of the copy before him being incomplete; and partly to design, i.e. either because the matter omitted was deemed altogether spurious, or because, although allowed to have originally belonged to Ibn 'Ezra, it was known to have been suppressed by him in the final recension[2]. In the former two cases the

[1] For instance, on Num. xiv. 2, the printed editions accessible to us have: וילנו מבנין נפעל מהפעלים השניים לנפעל שלם, which, as one will see, gives no proper sense. The fact is, that the last two words belong to verse 3, and instead of לנפעל must be read לנפל, which will be easily understood. We may on this occasion make one general statement that in this MS. קדמונינו, חכמינו, המעתיקים, &c. occur, and only very rarely (58^b, 119^b, 200^b, 307^a, 308^b, 321^a, 324^a, 332^a) the term רבותינו, which is so frequently to be found in the printed editions. That the former are the only authentic readings is vouched for both by the attacks on Ibn 'Ezra on account of these expressions, and by the reasons pleaded in defence of them by his commentators. Whether the substitutions of R. Yehudah for R. Yonah (65^a), Daniyyel instead of Raziel (130^b), Rab Mebasser Hallevi instead of Haggaon Hallevi (272^a), Rabbenu בחיי instead of Rabbenu Hai (387^a) and others, are really of value (although they are probably so), must be further investigated.

[2] To the last of these causes may be ascribed the omission of the rhymes before the majority of the weekly Parshiyyoth in Exodus, which are to be found in the printed editions. By the way we wish to correct a mistake into which Friedländer (commentary of Ibn 'Ezra on Isaiah, &c., London, 1873, 8vo., p. xvi.) fell with respect to the meaning of one of these rhymes. He hints in a romantic conjecture that (the aged, feeble, and poverty-stricken) Ibn 'Ezra, was alluding by חצי לבו (in the rhyme before יתרו) to his wife. Friedländer mistakes Ibn 'Ezra either for Virgil of old or Lenau of our own time. Now, of all the matter-of-fact Jews (who, although they are allowed by common consent to

successive and learned owners have supplemented the omission (see later), and in the latter two cases we are yet without a supplement.

3. But it is the additions which are of the greatest possible importance. These are of a twofold nature, viz. such as belong to Ibn 'Ezra himself and such as belong to others.

(1) As regards Ibn 'Ezra's own, they generally bear the mark of genuineness on the surface, and are of the most varied kind, comprising lexicography[1], grammar[2], bibliography[3], theology[4], liturgy (leaf 64[b]), astronomy[5], ethnography[6], &c. Although these additions are most nume-

make the best of husbands, are known never to indulge in such romantic talk, fit only for silly boys and girls) Ibn 'Ezra was the most unromantic. When he says that the expression man comprises woman also, adding the remark כי האיש ואשתו הוא האדם (on Ex. i. 1), he announces a higher principle, a religious truth, and not a piece of romantic nonsense. The הלך חצי לבו is, undoubtedly, an allusion to his illness, caused not only by hard study, but also, and chiefly, by want. It is only another poetical description of what he wittily calls (in his dedication to R. Mosheh b. Meir of his grammatical commentary on the Pentateuch) his מכה חדשה גם ישנה (Otzar Nechmad, II., p. 223), which was no love-sickness but unromantic—poverty! The latter part of the first line of this beautiful verse is evidently an allusion to Job xxx. 11 and the עיני is, no doubt, a misprint for עוני, which, in its turn was a copyist's mistake for עני. The correct reading of the whole would be thus:

נאם אברם אסיר תקוה . אשר פתח עני יתרו .
עדי הלך חצי לבו . וענה הנדד יתרו .
וזה פרש בפרשה . תחלתה דבר יתרו :

[1] On the lexicographical additions we have to remark that they comprise three languages, Hebrew, Aramaic, and Arabic. The additions in the first-named language are too largely represented in this MS. to require a single example; for one in Aramaic see an interesting instance on leaf 29[a] (on שרוך, Gen. xiv. 23), and for one in Arabic see leaf 78[b] (on פרוכים, Ex. i. 13).

[2] Grammar is, as is known, our author's forte. Ibn 'Ezra declares of himself in his introductory rhymes to be bound by the ties thereof (לאברהם.... .... השר , ובעבותות הדקדוק נקשר....). The additions, on this head, are too numerous to be recounted.

[3] To give only one example, see 23[b], where his יסוד is here called יסוד הדקדוק; but there are also numerous other instances.

[4] See particularly the antichristiana, leaves 32[b], 46[a], &c.

[5] See leaves 339[b]—340[a], on Num. xxviii. 15. That something similar to this explanation, which in a marvellous way reconciles the Rabbis (T. B. Chullin, 60[b]) with the astronomers (on the relation of the moon to the sun), was to be found in the סוד העבור, is testified to by Ibn מטוט (MSS. Add. 1015. 2, leaf 71[b], and Add. 518, leaf 64[a]).

[6] See leaf 360[a], where on Deut. iv. 1, he says וכן ראינו ברומי רבתא.... and leaf 369[a], where on Deut. xxii. 22, he says: משפט הערלים להישראלים שוה (comp. the so-called Margalioth Tobah, leaf 145[a], and the commentators ibidem).

rous on Exodus, where from i. 13 to xxiii. 13 (and possibly xxxii. 1) a considerable part of the באור ... הקצר (ed. by Reggio; see above) is very skilfully interwoven with the ordinary commentary, they extend over all the five books, having even on Exodus whole passages the original existence of which cannot be traced to the so-called Short Commentary. Over and above these must be mentioned as also belonging to our author, the first two out of three treatises, or essays, which are to be found between the rhyme after the last weekly Parashah of Exodus (פקודי) and the end rhyme for the whole of that book[1].

a. The former of these essays commences (leaf 242):

יש במועד עצרת דבר לתמוה שהוא כולל הרבנים והמינים...

and ends (leaf 244ᵃ):

...ואילו לא היה לנו רק הקבלה הנגמרה מפי קדושי עליון היה מספיק לנו ואף כי הכת' יעיד לנו כי כל דבריהם אמת. ככה העתקתי במכתב (ממכתב) החכם כי שפתיו ישמרו דעת ״

The authenticity of this essay on Lev. xxiii. 11, although it is given here abruptly and without the smallest advertisement that it belonged to Ibn 'Ezra, is secured by the following facts. In the first place we read in the course thereof (leaf 243ᵃ) ...ואני אברהם אומ' כי פסח השם... and in the next place we have the testimony of one of the earliest commentators of Ibn 'Ezra to that effect. R. Shelomoh Ibn Ya'ish the younger, to whom this essay owes its preservation (see MS. 210. 2, leaves 49ᵇ—51ᵃ)[2] makes the assertion (ibid. leaf 51ᵃ), that he copied it from Ibn 'Ezra's own handwriting (ממכתב and not במכתב as here). As for ourselves we recognize in its every expression the diction of our far-famed author, and believe it besides to be the only true interpretation of the verse[3].

β. The latter of these essays commences (leaf 244ᵃ):

לך יוי הגדולה והגבורה ״ דע כי גדולת השם נשגבה מדעת חכמי לבב...

[1] For the author of these rhymes, which commence with the weekly Parashah משפטים (leaf 203ᵇ), and which are of no great value in themselves, see A, a, 3 (2) *β*.

[2] In MS. Add. 400. 12, leaves 45ᵃ—46ᵇ, this whole passage is very corruptly given.

[3] We may remark by the way that the difference in the interpreting this verse is not only the watchword of Rabbanites and Qaraites now, but was also one of the Pharisees and Sadducees of old, and was only second to the other one of immortality or resurrection; see T. B. Menachoth 65ᵃ; Matthew xxii. 23—32, Mark xii. 18—27 and Luke xx. 27—38. On the mistakes made on this point by Dean Alford with regard to the tradition of the Jews (in his New Testament for English Readers, Vol. I. p. 153), see Excursus III.

and ends (leaf 245ᵃ):

...כי השם שהוא נכתב ואינו נקרא הוא שם תפארתנו, כאשר פרשתי השם הנכבד.

This short essay is an explanation of 2 Chron. xxix. 11—13, which three verses have been used by many others, besides Ibn 'Ezra, as a convenient thread to string thereon cabbalistic doctrines. With our author they and their explanations formed the introduction either to his Excursus on the שם המפורש in Ex. iii. 15 or to that on the same subject in xxxiii. 23; more probably, however, the latter. The only evidence that this essay belongs to Ibn 'Ezra is that it is written in the style of his well-authenticated writings.

(2) As regards the additions by others, they may be conveniently classified under three heads, viz. either such as are to be found within the text and are supposed to belong to an anonymous disciple of our author; or such as are anonymously inserted after the last Parashah in Exodus, and at the end of certain other Parshiyyoth and books, whose author, however, can be traced either with certainty, or at least with high probability; and finally such as are to be found on the margins. As the marginal literature will be treated on below, in the paragraph on scribes and owners, we have to speak here only of the former two.

a. The first who made the remark that the so-called Long Commentary on Exodus did not belong to Ibn 'Ezra himself, but was the work of a disciple of his[1], was one of his most distinguished supercommentators, R. Yoseph b. Eli'ezer Hassephardi, the author of the צפנת פענח (see MS. Add. 510. 1, leaves 45ᵇ—46ᵃ). This Rabbi brought forward thirteen proofs in support of his view, the strongest of which is the *ninth*, in which he reminds the reader that in two places in Exodus (in the Excursus on iii. 15 and in the explanation of xii. 9) the writer must have been another than Ibn 'Ezra. Now this is quite true: not only the latter passage, which is also to be found in the printed editions, but the former passage also, for which the reader will look in vain there, is to be found in this MS.[2] (see leaf 88ᵇ and leaf 118ᵇ). Nevertheless, we must maintain that we cannot go the full length of this distinguished scholar, to deprive Ibn 'Ezra of the direct authorship of the פרוש הארוך on Exodus. This commentary is certainly in Ibn 'Ezra's own language, a language so peculiar that not even a disciple of his, and were he even of many years' standing (which none of his disciples

[1] Friedländer, in his otherwise instructive introduction (see above, p. 120, Note 2), p. xxv, forgets to state that this fact was already mentioned by our R. Yoseph. See מרגליות טובה, leaf 40ᵇ in the preface of the author of the Ohel Yoseph (under which name an extract from our R. Yoseph's work is given there), and comp. also Number 51 of this Catalogue below.

[2] For an inference of some interest to be made from this fact, see the paragraph on the use made of this MS. towards the end of this description.

ever were, or in fact, ever could be, owing to his continual peregrinations) could absolutely imitate. The utmost that can be admitted we will allow, viz. that these two and a few other phrases, are remnants of explanatory remarks made earlier or later, on the margins by teachers of, and commentators on, Ibn-'Ezra-literature, which have crept into the text afterwards[1]; an accident very often to be met with in Hebrew works, and one which is not unfrequent even in non-Hebrew works.

β. As stated before, there are to be found between the rhyme of the last Parashah of Exodus and the end-rhyme for the whole of that book three essays or short treatises, the first two of which only can be ascribed to Ibn 'Ezra, while the last belongs to somebody else.

This last essay commences (leaf 245ᵃ):

ודע כי הא׳ יסוד כל המספר כי ממנו יחל להיות כל המספרים כי לא יתכן לומ׳ בג׳ ...

and ends (leaf 252ᵃ):

... נמצא מספר השוה במעלה הרביעית שהם אלפים. והם ח׳ אלפי׳ וקכח״ ועל זה הדרך עשה לכל המעלות עד אין קץ״

This is an explanation of the famous Excursus by Ibn 'Ezra on Ex. iii. 15 (on the Tetragrammaton; see above)[2]. It is here anonymously given, but belongs to R. Shelomoh Ibn Ya'ish the younger, from whose supercommentary on Ibn 'Ezra on the Pentateuch it is an extract (see MSS. Add. 400. 12, leaves 22ᵇ—29ᵃ, and Add. 510. 2, leaves 20ᵇ—25ᵃ). To this explanation is attached an arithmetical Table (of the Hebrew Alphabet) in illustration of the foregoing. In the just-mentioned two MSS. such a Table is not to be found; nevertheless there can be little doubt that it belongs to our R. Shelomoh, even as the verses, or rather rhymes, at certain Parshiyyoth and books belong to him. (On the influence of this R. Shelomoh on the work as contained in this MS. see above p. 122 and below p. 125.)

b. Summing up all matters in connexion with the internal economy of this MS. the following are our impressions (we call them impressions only as, in part, they cannot be elevated into absolutely scientific convictions, because they cannot be mathematically demonstrated; they are however moral convictions).

[1] See for instance 34ᵃ, where in the text a ס״א occurs, and 343ᵇ, where in the text a long passage superscribed גליון occurs, and which is signed א״ב. For other arguments see Reggio in Kerem Chemed, IV. pp. 97—110. That Reggio did not entirely remove all the difficulties that beset this question, was owing simply to the fact of his not knowing the whole extent of them.

[2] This Excursus is also known under the name of סוד המספר or יסוד המספר or המספר simply (MSS. Add. 510. 2, leaf 20ᵇ, and 30ᵃ; Add. 400. 12, leaf 22ᵇ), and סוד השם (MS. Add. 510. 1, leaf 45ᵇ), &c.

(1) The whole MS., although ranging over a hundred years, was executed after one and the same model.

(2) That model, as far as the commentary is concerned, was either a direct, or, only by one or two links, indirect, copy made from the commentary as copied by Ibn 'Ezra's disciple and collated with Ibn 'Ezra's own handwriting.

(3) That MS. of Ibn 'Ezra's own hand contained the final, and consequently only authentic, recension.

(4) The almost direct copy so obtained was provided with a few marginal, and several other more extensive, notes, containing literature which either originally belonged to Ibn 'Ezra or to his annotators.

(5) The chief of these annotators was no less a personage than R. Shelomoh Ibn Ya'ish the younger, a teacher of, and a commentator on, Ibn-'Ezra-literature.

(6) The explanations of the difficult passages of Exodus (iii. 15 and xii. 9) in which a stranger's language and hand are traced, are partly the immediate disciple's and copyist's, and partly this R. Shelomoh's.

(7) And finally, these, the long explanations on the mathematical Excursus, &c. were the nucleus of this R. Shelomoh's supercommentary.

B.

External Matters in connexion with this MS.

a. The MS. as it now stands (excluding annotators, of whom we shall speak later under owners, &c.) is the work of five scribes, three of which were contemporary, one preceding and one succeeding them, so that the MS. is the product of three different ages.

(1) The oldest, or original scribe, was an oriental Sephardi writing his part of the present MS., at the latest, towards the middle of the xivth century. Although we possess now only leaves 14—36, 38—47, 49—120, of his hand, there is little doubt that he originally copied the whole work. Anyhow we possess absolute evidence that he must have written more than we have now in our hands of him, as the ends both of leaf 120 and leaf 140 clearly show. This scribe has a hand bold and full of character, and the part written by him is of surpassing correctness. Owing to this exactness and legibility, the MS. probably served as a standard copy from which fresh copies were continually made. While this fact accounts by itself for the uniformity of the present MS. in spite of the many supplements of which it consists, it accounts also, in conjunction with another fact (that of the paper not having been even originally strong; see leaves 15^b, 36^a, &c.), for the original MS. becoming defective so early.

(2) When the original MS. had, towards the close of the xivth century, become defective, first at leaf 140 and then again at leaf 120, the defect was supplemented by three contemporary Greek Sephardic scribes, first from leaf 141, and, shortly afterwards, from leaf 121. It is peculiar to the first[1] of the three contemporary scribes, to whom a good deal of the supplement, including the very last leaf, is due, generally to represent the Most Holy Name by ייי, whilst the original scribe gives it by יןי, and the other scribes write it either in the same way, or יי, which last mode is sufficiently current in our own days[2]. The second of these hands will be best identified on leaf 227ᵃ, while the third[3] will be most easily identified on leaf 377ᵇ. Leaf 194 has been left blank by accident; as leaves 193 and 195 read on.

(3) The MS. having within the first half of the xvth century become defective between leaves 233 and 306, a hand supplemented this defect. This hand is of Italo-Greek training; it is very legible, and the literature copied by it, being also on the latest manufactured paper, has the best appearance in the whole MS.

b. The influence of the scribes has not been the only one on this MS.; that of the various owners has also been great.

1) A Greek Sephardic owner of the xivth century, probably a Rabbanite, has some important corrections on the margins, &c. of the oldest part of the MS. He is best identified on leaf 47ᵃ.

2) A Greek Sephardic owner of the second half of the xvth century, whose hand we might almost describe as the sixth of scribes, has rendered considerable services to this MS.

(1) by supplementing leaves 37 and 48;

(2) by supplementing, chiefly on the margins, but occasionally also in the body of the MS., portions of the Ibn-'Ezra-literature, which had been accidentally forgotten by the various scribes; and

(3) by giving remarks of his own, but in connexion with the literature before him; these remarks are not without value. From the way the supplements are executed we see that he must have had an Ibn-'Ezra-copy uniform with that of the scribe's; and from his own remarks again, that he knew Arabic (238ᵇ), and must have been not only a Rabbanite (260ᵃ), but also a Cabbalist (154ᵇ).

[1] This scribe executed also a MS. of Rashi on the Pentateuch; see MS. Add. 1014. 2, which was attached to the inside of the binding of the present copy.

[2] For an explanation of all these modes of representing the Tetragrammaton, see Excursus VI. of this Catalogue.

[3] This scribe has sometimes literature of his own under the name of חדוש הסופר; comp. leaf 331ᵇ, &c.

3) The MS. came at the end of the xvth, or at the commencement of the xvith century, into the hands of a R. Shelomoh b. Shemuel. See next paragraph.

4) In 1505 (הרס״ה ליצירה) the just-named R. Shelomoh sold it to R. Shelomoh b. Daniyyel. See leaf 392[b]. Both these successive owners were, apparently, Qaraites; they have left no literary marks on the MS.

5) Within the last years of the xvith century the MS. must have been in possession of R. Ya'aqob b. Shemaryah Hakkohen, a Qaraite of Crimean training, and who, if we may judge from his spelling Hakkohen הכוהן (see leaf 392[b]), was of no literary capacity.

6) In the year 1625 (השפ״ה) the congregation of קריקיר were the owners of this MS., having received it on, or after, the death of the before-named R. Ya'aqob, from his son R. Chanokh, who presented it to them for holy purposes, i.e. for study (הקדיש...לקהל קדוש קהל קריקיר). The man who wrote this notice and who was probably the Chakham or minister of the congregation, also provided the MS. with notes of a double nature, i.e. supplements of omissions and remarks of his own. If the latter are not of great, they are of some, value. The only thing we must guard against is his remark on leaf 309[b]: מכאן חסר עלה א׳; in reality, there are *four* leaves wanting. His remark on 265[a] was at one time true; now the transposition he mentions there, is rectified. (The last three lines to be found on leaf 392[b], which contain a sentence not entirely finished, seem to have been intended only as a repetition of the foregoing; they are probably no distinct mark of an owner.)

7) A seventh owner has left his mark of ownership on this MS. in a somewhat ludicrous way. About the xvii—xviiith century an anonymous Qaraite pasted over the names of the previous owners, and wrote, on the paper covering them, a note purporting to give the names of the seven days of the week, as called by the Christians in Latin. Here is a specimen of this note: יר׳(צה) יום ראשון קראוהו סוֹלִים (Dies Solis) ויום ב׳ לוּגִים...: (Dies Lunae, he not being able to distinguish the נ, which he mistook for a ג &c.). He placed this note, probably, in explanation of leaf 138[b] (Ex. xvi. 1).

c. As regards the use of this MS. it will be convenient to divide our statement concerning it into two paragraphs, i.e. regarding it in connexion with the past and in connexion with the future.

1) In connexion with the past the following will be of interest.

(1) There is a great probability that this MS. (of course in its original state, when all or most was in the hand in which leaves 14—120 are now) was in the hands of R. Yoseph b. Eli'ezer Hassephardi, and that it was from this very MS. that he took his proofs against the authenticity of the

so-called Long Commentary on Exodus. For these are his words in the ninth proof alluded to before (A, a, (3), (2), *a*):

...והתשיעית בפרשת ואלה שמות הארוך בסוד השם כתוב הנה ביארתי לך מכתב לשון החכם כי הוא פירושו וזה צחות לשונו אשר אכתוב לך כן כתוב שם אות באות...

Now, although it is not impossible, that other copies contained the same (and indeed, copies either copied from ours or the one ours was copied from, must have contained it), ordinarily this phrase was not found in the so-called Long Commentary. We remind the reader only of two facts, in the first place that it is not to be found in the printed editions, and in the next place, that, had it been common, R. Yoseph would not have laid such stress upon it (אות באות); and moreover the matter would have been noticed before him. As we know from the Oxford MS. containing Ibn Ya'ish the younger's supercommentary, which was copied by this R. Yoseph in 1375 (see Numbers 47 and 51 of this Catalogue), that the latter lived for some time at Canea (Khania) in Crete (Candia), and as what he quotes is actually to be found in our MS., whilst it is not known to be found in any other, we have a moral conviction that it is this very MS. he made use of in writing the mentioned preface. It is probable that our MS. in its later parts was also executed in Canea.

(2) But another R. Yoseph, a man of the xviiith, or perhaps our own century, and a learned Qaraite (of the Crimean peninsula, if we may judge from his handwriting), made use of this MS. He left his mark on it, not by writing on the margins, or some such thing, but by leaving a little strip of paper inside of it, on which the following poem which gives the acrostic יוסף is written:

יודעי ספר מנעוריהם, אזל כסף מכיסיהם
ובכן רבים לא יוכלו הם ללמוד תורה כחפציהם
ספרי רבים תוך חדריהם עכבר רוקד על גבי(הם)
פִּזר עפר על קרשיהם כי לא נסו ללמוד בהם

This R. Yoseph is possibly the commentator of the מבחר whose name in full was Yoseph Shelomoh Yerushalmi, and who probably used this MS. while he was composing his supercommentary (see the description of MS. Add. 861 below, and especially note 2 there).

2) Having spoken of the use this MS. has been probably made of, we will urge on the learned the duty of using it (and this the sooner the better) for a critical edition of our great author's greatest work, the commentary on the Pentateuch. It is the peculiar gift of, and therefore, no doubt, the duty incumbent upon, our generation critically to reproduce the works of ancient authors. After a critical edition of Rashi on the Pentateuch has been attempted by Berliner (and this with considerable success; see No. 34 of

this Catalogue), it is unquestionably Ibn 'Ezra's turn to be reproduced in a more careful way than has been done hitherto. And we feel it the more our duty to urge the use of this MS. in such a case at once, because of its material condition.

d. This condition is indeed far from satisfactory. Besides the defects enumerated before, leaves 14—16 and 390—392 are seriously damaged, and more or less all the outer margins of the MS. are in process of decay. In various other places also the damp has done serious injury to this otherwise remarkable copy.

[Library-mark, Add. 1014. 1; bought in 1873 from Fischl Hirsch.]

No. 47.

Paper, in quarto, 8 in. × $5\frac{3}{4}$ in.; 97 leaves, 8-sheet quires, 23 lines; Rabbinic character, Sephardic handwriting of the XIVth century.

[פרושים על פרוש הראב"ע על התורה וכו']

Supercommentaries on Ibn 'Ezra on the PENTATEUCH, &c.; defective.

1. [פרוש על פרוש הראב"ע על התורה לר' שלמה אבן יעיש הבחור]

SUPERCOMMENTARY ON IBN 'EZRA ON THE PENTATEUCH, BY R. SHELOMOH IBN YA'ISH THE YOUNGER; defective.

1ᵃ, blank; 1ᵇ, *Genesis;* 20ᵇ, *Exodus;* 41ᵃ, *Leviticus;* 53ᵃ, *Numbers;* 63ᵃ, *Deuteronomy* (65 wanting); 68ᵇ, blank.

Begins (leaf 1ᵇ):

בראשית יש אומ' כי הבית נושא בלי טעם... על כן אמר בראשית. פי' כי מלת בראשית היא להרחבת הלשון כי לא יאמר ראשית ואחרית אלא בזמן והזמן תלוי בתנועת הגלגל...

Ends (leaf 68ᵃ):

...ומענין האותות והמופתים כבר אמ' בפסוק שלפני זה „ תם ונשלם תהלה לאל עולם" בד"ח לב"א (בריך דיהב חילא לעבדיה בר אמתיה[1])

[1] For this phrase see Biscioni (8vo ed.), p. 226, and the ed. princ. of Ramban on the Pentateuch (at the end of Exodus), where however it is given, not as an abbreviation, as it is here, but in full.

From whatever point of view we look upon this copy, whether as a book, or as a MS. as such, it claims the greatest attention. As a systematic exposition of Ibn 'Ezra, it is in age the second or third, whilst in power and perspicuity it is second to none. This superiority is enhanced by the fact of the author's possessing Ibn 'Ezra's autograph copy; see leaf 51ª, lines 8 and 9 and Number 46 of this Catalogue, pp. 122, 125. That a very favourable opinion was long entertained of this work, will be seen from the fact, that, for hundreds of years, the explanations, given here, have been substantially, if not literally, reproduced, both by anonymous authors (see this Catalogue, pp. 104, 106), and by others whose names are known, e.g. Ibn מטוט (MSS. Add. 1015. 2 and Add. 518), R. Yoseph b. Eli'ezer[1] (MS. Add. 510. 1), Ibn Mayor (MS. Add. 433), and Ibn Zarza (the מקור חיים), passim. (With respect to the plagiarisms of this last, see Auerbach in Geiger, *Jüd. Zeitschr.* IV. p. 297 and Steinschneider, ibid. VI. p. 129, although neither of these scholars suspected that his chief source was our author.) As a MS. it is as old as any known, the Bodleian copy (Uri 106, Neubauer 232) being of the year 1375, whilst this copy is at all events at least as old, if we may judge from both paper and handwriting. It certainly lacks the commentary on Ibn 'Ezra's preface, which is to be found in the Bodleian copy; but when we compare the style of that alleged exposition of the preface with that of the whole supercommentary we cannot but entertain grave doubts as to its genuineness[2].

As there is but little known concerning the Author[3] of this important work (see Steinschneider *Hebr. Bibliogr.* [המזכיר] VI. p. 115, Note), the following list of his authorities, and some of the peculiarities which he exhibits, will be welcome to the student of Hebrew literature. We will only add, that although he may have been born at Guadalaxara (Uri 106), he certainly lived for some time in Provence, where he probably studied (see p. 131, Note 1); and he perhaps immigrated into Greece also.

1. Authorities:

(1) נוגמייש (16ᵇ; Hieronymus);

(2) חיוג (55ᵇ);

(3) Se'adyah Gaon; independently of Ibn 'Ezra, 45ᵇ);

[1] That this R. Yoseph copied the Bodleian copy we have mentioned before (p. 128 of this Catalogue).

[2] See, however, Biscioni (8vo. ed.), p. 335.

[3] We have, as we believe, clearly shown in the preceding Number of this Catalogue, that our author was not merely a commentator on, and practical teacher of, Ibn 'Ezra-literature, but that he exercised also some influence on the present shape of that writer's commentary on the Pentateuch. This gives him an even greater importance than he would have had in virtue of his own literature.

(4) הרקמה, also השרשים, R. Yonah and also Ibn גנאח (4^a, 14^b, 43^b 44^b, 49^b);

(5) Rashi, also Rash (20^a, 45^b, 47^b, 48^a, 48^b, 58^a, 61^a, 61^b, 62^a and 67^b);

(6) Yeshu'ah (20^a); (7) Sepher הכוזרי (41^b);

(8) Rambam (8^b, 19^a, 57^a, 61^b);

(9) R. Shemuel Ibn Tibbon (63^b);

(10) R. Mosheh Ibn Tibbon (6^b, 34^a);

(11) ... הראב״ד השיג (i.e. R. Abraham b. David of Posquières, 61^b);

(12) R. David Qimchi (18^a, 42^a, 45^b);

(13) Rab Nissim (40^a);

(14) ... מה ששמעתי מרבותי (without further specifying them, 31^a);

(15) ... אדוני אבי ר׳ מאיר בר׳ דוד ז״ל, also without אבי and again with צבי [i.e. צדיק בימיו יפרח, in allusion to Ps. lxxxii. 7] after the name (13^a, 28^b, 35^a, 38^a, 60^a);

(16) מפי ר׳ לוי הכהן, also ... כך קבלתי מפי, and ... מפי אדני ורבי (36^b, 37^a, 39^b and 52^b);

(17) ... זה פי׳ דון קומפרד דארלדי[1] (52^b);

(18) פלוני אלמוני (30^b; the matter is to be found in the supercommentary of R. Shemtob b. Yehudah Ibn Mayor, who cannot, however, have been the original author, as this MS. was, no doubt, executed before he was born; see MS. Add. 433, Number 52 of this Catalogue).

2. Peculiarities:

(1) צ״ע and כלומר are standing phrases with him;

(2) Although he professes to comment on Ibn 'Ezra, he often contradicts him (see passim, but particularly 63^a, where he indignantly rejects Ibn 'Ezra's well-known view, that there are thirty-three verses in the Pentateuch not written by Moses himself).

(3) For the ordinary בעזרת (בעזר) השם &c. he has (leaf 25^b):

כאשר נפרש בעזר שלום עמו דורש יפקח אוזן חרש לדעת שורש[2]...

[1] Don Comprad of Arles. The name Comprad occurs in Provence (Avignon) a hundred years later also; see Zunz, *Literaturgesch. d. synag. Poesie*, p. 525, under Jacob b. Chajim.

[2] It is on the strength of these verses, or rather rhymes, that we ascribe to him the rhymes to be found in the MS. described in the preceding Number; which rhymes commence with the pericope משפטים and go on, with very little interruption, to the end of the Pentateuch.

(4) On the much-discussed פרוכים (Ibn 'Ezra on Ex. i. 13; Steinschneider in Geiger's *Jüd. Zeitsch.* vi. p. 124) he has the following:

...כלומ׳ כי מלת פרך אינה מספקת בעצמה ואינה נאמרת כי אם בהסמך לה מלת עבודה או יש לקרות פרכים כלומ׳ יקבץ. פ״א ולומר פרוכים לא יתכן וזה אמ׳ כנגד אביתור הפייט שיסד ברהוטה את מי זנחת לנצח מכל מעונים אני לפלא ומכל פרוכים אני למופת. וכוונת החכם כי לא נמצא ממנו פועל על כן לא נוכל לומ׳ פרוכים. זה שמעתי מפי החכם הנכבד אדני רבי ר׳ מאיר ב׳ר דוד.

(5) The explanation of the mathematico-theological Excursus in Exodus, occupying eight leaves (20[b]—28[a]), precedes that of the ordinary commentary on that book. It is, no doubt, the author and not the scribe, to whom originally belongs the notice כבר כתוב למעלה המספר, which is to be found where this Excursus and its explanation would ordinarily stand.

(6) This commentary extends over all the Parshiyyoth of the Pentateuch, except תצוה, with respect to which the author says (leaf 36[a]): ...בואתה תצוה לא נצרכתי לפרש. For additional information on this work see the description of MS. Add. 400. 12, and for additional information on this MS. see below, and the description of MS. Add. 510. 1.

2. [פרוש סודות אבן עזרא על התורה לר׳ יוסף אבן כספי]

SUPERCOMMENTARY ON IBN 'EZRA ON THE PENTATEUCH, BY R. YOSEPH IBN KASPI.

Leaf 69[a], *Supercommentator's preface;* 69[b], *Explanation of commentator's preface;* 70[b], *Genesis;* 77[a], *Exodus;* 86[b], *Leviticus;* 89[a], *Numbers;* 91[a], *Deuteronomy.*

Begins (leaf 69[a]):

בשם אל עולם אתחיל לפרש פי׳ הסודות אשר לר׳ אברהם אבן עזרא. לא מפני היותי איש חכם בעיני פתני לבבי...

Ends (leaf 96[a]):

...אבל מניחו כפי אשר גזרה חכמתו ואין לאיש להבין בו וזה הוא שאמר סוד גדול: תם ונשלם ביאור הסודות תהלה לאל אשר לא נעלמו ממנו הנסתרות א״א (אמן אמן).

As far as the literature, on the whole, is concerned, this supercommentary is identical with MS. Add. 377. 3. 6 (No. 35. 6 in this Catalogue). As there, the following pericopes, because without the so-called Sodoth, are here also without a commentary: תולדות, וישב, מקץ, ויגש and ויחי in Genesis; וארא, בא, בשלח, תרומה, ויקהל and פקודי in Exodus; צו, שמיני, תזריע, מצורע, אמר and בהר in Leviticus; במדבר, בהעלותך, שלח לך, קרח,

מטות, חקת and מסעי in Numbers; שפטים, כי תבא, נצבים and וזאת הברכה in Deuteronomy. As a MS. however, this copy is greatly superior. For more information concerning the rank which this commentary occupies in Ibn Kaspi's writings, see MS. Add. 857. 2 and Excursus II.

3. [סוד הערכים לר׳ יוסף אבן כספי]

REASONS FOR THE SCALE OF VALUATION AS DETERMINED IN THE TWENTY-SEVENTH CHAPTER OF LEVITICUS, BY R. YOSEPH IBN KASPI; defective.

Begins (leaf 96[b]):

טעם הערכים הנה ידוע לנו כי יצירת הולד למ׳ יום וכנגדם ימי טומאה וטהרה...

Breaks off (leaf 97[b]):

...וזה האדם כמה עלו ערכיו ערכה חמש ועשרים וחמשים הרי ע״ה כמה נשאר עליו עד תשעים ט״ו כי |

This essay is, unquestionably, one, and probably the first, of the so-called Sodoth by Ibn Kaspi mentioned by R. Shelomoh, the owner of MS. Add. 377, in his Postscript (leaf 70[b], outer margin); see this Catalogue, pp. 61, 62. As, unfortunately, this MS. breaks off with the third page, it is impossible to say of what extent this essay was, much less, of what extent the other essays were; and with respect to these latter, beyond the mere titles, what they contained[1]. To judge, however, from this fragment, all had somewhat cabbalistic tendencies, despite the author's distinct assertion elsewhere[2], that he was no depository of cabbalistic lore, as he had "received nothing".

The scribe's name was probably Se'adyah, as that name is once distinguished by points (leaf 50[a]). He must have been a superior man alike in intelligence and conscientiousness, as the remarks in his hand on the margins amply show. He either lived in Africa, or was an African either by birth or education; probably both. The same kind of paper on which this MS. is written was to be had at Mostaganem about the middle of the xivth century (see MSS. Dd. 5. 38 and Dd. 11. 22).

[1] The סוד היבום is, apparently, different from the matter which is to be found here on leaves 78[b]—80[a], since R. Shelomoh, the index-writer of MS. Add. 377, would have noticed their identity on leaves 74[a]—76[a] there and would not have re-copied the matter at the end of the Maamar Haskel; see MS. Add. 377. 3, leaf 70[b], outer margin.

[2] In the second Maphteach of the Menorath Keseph (on the מעשה מרכבה) he says:

...דע בני שלמה..., והפנים שניים כי אולי אין אני מגלה דבר ממה שהוא על אמתתו כי יודע אלהים כי מעולם בענין זה או בשום סוד מסודות לא באה אלי קבלה כלל לא מפי סופרים ולא מפי ספרים... See MS. Add. 857. 3, leaf 1[a].

The following traces of ownership are to be found:

(1) An Ashkenazic hand of the xiv—xvth century has numbered the leaves on the lower margin (the only traces of which numbering are to be found on leaves 40—43, 45—47 and 49). This scribe has written scientific and Talmudico-Rabbinical notes, &c. on leaves 1[b], 7[a], 21[a], 21[b] and 45[a]. From leaf 60[b] we see that it is this hand which has supplied the designs in red, occasionally to be found, chiefly at the commencement of the weekly Parshiyyoth, but now and then also at fresh sentences.

Another Ashkenazic hand of the xv—xvith century has written the names of some of the Parshiyyoth and has re-numbered the leaves on the lower margin, and the greater portion of this numbering exists to this day. There are some learned notes on the margins of leaves 15[a], 15[b], 27[a] and 28[a] by the same hand.

Another owner was R. Yoseph Shelomoh Graziano (see No. 40 of this Catalogue), who has written, in Italian Rabbinic, on leaf 1[b], בה"א (בשם ה' אמן) ביאור על הר"א ן' עזרא בפירוש התורה . אי"ש ג"ר חאו"ע; and on leaf 69[a], except that instead of בה"א is ב"ה and that the last three words are left out altogether, the same phrase is to be found again. He did not know to whom either of the two commentaries belonged (see MS. Add. 510. 1, Flyleaf).

(2) A still later owner was R. Yeudah Zerachyah Azulai of Jerusalem, a grandson(?) of the great Bibliographer[1], who has written on leaf 1[a] זה שמי וזה זכרי לדור דורים הצעיר יאודה זרחיה אזולאי ס"ט (סופי טוב); and again a second time the name and the above abbreviation only. These are in Rabbinic Sephardic writing. To him, probably, belongs also the entry, ביאור לביאור התורה להרב רבי אברהם בן עזרא זכר צדיק לחיי העולם הבא, which is to be found on the same page, but which is in square Sephardic. This owner also did not know to whom either of the two commentaries belonged (see as above).

Besides the defects enumerated, the first leaf is a little torn, and the whole MS. is slightly stained. Part of it is also somewhat damp, and leaves 66—94 are bored through in one place, probably by the authorities of the Quarantine (in Italy?). The paper, however, is stout; and the MS. is not in bad condition.

[Library-mark, Add. 510. 2; bought in 1869 from H. Lipschütz.]

[1] According to a testimonial by RR. Yoseph b. Rephael and Betzaleel b. Yisrael Mosheh Hakkohen, the Rabbis of Wilna (הלבנון, x. No. 5, p. 40), our R. Yeudah Zerachyah was a grandson (נכד) of R. Chayyim Yoseph David Azulai, the author of the Shem Haggedolim, &c. He is there asserted to have owned, besides other valuable MS. works, the Yerushalmi of Seder Zera'im and Massekheth Sheqalim with the commentary of R. Shelomoh סירילי'או. (On this last-named Rabbi see our description of MS. Oo. 1. 24. 2.)

No. 48.

Paper, in quarto, 8 in. × 6 in.; 64 leaves, mostly[1] 6-sheet quires, 24 lines; current character, German Ashkenazic handwriting of the XV—XVIth century.

[פרוש על פרוש הראב״ע על התורה לר׳ שלמה אבן יעיש הבחור]

Supercommentary on Ibn 'Ezra on the PENTATEUCH, by R. Shelomoh Ibn Ya'ish the younger; incomplete.

Leaf 1ᵃ, *Genesis;* 22ᵇ, *Exodus;* 39ᵇ, *Leviticus;* 47ᵇ, *Numbers;* 56ᵃ, *Deuteronomy;* 62ᵃ—64ᵇ, blank.

Begins (leaf 1ᵃ):

בראשית...י״א כי הבית נושא בלי טעם...בראשית כי מלת בראשית היא להרחבת הלשון כי לא יאמר ראשית ואחרית אלא בזמן...

Breaks off (leaf 61ᵇ; in Ibn 'Ezra on Deut. xxxiii. 6):

...ומספרם לעד גם נשיאים (נהרג) או |

The way in which this MS. of a most valuable work (it is identical with part 1 of the preceding number) breaks off here, is a fair sample of the mode of the execution of the whole. It must have been transcribed from a copy full of mistakes and lacunæ. Thus the greater portion of the most interesting passage on Paradise (by Ibn גברול; see No. 44 of this Catalogue) is missing, as are also the important passages on the omniscience of God (11ᵇ) and the creation of the world out of nothing (47ᵃ). The explanation of the Parashath תזריע is promised to come after וזאת הברכה; but part follows this promise immediately, while the other part is not given at all. The Parashath בחקותי in Leviticus is to be found between the first and second Parshiyyoth of Numbers (48ᵇ). In Parashath נשא the passage on the Nazir is almost entirely missing; as are also, in various places of the MS., the most important names and most instructive passages. Yet this MS. is far from being utterly without value. In the first place this MS. is not defective where the other copy is, and secondly it represents a wholly independent text. We find, on leaf 57ᵇ, a quotation, not to be found in the other copy, which is there (leaf 65) defective, from an earlier *Sepher Yochasin* (a halakhic treatise on inheritance, &c.) than the one so well known. We learn also, that when the author in one place calls R. Meir b. David אבי, he does so out of mere veneration for his teacher[2], and not

[1] The exception is the last quire, which has 8 sheets.

[2] 2 Kings ii. 12 and iii. 21.

because he was really his father, seeing that he gives the same title, according to this copy (38ª), to his other teacher R. Levi Hakkohen (מפי... מורי א"א[1] ר' לוי הכהן).

The scribe's name was Ya'aqob (see 6ᵇ, 14ᵇ, &c., where this word is distinguished by points). This Ya'aqob is also the copyist of other parts of MS. Add. 400.

The leaves of MS. Add. 400 having been twice numbered (in the upper margin), once in Hebrew and once in Arabic; this work occupies leaves 362ª—425ᵇ in the former and 781ª—845ᵇ in the latter numbering.

For owners see the description of MSS. Add. 400. 1 and 2 below.

The material condition of the MS., except that it has been pierced quite through in two places, probably by the authorities of the Quarantine (in Italy?), is excellent.

[Library-mark, Add. 400. 12; bought in 1868 from H. Lipschütz].

No. 49.

Paper, in folio, 10⅞ in., × 8⅞ in.; 92 leaves, 5-sheet quires, 29 lines; Rabbinic character, fine Sephardic handwriting of the XIVth century.

מגלת סתרים [והוא פרוש על פרוש הראב"ע על התורה לר'] שמואל בן סעדיה אבן מטוט.

Supercommentary on Ibn 'Ezra on the PENTATEUCH by R. Shemuel b. Se'adyah Ibn מטוט[2]; defective.

[1] i.e. אדוני אבי.

[2] From this copy (leaf 1ᵇ), MS. Add. 518 (leaf 1ª, see next number of this Catalogue), and the copy preserved in the Court-Library of Vienna (see Goldenthal, *Die neuerworb. handschriftl. hebr. Werke*... Wien, 1851, 4to, p. 6), but particularly from the acrostic with which commences the author's משובב נתיבות (see the decription of MS. Add. 1015. 1, below), and which gives Shemuel ben Se'adyah Ibn מטוט (...מישך טוב ודעת טעם...; see the Bodl. copy, Mich. 545, olim 138, leaf 131ª), it will be seen that the transliteration *Motot*, as most give it, is, to say the least, as yet insufficiently certain. This was, no doubt, instinctively felt by the exact Wolf (*Bibl. Hebr.* III., p. 1113); who, however, wavers between Mothoth and Mittoth (!).

Leaf 1[a], blank; 1[b], *Supercommentator's preface;* 2[a], *Explanation of commentator's preface;* 5[a], *Genesis;* 26[a], *Exodus* (30 wanting); 50[b], *Leviticus;* 64[a], *Numbers;* 75[a], *Deuteronomy;* 92[b], blank.

Begins (leaf 1[b]):

מגלת סתרים והוא ביאור פירוש התורה לר׳ אברהם ן׳ עזרא ז״ל„ בהיות דרך ר׳ אברהם בן עזרא„ על יסוד הדקדוק וטעמי המקרא„...

Ends (leaf 92[a]):

...ולכן השאיל הכתו׳ מלת נס על כי היבושת תנים כל לחה מן הגוף„ בעבור כבוד משה שהיה חי ועומד עליהם„ תם ונשלם„ שבח לבורא עולם„ ביל״א ו (ברוך יי׳ לעולם אמן ואמן Ps. lxxxi. 53) בנל״ך ואע״י„ אלץ[1].

Although this supercommentary has been printed twice (Venezia, 1553, 4to; Amsterdam, 1721, Folio), something more concerning it, its author, his other works and the authorities he quotes in this work, will not be deemed out of place.

If Steinschneider (Bodl. Catal. p. 2457) states, and his statement is correct enough, that the Amsterdam edition (of the so-called מרגליות טובה) contains only an abridgment of the Venice edition, it must be added, that the latter in its turn seems to be another (and earlier?) recension, and but a poor representative, of the work as it lies before us in the present MS.; a fact which may be ascertained by a cursory collation of most passages. This MS., as well as also MS. Add. 518, and finally also that belonging to the Court-Library of Vienna (see above, p. 136, Footnote 2), are a (later?), fuller and considerably better recension[2]; and of these three again this copy is, whatever its shortcomings may be as a manuscript, the more valuable one when viewed as a work.

[1] This is probably an abbreviation of אזכיר לבדך צדקתך, which is the latter part of Ps. lxxi. 16, slightly transposed. It is possible that it is, at the same time, a contraction of the scribe's name, which would explain the transposition. That it cannot be a simple contraction of the scribe's name, however, is clear from Add. 1015. 1, at the end of which it also occurs, but with this difference, that it is there placed before the formula ביל״א ו.

[2] There are only a few passages which are more fully worded in the printed edition than here, e.g. the mathematico-astronomical Excursus in the pericope כי תשא, where we here miss the quotations from Ibn Ezra's אגרת השבת (see MS. Add. 475), and which is to be found in the Venice edition, leaf 35[a] (i.e. 33[a] as the pagination there is wrong), col. 2; and the pericope ויקהל which has no commentary and concerning which it says (leaf 49[b]) אין בפרשה הזאת דבר שצריך ביאור (see MS. Add. 518, leaf 47[a] where the same words are to be read), whilst the Venice edition (34[a]) has one on the so-called Other Recension, i.e. the ordinary, or Long Commentary (see later). In most cases, however, the matter of the passages apparently fuller in the printed editions, is not missing, but is to be found in other places.

The author was an Arabic-speaking[1] Rabbi of the xivth century and lived at Guadalajara (Guadalaxara[2]), of which place he probably was a native. He was a man of great eminence in Talmud, Qabbalah, Philosophy, &c. In Philosophy (particularly in Astronomy and Astrology, both of which formed at that time part of it) he was a zealous follower of Ibn 'Ezra (see passim, but particularly leaf 15[a], where he says: ...ודעתו עמוקה מאוד בחכמת המזלות ונשגבה ולא אוכל לה.., and leaf 60[a], where he says: ...ודעתו רחבה מאוד בחכמת (המזלו)ת ותהלוכות המאורות). In Talmud and Qabbalah, on the other hand, he was a zealous follower of Nachmanides (see passim, but particularly in the pericope וילך, leaf 87[b], where he says: ...הוא אשר יגדיל כבוד התורה ולכן יכפיל אלהים שכר הרמב"ן ז"ל...; compare also leaf 73[a]). And although he defends Ibn 'Ezra against the charges, brought against him by Nachmanides and many others, that he thought and spoke lightly of the Rabbis, he does so, apparently, to guard himself, as his commentator, against similar reproaches (see preface, after the word לצנועים, leaf 1[b], which portion is not to be found in the printed editions). But he has a small opinion indeed both of Ibn Ezra's orthodoxy and of his knowledge of Talmud and Qabbalah. He repeatedly charges him with having unlawfully dislocated well-connected verses (see, for instance, leaf 87[b], where he says: והנה הוא מבלבל...וחס ושלום שיהיה כן הנכון) and with not having penetrated deeply enough into the cabbalistic spirit of the rabbinical sayings (see leaves 27[a], 35[b], 36[a], 48[b], 56[b]).

Of his other works the author mentions here only the מגלה עמוקות, a direct cabbalistic commentary on the whole Pentateuch (although now there are only fragments of it known) and the משובב נתיבות, a cabbalistic tripartite compendium, the middle part of which is a commentary on the ספר יצירה (see the description of MS. Add. 1015. 1 below). The Megalleh 'Amuqoth he mentions on almost every page and sometimes twice or even thrice, whilst the Meshobeḅ Nethiboth is only occasionally mentioned by him. R. Abraham b. David Hallevi's work (العقيدة الرفيعة) he seems not to have translated when he wrote the present work, as he mentions that work by its Arabic name (see later). Neither had he, at

[1] That our author was an Arabic-speaking Rabbi will be seen not merely from the *Ibn* prefixed to the surname, but also from the numerous technical terms in Arabic occurring in this, and another, work of his (MS. Add. 1015. 1). He was, moreover, the translator of R. Abraham b. David Hallevi's אלעקידה אלרפיעה (see later) into Hebrew (Steinschneider as above).

[2] See MS. Add. 1015. 1, in the last line but one of which it says: ... וכתבתים בשנת שלשים ומאה לפרט היצירה בואדאלחג'ארה. That our author lived in 1370 was known to Zunz more than thirty years ago (see *Eine merkwürdige Medaille* in Jost's *Annalen*, II. p. 156, col. 2); but both he (in 1840) and Steinschneider (in 1862) were apparently ignorant of the place where this author wrote.

that time, written his other two (?) works, on בחיי (if he ever did so at all) and the תהלות ה' (discovered by Steinschneider; see Bodl. Catal. as before); at least, he makes no mention of these.

Of the authorities, and works by others, which he quotes in this supercommentary, we need give references only to the productions of Ibn 'Ezra and such as belong to periods after him, stating only in a general way, that our author mentions repeatedly the works of Aristotle and their Arabic commentators (see also p. 141 below, Note 1); and that of Jewish authorities before Ibn 'Ezra he mentions the בהיר (40[b]); but not the זוהר, although he knew of it; see description of MS. Add. 1015. 1 below), Se'adyah Gaon, R. Yonah, Ibn גברול, R. Yoseph Ibn אביתור, Rashi and others.

1. Of Ibn 'Ezra's works he quotes the following:

a. Commentaries on the Bible.

(1) The so-called Other Recension to Genesis, by which is meant the commentary, of which a fragment is to be found in Otzar Nechmad, II. p. 218. It extended unquestionably over the whole of that book (and not as Mortara thinks); see leaf 22[b], where a reference to it as late as on וישלח (Gen. xxxii. 20) is given[1]. He quotes this commentary sixteen times.

(2) The so-called Other Recension to Exodus, by which is meant the commentary ordinarily to be found in the Bible editions, since our author as well as other supercommentators (see MSS. Add. 510. 1 and Add. 433, &c.) commented on the Short commentary (see p. 90 of this Catalogue). He quotes this commentary thirty-six times.

(3) On Joshua, concerning which it says here (leaf 88[b]):

...ואין פירושו לספר יהושע נמצא אצלנו להתבונן ממנו...

(4) On Isaiah, which he quotes three times (5[b], 36[a] and 55[a]).

(5) On the Minor Prophets, which he also quotes three times (86[a], Haggai, 19[b] and 85[b], Zechariah).

(6) On the Psalms, which he quotes six times (6[a], 6[b], 13[a], 15[b], 18[a], 19[a]).

(7) On the Proverbs, concerning which he says (48[a]): ...ואין פירושו ..אצלנו, see p. 90 of this Catalogue.

(8) On Job (2[a]).

(9) On Lamentations (63[a]).

(10) On Ecclesiastes, which he quotes five times (6[a], 11[b], 78[a], 79[b], 80[a]).

(11) On Daniel (6[a]).

[1] Whether the MS. in possession of Jellinek which is supposed to contain this Other Recension does really contain it needs further investigation; see our description of MS. Add. 510, 1, below.

b. Other treatises of grammatical, theological, mathematical and astronomical (astrological) import:

(1) צחות (5^a, 18^b, 26^b). (2) שפת יתר (26^b).

(3) מאזנים (22^a, 74^a, 76^b). (4) ספר היסוד (73^b).

(5) ספר האחד (11^b, 28^a, 29^b). (6) ספר השם (6^a, 22^b, 31^b, 35^a).

(7) יסוד מורא, which he quotes twelve times (7^b, 13^b, 26^a, 27^a, 29^a, 31^a, 38^b, 44^a, 46^b, 56^b, 61^b, 63^b).

(8) ערוגת המזימה ופרדס החכמה (5^b; which is, no doubt, not only identical with the book of the same name in MS. Dd. 10. 68, leaves 248^b—250^a, but also with the ערוגת החכמה ופרדס המזימה, MS. Add. 400. 11. 2 and the ערוגת הבושם ופרדס החכמה quoted in MS. Add. 518, leaf 6^a; comp. Kerem Chemed, IV. pp. 1—5).

(9) Commentary on the ספר יצירה ((5^b, 7^b, 8^b, 18^b, 29^a).

(10) סוד העבור (72^b). (11) ספר העצמים[1] (40^b, 49^b, 70^a, 80^a).

(12) ראשית חכמה (7^b; see MS. Add. 481).

(13) ספר המולדות (11^a, 13^a, 20^a, 91^a; see MS. Add. 481).

(14) משפטי המזלות (11^b). (15) שמוש המזלות והמשרתים (40^b).

(16) שמוש המשרתים (43^a). It is not impossible that the last-named three titles may mean only one and the same book; the last two very probably do so.

2. R. Abraham b. David (דאוד) Hallevi, or the Elder (22^b, where he also mentions his אלעקידה אלרפיעה, and 35^b).

3. Maimonides (25^b, whose משנה תורה he quotes).

4. R. Yoseph Qimchi (89^b; see MS. Add. 518, leaf 77^b, where it reads David instead of Yoseph).

5. Nachmanides, whom he quotes fourteen times (15^b twice, 22^b, 33^b, 42^b, 44^a, 55^a, 61^b, 66^b, 69^a, 73^a, 82^a, 86^a, 87^b).

6. יסוד עולם (i.e. R. Yitzchaq b. Yoseph Ibn Yisrael, 2^a, 34^a, 58^b, 64^b; see MS. Oo. 6. 68).

[1] This book was, according to R. Shemtob b. Yehudah Ibn Mayor (MS. Add. 433, leaf 127^b), originally written in Arabic and afterwards translated (by whom?) into Hebrew. Compare No. 52 of this Catalogue, below.

7. R. Chayyim Ibn Yisrael (the brother of the foregoing; 11ª, where he also quotes his מאמר גן עדן, 11ᵇ, 14ª; see the description of MS. Add. 433 below).

8. R. Yoseph Ibn וקאר (i.e. Don Yoseph b. Abraham; 9ᵇ. See this Catalogue, p. 109 and the Bodl. MS., Mich. 545, olim 138, leaf 136ª, where our author quotes Ibn וקאר's work מאמר הכולל).

9. R. Yehudah (MS. Add. 518, leaf 8ᵇ, has חסדה) b. Nissim b. מלכה (8ª).

10. המקובלים (15ª, 35ᵇ, 36ᵇ, 38ᵇ, 40ᵇ, 61ᵇ).

11. האצטגנינים (15ª, 21ª, 44ª, 47ª, 80ª, 80ᵇ).

12. חכמי המזלות (9ᵇ, 23ª, 29ª, 84ª).

13. חכמי הטבע (13ª). 14. חכמי המחקר (32ª).

15. הפילוסופים (38ᵇ, 40ᵇ, and חכמי הפילוסופים 67ᵇ, 82ª).

16. חכמים מן הישמעאלים[1] (9ᵇ).

Regarding the original scribe we may say, that, although we know him neither with precision, nor even with certainty, his name probably lies within the Chiffre אלץ (see p. 137 above, Note 1). His individual name may have been Eliyyah, El'azar or some other, commencing with אל whilst his surname was Ibn Tzur, or Tzaddiq, or some other, commencing with צ[2]. But he was, no doubt, an Arabic-speaking Sephardi, as the peculiar character of several of his letters warrants us to believe (the ף, ק, &c.). He, probably, also belonged to Guadalajara, or its neighbourhood, for as this copy can scarcely have been executed much later than 1375 or 1380, the MS. was probably copied where the work had been composed. The hand is of singular beauty and the work of surpassing correctness. His only fault is, that the spaces left for the diagrams on leaves 2ᵇ and 28ª have been left blank[3].

A later hand, of the xv—xvith century, and also that of a Sephardi, who, was in all probability, an owner, has made some entries on leaf 92ᵇ, the whole of which had been left blank by the original scribe. The matter relates to Ibn 'Ezra's commentary on the Pentateuch, and consists partly of short explanations and partly of what the scribe considered the correct

[1] Of these are specified: Ibn Sina (Avicenna), 7ᵇ, 9ª, 11ª, 14ª; Abunazr, 7ᵇ, 9ª, 15ª, 44ª; Abuchamid, 9ᵇ; Ibn Roshd (Averroes), 7ᵇ, 15ª. On this last-mentioned page he speaks of his (Averroes') ספר הסגולות.

[2] Anybody who knows the importance of the smallest clue to an anonymous scribe's name will appreciate even the reduction of a doubt from within a vast, to one within a small, range of speculation.

[3] The same has, no doubt, also been the case with respect to the diagram, which ought to have stood on leaf 30, now missing.

readings of the text. The whole amounts to eight pieces, all of which refer to the first Excursus of Exodus. A considerable portion, however, is absolutely illegible, and some of the rest can be read only with great trouble.

Another Sephardic owner, of the xvi—xviith century, has written emendations on leaves 20[b] and 25[a]; the writing on the latter leaf is more of the current character.

Another Sephardic owner, of the same period, but somewhat later, has re-written the antichristian passage on leaf 24[a], which had been erased by an anonymous censor. He has also written an emendation on the outer margin of leaf 66[a].

A fourth owner, of the xvii—xviiith century, and also a Sephardi, has written, in Rabbinic character, the title of the book (מגלת סתרים). To this hand are also due: (1) the catchwords at the end of the lower margin, and (2) the numbering of the quires there, which numbering, however, is wrong.

A fifth owner, a Sephardi of the xviiith century, has written on leaf 1[a], in square character, the title of the book, and, also on 50[b], under the original scribe's writing of the same, the first three words of Leviticus.

To a sixth owner, a Sephardi, and also of the xviiith century, are due the words ונקרא ס׳ מוטות, on leaf 1[a].

For the connexion of this MS. with the Colleges of R. Yomtob Ibn בנבשת and R. Mosheh Shime'on Shelomoh, &c., see the description of MS. Add. 1015. 1, below.

The state of the MS. is unfortunately, very unsatisfactory. Most of the margins have suffered considerably from damp; which makes the MS., in very many places, quite illegible, and leaves 2—21 are worm-eaten. Yet, considering both the age and the correctness of the transcription, and, above all, its value for the textual criticism of Ibn 'Ezra's commentary[1], few MSS. will be able to stand a comparison with it.

[Library-mark, Add. 1015. 2; bought in 1873 from Fischl Hirsch.]

[1] If R. Shelomoh Ibn Ya'ish had the advantage of using Ibn Ezra's autograph copy, our author had, in his turn, the advantage of collating a great number of old copies of it, which he critically sifted. Thus we find, on almost every page, one or other of the following phrases: ומה שכתוב . . . משובש, העתקות, מקצת ספרים, מקצת העתקות, כן היא גרסתו הנכונה, כן נמצאו דבריו, ואם הוא משובש, בשום העתקות, כן הוא לשונו האמתי, ונראה שהוא טעות, יש ספרים . . . של הארץ הזאת, &c. The phrase, however, most frequently used in connexion with this critical sifting is כן הוא לשונו.

No. 50.

Paper, in quarto, $8\frac{1}{2}$ in. × $5\frac{5}{8}$ in.; 80 leaves, 8-sheet quires, 40—42 lines; Rabbinic character, Sephardic handwriting of the XVth century.

מגלת סתרים [והוא פרוש על פרוש הראב"ע על התורה לר'] שמואל ב'ר סעדיה אבן מטוט

Supercommentary on Ibn 'Ezra on the PENTATEUCH, by R. Shemuel b. Se'adyah Ibn מטוט; defective.

1^a, Supercommentator's preface; 1^c, Explanation of commentator's preface; 5^a, *Genesis* (17 wanting); 27^b, *Exodus;* 45^b, *Leviticus;* 57^b, *Numbers* (65—67 wanting); 68, *Deuteronomy* (78—80, the last leaf probably blank, wanting).

Begins (leaf 1^a):

מגלת . . . בפירוש התורה לר' אברהם אבן עזרא . . . בחיות הד . . . המקרא והחכם . . . רומז דעת עליונים במשפט . . . ובמעשה בראשית . . .

Breaks off (leaf 77^b, on Deut. xxxii. 13; Venice ed. leaf 51^b, col. 2):

. . . כי מן התאר הזה ימצאנו פעולה כמו שכתו' יפתח וישדד אדמתו וטעם הפסוק והמפותח מן האדמה ובא על משקל ׀

This MS., as a work, agrees, on the whole, with the work described in the preceding number; the few deviations are pointed out there. As a MS., however, although originally much inferior to MS. Add. 1015. 2, it has its own peculiarities and its own history, which deserve to be pointed out. The scribe's name was, probably, Zerachyah as 'זר is to be found twice (leaves 43^a and 76^a) at the head of marginal notes by the original copyist. He has the peculiarity of continually giving by abbreviation (כה"ל) the author's frequent phrase of כך (כן) הוא לשונו (see p. 142 of this Catalogue, Note). To this copyist belongs the drawing and filling out of the diagrams (with the exception of the filling out of that on leaf 29^a, for which see later). The words משא בערב, in elegant Sephardic square character, which are to be found on the inside of the binding, probably also belong to him. They, of course, refer to a much older work than Romanelli's.

The following marks of ownership are to be found in this MS.

(1) On the margins (passim) is to be noticed a Greek hand of the XVIth century which has supplied numerous corrections, &c. The same owner has filled out the second diagram (on 29^a) and also written on the inside of the binding a memorandum of a debt due to him and to his partner (or partners). From the coin (לבנים) there mentioned it is clear that the writer lived in Turkey.

(2) An ungraceful Sephardic hand has scrawled on leaf 1[a] the words: זה הספר של אברהם חכים. The writer of this belonged to the XVII—XVIIIth century; and he also lived, no doubt, in Turkey, where the Chakkims are found.

The condition of the MS. is, apart from the missing leaves enumerated before, far from satisfactory. The paper, originally brittle, has suffered much from damp. The MS. has, apparently, been immersed (in part) in salt water, so that the upper portion, particularly that of leaves 1—3, is almost entirely illegible. Leaf 18 is badly torn and the whole MS. is somewhat stained, soiled and worm-eaten.

[Library-mark, Add. 518; bought in 1869 from H. Lipschütz.]

No. 51.

Paper, in quarto, $8\frac{1}{16}$ in. × $5\frac{7}{8}$ in.; 96 leaves, 4-sheet quires, mixed (Rabbinic and current) character, German Ashkenazic handwriting of the XVth century.

צפנת פענח [והוא פרוש על הראב״ע על התורה לר׳] יוסף בן אליעזר בן יוסף [מסרקוסטה]

Supercommentary on Ibn 'Ezra on the PENTATEUCH, by R. Yoseph b. Eli'ezer b. Yoseph of Saragossa.

Leaf 1[a], *Supercommentator's preface;* 1[b], *Explanation of commentator's preface;* 5[a], *Genesis;* 45[b], *Supercommentator's preface to Exodus;* 46[a], *Exodus;* 75[b], *Leviticus;* 85[a], *Numbers;* 89[b], *Deuteronomy.*

Begins (leaf 1[a]):

בראשית(.) צפנת פענח(.) כל דורש מי מעדן · מצמאת לבו רותח · בא נא ושתה יין הרקח · עורי לב(!) אמר יוסף בר אליעזר בר יוסף ע״ם יש״ו (על משכבותם יבא שלום וינוח[1]) מגלות ירושלים אשר בספרד אחרי בואי אל אדמת הקדש...

Ends (leaf 96[b]):

...בעבור כבוד משה פי׳ בעבור כי יש בדרש שעשו כן בעבור שאהרן היה מטיל שלום בין איש לאשתו ובין אדם לחבירו״ ברוך ה׳ לעולם אמן ואמן · תם ונשלם תהלה לאל עולם:

[1] This phrase is somewhat rare. It is a transposition of the well-known יש״י עמה״ץ with a slight addition. This latter phrase is a contraction of Is. lvii. 2. See Index of Abbreviations at the end of this Catalogue.

An extract from this work is extant under the name of אהל יוסף in the so-called מרגליות טובה (see p. 123 of this Catalogue, Note 1), which latter contains, besides the text of Ibn 'Ezra's commentary on the Pentateuch, extracts from three supercommentaries upon it, i.e. the מקור חיים by R. Shemuel b. סנה Ibn Zarza (Mantova, 1559, Folio), the מגלת סתרים (numbers 49 and 50 of this Catalogue) and the צפנת פענח (the present work). As regards the value of this printed extract we may remark that it is not, and indeed cannot be, very great. For, apart from the fact of it being a mere extract, the peculiar reasons for it being so, which are partly given by the editor himself and partly by Jellinek and ourselves (see later), make it, when compared with a well-preserved and bona-fide copy of this work, almost wholly worthless. R. Yequthiel Lazi, the editor of the "Margalioth Tobah", assures us (see Editor's Note preceding the preface of the "Ohel Yoseph", that within that preface, as also that on leaf 153[b] and elsewhere), that the MS. before him was defective, illegible and worm-eaten, or he would have given us much more of this excellent work. On examination, however, we find that all the critical passages (such, for instance, as bear on the date of the composition of the Pentateuch, &c.) are missing. Now we are far from impugning the editor's veracity, and sharing Jellinek's views, that the omissions are due to fear on the part of the editor, and other but similar reasons (כוכבי יצחק, 27. Heft, p. 34); we think, on the contrary, that there can be little doubt, that it was an owner before R. Yequthiel Lazi, who had not distinctly called the "Tzaphenath Pa'neach" an excellent work, who removed all these critical passages. Anyhow, we must confess that, be this as it may, the printed extract does not represent this work in its most important points.

Our author was a Spaniard by birth, who travelled, however, to various other countries, as Palestine (leaf 1[a]), Syria (ibid.), Greece (p. 128 of this Catalogue). He composed this supercommentary for R. David b. Yehoshua' Hannagid (leaf 1[a], &c.), a descendant of the celebrated Maimonides, whose own and whose descendants' full genealogy[1] for thirteen generations we on this occasion get (leaf 1[a] and 1[b]). From this genealogy on the one hand, from a passage, in which the author attacks Nachmanides[2], on the other

[1] This genealogy runs thus: ...הנגיד הגדול ר' דוד ירום הודו, בן ר' יהושע הנגיד, בן ר' אברהם הנגיד, בן ר' דוד הנגיד, בן ר' אברהם הנגיד, בן ר' משה ראש הנגידים מורה צדק, בן ר' מיימון הדיין, בן ר' יוסף החכם, בן ר' יצחק הדיין, בן ר' יוסף הדיין, בן ר' עובדיהו הדיין, בן הרב ר' שלמה, בן החכם ר' עובדי'... Compare Maimonides' subscription to his פרוש המשניות.

[2] Leaf 69[b] (comp. Ibn 'Ezra's short Commentary on Ex. xxviii. 30), the following passage is to be found:
...ורמב"ן תפש עליו בזה וככה ר' יוסף שלודיל ושניהם לא הביטו (הבינו?) דבריו ואיך ישיבו עליו תשובות ואע"פ שרמב"ן גדול ממני כמה מעלות ואמ' שדבריו הם דברי קבלה הנה הוא בעצמו הרס קבלתו כאשר אמר בפרשת בראשית בפסוק ביום הששי ששנת קי"ח יבא משיח והנה עבר קי"ח והמשיח לא בא ואיה קבלתו...; comp. also Geiger's *Jüd. Zeitschr.* I. p. 222. (That, however, Nachmanides was not the author of this statement will be clearly shown in Excursus II.)

hand, and finally from the fact, that our R. Yoseph is the copyist of the Bodleian MS. containing the supercommentary of R. Shelomoh Ibn Ya'ish the younger on Ibn 'Ezra on the Pentateuch (see pp. 128, 130 of this Catalogue): we find that the work before us must have been composed during the latter half of the xivth century.

The literary means at our author's disposal for so important a work were, comparatively speaking, not very great. That he knew Arabic (a language, which was at that time absolutely necessary in order to be able to read the Greek-Arabic philosophers), we know from leaves 1^b, 28^a and 57^a, &c. But who could have believed that the Midrash Rabbah was only known to him at second hand (10^b)? That he was acquainted with synagogal poetry which is to be found only in the Ashkenazic ritual or its offshoots (46^b and 59^b), was an advantage for which he probably[1] was indebted to the fact of having visited Greece, where Ashkenazim had early settled (see the description of MS. Add. 542 below).

As alluded to before (p. 123 of this Catalogue), our author was one of the first to draw the attention of the learned world to the fact that others besides Ibn 'Ezra had something to do with the works that go by the name of the latter. This view is not only to be found in the second preface (to Exodus; leaf 45^a), but also on leaf 41^a, where he says: פי׳ הארוך שהוא מדברי תלמידו; leaf 64^b, where he says that כי תצא is a mistake for קדושים, and that this mistake is owing to one of his disciples; and leaf 46^a, where he distinctly names as one of these disciples, R. Yoseph ממרווייל, or המורייל (commonly מודוויל). Whilst he states this his conviction, no doubt, in the first place, in the interest of truth, he uses it next as one of the means gallantly to defend his author, whom he veritably idolises (leaf 1^a), against aspersions (leaves 57^a and 71^a, &c.). Otherwise we learn from this commentary only three more interesting facts in connexion with the works of Ibn 'Ezra, i.e. (1) that the so-called First Recension[2] on Genesis was in our author's hands; (2) that the commentary on Proverbs was not in his hands (indeed, no commentator but Ibn Kaspi seems ever to have seen it; see pp. 90, 91 of this Catalogue); and (3) that Ibn 'Ezra wrote *two* commentaries on Job.

[1] If this was our author's only visit to Greece, it would lead us to the conclusion that this commentary was composed after 1375.

[2] If the MS. believed by Jellinek to contain the First Recension on Genesis (כוכבי יצחק; 27, p. 34, Note; comp. this Catalogue, p. 139, Note) really does so, it can only be an incomplete copy; since the present MS. also cites the important passage (leaf 23^b) which Jellinek says is not to be found there. But it must not be forgotten, that there may be, or have been, several earlier Recensions on Genesis in existence, one that of which Mortara's is a fragment, and another, which forms, or formed, part of the grammatical commentary on the whole Pentateuch (*Otzar Nechmad*, II. pp. 222, 223, Note). Indeed, wherever he went on his travels, Ibn 'Ezra seems to have composed commentaries and other works at the request of his admirers (comp. Luzzatto, *Kerem Chemed*, IV. p. 132).

Of other authors he quotes:

(1) The 'Arukh (40[b]). (2) Qimchi (24[b]).

(3) Nachmanides (69[b]). (4) R. Yoseph שלודיל (42[b] and 69[b]).

(5) R.(!) Abraham אלזרקאל (83[b]).

There are a few more points of interest in connexion with this copy as a work to be mentioned:

(1) The author has the peculiarity of quoting any. passage from a prophet, if that constitute a prophetic portion of a week, by the name of the pericope to which it belongs.

(2) The pericopes שמיני, מצורע and קרח are without a commentary here, just as they are in the printed edition.

(3) Leaves 26[a] and 39[b] have two Antichristiana of some interest.

(4) The diagrams were, no doubt, originally conceived by the author.

As regards this copy as a MS. we remark, that it is, on the whole, exceedingly well copied, and that the lacunæ to be found on leaves 4[b] and 31[b], are in reality much smaller than one would at first sight think. The diagrams on leaves 2[a], 2[b], 7[a], 8[a], 18[a], 36[b], 85[a], are, if not artistically, yet intelligently, executed.

Two Italian censors have entered their names on leaf 1[a]:

Fr. Hipp. 1602, and Fra Gir[o]. da durallano(?) 1640.

Of owners we have on leaf 1[a] the following signatures:

פירוש וביאור על כמהרר"א ן' עזרא לפירושו על התורה אי"ש ג"ר חאו"ע (see p. 134 of this Catalogue), the last three abbreviations of which occur again on leaf 96[b], and יאודה זרחיה אזולאי ס"ט.

On the fly-leaf is the following entry by the former owner:

ב"ה ארבעה פירושים על פירוש החכם ר' אברהם ן' עזרא על התורה ואלו הם: ס' צפנת פענח מר' יוסף ב"ר אליעזר הספרדי, ושני פירושים של חכמים אחרים על ן' עזרא הנ"ל שהעלימו שמותם בספר וביאור ד' לן' עזרא על התורה הוא מהחכם השלם הרב ר' שמואל ביבא זצ"ל. אי"ש גֿר אנכי בארץ, חאו"ע.

On the same fly-leaf we read by the latter owner something similar:

ארבעה פירושים על הפירוש שפירש הראב"ע על התורה זיע"א (זכותו יגן עלינו אמן) ספר צפנת פענח והוא פירוש מודפס מרבינ' יוסף בר רבי אליעזר הספרדי ושני פירושים מחכמים שונים שהעלימו שמותם הקדושים וביאור רביעי להרב רבינ' שמואל בן ביבא. יאודה זרחיה אזולאי.

It will thus be seen:

(1) That while both these owners knew the title of the first of these four commentaries, the latter owner (Y. Z. Azulai), who lived after the

publication of the so-called Margalioth Tobah recognised the identity of the "Ohel Yoseph" and the Tzaphenath Pa'neach, as he speaks of the latter as existing in print (פירוש מודפס).

(2) That neither of these learned owners knew that the second and third of these four commentaries were those of Ibn Ya'ish and Ibn Kaspi respectively.

(3) That even as late as Azulai's time the fourth commentary (by R. Shemuel Ibn ביבא) still formed part of this volume. To our great regret such is no more the case, this fourth commentary having been cut out (and cabbalistic matter having been substituted; see MS. Add. 510. 3), before the volume came into this Library. This regret is the greater as very little is otherwise known of this R. Shemuel's commentary (comp. השחר, v. 4, p. 39.)

The MS. is in a most excellent condition.

[Library-mark, Add. 510. 1; bought in 1869 from H. Lipschütz.]

No. 52.

Paper, in quarto, 8¼ in. × 6 in.; 240 leaves, 4-sheet quires, 26—27 lines; mixed (Rabbinic and current) character, fine Sephardic handwriting of the XVIth century.

המאור הגדול [והוא פרוש על פרוש הראב"ע על התורה לר' שם טוב בן יהודה אבן מאיור יליד בירבישקה]

Supercommentary on Ibn 'Ezra on the PENTATEUCH, by R. Shemtob b. Yehudah Ibn Mayor, of Briviesca.

Leaf 1[a], Introduction of the supercommentator; 3[a], *Genesis;* 65[b], *Exodus;* 145[b], *Leviticus;* 183[b], *Numbers;* 208[b], *Deuteronomy;* 240[a], subscription of the copyist; 240[b]; blank.

Introduction begins (leaf 1[a]):

בה"א עמ"י עש"ו

בשם האל הנכבד והנו(רא). אחל ביאור לפירוש התורה, להחכם השלם השכליי
ר' אברהם ן' עזרא. אנא מעון הנשמות. ויסוד העולמות. ה(טוב) הנצחי...

Supercommentary begins (leaf 3[a]):

בראשית. ואלו היה טעמו כן היה הבית קמוץ בק"ג, כ"ה (כונת המחבר) שאלו
היה הבית נוסף לא יתכן לא בנקוד השוא כאשר בא...

Ends (leaf 240ª):

...והעד כי סמך משה, כ"ה, כי אמרו כי סמך משה עדות והוראה להיות מלא רוח חכמה[1]. פנים אל פנים פירשתיו. כ"ה בתפלת משה רבינו עליו השלום„ תושלב"ע בנל"ך ואע"י

אמר המעתיק אל ישם עלי חטאת קורא בספר זה אם ימצא בו איזה שגיאה או טעות במקום יחיד רבים ובמקום עתיד עבר בהיות כי כן מצאתי בהעתק וגם כי ברוב המקומות היה מטושטש כי ההעתק היה ישן נושן ואל בינתי לא נשענתי להגיה במקומות ההם אבל ברוב המקומות כתבתי בחוץ מה שנ"ל או ציינתי חוט בדיו כדי לישאל עליו„ ותשלם המלאכה מלוכה ערוכה בכל ושמורה בפי' ביאור התורה להראב"ע ז"ל היום יו' ג' ד' לחדש חשון שנת ישוב[2] יי' לשוש עליך, סדר הרימותי ידי אל יי' אל עליון קנה שמים וארץ„ פה סאלוניקי (Salonika) „ יוחנן בכמאא"ר אברהם ן' עזיז זלה"ה.

Although very young[3], our author was qualified, as few were either before or after him, for the difficult task of writing a supercommentary on a work so enigmatically worded as is Ibn 'Ezra's commentary on the Pentateuch. He possessed great natural talent, which both his eminent teacher[4] and he himself marvellously developed. Nor was he less favoured by local and historical accidents, in the production of this work. He was a Sephardi by birth and education, and therefore naturally familiar with Ibn 'Ezra's Sephardic attainments and style of writing. Even as Ibn 'Ezra he knew not merely the (agadic part of the) Talmud (see passim) and the Bible according to the whole extent of the Hebrew and Aramaic idioms, as extant in Text and Targum (see passim), but also Arabic and the philosophical works written in that language (see passim), and, in addition, he knew Latin also (leaf 55ª). He was born at Briviesca, a place in which not merely Jewish piety, but Jewish learning also was at home[5]. He came into the world in 1360[6], when the Jews of the Peninsula, although suffering

[1] This explanation is taken from Ibn Kaspi's *Larger Supercommentary*.

[2] According to Jahn's Tables, Tuesday 4 Marcheshvan 5318 corresponds to 28 September 1557 of the common era.

[3] When the author proceeded to the composition of this supercommentary he was only 24 years old; see leaf 2ᵇ, where it says: ...ואף כי איש כמוני בן ארבע ועשרים.... Compare also Steinschneider in Geiger's *Jüd. Zeitschr.* VI. p. 122.

[4] R. Barukh; see later on. Comp. also our communication respecting this MS., in *Jüd. Zeitschr.* VIII. p. 238.

[5] See leaf 1ᵇ, where it says: ...עיר הקדש תופשי התורה מה נורא המקום ההוא מקום בירבישקה.... Comp. also תשובות שאלות by R. Shelomoh b. Abraham Ibn אדרת (MSS. Add. 499 and Add. 500).

[6] Leaf 145ᵇ, we read the following: ...ונשלמה באלול שנת מאה וארבעים וארבע לאלף הששי.... According to this the supercommentary on Exodus was nearly finished in 1384; but, as our author was not much more than 24 years old when he wrote this (see Note 3 above), it follows that he was born about 1360.

terribly, suffered not so much as Jews as they did as Spaniards, and when, consequently they had not, despite the author's complaints, really degenerated, in a scientific point of view. Nor was the fate which befel his parents (ויומתו שם אבי ואמי) and his relatives (וכל לאמי, or the Jews in general?) and many others of his native city (נחרבה עירי, 1[b]), although very sad for him in every other respect, without advantage to him in reference to the production of this work, inasmuch as this catastrophe compelled him to produce something, were it only for bread. Even his youth proved with respect to this work an advantage. For while, on the one hand, it gave the author the energy necessary for his task, it on the other hand forced itself continually upon his mind and made him seek for information from others[1], older and riper, though perhaps not always more naturally talented, scholars than he was.

The importance of the work before us (of which one more copy[2] only is supposed to exist) lies in two circumstances:

(1) that it is a preeminently grammatical supercommentary, and as such it is unique. As is well known, Ibn 'Ezra's forte lay in the grammatical knowledge of Hebrew, of which he was not only one of the ablest teachers, but most distinguished founders. That he naturally brought this great knowledge to bear in a preeminent way on his Pentateuch-commentary has been alluded to before (p. 121 of this Catalogue, Note 2). Now Ibn Mayor, having justly the conviction that the point of gravitation in Ibn 'Ezra's writings was grammar, composed this supercommentary chiefly[3] with the view of explaining the grammatical remarks as extant in his author's Pentateuch-commentary.

(2) that it is an inexhaustible source of biography and bibliography. Not much more original, on the whole, than the Meqor Chayyim, and other, but similar, works, this supercommentary has a great advantage

[1] Leaf 2[a], we read thus: ...חזק ואמץ כתוב כל הסברות, תקבץ אותם, מכל מקומותם, אשר הם מפוזרות.... Upon this principle the author acted, although he claims originality, a few things excepted (see 2[b], ...וחדשתי מלבי דברי הרשום, לבד דברים מעטים שהחכמי' הקדומי' ממני חדשום...)

[2] This is in the Bodleian (Uri 128), and was written by the same copyist as ours, only two years later (Neubauer 228). Uri inadvertently describes it as by Shemtob Gafruth; probably because of an entry to that effect by a former owner. (See Steinschneider, Conspectus, p. 5, and Neubauer as before.)

[3] See leaf 2[a], where our author says, that he called this supercommentary *Hammaor Haggadol* (the greater light) in allusion to his family name (*Mayor* signifying in Spanish *greater*, while *Maor* signified in Hebrew *light*). They, he continues, who would study this work, would find in it *light* thrown on *every* hidden meaning (of Ibn 'Ezra), be it a mystical, grammatical, or exegetical one; but he (the author) would, although only briefly treating on the first and third points, dilate considerably on the second (grammar). Comp. also Steinschneider, in Geiger's *Jüd. Zeitschr.* VI. pp. 122, 123.

over these. For it contains not merely the best explanations known, on this head, down to 1384, but also the names of the eminent men from whose oral instructions they had been partly obtained; names some of which are otherwise utterly unknown. Nay, even on the works and authors which are to be met with here not for the first time, considerable and additional light is thrown by the way in which they are quoted here, as will be best seen from the following list.

1. Works and authors before Ibn 'Ezra[1].

a. Jewish works and authors.

(1) אשר בטוליטולה (sic) ספר הללו (109ᵇ). See this Catalogue, p. 32, Note 4. This celebrated Bible was, apparently, seen by the author himself.

(2) ספר דמשק (38ᵇ). This standard copy is only quoted from Ibn גנאח.

(3) חכמי החכמים (124ᵃ) and חכמי האמת (153ᵃ; the Rabbis of the Talmud and not the Cabbalists, as these latter are called by the author, on leaf 83ᵃ, ... הסכלים בעלי הקמיעות וההשבעות ...).

(4) Midrash השכם (26ᵃ). See this Catalogue, p. 54.

(5) R. Se'adyah Gaon (32ᵇ, 72ᵇ, 182ᵇ).

(6) קריש (sic) בן (69ᵃ). See *R. Jehuda ben Koreisch...Epistola de studii Targum utilitate*, ed. J. J. L. Bargès et D. B. Goldberg, Lutetiæ Parisiorum, 1857, 8vo.

(7) אביתור הפייט, i.e. R. Yoseph b. Yitzchaq (b. שנטאס) Ibn אביתור (68ᵇ).

(8) R. Adonim, i.e. דונש b. תמים (10ᵃ). See Jost's *Annalen*, II. pp. 320, 384.

(9) חיוג, who is quoted times too numerous for specification; see, however, next paragraph.

(10) R. Yonah Ibn גנאח. This grammarian and lexicographer also is quoted times too numerous for specification. He is identical with R. מארינוס, or מרינוס (i.e. מרונוס, Marwân ?), under which name he is very often quoted in this MS. (see our review of the *Kitab al-uzûl*... in the *Jewish Chronicle* of June 6, 1873, p. 161). Occasionally he is quoted here in connexion with the foregoing חיוג, for instance, 160ᵃ, where both are spoken of as ... ראשי הדקדוק החכם הגדול ר' יונה והחכם הקודם ממנו ר' יהודה חיוג.

[1] Some of these authorities are mentioned by Ibn 'Ezra himself; but as given here, they are quotations independent of him.

(11) R. *Yehudah*[1] b. גנאח (57^{b}, 218^{a}).

(12) R. Chananeel (195^{b}). (13) R. Yitzchaq Ibn גיאת (64^{a}).

(14) R. Mosheh Hakkohen Ibn גיקאטילה, who is quoted times too numerous for specification.

(15) R. Shemuel Hannagid (9^{a}, 234^{b}).

(16) Rashi (passim). (17) R. Yehudah b. בלעם (57^{b}).

(18) המדקדקים הקדמונים (20^{a}), המדקדקים הראשונים (55^{a}) and המדקדקים (passim), מדקדקי המערב (190^{b}).

b. Non-Jewish works and authors.

(1) Plato (אפלטון 167^{b}).

(2) Aristotle (ארסטו 111^{b}, 135^{b}, 155^{b}), הפילוסוף (111^{a}, twice, 125^{a}), ראש הפילוסופים (passim).

(3) Galen (גאליאנוס 156^{b}). (4) Hieronymus (55^{b}).

(5) הפילוסופים (142^{a}, 145^{a}), חכמי הפילוסופים (124^{a}), חכמי יון (95^{b}, 124^{a}, 155^{a}, 231^{b}), חכמי המחקר (112^{b}).

(6) Al-Farghānī (... בספר אלפרגני ... 85^{b}).

(7) Al-Fārābī (אבונצר בשם נמצא 34^{a}, אבונצר 202^{a}, אלפאראבי 182^{b}).

(8) בעלי התכונה (84^{a}), חכמי התכונה (85^{b}), חכמי הכוכבים (202^{a}).

(9) חכמי הספירות and חכמי המדות (124^{a}).

(10) הרופאים (158^{b}, 219^{b}, 229^{b}), חכמי הרפואה (124^{a}, 197^{b}), אומני הרפואה והפילוסופיא.

2. Works by Ibn 'Ezra.

a. Commentaries on the Bible.

(1) פרישה הראשונה on Genesis (6^{b}, 28^{b}, 42^{b}, 49^{b}).

(2) פרישה האחרת on the same Book (5^{b}, 9^{a}, 10^{a}, 28^{b}, 30^{b}, 32^{b} twice), also נסחא האחרת (7^{b}), and finally שטתו האחרת (32^{b}, 45^{a}). See this Catalogue, pp. 106, 139.

(3) שתי שטות on Exodus (92^{b}).

(4) פרישה הראשונה on the same Book (93^{a}), also נסחתו הראשונה (73^{b}, 98^{b}).

(5) נסחא האחרת on the same Book (131^{a}, 135^{a}), also שטתו האחרת (199^{b}, 128^{a}, 132^{b}). See this Catalogue, pp. 90, 139.

(6) פרישה האחרת on Leviticus (164^{a}).

[1] This R. *Yehudah* is, perhaps, a mistake for the foregoing R. *Yonah;* or is the b. גנאח a mistake for b. בלעם? See (17) later on.

(7) On the Former Prophets[1] (28^a).

(8) On Isaiah, which is quoted twenty-four times (15^b, 16^a, 28^a, 29^a, 32^a, 32^b, 40^a, 41^b, 42^a, 49^b, 51^a, 59^b, 73^b, 89^b, 107^a, 110^a, 132^a, 148^a, 161^a, 183^b, 202^a, 209^a twice, 217^b).

(9) On Joel (97^a).

(10) On Haggai (227^a).

(11) On Psalms (78^a).

(12) On Job (201^a).

(13) On Canticles (45^b).

(14) On Ruth (228^a).

(15) On Lamentations (160^a, 229^b).

(16) On Ecclesiastes (18^b, 206^a, 212^b).

(17) On Esther (222^a).

b. Other treatises of grammatical, theological, cabbalistical (?), mathematical and astronomical (astrological) import.

(1) צחות (33^b).

(2) שפת יתר (33^b, 69^a, 198^b).

(3) מאזנים (41^a, 58^b, 188^b).

(4) ספר היסוד (12^b), otherwise יסוד הדקדוק; see this Catalogue, p. 121, Note 3.

(5) A work not named by its title, but said to commence המשכילים יבינו מעלת לשון הקדש... (232^b).

(6) ספר השם (5^b, 106).

(7) יסוד מורא (63^a, 176^a twice, 176^b twice, 215^b).

(8) טעמי המצות (226^a), perhaps identical with the foregoing work (comp. ed. Creizenach, Hebrew part, p. 23).

(9) Commentary on (part of) the Sepher Yetzirah (34^b).

(10) On *Demonology* (שדים; 223^b).

(11) ספר המספר (180^b, 232^a).

(12) ספר העצמים[2] (127^b); see this Catalogue, p. 140, Note.

(13) ספר העבור (8^a); see p. 140 of this Catalogue, where this book is called סוד העבור.

(14) משפטי העולם (176^b).

[1] ...ובספר מלכי׳ יש מספרים כאלה ויבין אותם מי שראה פירושו לנביאי׳ ראשונים,, Comp. this Catalogue, p. 139.

[2] This book is said here to have been originally written by Ibn 'Ezra in Arabic and afterwards to have been translated into Hebrew, as will be seen from the following: ...והנני מגלה לך דעתו ז״ל מאשר כתב בספ׳ העצמים בענין הנבואה וזה תוכן דבריו כי הוא לשון ערב ואני מצאתיהו מועתק בלשון הקדש... Our author here professes to give the substance only, and he does not give the name of the translator. The wording does not agree literally with the version by אלפנדרי so largely quoted by Ibn Zarza; and yet it is difficult to believe that this version was unknown to our author. There seems no way out of the difficulty until we get some further light from other sources. There is a copy of אלפנדרי at Oxford (Mich. 338, olim 316, Neubauer 1234).

3. Works and authors contemporary with Ibn 'Ezra.

a. Jewish works and authors.

(1) תוספות (55b, 56a, 215b). These Additamenta are, apparently, Sephardic, as none of them are to be found in the editions of the Babylonian Talmud.

(2) Maimonides (הרמב"ם 16b, 128b, [1]הר"ם passim, and once also רבינו משה ע"ה 144b).

(3) R. Abraham b. David of Posquières (206a).

(4) R. Shemuel Ibn Tibbon, whose Milloth are quoted (20b). See פירוש מהמלות זרות in the מורה נבוכים (Sabionetta, 1553, Folio).

(5) R. *Yoseph* Qimchi, whose פירוש למראות יחזקאל is quoted (128b).

b. Non-Jewish works and authors.

(1) Ibn Roshd (ב"ר 124a, בן רשד 142a, ספר השמע 6a, השמע הטבעי 215a, השמים 16a, ספר הנפש 17a, אבן רשד בקצורו בהגיון 34a, ספר בעלי חיים 155a, שינה והקיצה).

(2) An Arabic Philosopher, who is the author of the אלפנז[2] (128b).

4. Works and authors after Ibn 'Ezra.

a. Works and authors named distinctly.

(1) R. Yoseph Ibn עכנין (128b).

(2) R. David Qimchi (18b, 57b, 90b, 106b, 235a).

(3) Nachmanides (הרמב"ן 148a, הר"ם, 211a, 213a; see Note 1 below).

(4) R. Mosheh Ibn Tibbon (12a).

(5) R. Nissim[3]. He explains Ibn 'Ezra (36a) and is also to be met with five times besides (92b, 129a, 178a, 196b, 216b).

(6) R. Chayyim Ibn Yisrael of Toledo, also רח"י (and by mistake also R. *Yitzchaq* Yisrael, 14b, 17a, 18a).

(7) R. Levi b. *Gershom* (Ralbag, whom our author calls הרלב"ג, התוכן הגדול, הפילוסוף המעולה, החכם, מאישטרי ליאון די ניולש, or with all

[1] See, however, later under Nachmanides, who also is occasionally called הר"ם.

[2] This is, to judge from the quotation, a treatise on Metaphysics. Is אלפנז a mistake for אלכנז (الكنز) or אלפוז (الفوز)?

[3] Of Marseilles? see החלוץ, VII. pp. 102—144.

these titles together (17a, 33a, 53b, 64b, 74b, 111b, 112a, 128b, 141a, 142a, 143a, 143b, 156b, 157a, 163a, 168a, 212b)[1].

(8) R. Shelomoh Ibn Ya'ish the Elder (היעישי, 46b). This Ibn Ya'ish wrote originally in Arabic; compare Meqor Chayyim in the so-called Margalioth Tobah, leaf 116a.

(9) R. Shemuel b. סנה (צרפה ז"ל 202b). This compiler died in 1368; see Zunz, *Eine merkwürdige Medaille* in Jost's *Annalen*, II. p. 166, col. 2.

(10) Prophiat Duran (אפ"ד[2], whose explanation of Gen. xlix. 14 is here communicated; 63a).

(11) R. Barukh (81b). This is the author's teacher; see this Catalogue, p. 149, Note 4.

b. Authors not distinctly named.

(1) בן רש"ף, also השרף. He mentions this writer always with some questionable epithet, as may be seen on almost every page. According to Steinschneider this is R. Shelomoh Franco the author of the סוד ה' (Geiger, *Jüd. Zeitschr.* VI. p. 122).

(2) בעל הסודות, also בעל הסוד, or ב"ה. He is quoted, even as the foregoing, on almost every page. That he is not identical, however, with him will be seen from leaf 161a, where they are both quoted on one and the same passage, and where they are said but slightly to differ in the explanation thereof. Nor does Ibn Kaspi seem to be identical with this Ba'al Hassodoth, as in no instance could we trace an explanation, given under this head, either in MSS. Add. 377. 3. 6 and Add. 510. 2. 2, containing his Sodoth, or in his larger commentary which we have examined for the purpose at Oxford (Mich. 313, olim 100). On the other hand, some of the matter is to be found in the Meqor Chayyim, many of the sources of which remain still unknown to us.

(3) עזיאל החולם (113a). This must have been a supercommentator on Ibn 'Ezra on the Pentateuch.

(4) חולה הנפש (122a).

(5) הנעדר (172b, 188b). This was, probably, a convert to Christianity.

(6) חכם אחד מחכמי ההר, i.e. of Montpellier; see this Catalogue, p. 87 (201a).

(7) המקובלים (106a), חכמי הקבלה (144b)[3].

[1] Our author refers mostly to this brilliant philosopher and divine either in reference to his commentaries on the works of Aristotle, or to his מלחמות ה'; sometimes also to his commentaries on the Pentateuch and Job.

[2] From this it will be seen that R. Yitzchaq b. Mosheh Hallevi (see this Catalogue, p. 92) used not merely the name *Prophiat Duran*, but also the abbreviation אפ"ד, long before 1391. Friedlaender and Kohn's conjecture as to the cause of the latter (מעשה אפד, p. 2) is, therefore, untenable.

[3] The date of these two last (6 and 7) is not quite certain, and they may belong to a somewhat earlier period.

In addition to the explanations, the sources of which are more or less clearly acknowledged by Ibn Mayor, there are some which he, apparently, passes off as his own, the real source of which, however, can be traced to others.

(1) Such is, for instance, an interesting explanation of an otherwise utterly unintelligible passage of Ibn 'Ezra on Exod. xxxi. 3, in which that author refers to his (now lost) commentary on Proverbs (see p. 90 of this Catalogue). Lines 2—12 of leaf 137[b] (אמר שם שיש במוח...ובינת נבוניו תסתתר) are literally copied from Ibn Kaspi's *Perush* or *Biur Hassodoth* (compare MSS. Add. 377. 3, leaf 83[a] and Add. 510. 2, leaf 86[a]). It is, of course, not impossible, that the words ...ע״ד ר׳ יוסף כספי... had fallen out in the copy before our scribe (see his subscription given on p. 149 above and a little later on, under the paragraph on the scribe).

(2) But such an excuse can scarcely be pleaded in the following case, where Ibn Mayor has not simply copied, but also slightly altered, a whole treatise of R. Mosheh of Narbonne[1]. Leaves 140[b] (three lines from below) —145[b] (וטעם והתגדלתי...באורך נראה אור...) are, except a few slight alterations, in which a grammatical explanation by Ibn Mayor, and a metaphysical view by R. Levi b. Gershom, are introduced, absolutely identical with the matter published by *Pinsker* under the name of אגרת...מאמר פילוסופי in Stern's כוכבי יצחק, Dreissigstes Heft, pp. 25—33 (see particularly p. 27, the passage commencing נתיישר). Now this is the less excusable in Ibn Mayor, since he taunts Ibn רש״ף most bitterly for a like offence (18[b]...כתוב לבן רש״ף בסוד הזה שגנבו מר׳ דוד קמחי...).

This notice would be incomplete were we to omit the mention of a few peculiarities and other points of interest in connexion with this work.

a. Peculiarities.

(1) While he takes as his text the *ordinary* commentary on Genesis and the *brief* commentary on Exodus, as most other supercommentators have done, he nevertheless finds room to remark upon all the difficult and interesting passages to be found in the other commentaries on Genesis and Exodus respectively. He is most instructive also on those on the other three books, and he is particularly suggestive as regards the various נסחאות of the whole.

(2) There are, in this work, four extensive Excursuses: (1) on the Most Holy Name (77[b]—86[a]); (2) on Angels (125[a]—129[a]); (3) on the Anthropomorphism of the שעור קומה on Ex. xxxii. 21 (139[b]—145[a]; comp. the paragraph on R. Mosheh of Narbonne above); and (4) on Intercalation (173).

(3) Each explanation commences with the phrase כ״ה (i.e. כונת המחבר; see above, p. 148), to which, in case the explanation should have been con-

[1] On this author and his time see the description of MS. Dd. 4. 1, below.

fessedly taken from some one else, another phrase ע"ד, i.e. ...על דעת is added.

(4) The term כלומר, which is here often used, is once (113^a) written כלו אמר (כאלו), which is the real solution of the origin of this word.

(5) Ibn 'Ezra is here continually called השלם; and is, indeed, considered by our author as the most perfect scholar, even in regard to Geography (see 98^b, ...והוא ידע הגבולים...). Ibn Mayor rarely disagrees with him in anything, and least of all in grammar; when he does disagree with him he uses the term of respect וכבודו יהיה מונח במקומו, as for instance, 191^b, &c.

(6) Our author describes very tersely (171^b) Ibn 'Ezra's position with regard to the Rabbins of the Talmud (together with an apology for such a position) thus: ...וזה הכלל קח בידיך במנהג זה החכם שעל הרוב סובר אליבא דלא כהלכתא כמו שאמר בזה...וככה דרכו בכל מקום וזה לפי שראה שאין האדם נותן לבו כי אם לפסק ההלכה... (see also 172^b, &c.).

b. Other points of interest.

(1) Our author evidently knows of a weekly Parashah ויפן (Ex. xxxiii. 15) within that of כי תשא (see leaf 138^b and compare p. 15 of this Catalogue).

(2) Concerning the prayer היום הרת עולם, which is here explained, and exhibits some notable variations in the text, Ibn Mayor (or rather R. Mosheh of Narbonne; see above) has (142^b) the following: ...להורות על היותו ית' התחלה הזה תקנו מסדרי התפלות של ראש השנה ויום הכפורים היום הרת עולם... (see also כוכבי יצחק as before, p. 29).

(3) Antichristiana are to be found 35^a, 55^a, 161^a[1], 238^b[2].

(4) Of the morals of some of the Jews of his time, particularly as contrasted with their intellectual superiority (which latter he traces to the dietary laws of the Pentateuch), our author gives a very disheartening

[1] Among others we read also the following remark on certain terrible diseases called after Christian Saints:

...כי לזה סמכו הנוצרים לכל החליים שהם קשים לרפאתם לפי חכמת הרפואה סמכו אותם אל אנשים קדושים מהם לפי דעתם כמו הצרעות לש' (Santo) לאזארו י"ש (ימח שמו) וכן כולם...

[2] This remark belongs to Ibn רש"ף, in whose name it is quoted and is mixed up with, or rather proceeds from, an anti-mohammedan passage, running thus: ...שהישמעאלים מביאין ראיה על דתם מזה הפסיק (i.e. Deut. xxxii. 2) ואמרו כי משה ע"ה ידע בנבואה שעתידים להיות אחריו שני דתות דת עיסי (Jesus) בן מרים ודת מחמד...

account[1], as he does also of the behaviour of the rich towards the learned poor.

(5) Witchcraft he illustrates (169^{b}) by an interesting story in which both he and a "wise woman" (אמגושית) of Tarragona (טראגונה) play a part.

(6) The הר הלבונה (Ibn 'Ezra on Gen. ii. 11) is given (12^{a}) as הר הלבנה (i.e. the Arabic גׄבל אל קמר), as he says he had found it in an Arabic book (of geography?).

(7) Leaf 158^{b}, the author speaks of a terrible disease, called the *Persian Fire*, and its cause[2].

(8) Diagrams, the original arrangement of which is traceable to the author, are to be found 77^{b}, 88^{b}.

Of R. Yochanan Ibn 'Azziz, the copyist of this MS. it is impossible to speak in too high terms. His intelligence is only equalled by his conscientiousness; and even editors of our own time could only rival but never exceed him (see passim, but particularly 47^{a}, 75^{a}).

The following marks of ownership are to be found in this volume.

(1) Every recto-page has the name of the weekly Parashah which is there found commented on. These superscriptions are in Sephardic Rabbinic, but not in the hand of the original scribe. They belong, no doubt, to an anonymous owner, of the xvi—xviith century.

(2) Another owner, of a little later date (xviith century), was R. Yitzchaq חנין (239^{b}, 240^{a}).

(3) Another owner again was R. Shemuel Yitzchaq חנין (9^{a}). This owner has Hebrew-Arabic notes on 138^{a}—139^{a}, and is, probably the son of the foregoing. He is, no doubt, identical with the Shemuel *ben* Yitzchaq חנין of 4^{b}, 112^{a}, 234^{a}, 240^{a}.

(4) The פי׳ על הרא״בע כ״י in Sephardic square character, which is to be found on the label on the back, belongs to an anonymous owner of the xvii—xviiith century. To the same hand belonged also the Library-mark No. 277, which number is now crossed through.

(5) The amplification of the title on the label on the back, running: המאור הגדול (פי על הרא״בע כ״י) ר׳ שם טוב בן יהודה ן׳ מאיור is in the handwriting of H. Lipschütz the bookseller.

[1] ...במה שנמצא באומתינו מחוזק ההכנה לחכמה יותר משאר אומות ועם קצתינו הפסיד השם הנכבד... (169^{a}).

[2] In connexion with this disease the following is to be read:

...וכבר הנידו הרופאים כי האשה ההרה בימי נדותה יהיה הנולד מצורע ובכלל הנה (הזה?) אם תתעבר אז הנה יקרה לנולד הפסד נפלא אם צרעת אם הדומה לו מההפסדים הנפלאים כמו האש הפרסי...

Attached to the inside of the binding at the beginning is a slip of paper, on which is set forth, in a few lines in Latin, the nature and value of this MS. This short and excellent, if not exhaustive, description belongs to the eminent bibliographer Dr Steinschneider, and is dated, Berlin, Nov. 8, 1867.

As regards the condition of the MS.: the first few lines of leaf 1[a] are not quite legible, leaf 240 is cut in the lower margin, a few leaves are disfigured by some cabbalistic (?) scribbling and arithmetical calculations (without connexion with the matter on the spot), whilst a few other leaves are somewhat soiled and stained. On the whole, however, this volume is as well-preserved as the matter it contains is valuable.

[Library-mark, Add. 433; bought in 1868 from H. Lipschütz.]

No. 53.

Paper, in quarto, $6\frac{7}{8}$ in. × $5\frac{1}{4}$ in.; 72 leaves, 4-sheet quires, 28—31 lines; Rabbinic character, fine German Ashkenazic handwriting of the XIVth century.

[פרוש על התורה. על שיר השירים ורות. ועל איזה הפטרות
כמנהג האשכנזים. לר׳ זלטמן נין ונכד לרבנו משלם הגדול]

Commentary on the PENTATEUCH, CANTICLES and RUTH, and some of the PROPHETIC PORTIONS according to the Ashkenazic rite, by R. זלטמן, great-grandson of Rabbenu Meshullam the Elder; defective.

Leaf 1[a], *Genesis;* 28[b], *Exodus;* 52[a], *Leviticus;* 60[a], *Numbers...;* 72 and all that followed wanting.

Begins (leaf 1[a]):

בראשית ברא אלהים את השמים וגו׳ למה נאמ׳ את. אם לא אמ׳ את הייתי
אומ׳ השמים והארץ בראו כביכול עתה אינו קאי כך משמ׳ שהק׳ בראם את
השמי׳ וכו׳. בראשית אמ׳ ר׳ יצחק לא היה צריך...וא״ת מילה וז׳ מצות...
מכלל בני נח לא יצאו וזאת ממד׳ (ממדרש) דר׳ יצחק אמנם כל בעלי
מדרשי׳ בדקו אחריה ולא מצאו מקומה אך קבלה היא שרבי׳
שלמה אמרה בש׳ אביו והוא פתח פי׳ החומש בא׳ וסיים בתיו...

Breaks off (leaf 71^{b}, on Num. xxxiv. 19—28):

...שנ׳ וינחלו בני שמעון בתוך נחלתם לפיכך לא הוצרך להזכיר בו נשיא ושניי׳ מחמ׳ שאירע בהם עבירה שעשה זמרי נשיאיהם (נשיאם) על כן לא נזכר בו נשיא · ובספר בינה שעשה הר׳ אלעזר מוורמשא ראיתי שמאותו מעשה ואילך לא נעשה משבט שמעון לא שופט ולא מלך ובשבט בנימין יש מפר׳ לפי שגלוי וידוע לפני ׀

Neither this MS. nor its fellow-MS. Add. 699, 1, as stated before (p. 66 of this Catalogue), have received due justice at the hands of their sometime owner, the late S. D. Luzzatto, in his description of them (Kerem Chemed, VII. pp. 68—71). If further proof were wanted for the truth of this assertion it would be found in the simple fact, that in the just-mentioned description not even the name of the author, which is distinctly to be found in the MS. (60^{b}—61^{a}), has been communicated. We will supplement this and other omissions; and we hope to be forgiven, if we shall, for the sake of completeness, now and then re-state a fact already to be found in Luzzatto's description.

We learn from the work before us, that the author's name was זלטמן[1] and that his father was the son of a daughter of Rabbenu Meshullam the

[1] ...אחר פט(י)רת א״מ (אבי מורי) נזכרתי כי בחיי(ו) בסוף אמר מ״א (מורי אבי) כמדומ׳ לי שהיה מק(שה) למה בארון כתו׳ ושמו בדיו...או כך ושמו בדיו ולא את הבתים על המוט הלוים אילו שתי תירוצי׳ לא שמעתי ממנו אני זלטמן. (Leaves 60^{b}—61^{a}) The name זלטמן, according to Zunz (see further on) signifies *Saltman;* this name, however, although not exactly without meaning (as it would be the equivalent of *Salzmann*) is absolutely without connexion with the original Hebrew, as given by him (*Jehuda*). We, for our part, think that it may with more propriety, signify either *Slotman* (the modern *Schlottmann*, i.e. *Schlossmann*) or *Soltman* (i.e. *Soldmann*, an equivalent of *Söldner*). And although one would, certainly, in either of these cases have sooner expected the so-called holy name (see further on) to have been יששכר (שכר, סכר, סגר), one must, with respect to the Jewish custom of using double individual names, bear in mind the fact, that the German Jew has to translate the Jewish name (biblical or post-biblical) into German and not vice-versâ, and moreover that it has been the habit of the German Jews from time immemorial, in naming their children doubly, not so much to translate the meaning of the biblical or post-biblical names, as to accommodate these to names already existing in the vernacular. Such, of course, can, in most cases, only be accomplished by preserving a mere similarity of letters however slight, and sometimes even only of mere sounds, e.g. the biblical Reuben is given by Robert, Asher by Anschel (i.e. Anselm), Gershom, or Gershon by Georg, while the post-biblical Alexander is given by Suisslein or Sussmann, &c. Now *Slotman* or *Soltman* have not merely several letters in common with the original name as given and proved by us (Shemuel; see further on), but are not so very far removed from its signification, at least, according to the derivation as given in 1 Sam. i. 20.

elder[1]. He was, certainly, a pupil of the celebrated R. Yehudah b. Shemuel (commonly called R. Yehudah Chasid). He was, in all probability, also a fellow-pupil of R. El'azar b. Yehudah (commonly called R. El'azar of Worms), who is well-known as Talmudist and religious poet (פייטן), and far more famed even than his relative[2] and master as Cabbalist. Like both his master and his fellow-pupil, our R. זלטמן was, no doubt, a German[3], although he had also probably studied in France[4] and resided in Bohemia[5] as well as in Germany.

As to the name זלטמן, though very uncommon, it is found in at least two other places. First, there is a MS. Machazor in the Bodleian Library (Mich. 617, olim 449, Neubauer 1035) which was copied in 1258 by one Yehudah b. Shemuel המכונה זלטמן[6]. Secondly, in the margin of a commentary on the Prayers, &c., by R. El'azar of Worms (Bodleian MS. Oppenh. 160, olim Folio 1010, Neubauer 1204, leaf 180ᵃ) occurs the following passage:

מטעמי רבינו יהודה חסיד זצ״ל העתקתי זה והקשה הר׳ זלטמן בנו...

[1] See leaves (37ᵃ—38ᵇ):

...והנה בשנה לפני מותו אמרתי לו למ״א מה דוחקך לזה... ועיד הק(שתי) לו בלום קבלת אילו הסודות מאבי אמך ר׳ משלם הגדול שתיקן תרגו׳ של עשרת הדברות...

This Rabbenu Meshullam Haggadol (or the elder) is supposed by Luzzatto (*Kerem Chemed*, VII. p. 70) to have been M. ben *Qalonymos* (of Lucca), but Zunz (*Literaturgesch. d. synag. Poesie*, p. 162, Note 1), with greater probability, takes him to have been M. ben *Mosheh* (of Mainz). See our descriptions of MSS. Add. 374, Add. 375 and Add. 667. 1.

[2] That El'azar of Worms must have been related to Yehudah Chasid will strike every one who examines their respective genealogies. The one is *El'azar* b. *Yehudah* b. *Qalonymos*, and the other is *Yehudah* b. Shemuel b. *Qalonymos* b. Yitzchaq b. *El'azar* (see this Catalogue, pp. 58, 59).

[3] This is proved even more than by his name, which is unquestionably German, by the thorough knowledge of that language, which he displays; see 1ᵇ, 2ᵃ, 6ᵇ (?), 18ᵃ, 22ᵃ, 27ᵃ (2), 28ᵇ, 36ᵃ, 37ᵃ (?), 45ᵃ, 52ᵇ (?), 54ᵃ, 54ᵇ, 59ᵇ (2), 63ᵃ, 65ᵃ, 68ᵇ, where he employs, at least, sixteen German words and phrases.

[4] That he, as a German, should have studied in France will not surprise any one who takes into consideration, that although the German Rabbinate counted, in the XIIIth century, hundreds of distinguished men, the greater portion of them had, down to almost the close of that century, been educated in France. This accounts for the French words on 1ᵇ, 2ᵃ (2), 6ᵇ (?), 7ᵃ, 17ᵇ, 37ᵃ (?), 52ᵇ.

[5] This alone accounts for his giving an explanation in Bohemian (לשון כנען; 1ᵇ) in addition to the one in French, which is subsequently augmented by one in German. Philologists, in our sense of the word, did not exist in his time.

[6] Zunz (*Gesch. u. Lit.* p. 207) calls this copyist *Jehuda Saltman;* but in our estimation זלטמן is the every-day-name (המכונה) of the copyist's father, which is the more certain as the so-called holy name (שם הקודש, which is used for religious purposes, as for instance, in publicly reading the Law, &c.) of the latter was unquestionably שמואל.

It seems to us to be an almost irresistible conclusion from these facts that the father of the copyist of the Bodleian Machazor was identical with the author of our MS., and that the latter again was identical with the R. זלטמן, son of R. Yehudah Chasid, mentioned in the above extract. If this be so, it follows that the mother of R. Yehudah Chasid was a daughter of Rabbenu Meshullam Haggadol. The following stemma will help to make this clear:

Meshullam Haggadol
|
Shemuel Chasid = a daughter
|
Yehudah Chasid
|
Shemuel, called זלטמן
|
Yehudah[1].

It is true that in the MS., as we have it, our author's father is not absolutely identified with R. Yehudah Chasid, but this is probably owing to various reasons, the chief of which are the incompleteness of our MS., and the carelessness, or ignorance, of transcribers (see later).

The greater portion of the matter given here is of considerable interest[2] and more critically instructive than one would have expected from the age in which it was produced. The commentary extends not merely over the Pentateuch, but also over select passages of the two Megilloth, Canticles (56ª; inserted between the Parshiyyoth קדושים and אמר) and Ruth (61ª; between במדבר[3] and נשא), and the Haphtaroth, according to the Ashkenazic rite, of חיי שרה (15ª), יתרו (41ª), זכור (45ᵇ), כי תשא (50ᵇ), ויקהל (51ᵇ), שקלים (52ª), מצורע (55ª), אמר (58ª), בהר (59ª), מחר חודש (61ᵇ), נשא (62ᵇ), קרח (66ª), and בלק (70ª). Little however is in reality due to R. זלטמן himself; the explanations contained in this commentary are chiefly due to his father, R. Yehudah Chasid, and R. El'azar of Worms, in whose names they are honestly given. The matter given here in his father's name[4],

[1] This Yehudah is possibly the father of the R. David b. Yehudah Chasid who wrote the מראות הצובאות (MS. Add. 664) and the אור זרוע (MS. in the Almanzi collection now in the British Museum). See more under the description of MS. Add. 664, below.

[2] In explanation of Exod. xix. 8 we read (leaf 37ª) the following: ...כל זה אינו שוה לעולם יאמרו ישר׳ בכשפים אתה מדבר כמו אות׳ לצנים ששוחקי׳ בקופולט ב״א (כ״א?) משמיע קול משונה כאילו אדם אחר מדבר ואינו אלא קולו של עצמו אלא תעמוד בינינו ונראה אותך לתוך פיך ואתה תדבר להק׳ שידבר עמנו פה אל פה ואז נצא מכל הספיקות...

[3] Read *Be*midbar and not *Ba*midbar, as both the Book of Numbers and the weekly Parashah are commonly, but erroneously, transliterated.

[4] We must not omit to mention on this occasion, that sometimes matter which is to be found here is also to be found in MS. Add. 669. 1 (No. 36, above); and this not merely as far as the essence goes, but even word for word. Curiously enough, even as here it is also there given in the name of the compiler's (or author's) father. Of the two theories possible, we discard

R. זלטמן received, singularly enough, only to a small extent in a direct way, the greater part having been communicated to him by a R. Yitzchaq of Russia[1], who seems to have been the father's pupil and the son's friend. Once (35^{a}) also a R. Yitzchaq of Poland (מפולין), another time a R. Mordekhai of Poland, a third time (16^{a}) a R. Aharon, a fourth time (50^{a}) an anonymous Rabbi, a fifth time (68^{b}) a R. Menachem, and a sixth time (58^{a}) a R. Nathan of Bamberg (מבבנברק) also communicated to the compiler explanations by his (the compiler's) father. The explanations for which the compiler cites R. Yehudah b. Shemuel by name are more direct, while those attributed to R. El'azar b. Yehudah are again less so.

Of greater interest, however, than the explanations, are the authorities quoted in this book; and of these again such especially as were either contemporaries of the compiler or his immediate predecessors.

1. His earlier authorities are:

(1) הפייט (9^{b}, margin, but by the original scribe; 19^{b}, 38^{b}, 43^{b}); הקליר (8^{a}), Eli'ezer (El'azar) הקליר (17^{b}, 45^{a}[2]).

(2) ...אמיתי גאון שעשה הפזמון יי' יי'... (49^{b}).

(3) R. Yoseph Tob-'Elem (34^{a}).

(4) R. Yoseph b. Shelomoh of Carcassonne (...ביוצר של חנוכה לבשה רוח את יהודה..., 70^{a}, without, however, the mention of the author's name).

(5) הערוך (28^{a}). (6) Rashi, Rabbenu Shelomoh (passim).

(7) Rabbenu Meshullam Haggadol, his great-grandfather (38^{a}).

(8) R. Shimshon (ben ?) Meshullam (38^{b}).

(9) R. Se'adyah (מ"א משום; not the Gaon, 38^{b}).

2. His more recent predecessors are:

(1) R. Shemuel b. Meir (35^{b}), קונטרס ר' שמואל (62^{b}).

(2) Rabbenu Tam (5^{b}). (3) Rabbenu Yoseph Bekhor Shor (64^{a}).

that of plagiarism and incline towards that of considering the compiler of the work contained in MS. Add. 669. 1 to have been the son of our R. זלטמן and also the copyist of the Bodleian Machazor mentioned above.

[1] The name occurs: 14^{b}, 16^{a}, 16^{b}, 17^{a}, 18^{b}, 26^{a}, 27^{a}, 29^{a}, 31^{a}, 32^{b}, 35^{a}, 35^{b}, 36^{b}, 38^{b}, 39^{a}, 43^{a}, 44^{b}, 49^{a}, 49^{b}, 51^{a} (2), 51^{b}, 53^{a}, 53^{b}, 54^{b}, 55^{b}, 61^{b}, 62^{b}, 64^{b} (2), 68^{b}. Out of the explanations communicated by R. Yitzchaq, and to be found in these places, one (49^{a}) belongs to R. El'azar of Worms, whilst another (54^{b}) belongs to himself. Two (29^{a}, 39^{a}) may or may not be his own; all others, however, are distinctly given in the name of the compiler's father.

[2] On this page we read the following: ...והיינו מה שיסד ר' אליעזר הקליר באתה כוננתה בסדר של יום הכפורים. Compare Zunz, *Literaturgesch. d. synag. Poesie*, pp. 34 (Note 1), 58.

(4) Rabbenu אפרים (Abraham) Ibn 'Ezra (7^b), Rabbenu Abraham (8^a), הר' Ibn 'Ezra (32^b), R. Mosheh (Abraham) Ibn Ezra (67^a).

(5) R. Elchanan, the Tosaphist (3^b, 23^a).

(6) R. Yitzchaq Hallaban (4^a). (7) R. Aharon b. Yoseph (8^a).

3. His own contemporaries are:

(1) The author's father (מ"א, א"מ, passim).

(2) The author's teacher (החסיד, passim). A record of his death and some other interesting matters in connexion with it are to be found 45^b—47^a. It has been shown above that these two authorities are probably identical.

(3) R. Yitzchaq of Russia (see above, p. 163). His communications are occasionally followed by כ'ה'ל' ר'ימ' משמ'א (א'מ), which signifies כן הגיד לי ר' יצחק מרוסיא משם מורי אבי (אבי מורי).

(4) R. Yitzchaq of Poland (see above, p. 163). It is not impossible that this is a mistake either for the just-named R. *Yitzchaq* of Russia, or for the following R. Mordekhai of *Poland*.

(5) R. Mordekhai of Poland (see above, p. 163).

(6) R. Aharon (see above, p. 163).

(7) R. Menachem (see above, p. 163).

(8) R. Nathan of Bamberg (see above, p. 163).

(9) R. Eli'ezer of Forchheim (מבורכחיים, 54^b, see above, p. 66, Note 1).

(10) R. El'azar of Worms (see above, p. 163).

(11) R. Yehoshua' b. Yitzchaq (70^a). He bears testimony to the fact that a certain explanation had been given in a certain way by the compiler's father. He was, perhaps, a son of R. Yitzchaq of Russia.

(12) An anonymous Rabbi (. . . הוגד לי' . . . 50^a; see above, p. 163).

In addition to these ought to be also mentioned a R. Simchah (59^a); but it is impossible, from the context, to find out, whether he was the compiler's contemporary R. Simchah b. Shemuel, or indeed, whether he was not the R. Simchah of Vitri-le-François (the author of the Machazor Vitri; see our description of MS. Add. 667. 1).

A few words about the scribe of this copy as well as the previous copyists of the work contained in this MS. will, we hope, not be without interest.

1. The copyist of this MS. is anonymous[1] but identical with that of MS. Add. 669. 1 (see above, No. 36); and he exhibits in both MSS. great

[1] The vacant spaces at the end of lines in both MSS. are filled up with part of the word on the next line, but very often also by a ר (see Excurs. I.).

talent as a scribe, which, however, does not prevent him from occasionally making grievous mistakes.

2. Even as he cannot have copied MS. Add. 669. 1 from the autograph, so there must have been one intermediate copy at least, between this copy and the original composition, since in various places (56ª, 59ª; 65ª, 70ª) additions are found by an earlier scribe, which additions, stood, no doubt, originally on the margin, but are now in the body of the work. They announce themselves, however, clearly enough, by the phrase תוספת, תוספ' סופר, &c. being placed either before or after them, as the work of an earlier scribe.

3. This earlier scribe's name was R. Shelomoh; a relative of his (65ª) was R. Shemuel (b. Qalonymos?), and one of his contemporaries (56ª) was a certain R. Yechiel b. Shemuel Hakkohen, who as well as another unnamed (70ª), communicated to him matter belonging to R. El'azar of Worms (the R. נטרונאי b. Menachem, disciple of R. Mosheh of France quoted by him on 59ª, was, surely, an older authority).

4. This R. Shelomoh is, if we mistake not, identical with the earlier scribe (or compiler) of part of the works contained in MSS. Add. 394 and Add. 561. He belonged, at all events, to the middle of the xiiith century, and his name in full was R. Shelomoh b. Shemuel.

As regards the literature to be found on the margins, the following few remarks will suffice.

1. The original copyist has emendations and remarks on leaves 1ª, 9ᵇ (in which הפייט is mentioned; see above, p. 163), 33ª, 56ª (upper margin).

2. Of the owners who left their marks of ownership on MS. Add. 669. 1 only two can be traced here, viz. the German Ashkenazic hand of the xivth century (early) and the Italian hand of the xv—xvith century. The former wrote all that is to be found on leaves 25ª, 32ª, 35ᵇ (in which R. Shema'yah is mentioned), 41ª, 54ª, 54ᵇ, 55ª, 55ᵇ, 56ª (inner margin), 57ª, 57ᵇ, 58ª, 58ᵇ, 61ᵇ, 62ª, 67ᵇ; and although, at the first glance, it may appear different, on strict examination it will be found that it is one and the same hand, only writing at various periods. To the latter hand is due the transliteration of the German words on leaves 27ª, 68ᵇ. For other owners, see this Catalogue, pp. 66, 67.

The condition of the MS. is, if possible, even worse than that of MS. 669. 1. Of leaf 57 scarcely one-third is left, while leaf 71 is very seriously injured, and even that part which is entire is so soiled and stained that it is almost illegible. But as if in compensation, the very last lines, which we have, after a great deal of trouble, succeeded in transcribing (see above, p. 160), contain an important piece of bibliographical information.

[Library-mark, Add. 669. 2; bought in 1869 from S. Schönblum.]

No. 54.

Paper, in folio, 10 in. × $7\frac{3}{4}$ in.; 344 leaves, 8-sheet quires, 30 lines; Rabbinic character, Sephardic handwriting of the XIVth century.

חדושים בפירוש התורה [לרבנו משה בן נחמן ירונדי[1]]

Commentary on the PENTATEUCH, by R. Mosheh b. Nachman of Gerona (Ramban, Nachmanides[2]), in two parts[3]; defective.

I. GENESIS—EXODUS. Leaves 1—128 (containing the whole of *Genesis* and part of *Exodus*) of this part are now wanting; but leaf 128 has been supplied by a leaf now numbered 128*[4].

[1] *Mosheh b. Nachman* (ירונדי) *Yerondi* (i.e. G*e*rondi, and not G*i*rondi, as Steinschneider writes the name in the Bodl. Catal.), with the common concluding phrase *Chazaq*, form the acrostic of the מסתגאב for the מלכיות of New Year, commencing: ...מראש מקדמי עולמים. (For the original of this soul-stirring, cabbalistic poem, see Geiger's Melo Chofnajim, Berlin, 1840, 8vo. Hebrew part, pp. 39—41, and Sachs' Die rel. Poesie d. Juden in Spanien, Berlin, 1845, 8vo. Hebrew part, pp. 50, 51.) Gerondi is written יירונדי by R. Yitzchaq ben Yehudah Gerondi, as may be seen from the poetical pieces for the New Year's service according to the rite of Algiers (מחזור קטן...ארגיל, Livorno, 1861, 8vo. leaves 64ᵃ, 65ᵃ, 66ᵇ).

[2] The Hebrew equivalent of this name, נחמני, is used by Don Yitzchaq Abarbanel (who died in 1508); see ישועות משיחו, passim. Another form נחמוני, used by at least two authors, is based on a false analogy with such names as מיימוני, חזקוני, &c. Of these two authors, one is the anonymous writer of the שם הגדולים (who was a grandson of R. Shemuel of Schlettstadt and therefore may be presumed to have lived in the XVth century); see Werbluner, *Debarim Attikim*, Part 2 (Leipzig, 1846, 8vo.), p. 9. The other is the anonymous writer of the דקדוקי רשי (Riva di Trento, 1560, 4to.), leaves 42ᵇ, 43ᵇ; see Zunz, *Gesch. u. Lit.* p. 121, Note d.

[3] After the whole of the introduction to the book, and a portion of the commentary on the pericope ויקרא, had been, by mistake or otherwise, written on leaf 160, the scribe recommenced the introduction on leaf 162ᵃ as a fresh part.

[4] That leaf 128* is a *bona fide* supplement to this MS., and not to MS. Add. 524. 1, is easily proved: (1) While a small portion of the last line in the supplement is blank, because no more matter was wanted to make this MS. perfect (at that particular time and in that particular place), there ever must have been between this supplement and MS. Add. 524. 1 a defect amounting to more than a page or so. (2) As in this MS., so also in the supplement, the verso-page has the catchword on the last, and not on a fresh, line, as in the case in the fellow-MS., so that one clearly sees that the supplement was written for the accommodation, even as it was written on the model, of this MS.

II. Leviticus—Deuteronomy. Leaf 161, perhaps[1] blank, wanting; 162[a], *Leviticus* (176 wanting); 227[a], *Numbers;* 281[a], *Deuteronomy* (286, 303, 336, 337 [which last leaf is, however, supplied by 337*], 341—344, wanting).

Begins (leaf 129[a], on Ex. xxii. 26):

צעקת כל מתחנן לו . . .

Breaks off (leaf 340[b], on Deut. xxxiii. 16; printed edd. on 13):

. . . ועל דעתי מגד ארץ ומלואה

This commentary is not merely philosophical and cabbalistic[2] (as Steinschneider states in the Bodl. Catal. p. 1960), but also, to a great extent, Midrashic, and, as far as Ibn 'Ezra and to a certain degree also Rashi and Maimonides are concerned, also polemical[3]. It has been printed many times, both with and without the sacred text[4]; and it has been twice,

[1] Leaf 160[b], certainly, looks as if the matter found there was to be continued on the immediately succeeding page; on the other hand we have now the introduction to Leviticus actually re-written on leaf 162[a]. These facts coupled with another, that leaf 161 is now lost, make it doubtful, whether this last-named leaf had ever been written on and afterwards cancelled, or whether it had remained blank, totally or partially, and had been afterwards lost.

[2] For a purely cabbalistic commentary on the Pentateuch by our author (consisting of a literal extract of all the cabbalistic matter from this work by an anonymous writer) see MS. Add. 493 below.

[3] The assertion, however, made by Chayyim Goldschmied that our author's *Pentateuch*-commentary was, on account of the polemics against Rashi and other commentators contained in it, called מלחמת הרמב"ן (see Landau's edition of the 'Arukh, iv. p. xxxi, Note 2) is incorrect. At least the authority adduced for it has yet to be found. We have certainly read through the 316 closely-printed pages of the יד מלאכי (Berlin, 1851, 4to.) without finding any trace of it.

[4] A word may be said here of the earliest printed editions of this commentary. (1) The dateless edition of 'Obadyah, Menassheh and Binyamin of Rome, of which a fine copy is in Christ's College Library (G. 4. 8), for the repeated use of which we here record our thanks to the Master (Dr Cartmell). (2) The Lisbon edition of 1489, of which copies are in the University Library and at Clare College, the latter (A. 5. 8) perfect at the end. (3) The Naples edition of 1490 (in the University Library), which, notwithstanding the assertion of the editor (or editors) to the contrary, labours under many shortcomings, owing both to the incorrectness and defectiveness of the MS. from which it was made; see passim. (The introduction to Deuteronomy, which is wanting in its place, is, however, to be found at the end of the whole work.) Its only merit, if merit it be, is its consistently conforming to the Naples editions of other works at that period, in which the names אלהים, אלהי &c. are given by אלדים, אלדי &c. (4) The Venice edition of 1545 (ש"ה, ובהרמב"ן, or אליהו המדקדק), for the loan of which we have to thank Dr Cookson, the Master, and Mr Wordsworth, Fellow and Librarian of St Peter's College. This edition, though not exactly a reprint of

at least, translated into Latin (see our description of MS. Gg. 4. 34, below). Author and work, then, being well known, we will confine ourselves to describing briefly the MS. before us.

The copy before us conforms, on the whole, to the printed editions; but has, nevertheless, several various readings of considerable value. Perhaps the most interesting, even if not most valuable, are the rhymes at the end of Exodus, which here stand thus (leaf 160ª):

...ירמוז אל הכבוד השוכן בקרבו.
והנה נשלם ספר הגאולה אשר יי׳ אלהי ישראל בא בו
לבני ישראל עם קרובו
הושיעו מיד שונאו וגאלו מיד אויבו
ואליו יבא
באלפי שנאן ורכב רבוא
לתת לו תורת אמת להנחיל יש את אוהבו
בנה בניתי בית זבול לשכן שכינתו על כרובו
ומקדש למקדש שהמלך במסבו
וברוך יי׳ החפץ שלום עבדו אשר עד הנה עזרו לבא
המחדש נעוריו בשיבו   המשביע בתורתו רעבו
ויניקהו דבשו וחלבו   כי הכין כל לבבו
ולשמו יברך בקרו וערבו   ברוך שאכלנו משלו וחיינו בטובו
חזקו ידים רפות ועינים כושלות אמצו״   בנל״ך ואע״י.

Of these lines, 5—9 are not to be found in any of the editions except the first (leaf 123ᵇ); and there only in an inferior state; while the last line, which may, however, be due to the copyist, does not occur even there.

The name of the original scribe was, perhaps, Mosheh[1], as that name, whenever it occurs at the commencement of a line, is distinguished by three or five points being obliquely placed against it (see passim). He

the Naples edition, stands in close connexion with it, as may be seen passim, but particularly from the commentary on Gen. ii. 11 and the rhymes at the end of Numbers (leaves 6ᵇ, col. 2 and 129ᵇ, col. 2). Steinschneider should scarcely have called this an *editio castrata*, seeing that, a few Antichristiana (?) excepted, it is as full as, and, in some respects, even fuller than, the preceding editions. (5) If there be a Venice edition, which deserves so disparaging an epithet, it is that of 1548 (King's College Library, A. 5. 1 and Trinity College Library, A. 14. 9); although, on the other hand, it must be remarked, that in this edition the commentary is a mere accessory. The first three editions must have been derived from three different MSS. The other early editions are not accessible to us.

[1] It does not necessarily follow, that a name, distinguished by points, &c., in a MS., is always the scribe's; it may be that of the original owner (see Excursus I.). In this case there is the less certainty in assigning the name Mosheh to the scribe, as the letters ה and ה are invariably used by him for the filling up of the vacant spaces of the lines.

was, if one may judge from his hand, a Sephardi of the Peninsula, and lived about 1330—1380. He must have been a superior man in point of learning, if not in that of calligraphy. The following peculiarities, which one or all may however be due to the copy before him, are worthy of note:

1. Instead of the בע"ה of the printed editions, he has בג"ה[1] (see, for instance, leaf 282[a]).

2. Rashi he gives invariably by ר"ש (see this Catalogue, pp. 40, 48, 67).

3. He occasionally divides a word, placing part of it on one line, and part on the next line (see, for instance, leaf 272[b], lines 10 and 11).

In addition to this scribe, others (owners or otherwise) have left their marks on this MS:

1. A Peninsular Sephardi of the xvth century, who wrote on the margins and in current character (see passim).

2. Another Peninsular Sephardi of the xv—xvith century, who wrote on the margins and in Rabbinic character (see 131[a], 134, 135).

3. A third Peninsular Sephardi of the xvith century, who also wrote on the margins and in Rabbinic character (see 145[a]).

4. A fourth Peninsular Sephardi, who wrote leaf 128*. The MS. must have become defective, at the latest, towards the middle of the xvith century, which defect was, however, made good by the insertion of this leaf about that time. It is in Rabbinic character, numbering 33 lines to the page.

It begins (on Ex. xxii. 15 and 16; printed editions 15):

ירבו עצבותם אחר מהרו...

And ends (on Ex. xxii. 26):

...כי חנון הוא ושומע צעקת

5. A Greek Sephardi, who wrote leaf 337*. It is written in Rabbinic character of the latter part of the xvith century, and contains 34 lines to the page.

It begins (on Deut. xxx. 43; printed editions 40):

כי בבנין בית שני לא הרנינו גוים עמו...

And ends (on Deut. xxxiii. 3):

...יאמר גם עתה

6. Another Greek Sephardi of the xvi—xviith century, who wrote in an inelegant Rabbinic character, on the margins of 139[a], 214[a], 304[a], 318[a], 319[a], 319[b].

The state of this MS. is, when compared with Add. 524. 1, not very bad. In addition to the losses of leaves enumerated above we must

1 This is to be added to the instances given by Zunz in his interesting article on א"ה and בע"ה in Steinschneider's המזכיר, x. p. 50.

however mention: 1. That leaf 223 is torn; but there is nothing missing; 2. That the outer margins of leaves 276 and 296 have been cut away by the bookbinder, by which process some valuable notes have been destroyed; 3. And that the whole MS. is a little stained, soiled, and worm-eaten; but the paper, except in two places (288ᵇ and 329ᵇ), where its texture was originally rather loose, is fairly strong to this day.

[Library-mark, Add. 524. 2; bought in 1869 from H. Lipschütz.]

No. 55.

Parchment and paper, in folio, 10 in. × $7\frac{5}{8}$ in.; (originally 344 leaves, 8-sheet quires, the inner and outer sheets parchment, the rest paper), 33 lines; Rabbinic character, Greek Sephardic handwriting of the XIV—XVth century.

חדושים בפירוש התורה [לרבנו משה בן נחמן ירונדי]

Commentary on the PENTATEUCH, by R. Mosheh b. Nachman of Gerona (Ramban, Nachmanides); defective.

Leaf 1, blank; 2 (wanting) Introduction; 3ᵇ, *Genesis* (17, 19—30, 32, 33, 35—38, 40, 41, 43—46, 48, 49, 51—54, 56, 57, 59—62, 64, 65, 67—70, 72, 73, 75—77, 79—81, wanting); 82ᵇ, *Exodus* (83—86, 88, 89, 91—94, 96—98, 100—115, 117, 118, 120, 121, 123, 125, 126, 128 and all afterwards wanting).

Begins (leaf 3ᵃ, in the introduction):

בחזקיא וספר תאגי הראה להם והם...

Breaks off (leaf 127ᵇ, on Exod. xxii. 7):

...והנכון שיקרב אל האלהים לישבע שגנב כמו שהוא

From the enumeration of leaves given above, it will be seen that this MS., as it now stands, is a mere fraction of what it originally was. It is nevertheless of no small value. For although it conforms on the whole to the printed editions, it yet not only favourably contrasts with them in point of general correctness, but also in occasionally containing matter not to be found in them[1].

[1] Of the several readings found here, and not in the printed editions, we will only mention one, in which it says, that *Noah saw Adam* (MS. leaf 22ᵇ, on Gen. x. 2—6), because the passage had been severely commented upon by the author of the work contained in MS. Add. 508. 4 (R. Zekharyah Hakkohen; see No. 59 of this Catalogue below). The passage in question runs here thus:

...ויעיד להם על נח ובניו שראו המבול והיו בתיבה והנה הוא עד מפי עד בכל ענין המבול ועד שלישי על היצירה כי נח ראה אדם הראשון ויצחק ויעקב ראו שם...

It is not improbable, that this very MS. was in the hands of R. Zekharyah Hakkohen, and that he took from it his points of attack against our author (see the foregoing Note), although this is not the only copy in which the objectionable passage alluded to occurs (see No. 56 of this Catalogue).

The vacant spaces at the end of lines are filled up with part of the word on the next line, and occasionally by an א (see Excurs. I.).

The following have left marks of their ownership on this MS.:

1. An anonymous Greek Sephardi of the commencement of the xvth century, by writing notes on the margins. These contain a few supplements of words and phrases forgotten by the original copyist, and now and then also an emendation or suggestion belonging to the annotator himself (7ª, 7ᵇ, 92ᵇ, 123ᵇ). Any other marginal supplements in a Greek Sephardic hand, belong to the original copyist himself.

2. The anonymous writer of the words: חדושי התורה מהרמב"ן ז"ל (leaf 1ᵇ). The writing is in Sephardic Rabbinic character, of surpassing beauty, and belongs to the end of the xvth century.

3. R. Elqanah קפשלי (leaf 1ª [1]). This name is written in bold Sephardic Rabbinic character (not Greek Sephardic, which one would have expected). The writing belongs to the xv—xvith century.

4. An anonymous annotator, who wrote between the lines and on the margins of leaves 4ª, 6ª. The writing is Sephardic Rabbinic character of the xvith century.

5. R. David b. Meir Ibn בביניישטי (?Benevenisti). This name is written in Sephardic square character (leaf 1ª). The writer seems to have belonged to the xviith century, and lived, no doubt, in Turkey.

6. On leaf 1ᵇ are two entries, recording money transactions, in 'Spagnol' (Judæo-Spanish) and written in Sephardic current character. The following names occur: (1) of persons: R. Yomtob אלנקוה, R. Mosheh שבת, and R. Mosheh b. אלחאת; (2) of places: Constantinople (אישטאנבול); (3) of money: Reals (ריאליש). These entries belong, apparently, to the xvii—xviiith century.

7. R. Abraham Hallevi ס"ט. This name is to be found on leaf 4ª, outer margin. It is a signature, somewhat artistically executed, in Sephardic current character of the xviii—xixth century. For some time past this MS., with the one described in the last No., have formed one volume, but the matter missing between them amounts to more than a page[2].

[1] As of this name there is only left the faintest trace possible we specify it minutely as being 3 in. from the upper, and $3\frac{7}{8}$ in. from the outer, margin. Is this the father of R. Eliyyah קפסלי?

[2] The matter missing is from ... טוען אם לא שלח (Ex. xxii. 7) to מהר ... ... לשון קישור וכן (Ex. xxii. 15 and 16).

The entry, partly in Rabbinic and partly in current (Polish) character, on fly-leaf 2ᵃ, is in the hand of H. Lipschütz, the bookseller; it runs thus: פי׳ רמבן על התורה חסר מן ההקדמה ומן פרשת וזאת הברכה. This statement refers to the time, when MS. Add. 524. 2 was bound at the end of this MS.

The condition of the MS. is not good; as, besides the defects enumerated above, leaf 3 is almost gone, as is also part of 66, while 115 is badly torn; and damp as well as worms have done considerable injury to this otherwise very interesting copy.

[Library-mark, Add. 524. 1; bought in 1869 from H. Lipschütz.]

No. 56.

Paper, in quarto, 8⅝ in. × 6 in.; 202 leaves, mostly[1] 5-sheet quires, 21 lines; Rabbinic character, Egyptian Sephardic handwriting of the xvth century.

חדושים בפירוש התורה [לרבנו משה בן נחמן ירונדי]

Commentary on the PENTATEUCH, by R. Mosheh b. Nachman of Gerona (Ramban, Nachmanides), in several parts[2]. Part 1; defective.

I. Genesis. Leaves 1—3 wanting; 4ᵃ, *Introduction;* 6ᵇ, *Genesis* (12 wanting); 202, probably blank, wanting.

Begins (leaf 4ᵃ, in the Introduction):

אמר שיהיה בבריאת המחצב שער בינה בתולדותיו...

Ends (leaf (201ᵇ):

...ויובן הענין במסכת שבת ובמסכת כתובות[3]. תם ונשלם של״הע (שבח לאל העולם) מעתה ועד העולם.

אתחיל לכתוב ספר ואלה שמות[4] בעזרת האל השוכן מרומות אמן.

[1] The first quire has six sheets.

[2] That the scribe wrote this commentary in several (probably five) parts, is clear, from the phrases with which he finishes, on leaf 201ᵇ, Genesis and introduces, or rather announces, Exodus. It is, therefore, also very probable, that leaf 202 remained blank; and being blank, it was ultimately lost.

[3] From these short quotations even it will be seen, how rich in omissions this copy is; for not only is in each line one word less than even in the commonest editions, but there is the whole of the concluding rhymes, after that book, omitted.

[4] See Note 2.

Although this MS. conforms, on the whole, to the printed editions, from which it, in most cases, only differs by the omissions and mistakes (of which latter it has not a few), it is, nevertheless, of great importance for the following two reasons:

1. Like MS. Add. 524. 1 it has (leaf 51ª) the rare reading, that Noah saw Adam (see this Catalogue, p. 170, Note).

2. It has (leaf 34ª, on Gen. iv. 22) between אין בזה טעם להזכירה בכאן and ומדרש אחד לרבותי' the strange phrase הוסיף המחבר ז"ל; and again between בפרקי ר' אליעזר and ואחרים the phrase ע"כ. Now, this is an important key. It is, in our opinion, an indication, wherever the עד כאן occurs in this commentary (and it occurs several times even in the printed editions; see passim), that just shortly before that, an addition had been made by the author himself at the second[1], or even a later recension[2].

The original scribe's name was, probably, Abraham, as the letters א and מ are frequently to be found at the end of lines (see Excursus I.). This scribe was a Sephardi, and either a native of Egypt, or, at all events, trained there (probably both); as his peculiar handwriting (besides the consistent omission of the use of the ף, where others would place it) will testify to. This scribe has a few peculiarities worth mentioning:

1. He always repeats the last word or two of the verso-page (being the last of the line, or on a line by themselves) on the next leaf; thus forming a species of catchword.

2. He very often leaves spaces for large initial words and phrases, some of which spaces either he, his assistant (see later), or a later scribe (or owner, see later) fills out. Some of these spaces are filled out with smaller letters than originally intended, while others are still blank.

3. Sometimes he leaves spaces, as if there was something missing, whilst in reality such is not the case; and although part of this is no doubt owing to the brittleness of the paper, this cause alone will not account for every case.

An assistant apparently, of the original scribe, a Peninsular Sephardi, wrote the latter part of leaf 56ᵇ, the whole of 201ᵇ, filled out a few of the vacant spaces, and made also some corrections.

Others, however, besides these two scribes, have contributed to this MS. as it now stands; these were probably owners.

[1] That, at least, a second recension was made by the author is well known from his remark on Gen. xxxv. 16 (not 17, as in Steinschneider, probably by a misprint).

[2] The final recension was made, shortly before the author's death, somewhere in Palestine (? at 'Acco, i.e. St Jean d'Acre); this final recension, however, seems to have been at least a third, as a second had most assuredly been made at Jerusalem itself (. . . ועכשיו שבאתי לירושלם . . .; see the preceding Note).

1. A Peninsular Sephardi of the xv—xvith century, by supplying omissions (which he did by filling out vacant spaces, and insulated words over some of the lines). He wrote in Rabbinic character.

2. Another Peninsular Sephardi, also of the xv—xvith century, by supplying corrections on the margins. He wrote in current character. Twice (leaves 60ᵃ and 138ᵇ) he has supplied also drawings (as a 'hand,' &c.) to draw the reader's attention to a particularly striking passage in the commentary.

Three other owners have left their marks of ownership in a less pretentious way:

1. A Peninsular Sephardi of the xvith century, by writing the words עמ"י עש"ו (on leaf 4ᵃ) in Rabbinic character.

2. An Italian, also of the xvith century, by writing (on leaf 4ᵃ) the words ספר בראש' להרמב"ן ז"ל in Rabbinic character.

3. Another Italian, but of the xviith century, by writing in mixed (Rabbinic and current) character the abbreviation בהנוא"ל (i.e. בשם ה' נעשה ונצליח אמן לעולם).

The state of the MS. is very bad, owing partly to the original brittleness of the paper (see above), partly to the corrosive nature of the ink, and partly to damp. Between these three causes the MS. has been almost ruined. From leaf 37 onwards, there are few leaves indeed, which have not lost whole words, or even whole lines; from leaf 100 to leaf 133, however, entire pieces of the middle have fallen out and continue to do so to this day, on the slightest touch. From 134 onwards, however, the leaves are in tolerable condition.

[Library-mark, Add. 525; bought in 1869 from H. Lipschütz.]

No. 57.

Paper, in folio, $11\frac{3}{8}$ in. × $8\frac{1}{2}$ in.; 602 leaves, mostly[1] 5-sheet quires, 24 lines; the text (on the verso of each leaf) in Sephardic Rabbinic character, and the translation (on the recto) in Italian handwriting of the xv—xvith century.

חדושים בפירוש התורה [לרבנו משה בן נחמן ירונדי עם העתקה רומית לפלוני אלמוני]

[1] The exceptions are quires 17 (which has four), 18 (which has seven), 27 (which has again four), and 35 (which has six sheets).

Commentary on the PENTATEUCH, by R. Mosheh b. Nachman of Gerona (Ramban, Nachmanides), with a Latin translation by an anonymous author, in several parts[1]; defective.

I. GENESIS—EXODUS. Leaf 1ᵃ, blank; 1ᵇ, 2ᵃ, rhymed preface; 2ᵇ, 3ᵃ, general introductions to the whole Pentateuch; 12ᵇ, 13ᵃ, *Genesis* (291—300 wanting); 544ᵇ, 545ᵃ, *Exodus;* leaves 603—612 and all afterwards missing.

Begins (leaf 1ᵇ with the usual formula of commencing a book, the superscription of the work and the text of the rhymed preface):

ב"ה חדושי התורה לרב רבינו משה בר נחמן תנצב"ה. באימה ביראה ברתת...

and (leaf 2ᵃ with the translation of the superscription and the preface):

Innouationes i*n* lege*m* Mag*ist*ri Mag*ist*ri n*ost*ri Moyse bar nama*n* sit a*nim*a sua ligata in ligamine vit*ae*. Cum timore cum metu cu*m* tremore...

Breaks off (leaf 602ᵃ, in the translation of the commentary on Ex. vi. 13):

... qui[a] tibi o*mn*ia verba no*n* ad aaron tecum et te

and (leaf 602ᵇ, in the text of the commentary on Ex. vi. 14, and with seven words of Ex. vi. 15, in the sacred text):

...ועוד כי הם בעצמם חסידי עליון ראויים לספר בהם כאבות העולם. ויקח אהרן את אלישבע בת עמינדב אחות

The Rabbinic text, in this MS., was either copied from the very MS., which served as copy for the Lisbon edition, or from that edition itself; more probably, however, the latter was the case, as our MS., except that it has throughout אלהים for the אלים of the Lisbon edition, too minutely reflects the advantages and disadvantages of that edition, not to stand in an absolute connexion with it[2]. The various readings taken

[1] The whole commentary, together with the translation, was written either in two parts (I. Genesis, Exodus; II. Leviticus, Numbers, Deuteronomy), or, which is even more likely to have been the case, in three parts (I. Genesis and part of Exodus; II. the remaining part of Exodus and the whole of Leviticus; III. Numbers, Deuteronomy). From the way in which Genesis ends and Exodus begins, on the one hand, and the way in which the latter breaks off, on the other hand, we see that Genesis and Exodus (be it only part of the latter) were to form one volume, and that, at all events, something was wanting to make up this first part.

[2] We will only give a few striking examples. Leaf 53ᵇ (on Gen. ii. 3) we miss, as in the Lisbon edition, the whole of the passage: ...ויהי זה קי"ח אחר חמשת אלפים... (see this Catalogue, p. 145). Leaf 61ᵇ (on Gen. ii. 11) we have ...באלסכנדריאה... as in the Lisbon edition (the Naples edition has ...באלכסונה...). Leaf 85ᵇ (on Gen. vi. 1) is even to be found the very abbre-

from MSS. (נ״א), or such as are of the scribe's own suggestion (נ׳), which are occasionally to be found on the margins, are, no doubt, a mere afterthought on the part of the copyist, as is also the partial supply of vowel-points (on leaves 1ᵇ—10ᵇ, 21ᵇ—87ᵇ, 91ᵇ—94ᵇ, 98ᵇ—100ᵇ, and insulated words to almost the end of the volume). The copyist's name was, probably, Hillel, as the letter ה serves a good many times to fill out the void spaces of the lines (see Excursus I.). Although his Latin handwriting was of Italian training, he must have learnt to write Hebrew from a Peninsular Sephardi.

The translation, whether it be viewed with respect to Rabbinic, or to Latin lore, is no monument of great learning. One, certainly, could have forgiven the translator the inelegance of his Latin diction, seeing that he had to contend with a treble difficulty: he had to render into Latin, thoughts that had been conceived almost three hundred years before in another language, and this not merely in the ordinary Rabbinic, but in the peculiarly coloured, cabbalistico-poetical, Rabbinic of Nachmanides. But what one cannot forgive the translator is his evident and frequent misconception of the text before him[1]. The translator seems to have

viation of the Lisbon edition for 480 (ת״פ) which in the common editions is given in full. Leaf 406ᵇ the pericope וישלח leaves off, as in the Lisbon edition, with למלך המשיח ... and not as the other editions, with במהרה יגלה ... Leaf 411ᵇ (on Gen. xxxvii. 26) is not merely, as in the Lisbon edition, the commentary on a later verse given before that on an earlier one, but the very mis-spelling of the word לרחיצה (for לרציחה) is to be found, even as it is there.

[1] To give only two instances out of the many, we adduce: (1) that leaf 10ᵃ, he translates ... עוד יש בידינו קבלה של אמת כי כל התורה כלה שמותיו של הקדוש ברוך הוא ... by *Etiam est in manibus nostris cabala veritatis quia tota lex tota ipsa nomina sua de sancto benedicto ipso* ... and (2) that leaf 545ᵃ, he translates ... השלים הכתוב ספר בראשית ... by *Perfecit scripturam libri Beressit* ... A superior man alike in Rabbinic and Latin scholarship, seems, on the other hand, to have been another translator of Ramban's commentary on the Pentateuch into Latin. MS. R. 8. 2, in the library of Trinity College, in this University, includes a fragment, consisting of a single quire of eight leaves, which contains the commencement of this commentary on Exodus (Introduction up to iii. 12 inclusive). This translator (see later) gives the second of the two passages just quoted, thus: *Finivit scriptura librum Genes[eos]* ... which, at all events, shows that he understood the author he had before him. We take this opportunity of thanking the College for their liberality in granting us the use of that valuable MS. In return for their kindness, we will furnish them, in addition to correcting an unaccountable mistake, which has crept into their printed Catalogue, respecting the volume of which this work forms part, with fresh matter in connexion therewith, which was, at the time of the publication of the Catalogue, unknown to us.

1. Only the first of the three works contained in R. 8. 2 (Isaiah, Hebrew and Latin) was copied by the scribe who is the copyist of the MS. described in this No. (57); the second and third work (Moreh Maqom and the Fragment

been one of those semi-learned Physician Rabbis with which Italy literally swarmed after the heart-rending catastrophe in the Iberian Peninsula (1492—1507).

As regards the copyist of the translation, he is in our opinion identical with the translator himself; and the translation was, no doubt, copied at the same time as the text, as the identity of the ink throughout in both, the emendations (by the original copyist) both in text and translation (on the verso-page; see, for instance, leaf 42[b]), the occasional summaries (in Latin on the recto-page) on the margins, but above all, the boldness of the ductus which characterises both the Rabbinic and the Latin, and the fact of the contents of the respective pages closely corresponding with one another, will clearly show. If the translator as such cannot obtain the approval of the reader, he will do so, and this deservedly, as copyist, of this splendidly executed MS.

Five owners, all of whom were, apparently, Englishmen and of the XVI—XVIIth century, have left their marks of ownership in this volume, in various ways:

(1) A good hand; (a) by writing at the end (leaf 602[b]) sunt quinterniones 60; and (b) by numbering on the verso-page the leaves down to 290 inclusive.

(2) A hand full of character and distinctness: by writing mostly on the verso-pages, with more or less interruption, from leaf 71[b] to 421. The Hebrew interspersed in its remarks, which are written in Latin, is in Rabbinic character. Leaf 111[b], on occasion of Nachmanides giving the Rabbinic opinion (Bereshith Rabbah, cap. 33) that Palestine had not been subject to the Flood, the annotator has: *Terra ÿsrael non fuit inundata, o vanitas,* forgetting that one of the Prophets (Ezek. xxii. 24) must have had the same tradition.

(3) A trembling hand: by putting on leaves 232[b] and 235[a] the letters a and b respectively.

of Latin translation of Nachmanides' commentary on Exodus) were copied by Gabriel de Cingulo.

2. There can be no doubt, that, as the *Moreh Maqom* is the work of Elisha' of Viterbo, so is also the fragment of the translation of Nachmanides' commentary; and that, as the translation of that commentary on Exodus was certainly preceded by a similar one of that on Genesis, so it was, most probably, succeeded also by a similar one on the other parts.

3. This Elisha' of Viterbo is probably identical with Egidio of Viterbo, who, according to Rubin (סוד הספירות, p. 24; see השחר, v. 3), translated cabbalistic books (as the Zohar, &c.) into Latin. Rubin calls this Egidio a נוצרי (by which he understands a Christian pure and simple); if Egidio was, at all, a Christian, he was a מומר (i. e. a Jew converted to Christianity), but in no case a Christian by birth. This Egidio must, of course, not be confounded with Cardinal *Egidio*, Bishop of *Viterbo* and pupil of Elias Levita.

(4) A somewhat careless and intricate hand: by writing, mostly on the verso-pages, references, explanations of difficult words and phrases, &c. The whole, naturally written in Latin, has occasionally Hebrew words; these are in square character. The first trace of this hand is on leaf 1[b] and the last on 562[b]. Although there are many leaves left without notes, the greatest gap is to be found between 416 and 560[b].

(5) A neat hand: a) by writing on leaf 1[a]: רבי משה בר נחמן .i. רמב"ן. Rabbi Mosis filii Nachmanis in librum Bereshith .i. Genesin, et in sex priora capita Elleh shemoth .i. Exodi, vsque ad versum decimum quartum capitis sexti Exodi commentaria; b) by putting, on leaf 1[a] (the library-mark) 20. The writer of this seems to have been the last owner of this MS., Thomas Whalley, D.D., and Vice-Master of Trinity College, who presented it to the University, as the printed Latin label, on leaf 1[a], states.

The condition of the MS., except for the above specified defects, is very satisfactory.

[Library-mark, Gg. 4. 34; presented in 1637, by Dr T. Whalley.]

No. 58.

Parchment, 12¼ in. × 6¼ in.; 2 leaves (forming the outermost sheet of a 6-sheet quire), 2 columns, 32—33 lines; Greek Ashkenazic handwriting of the XIII—XIVth century.

חדושים בפירוש התורה [לרבנו משה בן נחמן ירונדי]

Commentary on the PENTATEUCH, by R. Mosheh b. Nachman of Gerona (Ramban, Nachmanides); a fragment.

This fragment constitutes the remains of a magnificent copy, full of variants, and which, no doubt, contained originally Ramban's commentary on the whole Pentateuch, although we have now only two disconnected pieces on Leviticus.

The leaf now marked 1 begins (on vi. 2):

(שנעלה האברים) מן הארץ למזבח בלילה...

and breaks off (on vi. 23):

...אבל אמ׳ לכפר שאם הכניסה

The leaf now marked 12 begins (on xii. 2):

(ראשה ואבריה כבדים עליה) לפירש״י ולא ידעתי מאיזה...

and breaks off (on xiii. 3):

...שהן גבוהין ממראה החמה (ואם כל מראה)

The following note of an owner in a mixed (oriental and Egyptian) Sephardic hand of the xviiith century, is to be found on leaf 1ᵇ:

מי טייני ח״ר יאודה ארריטי ה״י ספרים שבילי אמונה וחסד לאברהם
מר זקנו מהרחיד״א וס׳ כתיבת יד ממעשיות

This note if written in Egypt, was probably written during, or after, the time of R. Chayyim Yoseph David Azulai's sojourn in that country, whither he went to his daughter's marriage. See ככר לאדן (Livorno, 1801, 4°), leaf 202ᵇ, letter ב, 5. (For more information concerning owners, see MS. Add. 511. 1.)

Having served for some time as binding to MS. Add. 511. 1, it is in various places almost illegible; particularly leaf 12ᵇ, which has been more exposed than the rest.

[Library-mark, Add. 511. 2; bought in 1869 from H. Lipschütz.]

No. 59.

Paper, in quarto, 7⅝ in × 5⅞ in.; 24 leaves, 6-sheet quires, oriental Qaraite (Sephardic) handwriting of the xvith century.

[השגות על איזה מקומות בפרוש הרמב״ן על התורה לר׳
זכריה בן משה הכהן הרופא]

Strictures on select passages in Nachmanides' PENTATEUCH-commentary, by R. Zekharyah b. Mosheh Hakkohen the Physician; defective.

Leaf 1, wanting[1]; 2ᵃ, *Genesis;* 9ᵃ, *Exodus;* 9ᵃ, *Numbers* (12 wanting); 15ᵇ, *Deuteronomy;* 15ᵇ, date of the author's death and elegy on it by R. Abraham Hakkohen (the author's son?); 16 and all afterwards wanting.

[1] If any one, after following our description of the MS., will turn to החלוץ II. pp. 161, 162, and read the שיר על הרמב״ן which the Editor has there printed, we are satisfied that he will not fail to share our conviction that that poem was written by our author as an introduction to the work here described; and that, in all probability, it actually stood on the leaf at the beginning, which is now lost. The Editor of החלוץ appears to have found the poem copied separately into a miscellaneous volume in such a way as to afford him no certain clue to the authorship, though his clear-sightedness has enabled him to see that it must have stood at the head of some book containing answers to the attacks of Ramban on *Ibn 'Ezra* and *Maimonides.* Steinschneider (Catal. Codd. Heb. Bibl. Acad. Lugd.-Bat. p. 143) very nearly hit the mark when he suggested that this poem was written to precede the השגות of our author relating to the ספר המצות (Cod. Vat. CCXLIX); and had he seen this קונטרס itself, he would no doubt, have been the first to discern the fact.

Begins (leaf 2^a, on Gen. x. 2):

(מתושלח) ראה את אדם. שם ראה את מתושלח. יעקב ראה את שם. עמרם ראה את יעקב. אחיה השילוני ראה את עמרם. אליהו ראה את אחיה ועדיין הוא קיים,[1] הנה מאמרם מתושלח ראה את אדם יראה שנח לא[2] ראהו...

Ends (leaf 15^b, in Nachmanides' commentary, on Deut. v. 5):

...וזהו להגיד לכם לפרש להם לכל דבור ודבור ע״כ

יום ה׳ ט״ו לכסלו שנת האר[3] פניך ונושעה נעדר פלוסוף האלהי הנ׳ כ״ר זכריא כהן צדק בכ״ר משה רופא יש״י עמה״ן והנה הקינה שעשו

אקוב[4] זמני ואבכה על מרירות אבוי   אוי לי לזאת אשפוך רוח מררתי
ביום אשר חשכו כל המאורים וגם   אבלו ונבלו פני תבל בצרתי
רבה שאיה לכל חכמות ובינות ביום   נעדר גבירי זכריהו זכירתי
הנה בעת אזכרה אמרות טהורות בפז[5]   קינים אקונן תמורת שיר בשירתי
מי ים וגשם ומי כל הנהרות היו   (כ)לו הם לכבות לרוב עוצם מדורתי
כהן ומורה כמן יורה בעתו אשר   ירוה צמאים לזאת גדלה בעדתי[6]
האל אשר אין ערוך אליו אספו וגם   אזכה בחלקו אני בעת פטירתי
נפשו צרורה תהי בצרור לחיים לעד   מזיו שכינה באור עליון טהורתי

Our author was, no doubt, a Greek Rabbanite. He is known as a synagogal poet (Zunz, *Literaturgesch. d. s. Poes.* p. 378[7]). But he is better

[1] See T. B. Baba Bathra, 121^b.

[2] In the printed editions, accessible to us, as indeed also in many MSS. of Nachmanides' Pentateuch-commentary, the passage (that Noah saw Adam) against which R. Zekharyah here successfully argues, is not to be found. But in two MSS. preserved in this Library (Numbers 55 and 56 of this Catalogue) it is to be found. The age and locality, in which the former of these two MSS. was executed, make it not improbable that our author had that very copy in his hands, when he wrote this little, but valuable, work.

[3] The האר &c. is without the points usual on such an occasion; in all probability, however, the whole word stands for the date, which would give 1446.

[4] This elegy has the acrostic אברהם כהן, the sixth line having not merely the letter כ, but the whole word כהן. This Abraham Kohen is, probably, the author's son. The value of the acrostic was, apparently, noticed by an oriental Sephardic owner (a Rabbanite) of the XVI—XVIIth century, since he has written against the elegy the words אברהם כהן; although, singularly enough, he must have soon forgotten this fact, since he suggests for the fifth line (מ), which, because he could not understand the היו״ לו (היוכלו), did not please him, another line (כל הנהרות ומי הים יכלו ולא״ יוכלו לכבות לרוב עוצם מדורתי), which again deprived the poem of its מ and has only one merit, that of being slightly superior in diction to the original.

[5] So in MS.; read כפז.

[6] So in MS.; read בערתי.

[7] In a Greek ritual in this Library (MS. Add. 542) are to found three poems by our author, the first two of which are noticed by Zunz, one having no acrostic and one with זכריה, and besides these a third with the acrostic זכריה כהן, which begins זכרו לעולם זאת והתאוששו and ends שלש תקיעות תקעו שלשו.

known as R. Zekharyah the Philosopher (Assemani, CCXLIX. p. 207); the title *the Physician* belongs, apparently, to his father (see superscription of the elegy). The present work is, no doubt, the famous קונטרים[1], heard of by many, but, in modern times at least, seen by none, and, apparently,

[1] The word קונטרס (occasionally also קונטריס, קונטרוש, &c.) seems to mean a set of sheets, written on or not, forming a quire, or quires, of parchment or paper. It is probably a corruption of the late Latin *quaternus* (like the French *cahier*, old French *quayer*, and the English *quire*, old English *quayer*), a gathering of four sheets. In this sense we find the word used by Rashi (1040—1105), as may be seen from his commentary on T. B. Menachoth 32ᵃ, אטבא. The Tosaphists (North French Rabbis of the age succeeding that of Rashi and founded chiefly by his grandson R. Ya'aqob b. Meir, or, as he is more commonly called, Rabbenu Tam) use the word exclusively for Rashi's commentary on the several parts of the Babylonian Talmud. Subsequently the word was used again less exclusively for any smaller works and pamphlets, or single quires of larger works. This was especially the case from the XIIIth century downwards among Sephardic authors, scribes and others, who, however, write the word קונדרס. In this sense the word קונטרים is used by R. Menachem Tamar of Greece (see Steinschneider, Catal. Codd. Heb. Bibl. Acad. Lugd.-Bat. p. 143), and probably before him, by his grandfather, the author of this little work, himself. Elias Levita, misled by the immediate succession of the נ to the ו in קונטרס derives this word (תשבי s. v.) from the Italian *quinterno* (Latin *quinternus*), an expression with which he would become familiar in the Venetian printing offices of the XVIth century. But, though the words *quinternus* and *quinternio* may have existed as early as the XIVth century in the sense of a 5-sheet quire (Du Cange s. v.) there seems no trace of them at an earlier date; and, indeed, their formation shows that they could only have been invented after the use of *quaternus*, signifying a quire, had been long known. Zunz (Zeitschr. f. d. Wissensch. d. Judenth. p. 324, Note 55) takes קונטרס to be an abbreviation of the קומנטרים of the Gemara and the equivalent of the Latin *commentarius*; but it is clear, that מקומנטריסין (T. B. Gittin 28ᵇ), מקמנטריסים (Ibid. 29ᵃ), and מקמנטריסי (T. Y. Yebamoth XVI. 5) are used not of things but of persons; and therefore, as Buxtorf long ago suggested, the word קמנטרים represents the Latin *commentariensis*, and not *commentarius*. *Commentarienses* (see the passages quoted by Du Cange s. v.) were governors of prisons, to whom the execution of condemned prisoners was committed. Buxtorf perceived that, in the view of the Talmud, the contrast lay between persons and persons, between the בית דין של ישראל, who were incorruptible, and the קומנטרסין של נכרים, who were liable to be bribed; though, in explaining קומנטריסין by *judices criminales*, he has given the word *commentarienses* a sense for which there seems to be no authority. Landau ('Arukh s. v. קמנטרים) has fallen into a strange mistake (all the more strange, seeing the free use he has made of Buxtorf's labours), in stating that Rashi and the Tosaphists misunderstood the word קומנטריסין. We have no means of examining MSS. of Rashi on the passage in Gittin, on which he comments, to see whether the true reading of his words is ממונין ליהרג, according to the printed editions, or מְמוּנִין להרוג, as the phrase runs in the קרבן העדה and פני משה on the Talmud Yerushalmi (both of these commen-

only known from the mention of it by R. Menachem Tamar, whose maternal grandfather our author was[1]. In these strictures R. Zekharyah ostensibly professes to defend Ibn 'Ezra's remarks in his Pentateuch-commentary and Maimonides' views on anthropomorphism as extant in his Moreh, &c. But, if the truth must be told, our author's principal aim is less to defend these two great teachers than to attack Nachmanides, against whom he has an antipathy, probably on account of his predilections for Qabbalah, which he (R. Zekharyah), as a sober thinker, holds in utter contempt[2]. In this aim the author, being a master of style and logic, perfectly succeeds; for with all feelings of veneration for Nachmanides, both as a man and a scholar, one is irresistibly carried away by the style and arguments exhibited in this little book[3]. These attacks on Nachmanides' commentary are, naturally, only on select passages, so that one need not feel surprised that very little is found on Exodus and Numbers and nothing on Leviticus and Deuteronomy (the matter which belongs to this last being only part of the text of Nachmanides). But, although, to judge from the way our MS. concludes, the copy is incomplete, there is probably not much wanting[4],

tators, no doubt, having Rashi's words in mind). But in no case can Rashi be taxed with ignorance of the meaning of the phrase he explains. As for the Tosaphists, they merely repeated what Rashi had said before them.

[1] Steinschneider, as before, p. 142.

[2] See leaf 3[a], where he says that Nachmanides invented mysteries (בסודות בדה מלבו), and leaf 8[b], where he charges him with inconsistency and cowardice, as the following will show:

... ואם כן החכם יראה כי שלמון לא נכנס בארץ כי שם נולד אחר שנים רבות לבואם. אלא שערום יערים הוא (Nachmanides) ועל כן קדם לברוח אל עיר מקלטו אש' היא הקבלה. ובאמת אין זה אצלי אלא כאיש נשקף בחלון ביתו בעד אשנבו ויורה חציו על גבור חיל ואיש מלחמה ואחר אשר חציו יכלה בו נכנס וסוגר בעדו כי ירא פן ימיתהו מלמטה הגבור בגבורתו. כה משפט האיש הזה ומעשיהו טוען על רבים ונכבדים ממנו וחוקר תכלית החקירה לטעון כנגדם ובפתע פתאום בורח אל הקבלה ומהפך הכל אל הנסתר לגמרי ויסתר משה פניו כי ירא. ולמה היה פוסח על שתי הסעיפים. אם הוא מקובל יורנו בקבלה ויניח טענות והחקירה ואם בוחר בחקירה לא יברח אל הקבלה. ואם זרוע כר' אברהם לו ובקול כמוהו ירעם יעדה נא גאון וגובה והוד והדר ילבש ויעמד על הטענות ויראה אם יעמד לבו התחזקנה ידיו. וברוך אשר סכל עצתו היה לו לומר כי אדרבה שלמון לא נכנס בארץ...

[3] See leaf 8[a], where he has (on Nachmanides' remarks to Gen. xlvi. 7, ...וזה זהב רותח...) the following striking passage:

...איננו אמת ואף כי ברור בתורה ואדרבה ההפך ברור בכל המקרא,גם בתורה גם בנביאים גם בכתובים. אם לא נפיח כזבים. ומדוע לא יתחמץ לבבו וכליותיו ישתונן, וירא און ולא יתבונן, וממשה לא נס לחח רבן של נביאי' ואדונן, גם אברהם בצל שדי יתלונן, ועל ד' מלכים כגבור התרונן, ופרעה ואבימלך על אשתו התאונן, והנה רבקה גם ער ואונן, ואלישע רפא צרעת נעמן, בלא כסף ובלא מחיר ואתנן, ויותר הגדולות אשר עשה ברוב חשבונן ומנין...

[4] The leaves missing at the end (at least 9), although they were, probably, not blank (see MS. Add. 508. 4), contained at all events nothing in connexion with this little treatise, as the elegy following it clearly shows. That this treatise is incomplete at the end, is no doubt owing to the incompleteness of

as the whole work is only called a קונטרס even by the author's grandson (see above, p. 181 and Note 1 there).

Of the many points of interest to be found in these Strictures we will only single out two:

(1) That our author was very probably acquainted with Ibn 'Ezra's grammatical commentary on the Pentateuch; at all events, he must have been so with the poem preceding it (see this Catalogue p. 120, Note 2), since, in the course of his argument he has (leaf 6[a]) the following:

...כי יפלא בעיניכם גם בעיני יפלא אם חשב הרב שלא ידע החכם כי מנהג הזקנה הוא שתכהין העינים כי הוא ראה זקנים רבים בימיו והוא עצמו היה זקן כי היה בן ארבעה וששים כשהחל לפרש התורה בהעתקה הראשונה כאשר אמ' בשירו[1]. עזרו עד הלום חסדו ומספר. שני חייו שמנה על שמנה. שהם ס"ד ואף כי בהעתקה השנית...

(2) That Ibn 'Ezra's Short Commentary on Exodus (edited by Reggio; see this Catalogue, p. 90) was not only known to him, but is called by him (leaf 11[a]) העתקה האחרת (in contradistinction to the Long Commentary a little before quoted by him), which, seeing that he had studied and knew Ibn 'Ezra's style as few others, is a confirmation, that this Long Commentary was viewed by him as, on the whole, belonging to Ibn 'Ezra (see this Catalogue, pp. 123, 124, &c.).

The scribe of this copy, of whose name no trace is to be found here, is identical with that of MS. Add. 508. 4; and must have been a Qaraite trained, if not altogether living, in the East, as the Sephardic character of the writing sufficiently warrants one to believe. One peculiarity of his deserves being noticed. Because, as a Qaraite, he probably knew the Pentateuch by heart, he gives only two or three words of a verse, when he writes a quotation from the Mosaic records, giving the rest by single letters only; see, for example, leaf 4[a], where Gen. xxvi. 13 and 14 are represented by ויגדל האיש וילך הועכגמולמצובורואפ, and a little later on Gen. xxvi. 3 and 4 by גור בארץ הזאת ועכללואכההואהאנלאואזכהולאכההובכגה.

This MS. was, in all probability, at one time, owned by R. Yehudah b. Eliyyahu Tishbi, a Qaraite, living in the xvith century near Constantinople; see the description of MS. Add. 508. 6 below. Another owner was the anonymous oriental Sephardi of the xvi—xviith century mentioned above (p. 180, Note 4).

the copy before the scribe. Perhaps the author died just when about to comment on Deut. v. 5, and hence the singular fact of the treatise ending with piece of Nachmanides' commentary thereon.

[1] This line reads in the אוצר נחמד (p. 223) thus: עזרהו עד הלום ומספר—שני חייו שמנה על שמנה.

Except for the defect before enumerated, this MS. is in good condition.

[Library-mark, Add. 508. 5; bought in 1869 from H. Lipschütz.]

No. 60.

Paper, in quarto, 8⅝ in., × 6⅞ in.; 48 leaves, 28 lines; mixed (Rabbinic and current) character, occidental Qaraite (a mixture of Sephardic and Ashkenazic) handwriting of the XIXth century[1].

[מעיל שמואל]

Supercommentary on the Mibchar[2] on the PENTATEUCH, by R. Shemuel b. Yoseph of Kala, in the Crimea; defective.

Leaf 1ª, *Genesis* (5—10, 36 wanting); 46ª, *Exodus*...

Begins (leaf 1ª, on Gen. viii. 3; Mibchar I. leaf 32ª):

קנ״א אפשר שלא חשש בשביל הא׳ כמו אלה בני יעקב שנים עשר...

Breaks off (leaf 48ᵇ, on Ex. i. 19; Mibchar II. leaf 2ª):

...ופעמים יראה הוא״ו כמו ויודע הדבר למרדכי ופעמים יראה היו״ד

This is, if not the most recent, certainly, one of the latest commentaries on the much-cherished text-book of the Qaraites. It was composed within the last century, and the author, dying on 25 Shebat, 5514[3], never went in his interpretation beyond Leviticus (see Steinschneider, המזכיר, XI. p. 13). On the other hand, this commentary, as far as it goes, is superior even to the טירת כסף[4] of R. Yoseph Shelomoh Yerushalmi (see this Catalogue, p. 128), who must have known and made use of it, without

[1] The water-mark of the paper bears the date 1819.

[2] המבחר, &c., is by R. Aharon the Physician b. Yoseph the Qaraite, who imitated, and by no means unsuccessfully, the great Ibn 'Ezra's language and mode of explaining the Scriptures. This work, although composed as early as the end of the XIIIth century (1294, as will be seen in the שיר המחבר; comp. Steinschneider, Catal. Codd. Heb. Acad. Lugd.-Bat., p. 5), was not printed till 1834 (not 1835, as both Steinschneider and Zedner write), at Eupatoria (גוזלוו), Folio. The author was an inhabitant of סולכאט, in the Crimea; such was the case, at least, in the year 1279, as may be seen from II. leaf 14ᵇ (on Ex. xii. 2). Later Qaraites however assert that he lived at Constantinople; see Pinsker, לקוטי קדמוניות (Wien, 1860, 8vo.) p. רל״ג.

[3] According to Jahn's Tables, 25 Shebat 5514 corresponds to Sunday, February 17, 1754 of the common era.

[4] This commentary accompanies the printed edition of the Mibchar.

however naming this source. Our author is not only well versed in the literature of his author and the earlier grammarians, but also both in the Rabbis (whom, although in duty bound to attack, he often involuntarily praises) and in Aristotelian philosophy (as interpreted by the Arabic-Hebrew school). Of later authors of his own community he quotes R. Abraham the Crimean (קירימי) only (on Ex. i. 1; see leaf 46[a]).

The scribe's name was probably R. Abraham Habbachur b. Ya'aqob Shammash (i.e. servant of the Synagogue); see the printed edition, in this Library, of the grammatical work פתח תקוה by R. Mordekhai Sultansky (סולטנסכי), Eupatoria, 1857, 4to. (with which this MS. was formerly bound up), on the lower margin of the title-page.

As a MS. this copy is, apart from the defects, rather of inferior value, owing partly to the ignorance of the scribe, and partly to the incompleteness and inexactness of the copy before him. But its value ought to be determined by the fact that it is, as yet, only the third[1] copy known of this important work.

As regards the condition of the MS., 29 leaves are apparently wanting at the beginning, since what is now leaf 1[a] is marked ל, 2[a] ל"א, &c.; although it is difficult to understand how all these leaves could have been occupied. Leaves 5—10 are missing in the middle, as also leaf 36; and all after 48, at the end. The margins also are badly cut; the paper, however, is good.

[Library-mark, Add. 861; bought in 1871 from Fischl Hirsch of Halberstadt.]

No. 61.

Paper, in quarto, 8½ in. × 5¾ in.; 184 leaves, 4-sheet quires, 23 lines; Rabbinic character, fine Sephardic handwriting of the xiv—xvth century.

[זכרון טוב והוא פרוש על התורה לר' נתן הרופא בן שמואל]

Commentary on the Pentateuch, by the Physician R. Nathan b. Shemuel; defective.

Leaves 1—9 wanting; 10, *Genesis;* 32[b], *Exodus* (73, 80 wanting); 81 (wanting), *Leviticus* (88, 97 wanting); 106[b], *Numbers;* 146[b], *Deuteronomy;*

[1] One is to be found in the Imperial Library of St Petersburg (Neubauer, Aus der Petersburger Bibliothek, p. 49), and another is in the possession of Fischl Hirsch (Steinschneider, המזכיר, xi. p. 13, who considered the same in 1871 as unique).

181[a], Author's poetical subscription; 181[b], blank; 182—184 (probably blank) wanting.

Begins (leaf 10[a], on Gen. xiv. 1—24):

חושים והיסודות נוצחים באחרונה ולוקחים לוט ורכושו. בן אחי אברם רמז לשכל החמרי...

Ends (leaf 181[a]):

...כי היא עדות נאמנה על אמתת תורתינו אשר עינינו ראו ולא זר ובאזנינו שמע(נ)ו ולא אחר כמו שנ׳ ואתם עדי נאם יי׳ ועבדי אשר בחרתי ולפי׳ ראוי לו בכמו זה הענין אשרי העם שככה לו אשרי העם שיי׳ אלהיו תם ונשלם בעוז אל עולם

ידידי קח ספר המשולש   בעניינים ברור דעת צרופים
פשט ודרש ונסתר הם כאחים   מחוברים ויחדו נאספים
ועיין בפשט תמיד תחלה   נאום אדון לכל חוזים וצופים
ובמדרש ונסתר אחרי כן   ואז תמצא טעמים נחלפים
גלויים הם לעיני האמת גם   מתוקים מדבש נפת וצופים
ואיש זקן רפה כח אספם   בס״ז שנה עלי סך ה׳ אלפים
ונתן בר שמואלי[1] הוא מקרא   מכונה הם (sic) בפי זכים וחפים

תם

If the above subscription is not strictly poetical, it is something better; it is an instructive résumé of this, in many respects important, work; and it is on the whole borne out by the contents of the MS. before us, as will be seen from the following remarks.

1. Title and Nature of the Work. The זכרון טוב[2], contains a

[1] The points over this word may possibly mean that this MS. was copied for a person of that name (see Excursus I).

[2] We cannot pronounce this title, at least as far as the author himself is therein concerned, to be quite certain. On the one hand, nobody until now has ever properly examined, or, at all events, properly described, this work, while, on the other hand, the MS. before us is defective at the commencement (leaves 1—9; see above), just at the likeliest place for finding the title of a book recorded, if given by the author himself. The only resource left to us, therefore, is the subscription; but this subscription, although it does not exactly exclude the possibility of this title, mentions the book, as will have been seen, by the name of ספר המשולש alone. If the author himself really called this book זכרון טוב (for which there is a high probability, see later), he did so, no doubt, in order to hint thereby, that this work be taken for what it was in his eyes (and, on the whole, is also in reality), a זכרון טוב, i.e. a reproduction of excellent explanations taken from works which had been chiefly composed by others than himself, who was a mere collector. It is also very probable, that, in addition to this reason, the Rabbinical saying ואין טוב אלא תורה (T. B. Berakhoth, 5[a]) and the liturgical phrase זכרנו בזכרון טוב לפניך

triple commentary on select parts of the Pentateuch in the shape of פשט, מדרש (or דרש) and נסתר. The Peshat is exegesis in the ordinary sense of the word; and though not always original[1], it is always exceedingly good[2]. The Midrash (or Derash) reproduces, as will be almost self-understood, Rabbinical views and sayings from the Talmudim and Midrashim[3]. The Nistar, however, contrary to all ordinary expectations, gives but rarely cabbalistic matter, but furnishes mostly allegories in the sense of the so-called Maimonidean[4] school, with all the inconsistencies, and

(for the Ten Penitential Days), hovered before the eye of his mind, when he named this book thus. For the high probability, if not absolute authenticity, of the title זכרון טוב, it must be mentioned, that not only does R. Menachem Perigori (the sixth owner of the present MS., writing in 1469) call it so, but that the copyist of De-Rossi's Cod. 1140 (writing in 1400) does the same. R. Shabbethai Bass (writing in, or before, 1674) uses the name as if the book were universally known under this title. (The evidence given by Heilperin in סדר הדורות, ed. Friedensohn, II. leaf 248[a], and Ghirondi in תג"י, p. 274, No. 17, is, comparatively speaking, worthless, as the former unquestionably here simply wrote out R. S. Bass and the latter confessedly copied De-Rossi.)

[1] The matter given under this head is often taken from Ibn 'Ezra and Nachmanides, the author not deeming it worth his while to mention the real authors thereof by name, except on leaf 129[a], where the name of the former, and leaf 102[a], where that of the latter, is to be found (see later). What he does to these two princes of Jewish commentators, he does also to others, as R. Tobiyyah b. Eli'ezer and R. Ya'aqob b. Anatolio.

[2] We will give one instance only. Every one, on reading Gen. xlv. 25—27, must feel, even as did Rashi and the Rabbis before him (Midrash Rabbah on Genesis, cap. 95), the difficulty of the nexus: *And when he saw the waggons which Joseph had sent to carry him, the spirit of Jacob their father revived.* Our author has regarding this the following explanation:

הפשט ספר הכתו' כי כאשר אמ' לו עיד יוסף חי וכי הוא מושל בכל ארץ מצרים לא היה מאמין בדברי הממשלה כלל... ובראותו העגלות שקט לבבו מהמייתו וסר ממנו הספק כי היה יודע כי העגלות הנמשכות והנגררות בכח הסוסים מוצאים ממצרים במהיר (במחיר) גדול ובמצות המלך„ כי הנה מלכי ארם וזולתם היו מוציאים סוסים ממצרים לצורך מרכבתם...

[3] By the term *Midrashim* we understand this peculiar kind of Rabbinic literature down to, and inclusive of, the so-called פסיקתא זוטרתא (in reality the לקח טוב by R. Tobiyyah b. Eli'ezer; see the description of MS. Add. 378. 1 below), to which, although our author does not acknowledge the source, the cabbalistic explanation on leaf 150[b] can be traced; see פסיקתא זוטרתא (Venezia, 1546, Folio) leaf 67[a], column 2, towards the end.

[4] The endeavour to prevent gross material conceptions, with respect to the Divine Being, from taking root in the mind of the simple Bible-reader is, although much older than אונקלס, yet chiefly to be found in the Targum of that name. Maimonides, the well-known Talmudist and philosopher, relying, on the one hand, on this endeavour as manifested in this Targum, and on the other hand, on what is to be found in the Talmudim and Midrashim respecting anthropomorphism, produced, on this ground, his far-famed מורה. But this book, although it was full, besides the spirit of philosophy it breathed, of the

let us add, absurdities, attaching thereto[1]. This triple commentary is sometimes, though rarely, merged into one, as may be seen, for instance, in the pericopes יתרו and ואתחנן (leaves 55[b], 151[b], &c.). If we may judge from Exodus, Numbers and Deuteronomy (Genesis and Leviticus being defective at the commencement), each of the five books is preceded by a short, but instructive, introduction (פתיחה), while, now and then, the so-called Nistar is preceded by a yet shorter introduction (הצעה).

2. Time of the Composition of the Work. This work was composed in the year 1307, a time when R. Shelomoh b. Abraham Ibn אדרת (see the description of MS. Add. 1187. 1) was yet alive. This fact helps to explain our author's apparently strange conduct in this commentary. We find, that, on the one hand, he not merely fights the battles of Maimonides against his opponents, but he actually reproduces in his Nistar (and this almost literally) all the inconsistencies, eccentricities, and even absurdities of the school, then wrongly going by this great man's name; whilst, on the other hand, he, unlike that school, continually urges his readers, in spite of his apparently high opinion of the allegories of his Nistar, to give the preference to the Peshat over it (see passim), as the Nistar could never exist without this Peshat (see particularly leaves 49[a], 109). To us it appears that part of the author's conduct was due to his standing in awe of the celebrated Chief Rabbi of Barcelona, who, towards the end of his days, was looked upon (and justly so) as the teacher of all the Israelite Diaspora (רבן של כל בני הגולה), and who had only a year or so before this commentary was composed, given battle to the so-called Maimonidean school[2].

fear of God, soon experienced the unenviable fate of being misunderstood by both extreme parties within Judaism. While to the believer the explanations contained therein savoured of heterodoxy, they served in the hands of the mistaken rationalists (the so-called Maimonidean school), for divesting the most explicit narratives of Holy Writ of their plain and bona fide meaning. To give an idea of the length this school went, we will only adduce, that they explained Gen. xiv. 9 (ארבעה מלכים את החמשה) by, *the four elements warring against the five senses;* an explanation which was, no doubt, to be found in this MS., on leaf 9[b], as the first words of leaf 10[a] warrant us to believe. See the next two Notes.

[1] Thus, for instance, we read, in reference to the three measures of flour, which Abraham had commanded Sarah to prepare (Gen. xviii. 6), that they were an allusion to the three principal sciences: Mathematics, Physics and Divinity. From this it will be easily understood, that, if Abraham did not, in our author's eyes, exactly signify the Μορφή whilst Sarah signified the Ὕλη (see the next Note), the whole, according to him, was an *allusion to the command issued by the human intellect to the soul* (רמז לצווי השכל האנושי לנפש; leaf 13[a]).

[2] This school had its principal representatives in Provence, where the extravagance of its process of symbolisation, in the interpretation of the Scriptures, was so great, that it amounted to an absolute negation of all Biblical history. R. Levi (b. Abraham b. Chayyim, author of the לוית חן and בתי הנפש

3. Place of the composition of this Work. On the other hand, the absurdities, with which the Nistar of this commentary teems, would and could scarcely have been reproduced by a man of such sovereign good sense, as our author proves himself to be in his Peshat, had he not been obliged to pander to the foolish and unnatural cravings of his time and neighbourhood. We know what the once glorious congregations of Provence, so distinguished in 1200, and even later, in sacred as well as profane learning, had become towards the commencement of the xivth century; how their piety had become mere fanaticism and their philosophy mere sophistry (see above pp. 187, Note 4, and 188, Notes 1, 2). Now, our

והלחשים; see Geiger in החלוץ ii. pp. 12—24 and Otzar Nechmad ii. pp. 94—97) and other persons not further specified, held forth in public at Montpellier and other places that *Abraham* signified the Μορφή, *Sarah* the Ὕλη, *the four Kings successfully contending with the five*, the four elements which ultimately conquer the five senses, *the twelve sons of Jacob*, the signs of the Zodiac, *Amalek*, the evil desire, the *Urim* and *Tummim*, the Astrolabe, and such like (see שאלות ותשובות . . . רבנו שלמה בן אדרת, Wien, 1812, Folio, leaf 52ᵃ, col. 1, and מנחת קנאות, Pressburg, 1838, 8vo. pp. 31, 45, 47, 50, 52, 77, 89, 106, 153, &c.). At last R. Abbamari b. Mosheh b. Yoseph (Don Astruc de Lunel), an inhabitant of Montpellier, the collector, and to a great extent also the author, of the Minchath Qenaoth, appealed for help to R. Shelomoh Ibn אדרת, who, in conjunction with his Rabbinical College (בית דין) and the Elders of the congregation of Barcelona, decreed, in 1305, that nobody should be permitted to study Græco-Arabic philosophy (Medicine excepted) before he had attained his twenty-fifth year (שאלות . . . בן אדרת, leaves 52ᵃ, col. 2 to 53ᵃ, col. 2). Originally R. Abbamari and others desired this restriction to extend to the thirtieth year, to which Ibn אדרת had at first acceded (מנחת קנאות, pp. 61, 115); later, however, R. Abbamari himself, seeing the opposition waxing great (see later), proposed the twenty-fifth year (Ibid. p. 134). R. Asher b. Yechiel (הרא״ש; see MS. Add. 1209), who had immigrated, only a few years before, from Germany into Spain, and had become Chief Rabbi of Toledo and all Castile, only very reluctantly acceded to approve this decree, as, according to his opinion, the prohibition till twenty-five misled people to think, that it was allowed to study philosophy after that period, at a time when one ought to be engaged in the study of the Torah. However, R. Abbamari, more distinguished for piety and learning than for discretion, would not rest. For a moment, his zeal had a contrary effect; for, alarmed by these anathemas, real Maimonideans such as R. Ya'aqob b. Makhir, the celebrated translator of Euclides (see our description of MS. R. 14. 61 in Trinity College), and R. Yeda'yah Happenini בדרשי (MS. Add. 639. 6), protested against this decree (מנחת קנאות, pp. 62, 84, 86, and שאלות . . . בן אדרת, leaves 53ᵃ, col. 2 to 60ᵃ, col. 1). The Jews of Montpellier, however, having been banished in 1306, the study of philosophy suffered with other studies, and the so-called Maimonidean school soon ceased to exist. The fanatics ascribed this, of course, to the interposition of Providence; although, to their honour be it said, they prayed for their antagonists, as fervently as for themselves (Minchath Qenaoth, p. 179). (For the ungenerous treatment which R. Abbamari is said to have afterwards received at the hands of this Maimonidean school, see Graetz, *Geschichte*, vii. p. 288.)

author, if he was not one of those unnamed orators, who had publicly given the nihilistic explanations of the Pentateuch mentioned before (which we suspect he was), is certainly a faithful mouth-piece of theirs, only endowed with a considerable share of prudence and caution. At all events, one can scarcely understand the depth and range of the so-called Maimonidean school and the literature referring thereto, without having read this book. In our mind there is little doubt, that this work is the result of viva voce explanations given in Provence, and perhaps in Montpellier itself, although the finishing touch may have been put to it somewhere else.

4. The Author's age and native land. Our author speaks of himself, in 1307, not merely as being feeble, but also and especially as being זקן (see, besides the subscription, also leaf 48ª). Allowing for this expression 60 to 70 years, he must have been born somewhere about 1240. Now, at the time of our author's birth and even somewhat later, it may have been (considering the connexion between Aragon, Catalonia and Provence, which had terminated only some thirty years before) nothing extraordinary for a Provençal, particularly if he was a Jew, to be a good Arabic scholar; but at the commencement of the xivth century, this was, (a few cases excepted, as for instance the Tibbon family, &c.), although not exactly impossible, yet very improbable. Our author, however, to judge from the use he makes of Arabic[1], must have known it perfectly and spoken it fluently. He was, therefore, in all probability, a Spaniard (an Aragonese or Catalonian) by birth.

5. Works and authorities quoted in this commentary. These are, certainly, very few; but still they represent a fair portion of literary chronology from pre-gemaristic times down to the very days of the author; and they are:

(1) The ספר יצירה (12ᵇ, 108ᵇ). (2) The ספר (i.e. the ספרי; 175ᵇ).

(3) The Midrash Rabbah, on Genesis (20ᵇ, 45ᵇ, 89ᵇ, 95ª) and Exodus (48ª, 60ª).

(4) במדרש (48ᵇ, 74, 85ᵇ). This last is the so-called תנחומא.

(5) The משכילים ובעלי הקבלה (17ª), also בעלי הקבלה (50ª), חכמי הקבלה (50ª), and finally דרך הקבלה (98).

(6) רבנו שלמה (Rashi; 66ª). (7) Ibn 'Ezra (129ª).

(8) Maimonides (mostly under the name of מורה צדק; but also under ר"ם, as 27ᵇ, and more plainly, under רבינו משה, as 19ᵇ, &c.).

(9) R. Yoseph (Ibn) עקנין and his commentary on Canticles (22ᵇ).

(10) Nachmanides, whom the author calls החכם, i.e. the Cabbalist (102ª); see this Catalogue, p. 109.

[1] לשון קדר, or ערבי. Once (68ᵇ) both these expressions are placed as if they meant two different languages.

(11) The בעל המלמד, i.e. R. Ya'aqob b. Abbamari b. Shime'on b. Anatolio (22^b); see מלמד התלמידים (Lyck, 1866, 8vo.).

(12) ספרי הרפואה (83^a).

6. Curious and interesting matters to be found in this commentary.

(1) The Articles of the Jewish religion, as defined by Maimonides, our author calls the י״ג אמונות, and he finds all of them in Deut. vi. 4—9 (152^b—154^b).

(2) Leviticus, besides being called by the well-known title תורת כהנים, is also called by him ספר רפואת הנפש; and Numbers, besides being called חומש הפקודים (Mishnah, *Yoma*, vii. 1), is also called by him ספר המספר (או ספר המופקד) (106^b). For the names he gives to Genesis and Exodus, see the next number of this Catalogue.

(3) The resemblance between Jethro and Plato, not only in their excellence in philosophy, but in the very etymology of their respective names, is alluded to in the following passage (38^b):

...ועל חכמתו (i.e. Moses') המפוארה שלמד מחותנו כהן מדין שהיה חכם ופלוסוף גדול וכבר נאמ׳ עליו שהיה אפלאטון (Plato) הפילוסוף האלהי לפי שתוף השם הידוע...

(4) The idea of the Heavenly Jerusalem[2] being the final object of an Israelite's aspiration, is referable, according to our author, to a cabbalistic (or a philosophical) origin; for he has (106^a) the following on it:

...ואם רחוקים אנו מירושלם נשים לבנו ועינינו אל ירושלם שבשמים כי אליה תכלית הכוונה באמת לפי הסוד הידוע למשכילים...

[1] This resemblance appears then not to be an original suggestion of our author's. It originated, no doubt, in the fact of the name of יתרו implying largeness. According to the Rabbis (in the Midrash Rabbah on Exodus, cap. 25) he bore this name because he enriched (enlarged) the Pentateuch by one Parashah (ואתה תחזה, in Exod. xviii). Plato's name also has the same meaning. He is said to have been called Πλάτων from either his mental or his physical qualities. Diogenes Laertius (Lib. 3, Plato) says: *Πλάτων διὰ τὴν εὐεξίαν μετωνομάσθη, πρότερον Ἀριστοκλῆς ἀπὸ τοῦ πάππου καλούμενος ὄνομα, καθά φησιν Ἀλέξανδρος ἐν διαδοχαῖς. ἔνιοι δὲ διὰ τὴν πλατύτητα τῆς ἑρμηνείας οὕτως ὀνομασθῆναι· ἢ ὅτι πλατὺς ἦν τὸ μέτωπον, ὥς φησι Νεάνθης.* Seneca (*Ep.* 58) says: Plato ipse ad senectutem se diligentiâ pertulit. Erat quidem corpus validum et forte sortitus, et illi nomen *latitudo pectoris* fecerat. Servius (on Virgil, *Æn.* vi. 658, 'humeris extantem suspicit altis') says: Quasi Philosophum, ac si diceret Platonem. Alludit enim Poeta. Nam Plato ab *humerorum* dictus est *latitudine.*

[2] Compare the Epistle to the Hebrews xii. 22 (*Ἱερουσαλὴμ ἐπουρανίῳ*). The equivalent expression, ירושלם של מעלה (*ἡ ἄνω Ἱερουσαλήμ*) is used both in the Talmud (Babli Ta'anith, 5^a) and in the New Testament (Gal. iv. 26).

(5) The attacks of our author on the Christianity of his time in Western Europe are so fierce, that we should have been greatly surprised, how a book containing them could have escaped the well-known wrath of the censors and its practical consequences, as mutilation, &c., had we not reason to believe, that this MS. had been copied in liberal Provence, and did we not know it for a fact, that it soon afterwards passed into the East, where censorship was unknown. Our author expresses himself with remarkable boldness against images, confession, hebdomadal fasts, pilgrimages (154^b, 155^a, 163^a, 165^b, 166^a, 173^b, 178^b, &c.), for which last practice he also sits in judgment upon the Mohammedans (165^b).

The scribe's name was probably Yoab, Yochanan, Yoseph, or something of the kind, as we find a line filled up on leaf 15^a by ׳ and on leaf 84^b by יו. Although, apparently, a Peninsular Sephardi, he probably copied this MS. in Provence. Unfortunately, the elegance of his writing is entirely eclipsed by his ignorance (or carelessness); for who would, for instance, readily recognise in his השחוק בקרובים (170^a), the author's protest against gambling (בקוביא), or in his יקם (95^b), the טמטם mentioned by Maimonides (Moreh, III. 29, 37)?

Ten successive owners have left their marks of ownership in this volume.

(1) A Peninsular Sephardic hand, of the xvth century (early) by making emendations on leaves 13^b and 15^a and giving a solution of an abbreviation on leaf 96^a. The emendations on leaves 22^b and 117^b (which latter is wrong) much resemble this owner's hand, but they belong to the original scribe.

(2) A Greek Sephardic hand, also of the xvth century (early) by writing a cabbalistic remark on 174^b.

(3) A Greek Ashkenazic hand of the xvth century by making an emendation on 99^b.

(4) A Greek Sephardic hand, also of the xvth century, by writing a remark on the outer margin of 34^a.

(5) A Greek hand of about the middle of the xvth century, by suggesting an emendation on 133^b.

(6) An Italo-Greek hand, by writing on 181^b, the following Note of sale:

(ב)שלישי (בשבת) בששה ימי׳ לחדש תשרי שנת הר״ל (1469) (מ)ודה אני מנחם פריגורי (Perigori) ב׳ר שבתי פנלי (Finale) איך מכרתי ספר זכרון טוב זה לר׳ אבשל(ום) בונא ויטא (Bonavita) מקהל פנרי (Fanari) בסך ידוע בינינו וקבלתי הפרעון בשלימות וכתיבתי תעיד עלי כמאה עדים והכל שריר ובריר וקים.

אני יוסף כהן בכ״ר אברהם כהן סהיד.

The witness writes in Greek Sephardic; the character of all the hands hitherto enumerated is Rabbinic. R. Abshalom Bonavita has left no mark now remaining in this MS., by which his hand can be identified.

(7) An oriental Sephardic hand of the xvth century (late) by making in mixed (Rabbinic and current) character, on 181[b], the following statement:

ב"ה ברב(י)עי בשבת בשבעה ימים לחדש אלול קניתי אני יצחק אלקיחילי
ז' (בן) ר' דוד אלקיחילי זה הספר זכרון טוב מר' אבשלום בונה ויטא
מקהל פנרי בשישים לבנים למשא ומתן קושטנטינה

No year is given. The word לבנים means small white, i.e. silver, coins, known in Greek as *ἄσπροι* or *ἄσπρα*, and in Italian as *albi* or *bianchi*; all words meaning the same thing (compare Zunz, *Gesch. u. Lit.* p. 548). The concluding words mean 'as current at Constantinople.'

(8) A Peninsular Sephardic hand of the xvith century (early) by suggesting, on 120[a], an emendation, which is, however, without value (as the במחנה of the text must not be emended into במנחה, but into במדה).

(9) Another Peninsular Sephardic hand of the xvith century, by writing on 33[b], 34[a], 63—68[b], 137[b]—141[a], the titles of the pericopes (once also, i.e. on 34[a], the number of the leaf, which is, however, wrong) on the upper, and the catchwords on the lower, margin.

(10) A Sephardic hand of the xvi—xviith century, by writing on the upper margin of 10[a], the following:

זכרון טוב לרבי נתן בר שמואל.

In this owner's time the MS. must have been already defective at the commencement. The last three owners wrote in Rabbinic character. The words 5067 ספר זכרון טוב נכתב ס"ז לפ"ק, written in Polish Ashkenazic current handwriting on 11[a] (which at the time of sale was thought to be the first leaf), belong to the undermentioned bookseller, Lipschütz.

The condition of the MS. is not very satisfactory, as, besides the defects before enumerated, 10, 120 and 179 are torn, and various leaves are stained and soiled. Luckily, however, only the margins are worm-eaten, and there is very little of the writing which is not clearly legible.

[Library-mark, Add. 485; bought in 1869 from H. Lipschütz.]

No. 62.

Paper, in quarto, $8\frac{1}{2}$ in. × $5\frac{3}{4}$ in.; 48 leaves, 8-sheet quires, about 35—40 lines; mixed (Rabbinic and current) character, Italian handwriting of the xvi—xviith century.

מבחר המאמרים [והוא פרוש על איזה מקומות בתורה] לר' נתן הרופא [בן שמואל]

Commentary on select passages of the PENTATEUCH, by the Physician R. Nathan b. Shemuel.

Leaves 1, 2 (both perhaps blank), wanting; 3^a^, *Title and introduction;* 3^a^, *Genesis;* 18^a^, *Exodus;* 28^a^, *Leviticus;* 32^a^, *Numbers;* 37^a^, *Deuteronomy;* 41—48 (all probably blank) wanting.

Title (leaf 3^a):

בהנו״א

פירוש קצת ענייני התורה על דרך כלל והוא המכוון בדרך הנסתר מאשר חבר החכם כמר נתן הרופא נב״ש״ת (נפשו בצל שדי תתלונן) בפי׳ התורה שלו הנק׳ מבחר המאמרים :

Introduction begins (Ibid.):

ספר בראשית. אמ׳ המחבר נבש״ת דע ישכילך (האלקי׳) שהספר הראשון הזה מחומשי התורה בכללו הוא סובב על מעשה בראשית המכונה בחכמת הטבע והוא ג״כ נקרא ספר הישרי[1]. והספר השני סובב על מעשה מרכבה ונקרא ספר הגאולה[2]...

Work begins (Ibid.):

דע ישכילך האלקי׳ שהעניין הכללי בפרשה הזאת בא להודיע תחילה מציאות העולם הזה המחודש הנברא מאין ליש...

Ends (leaf 40^b):

...וט(עם) במותו קודם מותו והצדיקים אפי(לו) במיתתם קרויים חיים :

חזק.

This small work, which was printed some years ago (Livorno, מעינתך[3], 8vo.), is by the same author as the preceding (No. 61). It consists, besides large extracts from the זכרון טוב (chiefly from the *Nistar*), of the leading ideas to be found in the commentaries of Ibn 'Ezra and Nachmanides, which are sometimes reproduced verbatim, although without giving the authors' names, and sometimes appear in another shape, without however being so worked up as to conceal the real authorship; and finally also of some entirely new matter. The title מבחר המאמרים is, at all events, fully justified, as this little work contains mostly *choice* explanations[4], whether

[1] See T. B. 'Abodah Zarah, 25^a.

[2] This phrase occurs in Ramban's verses at the end of Exodus.

[3] Luzzatto (יד יוסף, Padova, 1864, 8vo., p. 62, No. 526), writing probably from personal knowledge, says that this little book was printed in 1840, and that the date-word ought to have had another י (מעינתיך). Zedner gives 1840 as the date, without any remark, probably knowing what Luzzatto had written.

[4] As a specimen of these we may mention one which is found on leaf 39^b, which leads us to the solution of a difficulty felt by many critical readers of the Talmud Babli (Berakhoth 6^a, 57^a; Megillah 16^b; Sotah 17^a; Menachoth 35^b; Chullin 89^a); namely how R. Eli'ezer Haggadol developed from Deut. xxxiii. 10 the meaning of אלו תפלין שבראש.

original, or taken from other authors, or from the writer's own זכרון טוב. It is also worthy of note, that in the work before us, the Targum אונקלס is frequently referred to and explained.

As regards this copy as a MS., it is not merely of recent date, but contains many gross blunders, though perhaps not more than did the MS. from which the printed edition was taken.

The scribe's name is יהודה. He is identical with that of MSS. Add. 1169 and Add. 1171.

This MS. seems to have been executed for one R. Shime'on Hallevi; see leaves 15[a], 17[b] and 32[a]. (For other owners see the descriptions of MSS. Add. 1169, 1171.)

Except a few water-stains, the volume is in good condition.

[Library-mark, Add. 1170; bought in 1875 from Jacob Saphir of Jerusalem.]

No. 63.

Parchment, 12⅝ in. × 9½ in.; 228 leaves, mostly[1] 4-sheet quires, 26 lines; mixed (Rabbinic and current) character, fine Sephardic handwriting of the XIII—XIVth century.

[פרוש על נביאים אחרונים לר' דוד בן יוסף בן יצחק אבן קמחי הספרדי יליד נרבונא]

Commentary on the LATTER PROPHETS by R. David b. Yoseph b. Yitzchaq Ibn Qimchi[2] Hassephardi of Narbonne (Redaq), in two[3] parts. Part 1; defective.

Leaves 1—8 wanting; leaf 9[a], *Isaiah* (137 wanting); 143[b], *Jeremiah;* 227[b], blank; 228, probably blank, wanting.

[1] The last quire consists of six sheets.

[2] The question of how to read and transliterate the name קמחי, *i. e.* whether קִמְחִי or קַמְחִי (see Neubauer in the *Journal Asiatique*, 5[e] série, tome 20, p. 267), will be discussed in the memoir preceding the critical edition of Qimchi's Commentary on the Psalms, now in preparation by the present writer.

[3] That the second part of the Latter Prophets (of which this is the first) was still in connexion with this volume about the middle of the XIVth century, may be gathered from a Note which is to be found on leaf 227[b]; comp. the paragraph on owners, below.

Begins (leaf 9[a], on ותעלולים, Isaiah iii. 4):

וחלשיא והדרש תעלי בני תעלי פי שועלים...

Ends (leaf 227[a]):

...לפניו פירשנוהו במלכים וכן כל ימי חייו: ברוך העוזר והסומך:

Redaq is not an original commentator (any more than he is an original grammarian[1]). Most of his explanations belong either to the Targum[2], or to the Rabbis in Talmud and Midrash, or to the grammarians that preceded him, or to his elder brother (R. Mosheh), or finally, and chiefly, to his father, whom he frequently quotes, and whose excellent explanations have to a great extent been thus preserved from entire oblivion (see later). But though not original, Redaq is unquestionably, after Rashi, the most popular biblical commentator. This is owing to the fact of his combining the characteristics of Rashi and Ibn 'Ezra. The childlike simplicity and faith of the former and the incisive criticism of the latter, of both of which Qimchi is a harmonious personification, have secured to him popularity among both Jews and Christians in times past and present. Of course this popularity of his commentaries varies. It is greater or smaller in proportion to the greater or smaller popularity of the biblical books he comments on. Thus, for instance, his commentary on the Psalms is the most popular (as the numerous MSS. and editions thereof amply testify), because the Psalms themselves are, on account of their devotional contents, the most read of all biblical books. In accordance with this theory, it will be easily understood, why, next to that on the Psalms, his commentaries on the Latter Prophets, and of these again, those on Isaiah and Jeremiah, should be considered the most important, even as of these, in their turn, that on Isaiah should be the most sought after. With these introductory remarks we proceed to the MS. before us, which we must pronounce to be of the highest value for the following reasons.

I.

Importance of this MS. as executed by the original scribe.

1. This MS., as issued by the original scribe, is, if not the very oldest, at least, one of the oldest copies extant of our author's commentaries on Isaiah and Jeremiah.

[1] See our Review of the Kitab al-uzûl... in the Jewish Chronicle of June 6, 1873, p. 161.

[2] This is an element of value in Qimchi's commentaries on the Prophets, of which it is impossible to speak too strongly. In almost every verse he cites the so-called Targum of Jonathan; and even judging from the present MS. and No. 69 below, it becomes apparent how extremely corrupt is the ordinarily received text of that Targum, and how easy it would be almost to reconstruct it from a few good MSS. of Qimchi. In this matter, unfortunately, the printed texts of Qimchi are of no service whatever, seeing that they either merely reproduce the ordinary faulty text, or give a bare reference and catchword, or else they omit all notice of the citation altogether.

2. It has deviations, both in the shape of substitutions and omissions, greatly superior to the text of the editions. Whilst it has the genuine poem and bibliographical remarks, introductory to Jeremiah, it lacks the rhymed lines commonly found at the end of Isaiah, which, to one acquainted with Redaq's style, must appear more than doubtful.

3. It has additions, which, no doubt, embody Redaq's own, but later and better, recension. They are too numerous to be specified.

4. But, above all, it has intact the notorious Antichristiana, which Qimchi extracted from his father's books *Haggalui* and *Habberith*[1], as the following passage (leaf 113^b) will show: ... ועתה אפרש הפרשה כמו שפרשה אדני אבי ז״ל בספר הגלוי ובספר הברית שחבר תשובה על המינין.

II.

Importance of this MS. as enriched in literature by later scribes.

The commentaries on Isaiah and Jeremiah, are, for their better understanding, accompanied on the margin by part of the Sacred Text of those books. This is the work of three different scribes, all of whom, however, belong to the early part of the xivth century.

1. *Work done by the first of these later scribes.*

(1) The text written by the first of these scribes is in Peninsular Sephardic, current character. It reaches from the commencement to leaf 147^b, embodying with very few exceptions (see later) the whole of Isaiah and part of Jeremiah (i. 1—ii. 22). The text of Isaiah is so regularly and carefully given, that, but for the omissions observable in xxxvi—xxxviii (where but little of the text is found, owing to Qimchi's not having commented on much of it), one might almost have classed this MS. under the previous subdivision of this Catalogue.

(2) But this scribe has besides this, many, though but short, marginal notes, which consist chiefly of emendations. He must have had a copy of the later recension of Qimchi's commentary on Isaiah before him, as we find leaf 71^b, inner margin (on xxx. 20), the following phrase:

ד״ת (דעתא תנינא) או אפשר שירמוז מוריך אל הקב״ה ר״ל שעיניך יראו

which words, the first abbreviation perhaps excepted, unquestionably belong to Qimchi, as the context clearly shews (comp. Rashi).

2. *Work done by the second of these later scribes.*

(1) The text written by the second of these later scribes is in oriental Sephardic, Rabbinic character. It reaches from leaf 147^b to 151^a, and

[1] These works themselves are generally believed to be entirely lost. More will be said of them in the memoir referred to on p. 195, Note 2 above.

comprises Jeremiah ii. 23—iii. 7, of which, however, we must except ii. 26—28, 30—33 (see later).

(2) This scribe furnished the vowel-points to Jeremiah iii. 7, written by himself, as well as those to ii. 22 written by the first of the three later scribes.

3. *Work done by the third of the later scribes.*

The work of the third of the later scribes is insignificant. It consists merely of the writing of the text of Jeremiah ii. 26—28, 30—33 (see above) on the margin of leaves 198[b]—199[a]; and this is in Greek Sephardic character.

III.

Importance of this MS. as furnished with varied literature and information by owners.

1. It is not impossible that 1 and 3 of the later scribes just mentioned were successive owners of this MS., and that scribe 2 was the son, or a relative of scribe 3. But be this as it may, towards the middle of the xivth century this MS. must have been owned by a Peninsular Sephardi, as may be seen from two lines, written in Rabbinic character, on leaf 227[b]. The full name of the owner, which followed them, is unfortunately erased; which is the more to be regretted, as the statement contained in them (פירוש מר׳ דוד קמחי מארבעה נביאים אחרונים ממני דנין) leads one to infer that this owner alluded therein to his possessing this very volume and its fellow-volume containing Qimchi's commentary on Ezekiel and the Minor Prophets.

2. In the years 1395—1400, this MS. was, apparently, owned by קרגוד Bonet de Sylvis (בוניט דשלויש), in whose handwriting (Sephardic Rabbinic) the following three documents, which are instructive in more than one way, are to be found on leaf 227[b].

a.

היום יום ראשון כ״ט לחדש תמוז שנת קנ״ה (1395) נשבע שבועת התורה חפץ
ביד הנעלה אברם קרגוד דקבשטייאן (Castejon[1]) שמעולם לא יתן
לאשתו אישטיש גט שלא מדעתה וקבל על עצמו ברצונו שאם חס ושלום יעבר
על שבועתו לתת גט לאשתו הנזכרת שלא ברצונה קנס מאתים פרחים (Florins)
מאה לאשתו הנזכרת או לבאים מכחה והמאה הנשארים להב״ד אשר תעשה
אישטיש הנזכרת שאלתה ובקשתה ותקרב ותבואה טענתה זה היה בפני
הנעלה דון בוניט מיימון ובפני אני קרגוד בוניט דשלויש ובפני

[1] This name is variously represented in Hebrew: קבשטייאן, קבסטון, קשטיון &c.

רבים מאנשי קהל שלון[1] אך העדים המיוחדים אנחנו קדם זכרנו ולנו נתן רשות לחתום וליפות החתימה בכל מיני היפויים על האופן היותר טוב...

b.

היום יום שלישי בעשרים וחמשה לחדש מרחשון שנת קנ״ו (1395) באה לפנינו מרת מנדינאה וקבלה שבועת התורה חפץ ביד שקבלה חמשה עשר פרחים מאת ראשי קהל שלון בנכוי: מאה פרחים היו מחויבים אל הנעלה בעלה נ״ע (נוחו עדן) והיא קבלה אותו החוב בעד נדוניאתה והודאת (והודת) בפנינו שקבלה מאותו החוב ט״ו פרחים ככתוב למעלה: אני עד והנשא מאישטרי (the rest erased)...

c.

היום כ״ד ימים לחדש אייר שנת ק״ם (1400) השיב (דנין יוסף לאברם מציף) ספר מדע ואהבה תחלת הקונדרס (ואמצעי) קלף ומקרא מנביאים אחרונים בקלף ופירוש מר׳ דוד קמחי מישעיה וירמיה תחלת הקונדרס ואמצעי בקלף היו אלה הספרים הנזכרים ביד דנין הנזכר במשכון על (ידי אשטרוגה חמות אברם מציף) הנזכר שמה אותם במשכון בשם חתנו (חתנה) אברם הנזכר והנה אברם הנז׳ קבל הספרי׳ הנזכרים מיד דנין יוסף הנזכר שהיו במשכון אצלו בעד ב׳ דנרין ואברם מציף קבל על עצמו לשלם כל נזק והוצאה יבאו אל דנין הנזכר בעד הספרים הנזכרים הן מצד חמותו אשטרוגה הנזכרת הן מצד זולתה כי כבר קבל הספרים הנזכרים כלם בשלמות כל זה היה בפני ובפני בונן קלוניא וקרשקאש קרגוד וקבל אברם מציף שבועה בפנינו מכל זה ביום הנזכר למעלה.

3. Within the first half of the xvth century this copy must have belonged to a Peninsular Sephardi. He has left his mark of ownership on this MS.: (1) by writing one verse of the sacred text (Jerem. i. 5; leaf 144ᵃ); (2) by various corrections in the body of the MS. (see passim); and (3) by supplying various notes on the margins. These last, although they chiefly supplement omissions in the commentary, which had escaped previous owners, are by no means confined to this (see, for example, leaf 87ᵇ, which contains an astronomical note on the full moon). This owner wrote a beautiful current hand, which may be best identified on leaf 19ᵇ.

4. In the xv—xvith century this MS. probably belonged to a Greek Sephardi, as a suggested emendation, in Rabbinic character, on leaf 206ᵃ, leads us to believe.

5. In addition to the marks of ownership just given and which are inseparable from this MS., there is one to be found on a paper leaf, which had been attached to the binding of this volume. It is couched in Spagnol and written in mixed (oriental and Egyptian) Sephardic, current character. It contains the names of ח(כם) אברהם פאריו, משולם, and חכם שמואל, and is signed יוסף מזרחי. It is, apparently, quite modern (xviii—xixth century).

[1] The learned men of שלון or שילון are often to be met with in old MSS.

As regards the condition of the MS., it is, on the whole, excellent. Leaf 163 has lost all three outer margins, and 185 is cut; 9[a] is somewhat stained and soiled, as are a few other leaves; yet, in most cases, the writing looks quite fresh, and there is absolutely nothing that cannot be read with perfect ease.

[Library-mark, Add. 482; bought in 1869 from H. Lipschütz.]

No. 64.

Paper, in quarto, 9½ in. × 7 in.; 28 leaves, 7-sheet quires, 38—40 lines; mixed (Rabbinic and current) character, fine Italian handwriting of the XVIth century.

[כלי כסף והם פרושים על משלי וארבע מגלות הראשונות ובראשם הקדמה קטנה הכוללת רשימה עיונית לעשרים ועוד מספרי המחבר לר׳ יוסף בן אבא מרי בן יוסף בן יעקב אבן כספי מכספי המקום]

Commentaries on PROVERBS, ECCLESIASTES, and CANTICLES, and on RUTH and LAMENTATIONS, preceded by a descriptive CATALOGUE of more than twenty of his other works, by R. Yoseph b. Abbamari b. Yoseph b. Ya'aqob Ibn Kaspi of Argentière[1].

Leaf 1[a], A *poem* by the scribe; 1[a], the *Catalogue;* 2[a], *Introduction* to *Proverbs;* 2[b], *Commentary* on *Proverbs*; 12[b], on *Ecclesiastes*; 19[b], on *Canticles;* 20[b], *Introduction* to the Rolls *Ruth* and *Lamentations;* 20[b], *Commentary* on *Ruth;* 21[b], on *Lamentations;* 26[b], blank (27, probably blank, wanting); 28, blank.

1. קבוצת כסף.

THE CATALOGUE.

Title, and poem by the scribe (leaf 1[a]):

בהנו״א

קבוצת כסף

פירוש משלי ומגלות ה׳	דקדוק סודותיהם אוסף.
חבר אותו בתבונה ה	חכם אבן כספי יוסף.
וקראתיו בשמו כי נחצב	משכלו אוצר הכסף.

[1] Being in Paris in 1874, we carefully inspected Codex Oratoire 105 (New Catalogue, No. 986) in the *Bibliothèque Nationale*, and we can relieve Steinschneider's mind of the doubts expressed in Ersch and Gruber's *Encyklopädie*

Catalogue begins (ibid.):

אמר יוסף אבן כספי כאשר בא יוסף זקן באנשים...

Ends (leaf 2[a]):

...אולי יחנן ה׳ צבאות שארית יוסף בהתודע יוסף„

This *Catalogue* is, if we except a number of insulated words, which differ for the better[1], identical with the קבוצת כסף published (after a copy made by Werbluner from the Munich MS. 365) by Benjacob, in the collection *Debarim Attikim*, II. (Leipzig, 1846, 8vo.), where it forms No. 2 and occupies pp. 10—14. While we miss here the poem, which is there to be found at the end, but which in our opinion belongs to one or other of the scribes, at all events not to our author, and certainly not to this *Catalogue*[2]; we have here, at the commencement (see above), a different poem, which apparently belongs to R. 'Ezra of Fano (see later, in the paragraph on the scribe).

The importance of the *Catalogue* lies chiefly in the following four points:

(1) It is, if not the only one, at least, one of only a very few Catalogues prepared by a Jewish author himself of his own works[3].

(2) It contains matters of interest partly appertaining to the author himself, partly to his own family, and partly to that of Maimonides.

(3) It makes us acquainted with the plan of no less than twenty important works by the author, all of which afterwards existed, although

II. 31, p. 59, Note 12. The original hand has clearly enough the word דלאנגליטרא (Steinschneider's דלאנגלטירא is evidently a misprint); comp. also Munk, Mélanges, Paris, 1859, 8vo., p. 496, Note 3.

[1] We need only give two examples. We read here (leaf 1[a], line 12): ...ויעבור פרפיניאן ברצלונה כי שם צוה ה׳ את הברכה לבנו ולבתו. As is well known, the ordinary reading (לבתו ולבנו) has been much discussed and has given considerable trouble to the bibliographers, not only because Ibn Kaspi would thus have named his daughter before his first-born son, but chiefly because this daughter is nowhere else heard of. By our reading, on the one hand, and by considering, on the other hand, the remarks of the Midrash Rabbah on Genesis, cap. 84 (on xxxvii. 35: אין אדם נמנע מלקרוא...ולכלתו בתו), this difficulty disappears altogether. Again we read here (ibid.) ואחר ארגי׳(ע) להפריד instead of the unquestionably corrupt ואחר ארגון להפריד. It is however possible that this passage should run thus: ואחר ארגון לספרד (i.e. and from Aragon to Castile), seeing that at our author's time Castile was emphatically understood by Sepharad (Spain).

[2] See the ספר המוסר by our author (in the טעם זקנים, Frankfurt am Main, 1854, 8vo. p. 54).

[3] This point has been already, though in our estimation not sufficiently, appreciated by Steinschneider (Ersch u. Gruber's *Encyk.* II. 31, p. 58).

at the time of the composition of the *Catalogue* only part of them had been actually written, while another part had then yet to be composed.

(4) It describes to us, besides these twenty works, the plan and nature of other and earlier works by the author, the identification of which would otherwise be for more than one reason if not exactly impossible, at least very difficult[1].

2. חצוצרות כסף.

COMMENTARIES ON PROVERBS[2], ECCLESIASTES, AND CANTICLES.

General title (leaf 2ª):

חצוצרות כסף הכולל שלשת ספרי שלמה משלי קהלת שיר השירים״

This work spreads over select portions of the three books of Solomon, and is therefore divided by the author into three parts (חלקים).

[1] Thus for instance we learn from it:

(1) That (leaf 1ª) at the age of thirty our author had composed a work entitled תרומת הכסף, containing a compendium (ביאור עם קצור, i.e. a combination of abridgment and commentary) of the *Ethics* of Aristotle and the ספר ההנהגה of Plato. The work of Plato is the *Politicus* according to Steinschneider (*Encyk.* p. 69), but the *Republic* according to Kirchheim (*Die Kommentare von Joseph Kaspi...zu Dalalat al Haiirin.* Frankfurt am Main, 1848, 8vo. p. xiii). The title Terumath Hakkeseph was suggested to the author at Mallorca by one שלמה אטיוס of Perpignan; see מלאכת שלמה in *Debarim Attikim*, II. p. 15.

(2) That at the same age he had composed another work under the name of צרור הכסף (see the description of MS. Gg. 6. 37 below).

(3) That he had composed another work again, just before he had commenced the *Catalogue*. Its name was כסף סינים, and it contained one hundred and ten difficult questions (and answers?) on the Pentateuch and the Prophets. (The existence of a copy of this work cannot, at this moment, be traced; that it, however, did exist, we know also from the author's commentary on Lamentations; see later.)

(4) But the work which interests us most is the author's earliest production, although he mentions it here accidentally third. It is the פרשת הכסף, which, although it does not do so now, contained originally (if our interpretation of the author's בימי בחורותיו עשה פרישה לספר הרקמה וספר אבן עזרא בתורה המכונה פרשת הכסף, on leaf 1ª, be correct) under *one* title (analogous to the *Terumath Hakkeseph* mentioned before) an explanation of the Grammar of Ibn גנאח and a supercommentary on Ibn 'Ezra on the Pentateuch. This latter, in one form or another, included also the explanation of the so-called *Sodoth* as extant in MSS. Add. 377. 3. 6 and Add. 510. 2. 2 (pp. 55, 56, 61, 132, 133 of this Catalogue); see Excursus II. According to the preface in the Munich MS. 61 (*Melekheth Shelomoh*, p. 16), these two or rather three works were executed at the early age of seventeen!

[2] This work was composed for, and addressed to, his firstborn son (לך בני בכורי; 4ª), then resident in Barcelona (see 4ᵇ, 12ᵇ). This eldest son's name was Abbamari, as we learn from Cod. 40 in the Town Library at Leipzig (see

Introduction to Part 1 (Proverbs) begins (leaf 2[a]):

אמר יוסף אבן כספי זה הספר הוא כספרי מוסרי הפילוסופי׳ ואין בו לפי דעתי הכרח שיהיו בזה תורות וסודות...

Commentary on Proverbs begins (leaf 2[b]):

משלי שלמה בן דוד מלך ישראל. בזה אמר שם הספר ושם מחברו ואחר אמ׳ כוונת הספר ותועלתו...

Commentary ends (leaf 12[a]):

...והנביאים איה הם הודיעם (היודעים) כי כן היתה כוונת משה ושלמה ולמה לא אמרו כן בפירוש אחשורש ומרדכי ואסתר ועשרת בני המן ואותו תלו היטיבה ה׳ לטובים ולישרים בלבותם״

Postscript ends (leaf 12[b]):

...תעלוזנה כליותי, כי תנחל נחלותי, ואשלחך בחיי אל עיר ידיעותי, עד הגבול, ואם כל אשר לי ארץ כבולי (כבול), ה׳ אלהיך ירצך, ויהי אלהים עמך״ נשלם פירוש משלי החלק האחד מחצוצרות כסף ונשארו השנים, בשה״א (בשם ה׳ אמן).

To judge from the commencement, both of the Introduction and of the work itself, and from the author's subscription of this commentary, as communicated by Werbluner (*Mel. Shel.* in *Debarim Attikim* II. p. 19), our copy differs somewhat from that at Munich (Cod. 265[1]).

This commentary is, like most of the works of our author, thoroughly permeated with the ideas of Greek-Arabic philosophy, of which he was perfect master; and although Jerusalem and Athens do not ordinarily agree, they are here, on the whole, peaceably and harmoniously placed

Delitzsch, *Catal.* p. 304) and Cod. 264 at Munich (*Mel. Shel.* p. 17). Kirchheim (*Die Kommentare*, p. iii. Note 2) maintains, against De-Rossi, that Ibn Kaspi had only one son, Shelomoh, and one daughter, whilst Steinschneider (*Encyk.* II. 31, p. 60, Notes 13[a], 15 and 17[a]) partly sides with De-Rossi. Now the expression ואתה בני אשר בברצלונה (MS. leaf 4[a], line 19), the force of which has apparently escaped all these scholars, unquestionably shows that our author must have had a son besides the one at Barcelona. This other son lived at Tarascon, and his name was Shelomoh (see this Catalogue, p. 133, Note 2); and Steinschneider is quite right in emending the בעירי, in reference to this son, into צעירי.

[1] Thus, for instance, the questionable בן סודי, after the author's name at the commencement of the introduction, is not to be found here; nor the subscription by the author, in which the place and time of the composition are given as עיר טרשקון...חדש שבט...חשעים (Tarascon, Dec. 1329 or Jan. 1330). We suspect however that Cod. 265 at Munich, which is said to consist of 37 leaves in quarto, contains something besides the commentaries mentioned in the Melekheth Shelomoh.

together. Viewed as an explanation of a biblical book, it is, if not exactly the only one by the author worth anything (Kirchheim, *Die Kommentare*, p. vii), certainly the best of his commentaries on the Bible accessible to us. Its chief interest however does not consist in the explanations themselves it gives of this philosophical book, but in the following points, which are for the most part only accidentally touched upon.

(1) Ibn Kaspi ascribes only the substance, and at most the single sentences, of this philosophical book to Solomon, whilst the book as such he declares to have been composed by the King's servants[1].

(2) Of Aristotelian works he quotes the following: (1) ספר הטבע (Physics; 2^{b}); (2) ספר המדות (Ethics; 2^{b}, 3^{b}, 12^{a}); (3) ספר בעלי חיים (De Animalibus; 4^{a}); (4) ספר המליצה περὶ ἑρμηνείας; 9^{a}); (5) אותות העליונות (Meteora; 9^{b}). We may as well here draw attention to the author's *naïve* statement (11^{a}), that he considers Aristotle inferior to Moses!

(3) The Massorets and Accentuators, whom he evidently identifies with one another (טעמי בעלי המסרת and בעלי הטעמים; 4^{a}, 8^{b}), he places so high, that he says of them אין לנו אחריהם כלום or אין אחריהם פירוש חדש.

(4) Of Maimonides' works he quotes only the Introduction to his commentary on the Mishnah by name (7^{a}); he mentions him however, besides, in three other places (5^{b}, 7^{a}, 9^{a}).

(5) Of his own works he quotes: (1) the ספר הסוד, which was afterwards called by him טירת כסף (2^{a}, 3^{b}, 4^{a}, 11^{b}); (2) פירוש התורה (3^{a}, 3^{b}, 4^{a}, 5^{a}); (3) ביתר ספרי; without further specifying them (4^{a}).

(6) The interpretations of vii. 20, xvi. 33, xxiii. 30 and xxiv. 21 (4^{a}, 7^{a} and 8^{b}) are of interest, chiefly from an ethnographical point of view.

(7) In a linguistic point of view we may note the word שירא (the Assizes in France; 4^{a}).

(8) Ibn Kaspi evidently knew the זכרון טוב and the לוית חן, &c. (see No. 61 of this Catalogue), and controverts their authors, although he neither mentions them nor the books distinctly (12^{a}). He protests against allegorically explaining not only the Pentateuch and the other (historical) books, but even this book (of Proverbs), beyond the apparent and absolute necessity (comp. also 2^{a}).

[1] Leaf 4^{b} we read:

...שלמה לא חבר כל הספר הזה בסדר מראשיתו עד אחריתו רק היה מאמרו למשרתיו ושריו כמו שכתוב אשרי עבדיך...

and again leaf 8^{b}:

...זה עד ג"כ כי שלמה לא חבר הספר כלו על הסדר אבל היה אומר או כותב מאמריו בסירוגין קצתו היום וקצתו אחר שנה או שנתים ואחר (ואחד?) אם בימיו אם אחריו העתיקו אנשי ירושלם...

Introduction to Part 2 (Ecclesiastes) begins (leaf 12[b]):

עתה נתחיל בפירוש קהלת שהוא החלק השני בעזרת שרי„ דברי קהלת... תחת השמש„ אמר יוסף אבן כספי הנה שלמה השלם הניח בראש ספרו שם מחברו כי הודיענו שהוא ע"ה חבר זה הספר וכנה שמו בקהלת לטעם שאמרו חז"ל שנקהלה בו החכמה וכן כנה שמו אגור מטעם אוגר בקיץ. ואחר שהודיע שם מחבר הספר כמנהג הפילוסופים הודיענו כוונת ספרו כלו והוא אמרו הבל הבלים...

Commentary begins (leaf 13[a]):

מה יתרון לאדם בכל עמלו... ומה שיאמר ג"כ אחר זה דור הולך... אין הכונה בזה להודיענו עם (אם) העולם נצחי או לא...

Commentary ends (leaf 19[b]):

...ואם תבין תראה שכלם אחד וברוב הוא לשון אחד כי כונתו קבוץ הפעולה בהכרחי עם השמחה ולכן אמ' ברבם לאכול ולשתות ולשמוח כי האכילה והשתיה ר"ל ההזנה הנאותה„ ובזה נשלם דעת (דעתי) בזה הספר„

Author's conclusion ends (Ibid.):

...לכן אחר שאני מצאתי זה החדוש ונכתבו על לוח לבי אלו ההקשים והפסקים מה מאוד יהיה(!)סכלותי גדול(!) אם בזאת לא אוסר לכן כונתי שיהיה זה הפירוש חתימה לחיים לכל אנחותי ומחשבותי ומהאלהים אשאל העזר והאמצה יתברך וית' אמן„ נשלם פירוש קהלת החלק השני מחצוצרות כסף

The apparent contradictions, nay heresies, to be found in Ecclesiastes, are no modern discovery; the Great Synod already knew of, and seriously reflected on, them. In consequence of this reflexion, the book barely escaped being excluded from the biblical Canon (Mishnah Yadayim, III. 5, Midrash Rabbah on Ecclesiastes i. 1, T. B. Shabbath, 30[b] &c.). Now the reasons for ultimately declaring this book canonical, although they certainly satisfy the believer, might or might not satisfy the philosopher, who is in the habit of sifting everything critically. Our author then solves this double difficulty of the apparent contradictions and heresies of Ecclesiastes, according to his wont, philosophically[1]; and the aim of this biblical book is, according to him, a twofold one:

(1) To point out to the reader the following philosophical truths: (1) That the motive of all human actions is to be found either in folly or in wisdom; (2) Whilst folly is in reality only one, and divisible only into degrees, wisdom consists essentially of two kinds, worldly and divine, both of which are divisible again into degrees.

[1] Singularly enough in a philosophical commentary on so philosophical a book as Ecclesiastes, the author mentions Aristotle only once (הפלוסוף; 15[a], line 13) and his own קצור המדות also only once (16[b], line 19), just as he mentions Ibn 'Ezra only once (17[a], line 14), when he controverts him.

(2) To bring home to the reader the following philosophical counsels: (1) That nobody should for a moment question the duty of avoiding folly of any, even the slightest, degree; (2) That of worldly wisdom only a certain amount, removed alike from both extremes, should constitute man's motives; (3) That, on the other hand, with regard to divine wisdom (under which our author understands partly the study of religion and partly speculative philosophy), the more a man inclines to the extreme, the better it is for him, as thus alone can he make himself fit for perfection, immortality, and the conjunction with the *Active Intellect* (שלמות ונצחות הנפש עד שתדבק אל המלאך הנק' שכל הפועל; leaf 19[a]).

Now, although the theory of the *Active Intellect* being an Angel, with whom the souls of the perfect become one by study, &c. is a mere creation of the Greek-Arabic school, and is now happily exploded; and although, further, this commentary is also from an exegetical point of view inferior to the author's commentary on Proverbs, it would be unjust to denounce it as being utterly without value (as Kirchheim and Steinschneider evidently think). The division of the book of Ecclesiastes (into ten parts) according to our author, and the logical evidences (twenty-one, of which, however the 19th is missing) developed out of the book itself, are certainly very creditable ideas. This commentary is moreover not utterly devoid of other matters of interest. Thus, for instance, we become, in the course of it acquainted with certain facts relating either to the author himself or to others, and with his views on various matters. Thus we learn: (1) That he knew Latin (leaf 15[a], line 9); (2) that he was fifty years old when he composed this commentary (leaf 19[b]), a statement which is an important, though indirect, key to the chronology of his whole literary activity; and further; (3) the curious way in which he connects the Pope's sojourn at Avignon with the cheapness of wine and the dearth of corn (in Provence[1]); and (4) his view on the institution of the double keeping, in the Diaspora, of the biblical Feast-days (שני ימים טובים של גליות), a point which has been much ventilated of late, particularly in England.

Part 3 (commentary on Canticles) begins (leaf 19[b]):

ועוד נשאר הקטן ספר שיר השירים ועתה נתחיל בו בעזרת שדי„ אמר יוסף אבן כספי אחר שקדם לנו פי' משלי וקהלת שחבר שלמה בחכמתו ראוי לנו שנכתוב דברים מה בפירוש שיר השירים שחבר ג"כ שלמה ואין אני צריך לפרש המלות כי כבר פירשום קודמים לפני והיטיבו ברבם לכן לא אדבר רק על דעת הספר הזה בכלל...

[1] He does this, on occasion of illustrating Eccl. iii. 2, in the following way: ...וזה אנו רואים היום בגבולנו (Tarascon) אשר בסבת ישיבת האפיפיור (the Pope) בארצנו (Provence) נטער בכל הארץ כרמים לאין מספר עד ששב היין בזול והתבואה ביוקר ועתה הם משחיתים הכרמים ועוקרים הנטיעות וישיבום לשדות ויזרעו שם תבואה כ"ש אם מחר או מחרתו ישב לו ברומי כי יהיו בתה בגבולנו שדות וכרמים לאין מספר ויהיו שממה...

Ends (leaf 20ᵃ):

...על דרך יין וחמר וגן ופרדס ומזה המין הפלגות נפלאות בדברי ר"זל כי לא נעלמה מהם חכמה אבל לא נכיר אנחנו זה. ודי באלו ההערות לפי זה הספר לפי כונתינו ולאל יתברך ההודאה ית' וית' תמו שלשת חלקי ספר חצוצרות כסף ת"ל.

The author, according to his own confession, did not intend to write a regular commentary on Canticles, since others had preceded him in such work, and had moreover done it on the whole very well. He wished to give a general idea only of the book and a few hints thereon; and even these were not due to himself, but to Maimonides (Moreh III. 51; וגם זאת הכונה לא מלבי כי המורה המאיר לארץ האיר עינינו בזה...). And, as if to gratify our author's wish in this respect, this opusculum, more than two hundred years after its composition, appeared in print[1] as a quasi-introduction[2] to the triple[3] commentary on Canticles, edited by R. Yitzchaq b. Abraham b. Yehudah עקריש[4], an exile from the Iberian Peninsula and from Naples.

3. כפות כסף.

Commentaries on Ruth and Lamentations.

General Introduction begins (leaf 20ᵇ):

כפות כסף הכולל שתי מגלות כף אחת מגלת רות וכף אחת מגלת איכה ואתחיל במגלת רות בע"ה:
אמר יוסף אבן כספי ראיתי את הארץ והנה תהו ויושביה כמו בן ימותון ולא ישאר מן העולם השפל רק החלק מן הנפש השכלי...

This work is divided into two parts, or כפות, as they are called by the author.

(Part 1 commentary on Ruth) begins (leaf 20ᵇ):

ויהי בימי שפוט השופטים. נכון וראוי היה מאוד ליחד ספר לכתוב יחס דוד...

[1] At קושטאנדינא, i.e. Constantinople, without date, but according to Steinschneider (*Encyk.* II. 31, p. 64) in or about 1577.

[2] Editor's preface, towards the end: ...שמתי במקום הקדמה פי' הרב ר' יוסף ן כספי.

[3] This triple commentary consists of (1) the present work; (2) the שאר ישוב or קדש הקדשים of R. Ya'aqob Provençal (פרובינשאל; editor's preface: ומצאתי כתוב ששם המחבר...); and (3) a commentary, without a special title, by Se'adyah (סעדיא) Gaon (?), translated by the editor from the Arabic.

[4] The book is very inaccurately printed; but the awful vicissitudes of the editor, which would suffice as an excuse even for graver shortcomings, must be taken into consideration; and we are bound to state, that we are indebted to R. Yitzchaq עקריש in this publication for many historical, biographical, and bibliographical notices of interest to be found in his preface.

Ends (leaf 21):

...כמו מעשה בראשית ומעשה מרכבה ויתר ספרי הנבואה ובאור הכל אוצר ה׳ יבא:

Apparently, this commentary as extant in this MS. agrees with that under the same name, which constitutes part of the Munich MS. 265 (Mel. Shel. in *Debarim Attikim*, II. p. 18). As, however, neither Werbluner, nor Kirchheim, nor finally Steinschneider, say anything on the internal nature of this commentary, the following few remarks may not be deemed superfluous:

(1) *Characteristics of the book of Ruth, &c. according to this commentary.*

While the ostensible purpose of this book, says our author, is to give the genealogy of David the *King*, sprung from the house of *Judah*, whose greatness Jacob had prophesied and Moses had confirmed, the undercurrent continually manifesting itself in this book, and indeed in all Biblical books, is to give the reader moral and religious instruction and information which will largely contribute to the improvement both of his body and his mind. (Compare 2 Tim. iii. 16.)

(2) *Value of this short commentary for various reasons.*

The interesting matter which this Commentary contains is quite out of proportion to the smallness of its size. Though very brief, the information to be found in it is as varied as it is valuable. It embraces points in Biblical hodegetic, lexicography and grammar (extending both to Hebrew, Aramaic and Latin), philosophy, ethnography and bibliography (which comprises several of his own works, as also some of those of Ibn נֹנאח, Ibn 'Ezra and Maimonides). The whole is seasoned with a quaint, but by no means irreverent, humour peculiar to our author.

Part 2 (commentary on Lamentations) begins (leaf 21b):

הכף השנית מגלת איכה

איכה ישבה בדד מבוארת כונת זאת המגלה שחבר ירמיהו אחר חרבן בית ראשון שבו נחרב עמנו...

Ends (leaf 25b):

...ועל זה המין אמ׳ רבו׳ הקדושים ז״ל שבעים פנים יש לתורה בעבור היות(ו) סך חשבון גדול והעד בשבעים נפש וכן שבעים ושבעה וביאור כלל זה הענין יקר מאוד והכל אוצר ה׳ יבוא״

נשלם השבח לבורא עולם״

This commentary has been edited by Reggio in his אגרות י״ש״ר II. (Wien, 1836, 8vo.[1]), where it constitutes almost the whole of the 26th *Letter*,

[1] Reprinted (in a double edition) in the Ritual for the Ninth of Ab (the day of mourning for the destruction of Jerusalem and the Temple) under the name of אלון בכות (Wien, 1853, 8vo).

and occupies pp. 45—61. But the MS. which the editor had before him must have been an inferior one, as the edition teems with mistakes, which, particularly as Reggio is known to have been ordinarily a very careful editor, cannot be accounted for on the score of mere misprints. Our copy, on the other hand, although itself not entirely free from mistakes[1], is, generally speaking, a fair exponent of this commentary, and in some instances, even superior to that part of the Munich MS. 265, which also contains it.

In addition to Steinschneider's instructive, but very short, notice on this commentary, both as extant in print and in MS. (*Encykl.* II. 31, p. 65), the following few remarks may not be unacceptable to the reader.

(1) Our author appears here as the champion of biblical and, if we may say so, altogether of Hebrew linguistic orthodoxy, and will not even allow that (as Ibn 'Ezra thinks) a ן might irregularly have been put instead of a ם (in the plural). Thus on the word שוממין (i. 4) he has (leaf 22ᵃ) the following:

נכון בעברי כמו שוממים ... וחלילה שיהיה אות תמורת אות בכל כתבי הקדש כמו שאמרו כל הקודמים וכ״ש שם תמורת שם כי א״כ אין לנו לא לשון ולא ספר ...

(The נכון בעברי is here a standing phrase with him.) On the other hand he objects to Hebrew micrology and micrologists, whom he calls sticklers (אנשים מקפידים), as may be seen from his remarks on i. 19 (leaf 23ᵃ).

(2) Here, even more than in his other works, Ibn Kaspi shows his great familiarity with Greek philosophy and philosophers, several of whom he names distinctly. The phrase בעברי ובהגיון occurs here no less than twelve times.

(3) While our author probably knew Greek philosophy by the channel of Arabic only (with which language he was very well acquainted, as is known), we learn here additionally (comp. above, pp. 206, 208), that he knew Latin[2] (דרך העברי גם הרומי; 21ᵇ).

[1] This MS., for instance, reads (leaf 25ᵃ, on v. 6) כי הראשון היה עול for the unintelligible עוף of the printed edition, both of which are unquestionably a mistake for פול (i.e. Phul, as Steinschneider, l. c. Note 40, already rightly transliterates). The mistake in this MS. originated, no doubt, in the great similarity of the letters ע and פ in the Italian current character in the MS. from which it was copied. (On Phul and his influence for evil on the independence of Judah and Israel, see the interesting article by Graetz, *Die assyrischen Invasionen und Eroberungen in Palästina, im samaritanischen und judäischen Reiche* in Frankel's *Monatsschrift*, XXIII. pp. 481—492.)

[2] We may as well, on this occasion, give our author's rendering (23ᵇ) of the familiar *Solamen miseris socios habuisse doloris;* it is אבל רבים חצי נחמה, which is not only correct but even elegant, particularly when compared with Benzeeb's incorrect and inelegant צרות רבות חצי נחמות (Ozar Haschoroschim, ed. Letteris, under the word נחם; comp. Zunz in Steinschneider's המזכיר, XV. p. 10, No. 39).

(4) Of his own works Ibn Kaspi quotes distinctly his commentary on Proverbs (22[a]), the כסף סיגים (25[a]; comp. above, p. 202, Note), and the אוצר ה' (passim). This last-named work he treats as a general literary receptacle, putting, or promising to put, into it all that he can only slightly touch upon here and elsewhere.

(5) Of other authorities and their works he quotes, besides Plato, Se'adyah Gaon's translation of the Pentateuch, and Ibn גנאח (already mentioned by Steinschneider), Aristotle, the undefined המפרשים, Ibn 'Ezra, Maimonides (whom he here several times simply designates by המאיר לעולם כלו), and Ibn Qimchi (for which the printed edition and probably the MSS. before Steinschneider also, by mistake read א"ע).

(6) Our author speaks so frequently here of סודות to be found in the Bible (סודות גדולים, סודות נפלאות, סוד גדול, &c.) that, even had he not been the author of the ספר הסוד, and of a work on the סודות of Ibn 'Ezra, &c., it would astonish no one to find him designated by the name of Ibn Sodi (בן סודי; *Mel. Shel.* p. 15).

(7) We have only to mention, in addition, two interesting explanations of his. The first is to be found leaf 23[b] (on בעטף, ii. 11) and runs thus:

...כטעם נפשי עלי תתעטף...ואחר שביארנו הוראת לשון עטוף וסוף עניינו הנה בארנו מה שאמרו רבו' הקדו' שלא נעלם מהם דבר אמת שהב"ה מתעטף בטל(י)ת וזה אמת מכמה פנים וכמו זה הלשון אמ' הפילו' שהשכל הנפרד מתעטף קצתו עם קצתו[1]...

The second is to be found leaf 24[b] (on והגיונם, iii. 62) and runs thus:

אין זה על מלאכת ההגיון...וכבר ביארנו שהוא שיחת הילדים שגנו רבו' הקדו' ז"ל[2]...

As regards the scribe, it is the well-known Cabbalist R. 'Ezra of Fano, teacher of the even better known R. Menachem 'Azaryah of Fano and other Cabbalists and Talmudists of the xvith century. The name עזרא מפאנו is to be found on leaf 15[a], lines 10—13 and 15—19, where four words had actually to be divided in order to bring about this desirable(?) result. Little ornaments above and on the side of the letters draw the reader's attention to this name. R. 'Ezra was in copying this MS. probably not influenced by his profession of scribe merely; it was more the Sod-literature, which attracted him.

1 The allusion to 'our holy teachers' refers no doubt to the Targum on Cant. v. 10, T. B. Rosh Hasshanah 17[b], Midrash Rabbah on Genesis, cap. iii., and the Peraqim of R. Eli'ezer, cap. iii.; that to 'the Philosopher' to Aristotle; see *Metaphysics*, Book xii. (according to the old editions, but xi. according to most modern editions), chap. 9.

2 T. B. Berakhoth, 28[b].

For owners see the description of MS. Add. 857. 1, below.

The condition of the MS. is excellent in every respect.

[Library-mark, Add. 857. 2; bought in 1871 from Nathan Coronel of Jerusalem.]

No. 65.

Paper, in quarto, 8 in. × 5⅞ in.; 66 leaves, two 8-sheet, and two 6-sheet quires, followed by one of 5 sheets, 27—30 lines; Rabbinic character, Italian handwriting of the xvth century.

[פרוש על איוב לרבנו משה בן נחמן ירונדי]

Commentary on Job, by R. Mosheh b. Nachman of Gerona, (Ramban, Nachmanides).

Leaf 1ª, blank; 1ᵇ, *Introduction;* 5ᵇ, *Commentary;* leaves 64, 65, probably blank, wanting; leaf 66, blank.

Introduction begins (1ᵇ):

(עמ"י) עש"ו

פירוש איוב הידוע אל הרב רבנו משה ב"ר נחמן ז'צ'ל
דבר ברור וידוע כי האמונה בידיעת האל ית'...

Commentary begins (5ᵇ):

איש היה בארץ עוץ מצאנו מלכי העוץ ומפורש מזה בת אדום יושבת בארץ עוץ...

Ends (leaf 63ᵇ):

...ויש בצדיקים שלא יאמר כן במעלתם כגון במשה ואהרן כי פירש במיתתם שהיא על פי יי' והיא מיתת נשיקה שיש לה סוד לדבקה בשם הנכבד..

והספר נשלם ברוך יי' אל עולם
(מנחם מקסטילטיץ[1]) הכותב ונשלם

This commentary has been printed three times (Venezia, 1517, Folio; Amsterdam, 1724—28, Folio; Fürth, 1842—47, 8vo.[2]).

In each edition it accompanies the sacred text: the first two being

[1] If we read the name of the place the scribe lived in, or came from, correctly (מקסטילטץ), we should be inclined to identify it with Castelluccio, otherwise *Castel d'Asso*, near Viterbo.

[2] This last is not mentioned by Frankel, *Monatsschrift*, xvii. p. 450.

whole Bibles; the last, the Prophets and Hagiographa only[1]. All these editions however (one seems to be a mere reprint of the other) represent only one MS., and that an incomplete and faulty[2] one, less valuable than the MS. here described and than others which are now known[3] of this important work.

Unfortunately, however, this commentary has been declared, by no less an authority than Dr Z. Frankel, to be spurious, and the author has been said by him, in addition, to be a forger (*Monatsschrift*, XVII. pp. 449—458). Frankel certainly admits that he cannot give either the name of the forger, or the time when the forgery was perpetrated; but, as the whole tenor of his article betrays, he evidently suspects R. Shemtob Ibn Shemtob, perhaps for the moment confounding, in his mind, Shemtob Ibn Shemtob with Shemtob Ibn Gaon. As we, however, on the one hand, for weighty reasons, utterly disagree with what Frankel advances for depriving Nachmanides of the authorship of this commentary, and as it is, on the other hand, of considerable literary importance to ascertain the real author, partly in reference to the Targumim, partly in reference to Rashi's commentary on Job, and partly in reference to other matters, we shall discuss the authenticity of this commentary in Excursus II (compare p. 36 of this Catalogue).

The original scribe's name being מנחם, the latter part of a ם is invariably used for filling up the vacant spaces of the lines (see Excursus I). This scribe must either have had before him a MS. full of orthographical errors, which he conscientiously and faithfully copied, or he must have been an ignorant copyist. But his calligraphy leaves nothing to wish for. His writing is very distinct; and the part of the sacred text interwoven by the author with his commentary, although it is not given by the scribe in a different character of writing, is conveniently made prominent by its being underlined.

This MS. has had, since it came out of the hands of the original scribe, several owners, who, in one way or other, have left their marks of ownership in this volume.

(1) An Italian of the XVI—XVIIth century, by marking the chapters, on the outer margin in square character, and on the upper margin in

[1] This edition was possibly meant to complement that of the Pentateuch, &c. printed at the same place in 1802—3 in 4to. The former is entitled דרך סלולה and the latter דרך מסילה.

[2] To give only one instance of each, all editions end with xlii. 15; and all editions have, on xv. 3, כענין החכם (רוחכם) אש תאכלכם, a mistake which furnished Frankel with one of his strongest proofs that Nachmanides could not be the author of this commentary, as he would never have called the *Prophet* Isaiah החכם; see further on.

[3] For instance MS. Ee. 5. 9 (No. 25 of this Catalogue), and others, such as the MS. which R. Shime'on b. Tzemach Duran must have had before him (see his אוהב משפט on xlii. 17).

Rabbinic. It was, probably, this owner, who crossed through, and then wiped out, the name of the original scribe on leaf 63[b] (see later).

(2) Another Italian of the XVII—XVIIIth century, who wrote in Rabbinic, and who must have been a superior man, by correcting the MS. throughout, by writing summaries of the commentary on the outer margin, and by making on leaf 63[b], lower margin, the following statement:

סימתי בקריאת והגהת הפי' הנכבד הזה להרמב"ן ז"ל היום יום ה' ח' שבט הת"פ ליצירה

We have no doubt that the handwriting is that of R. Shimshon Kohen Modon (comp. this Catalogue, p. 39).

(3) Judging from a small remnant left of the label on the back, this MS. must have belonged in recent times to Cav. Marco (Mordekhai) Mortara, the present Chief Rabbi of Mantua.

(4) An even more recent, but anonymous, owner, wrote in Rabbinic character under the original scribe's name, which had been carefully crossed through and wiped out (see above), the words מנחם מקסטילטין.

The condition of the MS. is not good, the inner and lower part of every leaf being stained by water, and leaf 17 being badly torn.

[Library-mark, Add. 1051; bought in 1874 from S. Schönblum.]

No. 66.

Paper, in quarto, $8\frac{1}{8}$ in. × $5\frac{5}{8}$ in.; 32 leaves, one quire of 9 sheets followed by one of 7, 26—30 lines; mixed (Rabbinic and current) character, Sephardic handwriting of the XIVth century.

[פרוש איוב לר' אבא מרי בן אליגדור]

Commentary on Job, by R. Abbamari b. Eligedor.

Leaf 1, blank; 2[a], Introduction; 3[a], Commentary; 30[b]—31[b], blank; 32, probably blank, wanting.

Introduction begins (2[a]):

ספר איוב כתבו משה אם היה ולא חברו. ואם לא (היה כ)תבו וחברו על שאלתו מפני מה (צדיק ורע לו ורשע וטו)ב לו על צד חלוקת הדעות בזה הדרוש חלוקה הכרחית על דרך השאלה ותשובת המענה...

Commentary begins (3[a]):

ספר המספר שהיה איש בארץ עוץ בן נחור אחי אברהם שהיה מבני קדם...

Ends (leaf 30[b]):

...וכשמת איוב מת זקן יושב בישיבה, מקובל ומהודר מאת הבחורים (בני?) מסה ומריבה, ולא מת נעזב כקטן מוטל בעריבה, ומת שבע (ימים?) יודע חסרון העולם שהוא עוזב ויתרון העולם הבא, אשרי מי שבא לזאת המדה. אל אלהי הרוחות יצליחנו בכל ההצלחות אמן אמן סלה.

The commentary before us enters, as a rule, merely into the meaning of the book in general, and that of the chapters in particular. Occasionally, however, it explains also the single verses and even the single words. But whatever it does explain it explains remarkably well.

The author (who wrote also a commentary on Canticles; see later, in the paragraph on the scribe) was apparently, a Provençal[1] of the XIII—XIVth century (see next paragraph); and his name Abbamari is rendered certain by several MSS.[2], of which the present is, apparently, the oldest known.

Except Aristotle (2[b]), the author quotes by name only Maimonides (Ibid. and 22[a]); indistinctly, however, he quotes also the Rabbis of Talmud, Midrash, &c. (passim), and the schools המעתזילה and האשעריה (2[b]); these latter, perhaps, from the Moreh only.

The copy before us was probably executed in Africa (Algiers?), and before the close of the XIVth century, as both the nature of the paper, its water-mark, and the handwriting clearly warrant us to assume, although the copyist may have lived in the very first years of the XVth century, as he calls R. Shime'on b. Tzemach Duran בעל התשבץ (see Note 3 below).

The copyist's name is neither given, nor even in the slightest degree indicated. From this negative fact (see Excursus I) and other positive facts (see later) we conclude that he could not have been a professional scribe.

[1] Four Le'azim, three of which are Provençal, are to be met with on leaves 26[b] (two) and 28[b] (two).

[2] These are: (1) Our own copy, which belongs to the close of the XIVth century. (2) Codex De-Rossi 1372 (where, by the way, the שן אשטרוג דשון must be transliterated *Sen Astruq de* שלון, the דשון being, no doubt, a mistake for דשלון). As it is well known that De-Rossi generally ascribes to his (undated) MSS. an age higher by a hundred years than they really are, his "sec. xiv." in this instance, means probably *fifteenth century*. (3) The defective Codex Vat. CCXLIV, which is avowedly of the XVth century (Assemani, p. 204). (4) The defective copy in 272 (4) of the *Bibliothèque Nationale*, Paris, which we know from our own inspection to be, at the earliest, of the XV—XVIth century. (The author's name is there, however, only given by a later hand.) Compared with this fourfold testimony, the heading and subscription of the Bodleian copy (Opp. 221, olim 281; known to us from inspection, to be, at the earliest, of the XVth century), which ascribe this commentary to R. Mosheh of Narbonne, become comparatively valueless, as, indeed, the value of their testimony has been ere now much doubted (New Catal. 353. 4).

The scribe copied this MS., probably for his own use, so that he may be legitimately looked upon as the first bona-fide owner of it. That he was so for some time, at all events, is proved by the scribbling in his hand which is to be found on leaf 1^a no less than from the three Notes[1] on leaf 1^b and the Notes on leaves 30 and 31^a[2]. This scribe-owner (if we may use this expression) possessed at the same time, and apparently also copied for himself, part of the commentary by our author on Canticles (compare, above, the paragraph on the author), and Abuchamid's כונות הפילוסופים, &c.[3]).

The next owner has left his mark of ownership in this MS. by writing two Notes (in connexion with Physics) on leaf 31^a and by scribbling on leaf 1^a. These marks are executed in somewhat blacker ink than that used by the original scribe; their character also is mixed (Rabbinic and current), and the handwriting also is Sephardic as practised in Africa, but evidently of a century later.

A third owner was a Sephardi of the xv—xvith century. He has left his mark by scribbling in Hebrew (Rabbinic) and Spanish characters on leaf 1^a. (For other owners see the descriptions of MSS. Add. 532. 1, 2, 4 and 5 below.)

As regards the state of the MS., while it is impossible to bestow too much praise on the scribe for his intelligence as exhibited in the correctness of this copy; yet the roughness of the paper, the paleness of the ink, and the peculiarity of the handwriting must have very early made the reading a matter of no small difficulty; a difficulty of course considerably increased now, and proportionately increasing with every day. The only leaves, however, in a particularly bad condition, are 1^a, 15^a, 16^b, 17^b, 18, 19^a, the writing of which has been additionally affected by damp. The worms, although they also have told upon this copy, have, happily, not injured any part written on.

[Library-mark, Add. 532. 3; bought in 1869 from H. Lipschütz.]

[1] Of these three Notes only the first has a reference to the book of Job, briefly explaining the Rabbinical view, in the T. B. Baba Bathra, 14^b, on Moses' authorship of this book; the other two refer to the difference between the first and second Adar (ואדר) and to the Lulab and the נענועים in connexion therewith (Lev. xxiii. 40) respectively. In Note 2 the בעל התשב״ץ is quoted and in Note 3 Maimonides' משנה תורה.

[2] These Notes are, if we except insulated words, now entirely illegible.

[3] Owing to the state of the Note on leaf 1^a, which gives this interesting information, we cannot make out whether this work in that copy was accompanied by R. Mosheh of Narbonne's commentary (although it probably was; see MSS. Dd. 10. 12. 3 and 4, &c.). What we can make out of it, runs thus: פירוש איוב וקצת משיר השירים אל אלהי הפילוסוף (הפילוסוף האלהי) ר׳אבא מרי ב״ר אליגדור . . . וכוונות הפילוסופים לאבוחמד אלגזלי . . .

No. 67.

Paper, in quarto, 8⅛ in. × 5⅝ in.; 84 leaves, 6-sheet quires, 25 lines; Rabbinic character, Sephardic handwriting of the xvth century.

באור [על איוב לר׳ יצחק אבן ארונדי]

Commentary on Job by R. Yitzchaq Ibn Arundi; defective.

Begins (leaf 14ᵃ, on vi. 6):

החלמות (כלומ׳) לובן הביצה לפי שאין לו טעם ערב בעצמו כן אין ראוי לח(שוב . . .) יעשה פועל רשום מבלי טעם וסבה . . .

Ends (leaf 84ᵃ):

. . . וברך אחריתו מראשיתו בבנים ובקנינים ובכבוד ובאריכות (ה)חיים הזמניים ויראו (וירא) בנים ובני בנים ד׳ דורות. ע״כ תם תם בילא״ו תם ונשלם שבח לאל בורא עולם.

Leaf 84ᵇ is blank.

Job is a philosophical book, and a commentary on it, if it is to be of any value, must be in accordance with its nature, i.e. philosophical. And, in truth, from time to time attempts, more or less successful, have been made to explain this difficult book philosophically; and if most of such commentaries labour under notable shortcomings, it is not because of the unsoundness of the general principle that guided their authors, but of the special application, i.e. because of the mistaken attempt to make this book an exponent of *Greek-Arabic* philosophy. True, Hebrew-Israelite-Jewish religious philosophy and Greek-Arabic philosophy are related to one another; but they are nevertheless far from being identical, and it is the former of which the book of Job is an absolute representative. The philosophical commentary before us, on the other hand, although pregnant with Aristotelian philosophy, with which the author is familiar as few others, successfully avoids most if not all the dangerous rocks which caused the literary shipwreck of even so brilliant a philosopher as R. Levi b. Gershom.

The author, whose family-name ארונדי[1] points to *Ronda* (Lat. Arunda)

[1] אמר יצחק המיוחס לבית ארונדי is found, as we know from inspection, in Codd. Paris 261. 1 and Bodl. Hunt. 613. The former is a beautifully written and perfect copy, though not without many mistakes, whilst the latter is tolerably correct, but only a fragment, containing, however, the introduction, &c., which is the most important part of the whole work. When Uri (cxlvii. 1) calls our author Arunas (ארונס) it is for no better reason than because a comparatively modern owner, or cataloguer, had written that mistake at the head of the fragment.

in Andalusia, was, certainly, an Arabic-speaking Rabbi, as may be seen from the numerous Arabic words that occur in this commentary, although he lived, probably, in a Christian[1] country, perhaps in Provence, or more probably in Italy. He, no doubt, flourished in the first half of the xivth century, thus being a contemporary of R. Levi b. Gershom, as may be deduced not merely from the negative fact of his never affixing the term ז"ל (so usual after the name of a defunct person) to the name of this author, whom he very often quotes; but also from the positive fact of his speaking very slightingly indeed[2] of him, which ordinarily no Jewish author would do of a fellow-author already dead.

The following statement characterizing the tendency and internal economy of the commentary, and giving the enumeration of the authorities and works quoted, and some of the other interesting matters mentioned in it, will, we feel sure, not be unacceptable to the reader.

a. *Tendency of this commentary.*

Like others, our author holds that the principal aim of the book of Job is to answer the momentous and intricate question: Why are there pious persons who suffer, whilst there are wicked ones who are prosperous? But, unlike many, particularly philosophical, commentators (for instance R. Levi b. Gershom, &c.), he denies that Job and his friends had an idea of immortality.

b. *Internal economy of the commentary.*

(1) The whole book of Job is explained as strictly forming one living and inseparable piece of art, the various Ma'anioth (ויען) forming, as it were, the skeleton which the various verses clothe with sinews, flesh, and skin. Although additional strength is sometimes obtained for the purpose of this explanation from the philosophy contained in other parts of the Scriptures, the Talmud, the Midrash, and the Greek-Arabic philosophical writings, care is always taken to develop the philosophy of the book from the book itself. As the Ma'anioth are indissolubly interwoven with the whole book, so every verse, or part of a verse, quoted is skilfully interwoven with its respective Ma'aneh.

[1] Leaf 39b we read the following:

...המשל בזה כי כאשר לא ידענו תאר אדנות הכליפה בהישמעאלים וידענו שתאר אדנותו אל הישמעאלי' הוא כיחס אדנות הקיסר אל הנוצרי' הנה בידיעתנו תאר אדנות הקיסר ידענו בידיעה מה תאר אדנות הכליפה...

From this it would seem that our author lived in a Christian country and within the dominions of the Holy Roman Empire; and if so, then very possibly in Italy.

[2] Our author seems to have had a personal *pique* against R. Levi b. Gershom. He not merely frequently declares his (R. Levi's) general and special conception of the book of Job to be utterly worthless, but he actually wrote an opposition work מלחמות to R. Levi's work of the same name.

(2) The Ma'anioth are connected with one another by the phrase וכאשר ראה ... אמר; the primary explanation of each verse, or part of a verse, is introduced by the phrase ר"ל, while the further explanation of it is signalized by that of כלומ'. If either of these explanations is brought into connexion with an idea expressed in another part of the Scriptures, the further phrase ע"ד is used. At the end of the minute explanation of each Ma'aneh the whole of it is summed up, and the number of parts (i.e. leading ideas) of which it consists is given; the whole being introduced by the stereotyped phrase:

הנה המענה הזה יקיף על...חלקים...וכאשר...

c. *Enumeration of authorities and works quoted in this commentary.*

(1) The Rabbis (passim). (2) Plato (54b).

(3) Aristotle, either by the name of ארסטו, or simply הפילוסוף, or finally by the mention of a particular work of his, without expressly mentioning his name. We may remark on this occasion that there are few works by Aristotle which are not quoted in the course of this commentary, even in the defective state in which we have it.

(4) Euclides (אוקלידס; 60b).

(5) ואחאנס הפילוסו' (? Johannes; 66b).

(6) The commentators of Aristotle, as Themistius (63b), and Ibn Roshd (56b, 63b).

(7) המורה הגדול (Maimonides; 64a).

(8) R. Levi b. Gershom (almost on every page).

(9) The author's own introduction to this commentary (פתיחת זה הספר or פתיחת זה הביאור; passim). This introduction is unfortunately wanting (see later in the paragraph on the condition of the MS.).

d. *Other interesting matters in connexion with the commentary.*

(1) Leaf 55b has a paragraph on Providence as manifested by the forewarning character of certain dreams. In the course of this the author says of R. Levi b. Gershom:

והנה כאשר יבחן גדר זה האיש בשהוא משתבח שהוא מעמיק בפילוסופי' יותר ממה שקדמוהו ומתהלל בכל מאמריו שהם מופתיי' מזוקקי' מכל סתירה יש להפלא...

(2) Leaf 61b the author expresses his disapprobation of such as think that the mere knowledge of the ceremonial laws is enough for a Jew, in the following very strong terms:

...ובזה השתבשו החכמי' ההלציים מאומתינו ר"ל המעיינים בפשט התלמוד מפרש המצות המעשיו' והדיני' וכשלו כשלון גדול...ובזה כשלא יתבאר המובן בהם בדקדוק יצאו ממנה שבושים וכפירות...

The scribe's name was probably Yehudah as the letters and ה are frequently used for the filling out of the vacant spaces of the lines (see Excursus I). He was not only a good copyist as regards calligraphy, but also as regards intelligence, as there are comparatively few mistakes in the copy before us.

Of owners we can trace here only one, and this one is an anonymous person of the xvith—xviith century. (Is this R. David Harophe? See our description of MS. Add. 532. 5 below.) He writes a far from ungraceful, though somewhat intricate, hand. The work done by him is in current character and Sephardic handwriting, and consists (1) of numbering the leaves on the upper, and (2) re-writing (in some instances; see later, in the paragraph on the condition of the MS.) on the inner, margins words which had been probably destroyed by an instrument used by the Quarantine officials. He does the latter work of course mostly by mere guess, in which he is not always correct. In most instances, however, he has not even attempted to restore the words lost. From the paging made by him we see clearly that the MS. was even then as defective as it is now.

The condition of the MS. is far from good. In addition to the 13 leaves missing at the beginning, by which, unfortunately, the whole introduction and part of the commentary (the most valuable of the whole; see p. 216 above, Note 1) was lost, there are also wanting leaves 37, 48, 74—83. Moreover, the whole copy is more or less stained by water and soiled; and particularly leaf 14[a], the upper part of which is scarcely legible. Leaves 28—49 in the upper and 25—40 in the outer margin, are worm-eaten, by which, however, luckily, the writing has suffered nothing. Not so leaves 67—84, which have been pierced through (probably by the authorities of the Quarantine), by which a good number of words have been irretrievably destroyed.

[Library-mark, Add. 532. 1; bought in 1869 from. H. Lipschütz.]

No. 68.

Paper, in quarto, $8\frac{1}{4}$ in. × $6\frac{1}{4}$ in.; 20 leaves, 5-sheet quires, 27—28 lines; mixed (Rabbinic and current) character, Italian handwriting of the xvith century.

[העתקה ופרוש למקומות קשי הבנה בתרגום על חמש המגלות לחכם לועזי פלוני אלמוני]

Translation into Rabbinic Hebrew, with explanation of the difficult parts, of the Targum on the Five Rolls, by an anonymous Italian Rabbi; incomplete.

Leaf 1[a], *Preface;* 1[a], *Ruth;* 4[a], *Canticles;* 15[b], *Ecclesiastes* (17[a]—20[b] blank).

Preface begins (1[a]):

בהנו״א אתחיל לבאר התרגו׳ של חמש מגילות מלשון תרגום ללשון הקודש למען ירוץ קורא בו.

ויהי בימי שפוט השופטים אע״פ שבזאת המגילה אין בה תוספת ביאור...

Work begins (1[a]):

ויהי בימי שפוט השופטים ויהי רעב וגו׳ כונת המתרגם לומ׳ שהיה זה הרעב חזק מאד בארץ ישראל...

Breaks off (16[b], on Ecclesiastes ii. 8):

...כנסתי לי גם אוצרות כסף וזהב ואף המשקלים ומאזני צדק עשיתי מזהב

Apart from the fact that the work before us is unfinished (it lacks the greater portion on Ecclesiastes and the whole on Lamentations and Esther) the author's assertion, that it contains *the Targum on the Five Rolls in Hebrew* (בחרתי להעתיק אלו החמש מגלות מלשון תרגום ללשון הקודש), must be taken *cum grano.* In reality only the more difficult parts of that Targum have been translated by our author, as he himself says in another place (ובמקום אשר לא יראה תוספת...אניחנו); and this not into Hebrew pure and simple, but into questionable Rabbinic. This latter fact considerably detracts from the interest awakened by another assertion of our author, that Hebrew was understood by the generality of the people (Jews) of his time (וכמו שהמתרגם כיון להועיל להמון...ג״כ אנחנו ראוי שנכון להועיל להמון ולהוציא דבריו בלשון הרגיל אצלנו...). But, if in one respect the author has overstated the value of his work, he has in another respect undervalued it. It contains something more than a mere translation of parts of the Targum in question; it contains also an explanation of them. This explanation is either introduced by one or other of the phrases כונת המתרגם, הרגיש המתרגם, דייק המתרגם, פירש המתרגם, or succeeded by וזהו אומרו, וזהו שאמר, &c. In it the author points out the word, or the turn, of the sacred text, which justifies the Targumist in his deviation, or at least induced him to deviate, from the apparently more natural meaning of the verse (see, for instance, leaf 3[b], on Ruth iv. 7[1]; leaf 9[a], on Cant. iii. 6, &c.). Taken as a whole, this small work may be safely pronounced to be of no small value; the more so, as we become acquainted through it occasionally with a piece of Targum-text which is not to be found in the printed editions (see, for instance, leaf 11[a], on Cant. v. 10).

[1] The Targumist renders נעלו by נרתק יד ימיניה. What induced him to do so? Our author has the following remark on the point:
והוציא המתרגם מלת מנעלו (נעלו) מפשוטה לפי שדייק מה שנאמ׳ בתוריה ושלף נעלו מעל רגלו דמאצטרי׳ לומ׳ מעל רגלו נראה שמנעל (נעל) סתם בבל התורה נאמ׳ על מנעל היד שהוא הנק׳ גואנטי (גואנטו) בלע״ז.

The author, who displays great familiarity with Bible, Talmud and Midrash (and particularly with the last-named literary activity, which is the source sometimes, as it is at other times the efflux, of the Targumim; see Excursus II), must have been an Italian, as may be seen from the only בלע"ז to be found here (3[a]; repeated 3[b]). He probably lived in the xvith century, the unquestionable date of this MS. (see next paragraph).

To judge from the numerous corrections, &c. made by the scribe, this MS. seems to be an autograph; the scribe is certainly identical with the scribe of the first part of MS. Dd. 10. 14. 2 (see No. 39 of this Catalogue). There seems to be no trace of the work elsewhere.

There is no trace of ownership to be found in this copy; but, apparently, it belonged, at one time, to R. Yehudah Aryeh, of Modena (Leon Modena, see p. 72 of this Catalogue), as it afterwards certainly belonged to Yitzchaq (b. Menachem?) פראג'י (see ibid.).

The condition of the MS. is excellent.

[Library-mark, Dd. 10. 14. 3; presented in 1647 by the House of Commons.]

No. 69.

Paper, in quarto, 7¾ in. × 5½ in.; 174 leaves, mostly[1] 6-sheet quires, 30 lines; Rabbinic character, Sephardic handwriting of the xvth century.

[פרושים על חמש המגלות לא"ע ועל תרי עשר לרד"ק וכו']

Commentaries on the FIVE ROLLS, by Ibn 'Ezra and on the MINOR PROPHETS, by Redaq, with other matter; defective.

1. [פרוש על חמש המגלות לר' אברהם בן מאיר אבן עזרא יליד טוליטולה]

COMMENTARIES ON THE FIVE ROLLS, BY R. ABRAHAM B. MEIR IBN 'EZRA OF TOLEDO (הראב"ע).

1[a], *Ruth*[2]; 3[a], *Lamentations*; 9[b], *Ecclesiastes*; 34[a], *Esther*; 39[b], *Canticles.*

[1] The exceptions are quires 1, 2, 3, 14 (which have 7) and 4 (which has 5 sheets).

[2] The order observed here in the Five Rolls, is, no doubt, intended for that, according to which they are read in the Synagogue, i.e. Canticles, Ruth, Lamentations, Ecclesiastes and Esther. If Canticles is here placed last, it is either because the scribe of this very MS. began to copy it between Passover and

Begin (leaf 1[a]):

בשם אל תחזק ידי וזכרו יעמיד הודי:
וזה פי׳ מגלת רות לאברהם ספרדי
נאם אברהם בעבור היות דוד שורש מלכות ישראל נכתב בספרי הקודש יחס
דוד: שפט השופטים י״א שה׳ שפט שופטים...

End (leaf 48[b]):

...הם הררי ציון כי שם צוה יי׳ את הברכה חיים את (עד) העולם
נשלם פי׳ שיר השירים: שבח למעתיק הרים:

These commentaries, as extant in this MS., like those which are to be found in the Rabbinical Bibles[1], consist of single ones on Ruth, Ecclesiastes

Pentecost, or because he copied it from a MS. that had been commenced at such a time. Taking, however, into consideration the independent thought of our scribe (see later), the former reason gives the more probable account of the anomaly.

[1] Besides the single commentary on Esther and the triple one on Canticles, which are to be found in the Rabbinical Bibles, Ibn 'Ezra is known to have composed another single one on Esther and another triple one on Canticles. That on Esther was edited by Zedner from a MS. in the British Museum (London, 1850, 8vo; reprinted Berlin, 1873). That on Canticles was edited by H. J. Mathews from three MSS. at Berlin, Oxford and Paris (London, 1874, 8vo). We cannot allow this opportunity to pass without drawing the reader's attention to Mr Mathews' work. He has certainly placed Ibn 'Ezra's admirers, and the readers of his literature in general, under great obligations. Not merely has he carefully edited this interesting commentary, but he has also enriched it with an accurate translation, an instructive introduction and many valuable notes. But we must join issue with the editor, when he treats Ibn 'Ezra as he would treat an ordinary commentator and deduces (Preface, p. viii), from his expression (on Ruth i. 15) כבר פירשנוה בתורה, the conclusion that Ibn 'Ezra had actually written a regular commentary on the whole Pentateuch before he wrote his commentary on Ruth. Ibn 'Ezra was a man *sui generis*, and explained all parts of the Bible sporadically (if we may say so) before he had explained a single book regularly. His unsettled, migratory, mode of life caused him to write everywhere, at every time, and on everything, piecemeal, as the occasion demanded (see this Catalogue, p. 146, Note 2); so that the *negative* facts obtained from his statements (where he says in one work that *he is going to write* such or such another work, implying thereby that he had not already written it) alone have a value in determining the priority of his several works. For instance, when Ibn 'Ezra says (on Cant. iii. 10) כאשר אפרשנו במקומו, we learn from these words, that he regularly commented on *Canticles* before he had done so on Isaiah, even as we learn from his words (on Cant. vii. 3) וכן אפרשנו במקומו, that when he wrote them he had not as yet regularly commented on Proverbs (see further on). Thus we learn from his commentary on *Ruth* (i. 2, i. 16, iii. 11) that he had written it before those on Ezra, Isaiah and Proverbs. The same is the case with respect to his commentary on *Esther*, which he had composed before those

and Esther, a double one on Lamentations, and a triple one on Canticles. They are here, although not without mistakes, superior on the whole to those in the printed editions.

(1) This MS. has, particularly on Ruth, several omissions (of irrelevant matter), substitutions and additions.

(2) Several of the substitutions are accompanied (on the margin) in all the five books by various readings, sometimes with, and sometimes without, the announcement: ס"א. These various readings correspond with those of the printed editions.

(3) Many difficulties presented by the printed text of the commentaries on Lamentations and Canticles, in consequence of an explanation of one of the double or triple commentaries having been erroneously drawn into another, are here naturally avoided.

2. [קובץ וכוחים עם הנוצרים לפלוני אלמוני]

COLLECTANEA ANTICHRISTIANA, BY AN ANONYMOUS AUTHOR.

Begin (leaf 48[b]):

מצאתי בספר פירושי הנבואו' על הגאולה ממה שאמרו רוב הנביאים כולם מקובצים במקום אחד כדי שיוכל כל אדם למצוא תשובה על אפיקורוסי'· תחלה פרשה עתידה בישעיה בתחלת הספר והיה באחרית הימים נכון יהיה הר בית השם...וזה לא היה בבנין בית שני...ואם זה נאמר על מלכם...

on Ezra (i. 1), Canticles (i. 6), the Pentateuch, Samuel and Chronicles (i. 10), and Zechariah (ix. 30). But it by no means follows from the loose expressions כאשר פירשתי בספר דניאל (on Cant. vi. 5) and כבר פירשנוה בתורה (on Ruth i. 15), that the commentaries on Canticles and Ruth had been written after those on Daniel and the Pentateuch respectively. The commentaries on *Lamentations* and *Ecclesiastes* afford no evidence of priority either way; though the latter is positively dated from Rome in 4900=1140, and was probably the first *regular* commentary which he ever wrote down. We must now substantiate our view, which at first sight may appear somewhat strange. Ibn 'Ezra in his *Brief Commentary* on Exodus (which is on all sides acknowledged to be a genuine part of his Pentateuch-commentary, and is even believed by most critics to be the only one belonging to him on that book, to the exclusion of the *Long Commentary*) says (on xxxi. 3), ...ובפירוש משלי פירשתי; which ought to show that he had written the commentary on *Proverbs* before that on the *Pentateuch*. How then, could he in the commentary on *Ruth* mean by כבר פירשניה בתורה, that he had already written a regular *Pentateuch*-commentary, when on the same *Ruth* (iii. 11) he promises to write a commentary on *Proverbs?* These remarks are enough to show the extreme intricacy of the whole question; but it is hoped that they may tend in some measure to remove the difficulties so long felt by critics, and which have received such forcible expression in Halberstam's preface to his admirable edition of Ibn 'Ezra's ספר העבור (Lyck. 1874, 8vo.).

End (leaf 49[a]):

...כי לפי דבריהם החיה את המת ועשה ניסים שהיו (שלא היו) באפשרות הטבע

For the Jews, attacked as they and their religion have continually been, to compose Antichristiana, has been, as is well known, a common practice, particularly from the XIth century downwards. Some of these Antichristiana certainly occur as mere explanations of the Messianic passages of the Bible in a sense adverse to Christianity, as may be seen in the commentaries of Rashi and Ibn 'Ezra. Others, although of the same nature, and ostensibly composed for the same purpose, consist of shorter or longer excursuses in Biblical commentaries, and contain, besides the defence of the doctrines of Judaism, systematic, and sometimes even fierce, attacks on Christianity, as may be seen in the commentaries of *David* Qimchi on Isaiah and the Psalms and of Abarbanel on Isaiah. A third kind assume the proportions of whole independent works of controversy, in which the desire to refute the doctrines of Christianity is openly avowed, although, no doubt, this desire did originally spring from the ardent wish to defend Judaism. Such works are *Yoseph* Qimchi's הברית, Chasdai Crescas' בטול עיקרי הנוצרים, Shemtob Ibn Shaprut's אבן בוחן, Lipman's נצחון and others. But there exists, further, a fourth kind of Antichristiana, a species of second-hand compilations, which consists of books, treatises, &c. made up from all the before-mentioned three kinds. Even these, though they lack originality, have the advantage of giving the reader a general idea of the matter. To this category belongs Lopez' כור מצרף האמונות ומראה האמת and very probably also the treatise of which we find the commencement here.

As regards the author of this piece, though we cannot say who he is, we can with more certainty say who he is not. He is none of the above-mentioned writers, nor is it our scribe. Viewed as *literature*, it is written in the style of David Qimchi; but the MS. before our scribe must have been in a very bad state, and the difficulty of reading it extreme, if indeed it was legible at all. And this is no doubt the reason why after two half-pages, the scribe gave up copying entirely. For it must be clearly understood, that it is not a mere fragment inserted on a waste page, as might at first sight appear likely; seeing that the scribe has written it in precisely the same style as the rest of the MS. and that the rest of the volume, now occupied by Qimchi, was at his disposal.

3. [פרוש על תרי עשר לר׳ דוד בן יוסף בן יצחק אבן קמחי הספרדי יליד נרבונא]

COMMENTARY ON THE MINOR PROPHETS, BY R. DAVID B. YOSEPH B. YITZCHAQ IBN QIMCHI HASSEPHARDI, OF NARBONNE (REDAQ).

Leaf 49[b], *Hosea* (65 wanting); 81[a], *Joel;* 88[a], *Amos* (89, 100 wanting); 106[a], *Obadiah;* 108[b], *Jonah;* 112[b], *Micah;* 125[a], *Nahum;* 130[a], *Habakkuk;* 138[a], *Zephaniah;* 142[b], *Haggai;* 145[b], *Zechariah;* 167[b], *Malachi;* 173[b], blank; 174 (probably blank) wanting.

Begins (leaf 49^b):

דברי נביאים. במשל נשואים. כאשר קרואים. אינם מצואים:
נבון וחכם יתבוננו בם יודעי לסודם כאשר ברואים:
בהם דבריו ארכו ובהם קצרו כבשנים עשר נביאים:
אמר דוד בן יוסף בן קמחי הספרדי זה הספר מחובר משנים עשר נביאים...

Ends (leaf 173^a):

...ומצדיקי הרבים ככוכבים לעולם ועד
נגמר ונשלם פי' ספר מלאכי תהלה ושבח לאל סומכי:
בריך דיהב חילא לעבדיה בר אמתיה. כבודך ה':

This commentary, like most works of our author, has long enjoyed great popularity. Not merely has it been often printed in the original, but portions of it on most of these *Twelve Books* have been translated into Latin from time to time by various writers, and that on one (Żechariah) has been published entire in English. But this commentary, as extant here, has a value even beyond that of an ordinary MS. for the following reasons:

(1) It represents a better recension at the hands of the author; whereas the printed editions have only the ordinary text, and that in a more or less corrupt state.

(2) It has intact the Antichristiana, omitted or disguised in the editions.

(3) The quotations from the Targum are given here in full, so that its pristine text could be almost reconstructed from this and a few other MSS., as in the case of the Isaiah mentioned above (No. 63; p. 196, Note 2).

The name of the scribe was, probably, David or some other beginning with ד, since he invariably fills out the vacant spaces of the lines with this letter, unless he uses part of the first word of the next line. Although apparently a Peninsular Sephardi by birth, he seems to have been acquainted with the Ritual-Services of the Ashkenazim (see leaf 26^b, marginal Note). He probably lived either in Italy or Greece. The formula כבודך ה' given above points, however, rather to a Latin country, and therefore perhaps to Italy; see this Catalogue, pp. 42, 69. He was no mere scribe, though his handwriting is by no means ungraceful. The following points deserve remark:

(1) He makes few mistakes.

(2) He makes the reader's work more easy by placing various signs to distinguish the text from the commentary, &c.

(3) He often gives readings from other MSS. on both works (of Ibn 'Ezra and Qimchi), introduced mostly by ס"א, and in Qimchi also by נ"א, and three times by ד"ת. This ד"ת, though twice (91^b, 96^a) to be solved into דיוקא תנינא or דעתא תניתא (comp. this Catalogue, p. 197[1]), seems once (61^b) to stand for דברי תוספת.

[1] By an oversight on p. 197 a few words have fallen out. What is there printed "דעתא תנינא" ought to be "דיוקא תנינא or דעתא תניתא".

(4) He often adds marginal explanations from other authors. See, for example, leaf 18[b], where he has a Note, commencing ... מצאתי טעם, in which R. El'azar הקליר is defended from Ibn 'Ezra's attack (Eccl. v. 1) on him, on account of שושן being used by him in the masculine, whilst איומה is in the feminine.

(5) He occasionally gives explanations of his own (see, for example, leaf 17[b]).

(6) He marks some of the Haphtaroth occurring in the Minor Prophets.

(7) Once he makes the pious ejaculation ישמח לבינו ותגיל נפשינו בישועתך, where the unpropitiatory phrase והבתולו' לא תשמחנה ends a leaf (5[b]; in the פרוש הטעמים on Lam. ii. 10).

As regards owners, the following nine have left their marks on this MS.

(1) An anonymous Italian of the xv—xvith century by writing in mixed (Rabbinic and current) character, the running titles of several books of the Minor Prophets (see leaves 115[b], 116[a], &c.).

(2) An Italian of the xvi—xviith century by writing his name, מאיר פינצי, in Rabbinic character, on leaf 3[a], inner margin.

(3) An anonymous Sephardi of the xviith century, by marking in Rabbinic character the quires 26, 31, 32, 34, 35 on the upper inner margin. The numbers there still remaining, shew that the volume as we now have it must have formed quires 23—36 of a still larger Codex.

(4) An Italian of the xviith century by writing *Laudad°. Emanuel*, in Italian character on leaf 1[a], lower margin.

(5) An anonymous Sephardi, probably also of the xviith century, by marking the number of the quire (ל״ג) in Rabbinic character, on the upper margin of leaf 125[a].

(6) Again a Sephardi of the xvii—xviiith century, by writing in bold Rabbinic character the catchword on leaf 126[b].

(7) An Italian of the xviiith century, by writing in bold Rabbinic character the library-mark ד' קפ״ח on leaf 1[a]. This owner is apparently the father of the Physician Samuele Vita della Volta (comp. this Catalogue, p. 39).

(8) Cav. Marco (Mordekhai) Mortara, Chief Rabbi of Mantua, by writing (in a *Sephardic* Rabbinic hand) on the label on the back: ראב״ע פי' ה' מגלות רד״ק פי' תרי עשר קצור הערוך.

(9) The last owner, H. Lipschütz of Cracow, by writing on leaf 1[a] in Polish Ashkenazic current character ארי' צבי ליפשיץ and 'H. Lipschütz.'

The MS. is somewhat worm-eaten in the first three quires; but in all other respects is in good condition.

[Library-mark, Add. 403. 1; bought in 1867 from H. Lipschütz.]

No. 70.

Parchment and paper, in quarto, 8½ in., × 6 in.; (originally 56 leaves, mostly[1] 6-sheet quires, the outer sheets parchment, the rest paper), 30—31 lines; Rabbinic character, Greek Sephardic handwriting of the XIVth century.

[פרוש על שיר השירים לר׳ משה אבן תבון ואחריו יבואו מאמרים פילוסופיים שונים לר׳ זרחיה בן יצחק]

Commentary on CANTICLES, by R. Mosheh Ibn Tibbon, with other PHILOSOPHICAL PIECES, by R. Zerachyah b. Yitzchaq; defective[2].

[1] The last quire has 4 sheets.

[2] We have noticed above (p. 63) the fact, that one R. Shelomoh, a Greek Ashkenazic owner, has written at the end of Part 3 a Table of the contents of the whole Codex (now numbered Add. 377 in this Library) of which the present MS. forms Part 1. As the missing leaves (40 out of 56) contained many pieces of interest, we have thought it worth while to subjoin R. Shelomoh's list of the contents of this MS., with a few remarks, as supplementary to the notice of the three remaining fragments described in the text above. His list, which has already been made use of to some extent by Steinschneider (המזכיר, XI. pp. 42, 43), is as follows:

(1) אגרת התשובה וחסידות ומיני מוסרים ממה״ר אבינדור כ״ץ מא׳ עד ר׳ [Leaves 1^b—4^a]

(2) אגרת הרמב״ן ששלח לבנו ממדת הענוה מז׳ עד ח׳ [Leaves 4^b—5^a]

(3) אגרת הרמב״ן ששלח לבנו מענין מטבע מח׳ עד ט׳ [Leaf 5^a—5^b]

(4) אגרת הרמב״ן ששלח לבנו מענין ירושלי׳ ע״ה (עיר הקדש) ומבית הכנסת מט׳ עד י׳ [Leaves 5^b—6^a]

(5) פי׳ משיר השירים מאבן תבון מי״א עד ס״א [Leaves 6^b—31^b]

(6) כתבים מן המורה נבוכים שהשיב ר׳ זרחי׳ לר׳ יהוד׳ וגם מענין איוב ושטן ובני אלהים מס״ג עד ס״א [Leaves 32^b—40^a; 32^a being blank]

(8) הקדמה מספר האלהות לאריסטוטלוס מפ״ב עד פ״ג [Leaf 42^a—42^b]

(9) ביאור הקדמה על המורה בתחילתו בחלק ראשון מפ״ד עד פ״ח [Leaves 43^a—45^a]

(10) ביאור על הפרקי׳ מחלק ראשון מפ״ח עד ק״ט [Leaves 45^a—55^b]

(7) ביאור על המורה בפרק כ״ב מחלק שיני מע״ט עד פ״א [Leaves 40^b—41^b]

(1) This missing *Letter on Repentance* is, no doubt, identical with the MS. שערי המוסר in the Vatican (CCLI. 4; p. 214), which is superscribed: שערי המוסר מר׳ אבינדור כהן צדק, and begins: ...לעולם יהא אדם רץ לעשות רצון קונו מאהבה. The loss of this treatise out of the present Codex is doubly to be regretted, because it seems to have borne a title otherwise unknown, and because, besides the one in the Vatican, there appears to be no trace of any other copy, except that in the *Bibliothèque Nationale* at Paris (No. 839; formerly Ancien fonds 105),

Leaves 1—16 wanting; 17ª, *Ibn Tibbon on Canticles* (26—35 wanting); 36, *Letters of R. Zerachyah on the Moreh of Maimonides* (37—48 wanting); 49ª, *Commentary by R. Zerachyah on the Moreh* (52 almost wholly torn out, 56 wanting).

1. [פרוש על שיר השירים לר׳ משה בן שמואל בן יהודה בן שאול אבן תבון מרמון ספרד]

COMMENTARY ON CANTICLES, BY R. MOSHEH (OF MONTPELLIER) B. SHEMUEL (OF LUNEL) B. YEHUDAH (OF GRANADA AND LUNEL) B. SHAUL IBN TIBBON OF GRANADA; defective.

where, however, only the first leaf is at present to be found. On the author and his possible identity, not only with R. Abigedor b. Eliyyah of Vienna, but also with R. Abigedor, the uncle of R. Hillel b. Shemuel b. El'azar of Verona, see our description of MS. Add. 653 in the third Section of this Catalogue.

(2) This missing *Letter on Humility* is, no doubt, identical with the אגרת מוסר printed in the תפוחי זהב (Mantova, 1638, 8vo.), where it occupies leaves 107ᵇ—109ª. It is there introduced by: זאת היא האגרת מוסר ששלח הרמב״ן ז״ל לבנו וטוב לקרותה בכל שבוע. It begins: שמע בני מוסר אביך ואל תטוש והתנהג תמיד ...תכין לבם תקשיב אזניך. תקרא האגרת הזאת פעם א׳ בשבוע, and ends: לדבר בנחת... לא תפחות לקיימה וללכת בה תמיד אחרי השם למען תצליח בכל דרכיך ותזכה לעולם הבא הצפון לצדיקים: כבודך יי׳. (The last two words, of course, belong to the scribe of the MS. used by the printer; comp. this Catalogue, pp. 42, 69, 225.)

(3) This *Letter on a Coin* is, no doubt, identical with the piece to be found at the end of the early editions of Nachmanides' Pentateuch-commentary. It there begins: ...ברכני ה׳ עד כה, and ends: ...ונופו בעצמו עשרים גרעיני כרוב. The addition of the word ושלום at the close, in the first edition, seems to confirm the idea of this piece being a letter.

(4) This missing *Letter on Jerusalem, &c.* is, no doubt, identical with the letter sent by Nachmanides to his son Nachman, with which the Lisbon edition of the Pentateuch-commentary concludes. It is a brief résumé of what immediately precedes it (a meditation by the author on Jerusalem and its awful condition and a prayer for its welfare, which begin: ...עומדות היו רגלינו, and end: ...ברוך שומע תפלה אמן ואמן). This résumé is there superscribed: אגרת ששלח הרב ז״ל מירושלם עיר הקדש בימינו תבנה ותכונן לבנו האהוב: It begins: ...יברכך יי׳ בני נחמן, and ends: ...וגדול שלותם אמן. The loss of this letter out of this Codex is the more to be regretted, as it may, perhaps, have contained the year (after naming the month of Elul), which some give as '27 (1267) and others as '28 (1268). This little piece, though in the Lisbon edition, is not in the *editio princeps*. We take this opportunity of expressing our thanks to Dr Atkinson, Master of Clare College, for his kindness in allowing us the free use of the copy of the Lisbon edition in the Library of that College.

(5) Part of this *Commentary* still remains; it is therefore described in the text above.

(6) to (10). All these being R. Zerachyah's work on the *Moreh*, of which parts still remain, will be found described in the text above.

Begins (leaf 17[a], on iii. 11; printed edition, leaf 15[b]):

מקום כי אם לדודה בלבד...

Breaks off (leaf 25[b], on viii. 8; printed edition, leaf 22[b]):

...שהוא השכל הנקנה והוא רוח הקודש כי הדבור באדם הוא השכל ולכן נקרא

This commentary has lately been printed as one of the publications of the Society מקיצי נרדמים (Lyck, 1874, 8vo.). But, as the anonymous editor has given us only the text in its barest possible form (therein differing from an inferior MS. only in having an abundance of misprints), without critical introduction, without a single illustrative note of any kind (even to tell us from what MS. it is taken[1]), in which particulars it contrasts most unfavourably with some of its fellow-publications (notably the תגמולי הנפש and ספר העבור), enriched as they are with the editorial labours of Halberstam and Steinschneider[2], we are compelled to remark more at length upon this work itself in general and upon this MS. of it in particular.

[1] The MS. in the hands of the anonymous editor, as may be seen from leaf ט"ו *verso*, must have been in an oriental Sephardic handwriting. By oriental Sephardic scribes the letters רי are written with the י in inside the ר, which combination the transcriber for the press seems to have mistaken for ה; and as he also confounded נ' with ט, the result is הקטן for ריקנין. It is hardly satisfactory that the misprints in a book should be our only source of information as to the MS. from which it is taken.

[2] Steinschneider's contribution to the תגמולי הנפש is so full of valuable and instructive matter, that it seems worth while to add an elucidation of two little points which have escaped him. (1) The word לפנים (see p. 21) is applicable, of course, to both space and time (compare the Targumim, Talmudim and Midrashim passim). But though it is ordinarily used in Holy Writ in the sense of 'formerly' i.e. 'backwards,' yet it certainly occurs in Jeremiah vii. 24 (ויהיו לאחור ולא לפנים) in the sense of 'forwards' i.e. 'further on', as it is used here by R. Hillel. This whole difficulty of Steinschneider's, however, is based on the assumption that the word used by R. Hillel is the *Biblical* לְפָנִים; but may it not rather be the *Talmudic* לִפְנִים (itself the equivalent of the *Biblical* פנימה), as in the phrase לפני ולפנים, i.e. 'deeper and deeper in', 'further and further on' (T. Yerushalmi, Horayoth iii. 5, and T. B. Sotah 4[b], Horayoth 13[a])? (2) Again in the שלשה ענינים, &c. (leaf 50[a]), the original source of the saying of R. Yose the Galilean is to be found in the Siphra, Dibbura dechoba, Parashah XII, Pisqa 10; compare Bensly, *The missing fragment of the fourth book of Ezra* (Cambridge, 1875, 4to.), p. 28, Note 6. From the Siphra it was copied by R. Tobiyyahu b. Eli'ezer (לקח טוב on Lev. v. 16), by the Yalqut (§ 479), and by Rashi (on Lev. v. 16); but R. Hillel evidently took it (if not direct from the Siphra) from Rashi, who must have had before him a copy of that work in which the reading was היושב לו מן instead of השב מן. Whichever be the right reading, the phrase היושב לו can surely only mean 'who abstains,' 'whoever abstains.' (The Yalqut here has the ordinary reading; while R. Tobiy-

(i) *On this work itself in general.* Most, if not all, of the Hebrew literary productions of the middle ages, particularly if they are commentaries on the Scriptures and by authors nurtured in Greek-Arabic philosophy, are valuable to us rather for their accidents than for their essence. As elucidations of Scripture, they may be worth little; but they nevertheless deserve our attention, if only for the following three reasons:—(a) They reflect the spirit and taste of their own age; (b) they preserve to us the names of the most prominent men of times gone by; and (c) they rarely fail to enrich our vocabulary of post-biblical Hebrew with terms invented on the instant, as the occasion demanded. These are sometimes original, sometimes translated from Arabic or Latin, and sometimes only ordinary words, employed in an unusual sense; but always new to us. The commentary before us and its author form no exception to this rule either for good or for bad. Mosheh Ibn Tibbon, like his father and grandfather (and in some respects even more than these), was a diligent and successful translator of Greek-Arabic works of philosophy (in his time including not only mathematics and astronomy, but also medicine). But his original works, particularly his biblical commentaries, are, as far as scriptural interpretation is concerned, absolutely without value.

(a) To illustrate our statement, that the commentary before us reflects the spirit and taste of its age, we need only mention that it was so much in vogue for at least half a century after its composition, that the "Sages of Rome" actually requested 'Immanuel b. Shelomoh (whose poetry was so easy and graceful, but whose scriptural interpretation was so pompous and inflated), to explain the book of Canticles to them *in the style of R. Mosheh Ibn Tibbon, only a little more minutely!* (Comp. this Catalogue, p. 43.) Yet, apart from the fact that this commentary is full of absurdities (can any one imagine this lovely and peerless idyll being made to represent the hard and grinding metaphysical speculations of the Stagirite?), not only is the reader left in doubt, but the author himself is confessedly undecided, which of the various metaphysical ideas or terms a given verse or word may mean. Hence the continual recurrence of such phrases as: ואולי, או אמור, או, גם אפשר, או אפשר, ואפשר, &c.

(b) The references to the authorities and works quoted[1] here will be found of some interest. They are as follows:

(1) The "divine" Socrates (leaf י"ח *verso*).

(2) Aristotle (passim). (3) בעל ספר יצירה (p. 7).

yahu b. Eli'ezer works up the passage in quite an independent way of his own; so that R. Hillel cannot have taken it from either of these.)

[1] It is not the least of our anonymous editor's many faults, that he counts by *pages*, in Arabic numbering from 1 to 14 (Introduction and part of commentary); and then proceeds to count by *leaves*, in Hebrew from 8 to 26. This process makes his book very troublesome to quote.

(4) החכם, meaning sometimes King Solomon, sometimes Aristotle, and sometimes a Talmud-teacher (passim).

(5) רבותינו, the teachers of Talmud and Midrash (passim).

(6) The Talmud, by quoting various Massikhtoth, or various Peraqim of them, as: בפרק אין עומדין (p. 13), בע"ז (leaf ח *recto*), בפרק הבא על יבמתו (leaf י"א *recto*), בפרק המפלת (leaf כ"א *verso*).

(7) בראשית רבה (passim); אלה שמות רבה (leaf י"ד *recto*).

(8) ילמדנו on *all* the books of the Pentateuch (passim). Once also (leaf י *recto*) במדרש שיר השירים בילמדנו, which ought perhaps to be ובילמדנו.

(9) מדרש חזית (passim). (10) מסדרי התפלות (p. 11).

(11) הנוצרים (p. 12; leaf ח *recto*).

(12) הפילוסופים (p. 14). (13) יש מפרשים (passim).

(14) המשורר (not David; p. 7).

(15) וכן אמר (the poet; leaf ט *recto*).

(16) וכתב אחר (perhaps a mistake for וכתב אחרי כן; p. 10).

(17) אבונצר and his התחלות הנמצאות, also אלפראבי and אלפירב"י (pp. 9, 12, and leaf י"ח *verso*).

(18) בן גנאח and ר' יונה (leaves י"א *recto*, כ"א *verso*).

(19) ר' אברהם בן עזרא (leaf ח *recto*; this explanation however belongs not to Ibn 'Ezra, but to R. Se'adyah Gaon) and החכם בן עזרא (leaf י"ט *recto*).

(20) בן רשד (p. 10).

(21) הרב המורה, mostly, however, הרב simply (passim).

(22) R. David Qimchi (leaf י"ג *recto*).

(23) אבא מרי (passim); once (p. 6) שמואל בן יהודה.

(24) אדוני דודי החכם (i.e. R. Ya'aqob b. Abbamari b. Shime'on b. Anatolio, the author of the *Malmad*, whose sister was apparently the wife of R. Shemuel Ibn Tibbon, so that R. Ya'aqob was married to his own niece; pp. 11, 14, and leaves כ"ג *recto*, כ"ה *recto*).

(25) The author's own works (or parts of works): (a) the commentary on Genesis (leaves י *recto*, כ"ד *recto*); (b) the שער שבעה שבועות (p. 13); (c) the שער ההגדה (leaf י"ג *verso*); (d) the שער ספירת העומר (leaves י"ד *verso*, ט"ז *recto*, כ' *recto*, כ"ו *recto*); (e) שער הגן (leaf י"ח *recto*).

(c) But the chief value of this work lies in the unusual terms to be found in it; that is, either entirely new words and phrases, or common words and phrases used here in a new sense. The following (which struck us as such at a cursory glance, so that we will not guarantee all of them) may serve as specimens.

(1) איש הבינים (for אמצעי &c.; p. 11). (2) ואמרו ... אולם (for ואולם ... אמרו; unless the אולם be altogether a mistake for the frequent אולי; p. 13). (3) טובות (for virtues, commonly מדות טובות, but see פסקתא, Pisqa ותאמר ציון, where it is perhaps used in the same sense; leaf י״ג *recto*). (4) המתנגדים (for the, even with our author, otherwise usual ההפכים; p. 14). (5) עטוף על ... (for the, even with our author, otherwise usual שב אל ...; leaves כ״ב *recto* twice, כ״ג *recto*). (6) קדום ... אצל ... (perhaps after the *Moreh;* p. 9). (7) רעות (for vices, commonly מדות רעות, מדות מגונות &c., but see Jer. iii. 5, and פסקתא, as above; leaf י״ג *recto*). (8) רק (in the sense of '*but on the contrary*'; although this expression may belong to the author's father; p. 9). (9) לשון שניות (for pairs of things, commonly רבוי הזוגי &c.; pp. 13, 14). (10) We may on this occasion mention that there are also two Le'azim to be found, on leaves י *verso* (שושנה פרח אחד יפה שיש לו ששה עלים והוא הנקרא לזר״י) and ט״ז *recto* (או למעלותיו ושורותיו שקורין טוולאט).

(ii) *On this MS. of this Commentary in particular.* Apart from the defects arising from loss of leaves, the fragment of this commentary which remains is enough to show that it must have been copied from a faulty and defective[1] MS.; and that the Introduction (פתיחה), which is to be found in the printed edition, can never have existed here. Some passages, however, which had been omitted, were afterwards supplied in the margin by the original scribe. Nevertheless, with all these drawbacks, this MS. is not without value, as it is certainly one of the oldest copies of this commentary existing.

2. [אגרות ר׳ זרחיה לר׳ יהודה על שני מאמרים ממורה הנבוכים ופרוש על איזה פרקים מספר הזה לר׳ זרחיה הנזכר]

LETTERS OF R. ZERACHYAH TO R. YEHUDAH ON TWO MATTERS IN CONNEXION WITH THE MOREH; TOGETHER WITH FOUR EXTRACTS FROM A COMMENTARY ON THAT WORK BY THE SAME AUTHOR.

[1] Leaf 19b (on v. 7; printed ed. leaf י״ח *recto*, line 25) the scribe has: אני הכותב מצאתי כך כתוב מהעתק מתהילה (מתחלת) השורה של מעלה הנקודה בשבר ונ״ל (ונראה לי) שהיה טעות בספר ואני מניח מקום לתקנו. The printed edition, however, throws no light on this supposed deficiency, as the word שאחריו is there immediately followed by אמרו רבותינו ז״ל, even as it is here followed, after the Note just given, by the equivalent ואמ׳ רז״ל.

This article corresponds to Nos. (6) to (10) of the Table of contents given before on p. 227, Note 2. It will be convenient to notice the contents here in accordance with that Table, identifying the matter, even where now lost, with the corresponding passages in MS. Add. 1235, lately belonging to Carmoly (No. 39 in the sale Catalogue of his MSS. and frequently referred to in connexion with R. Zerachyah, in the *Otzar Nechmad* II., Frankel's *Monatsschrift* V. and Steinschneider's *Hammazkir* IV., &c.).

(1) *Letters to R. Yehudah.*

Of these explanations of the Moreh (which take here the form of letters in answer to R. Yehudah's questions), as they are found in MS. Add. 1235, only two seem ever to have existed in this MS. They are numbered (6) in the Table of contents, and formerly occupied leaves 32ᵇ—40ᵃ.

(a) On the עתה; a mere fragment.

Begins (36ᵃ):

שהעתה נחלק יהיה חלק מן הזמן ואין ראוי לקראו עתה...

Ends (36ᵇ):

...על (אל) תהי הורס ומהיר לפתום (לתפוש)

This will be found in MS. Add. 1235 from leaf 86ᵇ, line 17, to leaf 88ᵃ, line 14. Any remarks called for by this and the following explanations by R. Zerachyah will find a more appropriate place in our description of that MS. in the fifth Section of this Catalogue.

(b) On Job, Satan, and the sons of God.

This piece, which now no longer exists here, must have been identical with the corresponding passage in MS. Add. 1235, from leaf 92ᵃ, line 19 (אמנם אחי ומשיב רוחי...), to leaf 97ᵃ, line 1 (...שהכל כוונה אחת וענין אחד).

(2) *Four extracts from a commentary on the Moreh.*

(a) On Part III. Pereq 22. This extract, which now no longer exists here, is numbered (7) in the Table of contents. It extended from leaf 40ᵇ to 41ᵇ, and must have been identical with the passage to be found in MS. Add. 1235, from leaf 97ᵃ, line 1 (פרק כ״ב בחלק השלישי פי׳ ענין כוונת איוב...), to 98ᵇ, line 24 (השכלים הנפרדים). It will be observed that in the Table of contents it is called II. 22, not III. 22; but an examination of the Moreh shows at once, that, while II. 22, treating on cause and effect, &c., as introductory to the proof that the world was created out of nothing, would be here quite irrelevant, III. 22, which treats on Job, &c., is akin to the matter immediately preceding. Besides which, MS. Add. 1235 (which will be admitted to stand in some, if not close, relation to this our MS.) gives us on II. 22 nothing at all.

(b) Introductory remarks on the Metaphysics of Aristotle. This also does not now exist here. It is numbered in the Table of contents (8) and extended from leaf 42^a to 42^b. At first sight it might seem strange how this piece should have found a place in connexion with the Moreh; but, when it is remembered that the Moreh is founded on Aristotle's philosophy in general and on his Metaphysics in particular, the strangeness disappears. The phrase מספר האלהות looks as if it meant a mere translation of Aristotle's own introductory remarks to the Metaphysics; but, apart from the fact, that these could not have been compressed into two pages of our MS. (were they even those of the first chapter of the first book only), it is observable that the index-writer uses the preposition מן to signify *concerning*, *on*, *in reference to*, &c.; and so he appears to use the equivalent prepositional particle מ here in a similar sense. It is just possible that this may be the passage which is found in MS. Add. 1235 occupying much the same space. It there begins (leaf 136^b, line 23): כתו׳ בספר מה שאחר הטבע בהתחלתו..., and ends (leaf 137^a, line 23): ...והוא הנקרא צמיחה או הכרח״. Otherwise there seems to be no trace of it to be found in MS. Add. 1235, or other MSS. containing R. Zerachyah's works.

(c) On the introduction to the Moreh.

This again is lost from our MS. It is numbered (9) in the Table of contents; and extended from leaf 43^b to 45^a. It was unquestionably identical with what is to be found in MS. Add. 1235, from leaf 1^b, line 22 (אמר בהקדמה ויקחום...), to leaf 4^a, line 5 (ואחל מה שצריך לבאר בפרקים.).

(d) On certain Peraqim of Part I of the Moreh.

A considerable portion of this still remains. It is numbered (10) in the Table of contents, and originally extended from 45^b to 56^a. It is impossible to say what Peraqim were dealt with on the now missing leaves 45 to 48.

(*a*) On Pereq 36.

Begins abruptly (leaf 49^a):

שהגלגל חצי כדור...

Ends (leaf 49^a):

...שזולתו יהיה נעבד.

This is to be found in MS. Add. 1235, leaf 32^a, line 15, to leaf 32^a, line 20.

(*β*) On Pereq 46.

Begins (leaf 49^a):

פרק מ״ו אמ׳ בו והנה אמרו חז״ל מאמר כולל דוחה לכל מה שמראים אותו (אותן) אלו הספורים הגשמיים כולם אשר ישיגום הנביאים ר״ל באלו הספורים הגשמיים מה שהכתוב מספר...

Ends (leaf 50ᵃ):

...הם עניינים נבראים וכיוצא בזהו מה שזכר בב׳ אלו הפרקים כלומ׳ זה הפרק אשר אנחנו בו ובפרק ס״ה ובשאר המקומות שבפרקי המורה.

In the corresponding place in MS. Add. 1235 (leaf 37ᵇ) an explanation of Pereq 46 is to be found, which resembles the present in substance, though differing from it considerably in diction. At the same time, at the very end of that MS. (leaf 137ᵃ, line 23, to leaf138ᵃ), a second explanation of the same Pereq is given, which corresponds to the present more closely, though not word for word. We have found reason to believe that R. Zerachyah composed *two* commentaries on the Moreh (see our description of MS. Add. 1235 below). It is therefore probable that these two explanations of this Pereq represent the two different commentaries.

(γ) On Peraqim 51, 52.

Begins (leaf 50ᵃ):

פרק נ״א. אמר בו וזה ענין המקרה מחובר אל מה שיתחייב...פי׳ המחבר רצה בעניין זה לבאר שאחדות הבורא ית׳ הוא אחדות פשוט...

Breaks off (leaf 55ᵇ):

...או תהיה שבח לבורא

The explanations of these two Peraqim are to be found almost word for word in MS. Add. 1235, leaves 43ᵇ—51ᵃ. Though leaf 56 is now missing, it is evident, from the way the scribe has written leaf 55ᵇ, that he was drawing his work to a close, and as a matter of fact only six lines are needed to finish the explanation of this Pereq.

The scribe was R. Shabbethai Bilbao (בלבו; see No. 35 of this Catalogue), who seems to have executed the MS. for himself, as he was a dabbler not merely in poetry and Qabbalah, but also in religious philosophy.

Subsequent owners were:

(1) The before-mentioned Ibn Tarshish (see this Catalogue, p. 60), who has left his mark of ownership on leaves 17ᵇ, 18ᵃ and 19ᵃ.

(2) An oriental Qaraite of the xvth century (early), who has a few emendations on the inner and outer margins of leaf 19ᵃ.

(3) R. Shelomoh, the index-writer, who has only left his mark by writing on leaf 22ᵃ, &c. the running title שיר השירים.

For other owners again see our description of No. 35 above.

The state of this MS. is very bad, for, in addition to the (wholly or partly) missing leaves, it must be added, that this copy has suffered from damp, as well as from wax (or some such substance), which had been poured on it in a liquid state.

[Library-mark, Add. 377. 1; bought in 1867 from H. Lipschütz.]

No. 71.

Parchment, in quarto, 9½ in. × 7⅜ in.; 50 leaves, 5-sheet quires, 27 lines; Greek Ashkenazic handwriting of the XIVth century.

[פרושים על שיר השירים לר' אברהם הלוי. על רות. שיר השירים וקהלת לרש"י. על איכה לר' יוסף קרא. ועל אסתר לפלוני אלמוני]

Commentaries on CANTICLES by R. Abraham Hallevi, on RUTH, CANTICLES and ECCLESIASTES by Rashi, on LAMENTATIONS by R. Yoseph קרא, and on ESTHER by an anonymous author.

Leaf 1ª, *Introduction to Canticles;* 1ᵇ, *Commentary on the same book;* 22ª, *Commentary on Ruth;* 25ª, *Introduction to Canticles;* 25ª, *Commentary on the same book;* 34ᵇ, *Commentary on Ecclesiastes;* 44ª, *Commentary on Lamentations;* 48ª, *Commentary on Esther;* 50ᵇ, blank.

1. פרוש [על שיר השירים לר' אברהם בן יצחק הלוי]

COMMENTARY ON CANTICLES BY R. ABRAHAM B. YITZCHAQ HALLEVI (DON ABRAHAM HALLEVI, TAMAKH).

Introduction begins (leaf 1ª):

אמר אברהם הלוי ב"ר יצחק תמ"ך אמ' החכם אל תתהדר לפני מלך...

Commentary begins (leaf 1ᵇ):

שיר השירים אשר לשלמה. כבר הקדמנו שהספר הזה חברו המלך שלמה ע"ה...

Ends (leaf 22ª):

...ובהרמת השמאל והימין, ויגיענו לקץ הימין. אמן אמן והפירוש נשלם שבח לבורא אור עולם[1]״

This commentary has been printed twice (both times with the sacred text: Sabionetta, 1558, 16mo. [not 24mo. as Steinschneider, nor 32mo. as Zedner]; Prag, 1611, 8vo.). We will therefore on the whole confine ourselves to the MS. before us, making only such additional remarks as are absolutely necessary, either for rectifying the misstatements current

[1] This phrase, unlike those at the commencement and end of the five following commentaries (see later), belongs probably to the author himself.

with respect to our author, his age, &c., or supplementing a few omissions as regards the nature of this book.

(i) *On the author, &c.* Our R. Abraham b. Yitzchaq Hallevi cannot be the celebrated Provençal poet, of whom Steinschneider (*Bodl. Catal.* p. 693) speaks as having composed this work in 1380 and dying in 1393, seeing that the author of this work does not write as a great poet would (compare especially the rhymes at the end). Still less can he be the Don Abraham of Gerona, who wrote in 1400. He is, however, no doubt a man of an earlier date, and ought perhaps to be identified with the R. Abraham b. Yitzchaq Hallevi, who lived at Jerusalem (Zunz, *Literaturgesch. d. synag. Poesie*, p. 512), and who, though not a great poet, was a poetaster. What his original home exactly was it is difficult to say, as the Le'azim are not quite clear[1]. The work before us must have been composed, at the latest, towards the middle of the xivth century, as this MS. cannot be much after that date (see our description of MS. Add. 378. 1 in the third Section of this Catalogue). Respecting the תמ"ך, which is found at least as early as the eighth century[2] and which signifies תהי מנוחתו כבוד (compare Zunz, *Gesch. u. Lit.* p. 457), it ought to be remarked, that it is not altogether impossible that such a formula may have become in the course of time a family-name. (See Index of Abbreviations at the end of this Catalogue.)

(ii) *Supplements.* (1) The fact of our author not being a great poet did not, however, prevent him from writing a commentary of some merit, which is the more to be appreciated when we take into consideration the age he lived in. Like the rest of the school of Maimonides, to which he apparently belonged (although he seems to have been infinitely better in every respect than the majority of the men constituting it), he sees in everything, but especially in Canticles, an open and a hidden meaning (a נגלה and a נסתר), of which the latter was not a mystical or cabbalistical, but a philosophical signification. (2) Though this work distinctly names only Aristotle, Rashi, Maimonides and Nachmanides, its literature betrays, in the philosophical explanations, that the author knew the works of Ibn עקנין (or עכנין), Mosheh Ibn Tibbon, 'Immanuel b. Shelomoh, Ibn Kaspi and others, and, in the mystical explanations, those of R. Tobiyyahu b. Eli'ezer, and others (see leaves 2^b, 4^b, 5^b, &c.). (3) The author modestly acknowledges that he invented very little, and that the greater portion, if not all, of this work was due to predecessors. (4) Of all the curiosities which we find in this book, one exceeds everything else, i.e. the author's naïve confession (on vi. 8), that though the hidden meaning of the numbers 60 and 80 was known to him, the open meaning of them was not!

[1] The seven Le'azim are these: (1) רהיטנו=קְבִירוֹנְש; (2) חבצלת=רוֹשֶׁא; (3) שושנת=לִירִי; (4) לצמתך=קרין; (5) ושבלה=פַּלִידָה; (6) תרשיש=שָׁפִּילִי; and (7) חבר=רפיק (leaf 19^b). Some of them look French and some Provençal. The last is Arabic.

[2] See הלבנון, III., p. 63, &c.

(5) The terms constantly occurring in this book are: נגלה and נסתר and 'קצת' את קצת' (see Ibn Kaspi on Lam. ii. 11, and compare this Catalogue, p. 210). (6) For the better understanding of the commentary the sacred text accompanies it in full. This is evidently the author's own arrangement, and this description ought perhaps with more propriety to have found a place in the preceding section of this Catalogue.

2. [פרוש על רות לרבנו שלמה בן יצחק הצרפתי]

Commentary on Ruth by R. Shelomoh b. Yitzchaq of Troyes (Rashi, R. Salomo Isacides[1]).

Begins (leaf 22[b]):

ויהי בימי שפט השופטים ויהי רעב. זה הרעב היה אחד מי' רעבונים שנגזרו בעולם ולמה הוזקק הרעב לבוא באותו הדור לפי שהיו ישראל רשעים ומה שהיה (שהיו) השופטים ראוים לעשות להם. היו הם עושים לשופטים. לכך נאמ' שפט השופטים. על כי התחילו לשפט בשפטים. וזה אחד מן חמשה ויהי בימי שהם לצער. לפני מלוך שאול שהיו הדורות מתפרנסין ...

Ends (25[a]):

...שנ' ותורת חסד על לשונה וניתנה בשבועות „ חסלת פרוש רות

It need hardly be said that Rashi's commentary on Ruth has been printed times without number. But the MS. before us, while it has all that is in the editions, contains a great deal of additional matter, as may be gathered even from the beginning and end given above; but the body of this commentary is equally fruitful in new matter. This new matter has all the appearance of being genuine, although we must, of course, be very cautious with respect to the works of an author whose writings have been so much worked upon in early as well as later times, by learned and semi-learned (תלמידים טועים). The additions at the end are also to be found in the Naples edition of 1486, and bear some resemblance to the corresponding passage of R. Tobiyyahu b. Eli'ezer on Ruth[2]; a matter of no wonder, seeing that both writers drew from one common source, the Midrashim. It ought to be known however, that the לקח טוב on the Megilloth has, at some period, been supplemented by, or from, Rashi, as will be shown in our description of the copy of that work in this Library (MS. Add. 378. 1, below).

3. פירוש [על] שיר השירים [לרבנו שלמה בן יצחק הצרפתי]

[1] The י in רשי stands for יצחקי not ירחי; but in spite of the protest of Zunz and other scholars the name ירחי is still constantly used by less careful writers.

[2] Compare Berliner, *Magazin* I. No. 14, where this point is noticed. While, however Berliner corrects Steinschneider's mistake of Marcheshwan for Tishri, he himself erroneously makes the year 1487 instead of 1486.

COMMENTARY ON CANTICLES BY R. SHELOMOH B. YITZCHAQ OF TROYES (RASHI, R. SALOMO ISACIDES).

Introduction begins (leaf 25ᵃ):

בעזרת אל אלים נכתוב פירו׳ שיר השירים[1]״
אחת דבר אלהים שתים זו שמענו מקרא אחד יוצא לכמה טעמים...

Commentary begins (leaf 25ᵃ):

שיר השירים אשר לשלמה. שנו רבותי׳ כל שלמה האמור בשיר השירים קודש...

Ends leaf (35ᵇ):

...הוא הר המוריה ובית המקדש שיבנה במהרה בימינו אמ׳״

Both introduction and commentary are on the whole here what they are in the printed editions. But there is one passage, which cannot be passed over without notice, since, whatever its origin may be, it is here written quite as part of the text. It runs thus (on i. 4; leaf 25ᵇ): וראיתי כתוב בשם ר׳ יהודה אחי(!) נר״ו (נטריה רחמנא ופרקיה) משכני כמו משכתני ונתן דוגמ׳ תתנינו כצאן מאכל והוא נתתנו. וכן זה משכתני אחריך במדבר... It is at least enough to show how desirable it is that some scholar should begin to do for Rashi's other commentaries what Berliner has already done with so much success for his commentary on the Pentateuch (comp. this Catalogue, pp. 50, 128).

4. פירוש [על] קהלת [לרבנו שלמה בן יצחק הצרפתי]

COMMENTARY ON ECCLESIASTES BY R. SHELOMOH B. YITZCHAQ OF TROYES (RASHI, R. SALOMO ISACIDES).

Begins (leaf 34ᵇ):

פירוש של קהלת
דברי קהלת כל מקום שנ׳ דברי תוכחות...

Ends (leaf 44ᵃ):

...כגון נותן צדקה לעני בפרהסיא סוף דבר הכל נשמע נשלם פירוש קוהלת

Except for variations in the turn of expressions here and there, this is identical with the text as found in the printed editions.

5. פרוש [על] איכה [לר׳ יוסף בן שמעון קרא הצרפתי]

COMMENTARY ON LAMENTATIONS BY R. YOSEPH B. SHIME'ON קרא OF NORTHERN FRANCE.

Begins (leaf 44ᵃ):

זו פרוש איכה
איכה ישבה בדד העיר רבתי עם העיר שהיתה לשעבר...

[1] This phrase belongs, no doubt, to the copyist.

Ends (leaf 48ª):

‥ הוא שייסד רבינו גרשום דשו בו שועלים תחרש למשאות. השיבנו יי' אליך וגו'. נשלם פירוש איכה.

This commentary has been printed twice; as anonymous in the Naples Bible (Hagiographa) of 1486; and with the author's name in the דברי חכמים (Metz, 1849, 8vo.). Our MS. is superior in some points to both editions, but agrees more with the modern one, especially in respect to the Le'azim, of which the Naples edition has but two, and those Italian and peculiar to itself. Extracts from this commentary, contained in a Hamburg MS. (Cod. Hebr. 32), have been printed by the indefatigable Jellinek under the title פירושים על אסתר רות ואיכה (Leipzig, 1855, 8vo.). Although the editor was unable to verify the authorship of many of these extracts, yet his scientific instinct led him to suggest the real author; see his Foot-note on p. vii of the above work. It is not to be wondered at that he failed to decipher the Le'azim, which are there given in a very corrupt state, as may be seen from our MS., which though not quite correct, is yet much more so than any of the copies we have seen. From iv. 8 it might appear as if our author knew Greek; but the reference to a Greek equivalent may perhaps be an interpolation of the scribe, whom we know to have been a Greek.

6. פירוש [על] אסתר [לחכם צרפתי פלוני אלמוני]

COMMENTARY ON ESTHER BY AN ANONYMOUS RABBI OF NORTHERN FRANCE.

Begins (leaf 48ª):

זהו פירוש מגילת אסתר
ויהי בימי אחשורוש וגו' כשבת המלך אחשורוש כשנתיישב במלכותו שראה שנתקיימה מלכותו בידו דחיינו בשנת שלש שכבר הוחזק ובטוח במלכות…

Ends (leaf 50ª):

…ותכתוב אסתר וגו' את כל תוקף חוזק כלומ' כל כח וחיזוק שהיו יכולין מרדכי ואסתר לקיים ימי הפורים עשו״
נשלם פירוש מגילת אסתר שבח לאל יושב סתר חזק ונתחזק

Although by an anonymous author, and although no Le'azim are to be found in it, there can be little doubt, that this commentary is the work of a North French Rabbi, of the age immediately succeeding that of Rashi. It is of very great value. It is not printed, but is by no means unique. It is identical with two MSS. at Florence[1] (see Biscioni, 8vo. edition, pp. 347

[1] In fact these five commentaries on the Five Rolls appear to be identical with the five which occur as Nos. XIII—XVII in the second Florence MS. referred to in the text. Nos. XIII and XV, there anonymous, are by Rashi. No. XVI, there anonymous, is by R. Yoseph קרא.

and 367), and with one in the Bodleian (Opp. Add. 4to., 52). It certainly deserves to be edited.

The scribe's name was probably Nathan or some other commencing with נ, as may be seen from leaf 46[a], &c. He generally fills up the vacant spaces of the lines with the first letter, or letters, of the first word of the next line. Our scribe is in the habit of making a pious ejaculation, either הש׳ ישמרני מכל רע אמ׳, or ישמחני ו(י)חייני לאור׳ ימי׳, or הש׳ יחייני ו(י)קיימני, whenever an unpropitiatory phrase occurs in the text of his author; compare this Catalogue, p. 226 above.

Of owners we can trace here:

(1) The anonymous scribe of MS. Add. 378. 1, who copied that MS. in the year 1361. He has written on leaf 50[b] in square Sephardic character of great beauty the following sentiment: אצלך חפץ נזר השם טוב מכסף קנין דעת.

(2) An anonymous Ashkenazi of about the xv—xvith century has left his mark on this MS. by an emendation on leaf 22[a], outer margin.

(3) Another anonymous owner, whose date cannot be determined, has re-inked the MS. in various places, where the ink had sprung off (see later).

(4) One Nethaneel b. Shabbethai of Norcia, who has made the following entry on the last leaf: לעולם יכתוב (אדם) שמו על ספרו פן יבוא אחד מן השוק ויאמר זה הספר שלי הוא לכן כתבתי את שמי פה. שלי נתנאל בכמ״א שבתי מנורצי זלה״ה. He must have died in or about 1524. See our description of MS. Add. 378. 1 in the third Section of this Catalogue; where other owners of this MS. will be mentioned.

On leaves 49[b] and 50[a] are the entries of two censors: on the former that of 'Dominico Gerosolomitano 1595' and on the latter that of 'Gir. Dominico Carrett(o) 1607.'

The state of the MS. is excellent, except some parts of the smooth side of the parchment, where the ink has sprung off.

[Library mark, Add. 378. 2; bought in 1867 from H. Lipschütz.]

No. 72.

Paper, in quarto, $8\frac{1}{4}$ in. × $5\frac{1}{2}$ in.; 48 leaves, 8-sheet quires, 22 lines; Rabbinic character, Sephardic handwriting of the xivth century.

באור [על דניאל לר׳ לוי בן גרשם תושב פרובינצה]

Commentary on DANIEL, by R. Levi b. Gershom[1] of Provence (Ralbag, Gersonides, Leon de Bagnols).

1ª, blank; 1ᵇ, *Text;* 44—48 (44, 47, 48, cut out) blank.

Introduction runs thus (leaf 1ᵇ):

בשם אל חי

אמר לוי בן גרשום אחר התהלה לאל והשאלה ממנו להיישיר לפנינו דרכו (דרכנו?) ראינו לבאר דברי זה הספר כי נבוכו בו כל אשר לפנינו ולזה נאריך בביאורו ונספר התועלות המגיעות ממנו כמנהגנו

Commentary begins (Ibid.):

בשנת שלש למלכות יהויקים וגו׳ עד בלשצר מלכא ר״ל אחר שע(ברו) שלש שנים למלכות יהויקים ונכנסה השנה הרביעית...

Ends (leaf 43ᵇ):

...יתברך ויתעלה יוצר הכל אשר גלה לנו סודות„ והנה היתה השלמת הביאור הזה בירח אדר שני של שנת תשעים ושמונה לפרט האלף הששי והתהלה לאל אשר עזרנו ברחמיו וגודל חסדיו, יהי שמו מבורך ומרומם על כל ברכה ותהלה אמן אמן„

This commentary having been repeatedly printed[2] we may confine ourselves to the MS. before us as such; and this is of very high value for the following reasons:

(1) It is not merely one of the oldest, but possibly the very oldest, now extant, of this commentary, which was only composed in 1338.

(2) It is not merely fuller[3] than the editions, but the text also contains readings superior to those found in these editions[4].

[1] Not Gershon as commonly written.

[2] A word may be said here of the first edition (from which the other editions seem to be a mere reprint). Although executed with the very same type, with which the first edition of Nachmanides' Pentateuch-commentary was printed, it was not printed, as is stated in *Jüdische Typographie*, &c. (Ersch u. Gruber's *Encyk.* II. 27, p. 35, Note 15) by the three workmen (partners?), 'Obadyah Menassheh and Binyamin of Rome (comp. this Catalogue, p. 167, Note 4), but either by one of them alone, or by a successor to them all, as may be seen from the use of the singular number in the phrase which occurs in the printer's postscript to the first edition of Ralbag's commentary on Daniel (...וחלקי המחוקק). It was, however, probably printed after Nachmanides' commentary had been published, as that author's phrases at the end of Deuteronomy are almost literally imitated here by the printer.

[3] See, for example, the Introduction (1ᵇ), on ii. 5 (5ª), &c.

[4] Of these readings we will only mention one, viz. בנ״ה, which formula is regularly to be found here, wherever בע״ה is to be found in the printed editions. Now, בנ״ה is, no doubt, the formula used by the author originally here, just as it is used by him in his Pentateuch-commentary, which he finished and perhaps altogether composed in the same year as this commentary (1338). For the expression בנ״ה itself compare this Catalogue, p. 169.

The scribe's name appears to have been Zekharyah or some other beginning with ז, as may be seen from leaves 25ᵃ and 36ᵃ, where this letter is put at the *commencement* of 10 consecutive lines in one case and 4 in the other, without any connexion with the matter on the lines adjoining them (see Excursus I). He was apparently trained in Africa, if not a native of that part of the world; but, at all events, an Arabic-speaking Sephardi, as may be seen from his writing אלסכנדר, &c.

As regards owners, they form a goodly company; yet, except the original owner perhaps, they all lived in Italy, in one part or other.

(1) The oldest owner, who is anonymous and for whom the MS. was probably executed, belongs to the xivth century. The mark he has left in this MS. is of considerable value. He wrote on the margins, in Rabbinic Sephardic, numerous corrections and suggestions, mostly preceded by the letter ד (which, no doubt, stands for דיוקא). They are in most cases much to the point.

(2) The next owner is also a Sephardi, and his writing is also in Rabbinic character. He belongs to the xiv—xvth century, and his name, בינדיט כונת, occurs twice on leaf 1ᵃ. He was probably an ancestor, certainly a relation, of the Physician Abraham b. Shelomoh כונת, who was connected with the Hebrew press, which existed at Mantua from 1476 to 1480.

(3) A third owner, an anonymous Sephardi of the xvth century, wrote in Rabbinic on leaf 11ᵃ, outer margin.

(4, 5) Abraham(?) b. Eli'ezer of Pisa, from whom(?) the MS. passed into the hands of ...... b. David of Forli(?), both evidently Italians of the latter half of the xvth century. The actual names of both owners are lost, owing to the state of the MS., where the entry occurs (leaf 1ᵇ). Whichever of the two writes the entry, writes an elegant Italian current hand. The MS. seems never to have left Italy from the time of these owners till a few years ago.

(6) Another (anonymous) Italian owner of the xv—xvith century wrote on leaf 1ᵃ א' פי' דניאל ללוי ב"ג בנייר י. To this owner belong also several corrections, which are to be found between the lines of the text. He wrote in mixed (Rabbinic and current) character, and his hand is easily identified by the yellowish red ink with which he writes.

(7) Another anonymous Italian owner wrote a marginal note in mixed character; it is to be found on leaf 41ᵇ. He apparently belongs to the xvi—xviith century.

(8) Another anonymous owner of the xviith century left his mark by writing in Italian Sephardic (imitation) on leaf 46ᵃ the four words פירוש הר"לבג על דניאל.

(9) R. Sanson Cohen Modone of Mantua (see this Catalogue, p. 39) wrote on leaf 1^{b}, lower margin, in mixed (Rabbinic and current) Italian הספר הזה מהצעיר שמשון (כהן מודון); a statement which was probably repeated, though somewhat amplified, on leaf 43^{b}, lower margin, but which is now cut away by the binder. To this owner, who died in 1727, belong all the interesting and instructive summaries on the margins. He has marked the modern chapters, &c.; and twice (leaves 23^{b} and 37^{a}) he has made entries in Italian. Once (leaf 15^{b}) he has also written an emendation between the lines.

(10) After the foregoing owner's death this copy came into the hands of the father of the Physician della Volta (see this Catalogue, p. 39). In his time the MS. was very carelessly bound. In his writing are the title פירוש דניאל רלב״ג and the library-marks ה׳ ה׳ ט׳ and ה׳ ה׳ יו״ד on leaf 1^{a}. It is a bold, but very ungraceful mixed Italian hand.

(11) Samuele Vita della Volta of Mantua (see this Catalogue, p. 39) probably inherited this copy from his father with other books, but has left no mark on it himself. It is, however, possible that the words איסי בן on leaf 1^{a} belong to him. (Is there an allusion to his being אסיא, a physician?) These two words are in Rabbinic Sephardic and apparently belong to the XVIII—XIXth century. It must be noticed, that within the last hundred years, even the pure Italian Jews have adopted the Rabbinic Sephardic instead of their own less graceful Rabbinic.

(12) The next owner was Cav. Marco (Mordekhai) Mortara, Chief Rabbi of Mantua, as the words רלב״ג פירוש דניאל כ׳, on the label on the back, in his hand, clearly show.

Leaf 43^{b} contains two censors' entries: (1) 'Dominico Gerosolomitano 1597' and (2) 'Visto per me Gir. dominico Carretto 1618.' It may not be uninteresting to learn that, while the *suspected antipapal* passage, leaf 25^{b} (on vii. 26), has been struck out by the former of these censors, the *well-known antichristian* passages have been allowed to stand.

After the first leaf, which is a good deal damaged, this MS. is in very fair condition.

[Library-mark, Add. 397; bought in 1867 from H. Lipschütz.]

ADDITIONS.

כל אשר תמצא ידך לעשות בכחך עשה. קהלת ט׳ י׳.

The following notes are mostly the result of examining books and manuscripts received, or seen, too late to be of use while the preceding sheets were passiug through the press.

Page 8, last line (of text) but one. This use of יששכר (in the ביה שמו) has since been noticed elsewhere by Dr H. L. Strack, of St Petersburg, to whom we communicated our proof-sheets. See his article, *Die biblischen und die massoretischen Handschriften zu Tschufut-Kale in der Krim*, in *Zeitschrift f. d. gesammte luth. Theologie u. Kirche*, 1875, p. 603.

Page 23, line 13 from below. אכי״ר may also signify אמן כן יאמר רחום; see MS. Add. 1200 (a copy of the Yemen Machazor), leaf 145[a], where the last three out of these four words stand, written out in full, instead of the ordinary כן יהי רצון. Here, however, the אכי״ר was hardly used in a sense other than that given by us in the text.

Page 29, line 18. Another instance of the Qaraite formula of the dedication of a book to the use of a congregation, occurs in MS. Add. 1014. 1; see this Catalogue, p. 127, line 14.

Page 39, line 4. רז״ל may also signify רבותינו זכרם לברכה.

Page 40. This whole commentary (No. 28) has been transcribed and is being prepared for publication with the care which it deserves, by Mr W. Aldis Wright, of Trinity College. The Leipzig Glossary mentioned in the text, has been kindly sent over to Cambridge for examination and has been carefully collated by Mr Wright. Delitzsch (*Literaturblatt des Orients* v. No. 19) suggests the possible identity of the הרב quoted on Job with the הרב רבי ברכיה quoted on Canticles iii. 10 (not Eccles. as he and Zunz both print it). A comparison of the two MSS. at once reveals the fact that the citation in the Glossary on Canticles is actually taken from our Commentary on Job; and the authorship of our Commentary is thus rendered certain. Who the R. Berekhyah was, whether הנקדן or some other, remains yet to be discovered.

Page 44, line 19. בהנו״א has been commonly solved by בעזרת ה׳ נתחיל ונגמר אמן. We have, however, found the solution as given by us in the text, *written out* in many MSS., and it is further rendered certain by the amplified form בהנוא״ל, which occurs in MS. Add. 525 (see p. 174 of this Catalogue), where the current solution would, of course, be simply absurd.

Page 44, line 9 from below. כמ״ש with a quotation from the *Prophets* (as here) may also signify כמו שנאמר, &c.; with a quotation from the *Hagiographa* it might signify כמה שכתוב or כמו שכתוב, &c.

Page 48, line 8 from below. To ציטדין דפטרש add its equivalent (Cittadino di Patras).

Page 55, line 15 from below. אב"ע would be perhaps better solved here into אברהם בן עזרא (see p. 118 of this Catalogue, Note 1), as it is preceded by the title רבי'.

Page 56, line 10, דלטור should evidently have been written by the scribe דילאטור (Lat. *delator*), as otherwise the numerical value would be 249 instead of 260 (רכיל).

Page 56, line 9 from below. י"ל may, with equal propriety, be here solved by יחי לנצח, יחי לעולם, יזכר לברכה, or finally by יזכר לטוב.

Page 58, line 2. Is מפריש a mistake for מטרוייש? The matter is, certainly, identical with what is to be found in the לקוטי הפרדס (Venezia, 1519, 4to.), leaf 7[b], col. 2, line 15, &c., although some of it is in different order. Compare also פרדס הגדול (Warsaw, 1870, Folio), § 6.

Page 58, lines 6—8. Somewhat similar matter will be found in the לקוטי הפרדס, leaf 7[b], col. 1. The paragraph in our MS., though closing with the words סליק הטעם של קדיש, contains also some remarks on the קריאת שמע and the identity of its contents with the Decalogue.

Page 77, line 1. The same piece occurs in a MS. at Parma; see המזכיר, xii. p. 117.

Page 78, line 4 from below. א"ש, if not אוהב שלום, or איש שלום, as is possible, may perhaps be some equivalent of the title 'Knight of the Golden Spur' ('Sperone d'oro'), an order which R. Mordekhai Modena is known to have received from the Emperor Charles V; see Ghirondi, תולדות גדולי ישראל, p. 244, § 49.

Page 79, line 21. See on the subject of R. Yechiel of Paris an article by M. Adrien de Longpérier in the *Journal des savants* for 1874, p. 648.

Page 83, last 9 lines. The same piece occurs in the Parma MS. mentioned above; see המזכיר, xii. p. 116.

Page 84, lines 22—32. See this also in the Parma MS.; compare המזכיר, xii. p. 117.

Page 85, Note 1. On the family טרבוט, see p. 97 of this Catalogue; and Berliner, *Magazin*, ii. Nos. 4 and 24. The piece which contains this reference to that family, is also in the Parma MS.; see המזכיר, xii. p. 117.

Page 89, line 24. On חצר גדולה, comp. p. 111 of this Catalogue.

Page 89, line 3 from below. Since writing the remark in the text, we have examined the Paris MS. (No. 312 in the New Catalogue) to which Zunz refers; and we find that, though the narrative in our MS. treats on the same subject as that in the Paris MS., ours is altogether different and in every respect of greater value. (Is this R. Ya'aqob b. Nethaneel the same as the one to whom Maimonides addressed the אגרת תימן?)

Page 94, Note 4. R. Yechiel Mele, the compiler of the תפוחי זהב, was probably a son, certainly a relation, of this R. Pinechas Eliyyah.

Page 109, line 12 from below. The פשטים, &c. are on Ibn 'Ezra on the Pentateuch.

Page 111, last line of text. On חצר גדול, comp. p. 89 of this Catalogue.

Page 113, lines 25, &c. We have since found, that the matter contained in this piece is almost word for word identical with § 85 of the אגור of R. Ya'aqob b. Yehudah Landau, only with a different superscription. This discovery helps us to identify the בעל תפלין of the present piece with the R. Abraham מהייפארט (of Heufurt) b. Mosheh of Sinzheim, whose הלכות תפלין served as the ground-work of the ברוך שאמר of R. Shimshon b. Eli'ezer (Sklow, 1804, 4to.; see leaf 3[a]).

Page 119, last line of text. We have since seen the Paris MS., and our conjecture is confirmed (see leaves 72[b]—75[b] of that MS.).

Page 129, Note 1. This phrase will be found again, also in full, in MS. Add. 403. 1; see p. 225 of this Catalogue.

Page 131, line 13. צב"י may either mean צדיק באמונתו יחיה or צדיק בימיו יפרח. The first is an allusion to Hab. ii. 4; and, when used after the name of any one, it means 'May the just man (i.e. the one here named) live,' &c. The other is an allusion to Psalm lxxii. 7; and, when used after the name of any one, it means 'May the Righteous (i.e. the Messiah, see Zech. ix. 9) flourish in his days.' It is obvious from this, that while the latter phrase can be applied to any one, the former can be only with justice applied to men of *eminent sanctity*. We are satisfied that צב"י can only mean here what we have explained it to mean in the text. The solution suggested in המזכיר, xv. p. 77, Note 2, does not apply.

Page 134, line 21. We now know this Yeudah Zerachyah to have been b. Mosheh b. David. Compare the preface to his edition of the *Responsa* of R. David Ibn Abi Zimra (Livorno, 1818, Folio).

Page 136, Note 1. Steinschneider, to whom we sent a copy of this sheet and the next, objects (המזכיר, xv. p. 77, Note 2) to our solution on the ground that 'א"א gebraucht Niemand von seinem Lehrer.' He cannot, of course, mean that אדוני and אבי are not *singly* used constantly in all ages from biblical times downwards in this sense. And we can see nothing startling in this combination of the two phrases (even though not commonly used together), when we find them occurring in several MSS. of the very writer under consideration. We have already noticed the phrase אדוני אבי written in full and applied to another of his teachers (R. Meir b. David; see p. 135 of this Catalogue); and we may remark that it is also found in the Bodleian MS. (Neubauer, *Catalogue*, No. 232). So that, when we find the phrase in three wholly independent MSS., we have no reasonable ground for condemning it as a corrupt reading; an argument which we should be slow to resort to at any time. Otherwise, but for it having been written out in full elsewhere, we might perhaps have suggested the solution אדוני אלופי, or אָבִי אמי, or אָחִי אשתי, as R. Levi Hakkohen may have been the author's maternal grandfather or his brother-in-law for aught we know.

Page 136. No. 49. See המזכיר, xv. pp. 15—17; where Steinschneider gives an account of this MS. from an examination of it made before it came to England, though not published till long after our description was printed.

Page 144, lines 8 and 9 from below. The ו in יש״ו may also mean וינוחו, referring to the persons and not to peace.

Page 148, line 9. The missing fourth commentary cut out of this MS. has been lately brought to England, since the passage in the text was printed, and is now in the Bodleian Library (Opp. Add. 4to. 134).

Page 154, Note 2. We have since found, that this passage, as well as the one in which R. Yoseph Qimchi is quoted above, have been simply copied there by Ibn Mayor from the Parashath משפטים of the recension of Ibn מטוט which is in print (see p. 137 of this Catalogue), where the treatise in question is called אלפוו. Steinschneider (המזכיר, xv. p. 77, Note 2) refers us, on אלפוו, to p. 248 (it is really p. 247) of his Memoir on Al-fārābī (St Petersburg, 1869, 4to.); but, full of interesting matter as it is, we find nothing to our purpose on this point. The citations in question, having ceased to be Ibn Mayor's own, do not call for further investigation in this place.

Page 161, Note 2. Compare Gross in Berliner's *Magazin*, I. p. 108, Note 8, who speaks of having seen this relationship asserted by R. El'azar of Worms himself in a MS. commentary on the Prayers (no more precise reference is given) belonging to Baron Gunzbourg of Paris.

Page 176, line 6. The ה may perhaps be the final letter of the scribe's name, as is sometimes the case (see Excursus I).

Page 198, Note 1. קבשטייאן is generally represented by *Capestan*, or *Capestang;* see, however, Minchath Qenaoth, pp. 172, 173, where in one place it is given קבסטון and in the other קשטיון.

Page 210, Note 1. For the allusion to 'our holy teachers' see also פסקתא, Pisqa החדש.

END OF VOLUME I.

CAMBRIDGE: PRINTED BY C. J. CLAY, M.A. AT THE UNIVERSITY PRESS.

www.ingramcontent.com/pod-product-compliance
Lightning Source LLC
LaVergne TN
LVHW010249110826
845151LV00004B/1426